ALSO BY JONATHAN HORN

Washington's End: The Final Years and Forgotten Struggle

The Man Who Would Not Be Washington:
Robert E. Lee's Civil War and His Decision That Changed American History

THE FATE

OF THE

GENERALS

MacArthur, Wainwright, and the
Epic Battle for the Philippines

—◆—

JONATHAN HORN

SCRIBNER

New York Amsterdam/Antwerp London
Toronto Sydney/Melbourne New Delhi

Scribner
An Imprint of Simon & Schuster, LLC
1230 Avenue of the Americas
New York, NY 10020

For more than 100 years, Simon & Schuster has championed authors and the stories they create. By respecting the copyright of an author's intellectual property, you enable Simon & Schuster and the author to continue publishing exceptional books for years to come. We thank you for supporting the author's copyright by purchasing an authorized edition of this book.

No amount of this book may be reproduced or stored in any format, nor may it be uploaded to any website, database, language-learning model, or other repository, retrieval, or artificial intelligence system without express permission. All rights reserved. Inquiries may be directed to Simon & Schuster, 1230 Avenue of the Americas, New York, NY 10020 or permissions@simonandschuster.com.

First Scribner hardcover edition April 2025

SCRIBNER and design are trademarks of Simon & Schuster, LLC

Simon & Schuster strongly believes in freedom of expression and stands against censorship in all its forms. For more information, visit BooksBelong.com.

For information about special discounts for bulk purchases, please contact Simon & Schuster Special Sales at 1-866-506-1949 or business@simonandschuster.com.

The Simon & Schuster Speakers Bureau can bring authors to your live event. For more information or to book an event, contact the Simon & Schuster Speakers Bureau at 1-866-248-3049 or visit our website at www.simonspeakers.com.

Interior design by Kyle Kabel

Manufactured in the United States of America

1   3   5   7   9   10   8   6   4   2

Library of Congress Cataloging-in-Publication Data

Names: Horn, Jonathan, 1982- author.
Title: The fate of the generals : MacArthur, Wainwright, and the epic battle for the Philippines / Jonathan Horn.
Other titles: MacArthur, Wainwright, and the epic battle for the Philippines
Description: First Scribner hardcover edition | New York : Scribner, 2025.
| Includes bibliographical references and index.
Identifiers: LCCN 2024051725 (print) | LCCN 2024051726 (ebook)
| ISBN 9781668010075 | ISBN 9781668010099 (ebook)
Subjects: LCSH: World War, 1939-1945—Campaigns—Philippines. | MacArthur, Douglas, 1880-1964.
| Wainwright, Jonathan Mayhew, 1883-1953. | United States. Army—Officers—Biography.
| Allied Forces. South West Pacific Area. | World War, 1939-1945—United States.
| Generals—United States—Biography. | United States—History, Military—20th century.
Classification: LCC D767.4 .H676 2025 (print) | LCC D767.4 (ebook) | DDC 940.5400922—dc23/eng/20250111
LC record available at https://lccn.loc.gov/2024051725
LC ebook record available at https://lccn.loc.gov/2024051726

ISBN 978-1-6680-1007-5
ISBN 978-1-6680-1009-9 (ebook)

To Caroline, Laura, and Emma

Contents

CONTENTS

List of Maps

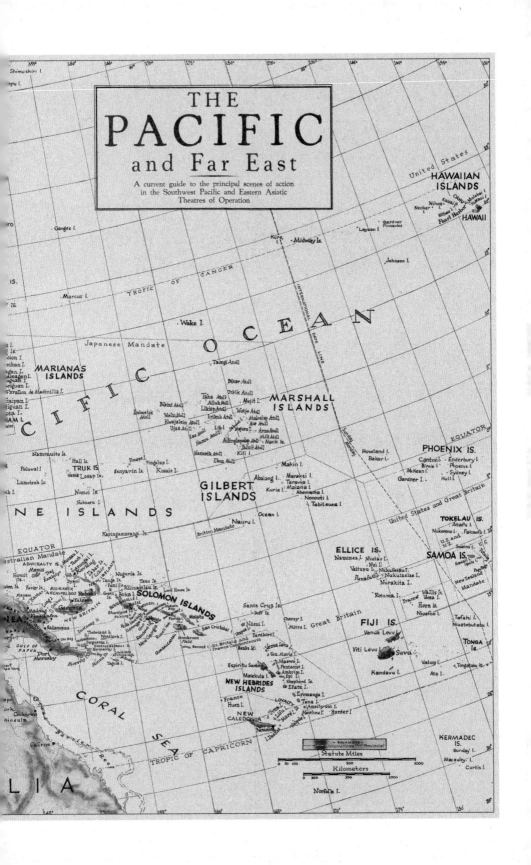

Paths to Honor

It would always be November 25, 1863, in the mind of Douglas MacArthur. Nearly a century later, he would recall the fighting in the present tense, as if he had been there. So many times as a boy he had heard the story of the 23,000 Union soldiers lying under the last line of trees and listening for the signal to rise, unfurl their flags, and step into the clearing as if actors entering a vast stage viewable from the ridges, hills, and mountains rung around it. Behind these men in blue lay Orchard Knob, the mound-like hill where their newly arrived commander, Ulysses S. Grant, watched, and behind him, Chattanooga, the crucial railroad junction where they had withered away on half their usual rations amid the weeks-long siege he had come to break. Ahead of them stood their adversaries, the Confederates lining Missionary Ridge, the steep heights running for miles on an axis penning the Union army into this town wedged into the winding Tennessee River.

At this point, two and a half years into the American Civil War, the soldiers had seen enough of rifle and artillery fire to recognize a suicide mission, and a frontal assault against a position as strong as Missionary Ridge had the look of one. Grant had done what he could to avoid it. He had tried to outflank the Confederates by attacking either end of their position: from above, where the railway tunneled through a hill, and from below, where towering Lookout Mountain had peeked out through the clouds the previous day when Union soldiers had seized it. By this day's dawn, the clouds had all disappeared, and the United States flag flew on the summit for all to see. But rebel flags still crowned Missionary Ridge. By the afternoon, both of Grant's attempts to outflank and roll up the Confederate line had stopped short. No choice remained but to order the men in the middle to advance. Grant had no expectation that they could carry the ridge. In fact, he specifically commanded that they not carry it, only seize the rifle pits at its base and then stop, in the hope of forcing the Confederates to divert resources from resisting the principal attacks on their flanks.

Sometime between three and four o'clock in the afternoon came the signal: six cannons discharging in rapid succession. The sound of bugles followed. Then out from the trees and into the amphitheater came two long lines of blue stretching two miles, marching in quick time toward the rifle pits at the ridge's base still hundreds of yards away, and drawing on an unseen reservoir of courage distilled in the despair and desperation of defeat. No one who saw the soldiers that afternoon would forget the pageantry with which they commenced their charge: their flags flying, their guns glimmering, their formations holding perfect as if on parade. The sound of officers shouting commands could be heard until the Confederate cannons atop the crest of Missionary Ridge unleashed their fire. Rather than retreat, the men doubled their speed as if racing one another to the ridge. Before any of them reached it, the Confederate soldiers lining the base began to give way. Those not succumbing to their shock at the surging blue wave sought to flee up the ridge toward their comrades entrenched on the crest.

Into the rifle pits the bluecoats swept. Stopping there, the two Union lines mixed together. Exhausted as the men were, they could not rest long. The rebel artillery atop the ridge began to find their range. Having come this far, the Union soldiers needed to go farther. The closer they stayed behind the enemy retreating up the ridge, the harder it would be for the Confederate infantrymen on the crest to shoot their rifles without striking their own ranks. The higher the bluecoats climbed up the slope, the more difficult the angle of fire would become for the Confederate cannons, which could not bow their barrels so low as to hit what was straight beneath them. Greater safety lay where glory began on higher ground. So out of the rifle pits rose the Union regiments, and up the ridge they went. "Who ordered those men up the ridge?" asked Grant, gazing from Orchard Knob. The generals gathered around him had no answer. The troops had gone on their own.

No orders could be heard over the roar of fire. And for a time, no order could be seen in the field. Many of the men could not even see their own officers through the smoke. All they could see were the banners their brethren had carried into the battle: the national colors and the regimental ones. Forward went the flag-bearers. And behind these brave men, others followed until the flocks they formed took on the appearance of inverted Vs with flags leading the way at their points. The generals watching from Orchard Knob could see a field full of such flags.

But Douglas MacArthur, imagining the scene long afterward, could see only one flag: the one picked up by his father, Lieutenant Arthur MacArthur, the adjutant of the 24th Wisconsin. He had not carried the staff into the battle. But when the sergeant whose job it was tired halfway up the ridge, Arthur rushed forward to rescue the flag from falling to the ground. The men cheered as he seized the staff and hoisted it up. They had not always respected him. He was but eighteen years old and looked even younger with ringlets in his hair and not the slightest stubble on his face. Not yet mature, his voice had broken and screeched the previous year when he had given orders to the men during their first dress parade. They knew he owed his commission to his influential father, the judge of the same name. The lieutenant went by junior, and seemed it, too. To his father's fine house in Milwaukee, Arthur had gone when he had fallen sick during the summer. He had not returned in time for the Battle of Chickamauga, the terrible defeat that had bloodied his regiment and forced it, along with the entire Union army, back into Chattanooga at the start of the fall. But upon hearing the news, he had raced to return: to rejoin the men and to share their suffering during the siege. Now they fanned out behind him and followed. Accounts of what he shouted to them differ. "On, Wisconsin!" was the version his son later accepted as true.

Down from the Confederate cannons on the crest came canister and grapeshot spraying metal balls everywhere. Finding refuge where possible in the ridge's jagged face and behind the stumps of trees the Confederates had cleared, the Wisconsin men dashed for cover before darting out again. But there was no hiding the flag. MacArthur held it high, even when a blast of canister tore through it. On he went at the head of the men pulling themselves up the ridge with their knees scraping the ground and their hands stretching for branches, rocks, or whatever else they could grasp. One final surge brought them over the crest and into the enemy's breastworks. Down the opposite side of the ridge ran the Confederates, as the Wisconsinites chanted, "Chickamauga! Chickamauga!" Its name no longer haunted them. They had avenged their defeat. MacArthur had not been with them then, but he was with them now and would have his moment. Near the house that had served as the Confederate headquarters during the siege, he planted the flag he had carried. Despite having the rim of his hat struck, he had suffered only a scratch. The flag, by contrast, was in tatters. MacArthur made a point of showing it to Brigadier General Philip Sheridan, who would soon become famous as Grant's cavalry commander but was then in charge of the division to which the 24th Wisconsin belonged.

Others also took notice of the regiment's flag. A newspaper correspondent hailed it as one of the first Union flags to clear the ridgeline and credited MacArthur by name for its appearance. A corporal who kept a diary noted MacArthur's infectious courage. So did a captain who wrote to MacArthur's father and made him a very proud judge. The lieutenant had the pleasure of seeing his name praised in the regiment's official after-action report. But no mention of MacArthur appeared in the higher-level report General Sheridan filed for the division as a whole.

In truth, it would have seemed strange for Sheridan to mention MacArthur given that his feat was, as one historian of the battle puts it, "no more intrepid than" those of many other soldiers whose flags lined Missionary Ridge at the end of one of the Civil War's most complete and surprising routs. There was the sergeant who ran ahead of his regiment, the 88th Illinois, into a trench still teeming with armed Confederates and, though alone among them, planted a Union flag with complete disregard for his own safety. There was a captain who picked up the flag of the 19th Illinois after its previous three bearers had fallen, and then carried the colors to the crest despite having fourteen bullets pass through his coat. There was the Indiana color-bearer who handed off his regimental flag upon suffering two wounds but, after seeing the men carrying it in his stead go down, picked it back up and brought it to the top, where he received a third wound.

Douglas MacArthur did not grow up hearing those stories. He grew up hearing his father's story and came to believe an account of it where Arthur reached the top of the ridge not with just a scratch but with his clothes as torn as the flag, his body "racked with pain" and "covered with blood and mud," and "his smoke-blackened face barely recognizable." In this version, General Sheridan came over on his own to the young lieutenant. "Take care of him," Sheridan said to the men around MacArthur. "He has just won the Medal of Honor."

If Sheridan did say those words, the 24th Wisconsin's commanding officer, Major Carl von Baumbach, did not hear them. He remained under the impression that his adjutant was not even eligible for the medal, which Congress had created only the year before. The law authorized the president to award medals to "such non-commissioned officers and privates as shall most distinguish themselves by their gallantry in action." As a lieutenant, MacArthur was a commissioned officer, which meant he did not qualify. In early 1863, however, Congress had passed a second law expanding eligibility to lieutenants, captains, majors, colonels, and even generals. But the change to the law went largely overlooked.

So, as a result, did many extraordinary acts of valor until decades after the Civil War, when the Medal of Honor began to acquire the prestige that would soon make it synonymous with courage "above and beyond the call of duty." Old veterans began demanding new consideration. Around this time, in 1889, Arthur MacArthur happened to take a new job as the army's assistant adjutant general, which put him in the Washington office overseeing the paperwork needed for a medal. He had stayed in the army all these years despite his conviction that it had denied him and other officers the honors their deeds during the Civil War deserved. He channeled his bitterness into legalistic letters to the War Department. A characteristic one ended, "I feel very reluctant to agitate the subject again," after having done so for six pages. In June 1890, a letter nominating MacArthur for the medal arrived from his old commanding officer, von Baumbach, who explained that he had only "very recently been informed" (surely by MacArthur himself) that officers could receive the award after all. "I think it no disparagement to others to declare that he was 'most distinguished in action' on a field where many in the regiment displayed conspicuous gallantry, worthy of the highest praise," von Baumbach wrote. Only days after receiving the letter, the army awarded MacArthur his medal.

Douglas was ten years old at the time and had followed his father to Washington, DC. It must have seemed as if the whole city was reliving his father's charge up Missionary Ridge. There was Douglas's grandfather, the still-proud judge, who had accepted a judicial appointment in the federal district and made a name for himself as a storyteller as skilled at entertaining the capital's elite as entrancing an impressionable boy happy to listen for hours. There were also the veterans of the 24th Wisconsin who sent affidavits backing up von Baumbach's claims. Curiously, none of them could swear to a memory of having seen Arthur as he ascended the ridge. They had only a hazy recollection of spying the flag at the top and hearing what was said of Arthur afterward. It made no difference to Douglas. When it came time for him to write his own account of the battle, he could see the scene as if it had happened only moments before. Rising above the ridgeline in the fiery light of the setting sun, the banner and its bearer blurred together into the seamless form he imagined "silhouetted against the sky." Where there had been many flags, there was now just one, and it was indistinguishable from the name MacArthur.

Eight years after receiving the Medal of Honor, Arthur MacArthur would once again be part of a flag raising, this time thousands of miles across the Pacific in a place called the Philippines. For what would transpire on those islands many years later during the early months of World War II, Arthur's son Douglas would fulfill a long quest to receive his own Medal of Honor but not without controversy. The medal would come to the younger MacArthur only after he had accepted orders to abandon his besieged army in the Philippines to starvation and surrender—to flee the very danger the medal salutes soldiers for facing. He would famously vow to make his way back and let no one forget the phrase "I shall return."

So quoted have those words been that they have obscured the memory of a no less dramatic vow: the one made by the general whom MacArthur left behind in the Philippines. His name was Jonathan Mayhew Wainwright IV, and he pledged to stay with his soldiers no matter the cost and to share their fate even if it meant becoming the war's highest-ranking American prisoner. To General Wainwright would fall an assignment as above and beyond the call of duty as any performed on Missionary Ridge and yet as different as the distance between victory and defeat: not lifting up the flag in battle but rather staying to see it taken down at the sickening hour of surrender. For the example he set, Wainwright would ultimately receive his own Medal of Honor but also the scorn of the second General MacArthur.

As the light dims on the last of the old soldiers who waged the Second World War, Wainwright has disappeared below the horizon of history's view, as if a footnote to the life of Douglas MacArthur, who stands above, as he envisioned his father, a singular hero silhouetted against the setting sun. The discovery of almost completely overlooked diaries and previously unexamined correspondence belonging to Wainwright and his family in military archives—boxes of primary source material not available the last time a biography of Wainwright appeared more than four decades ago—makes it possible, for the first time, to lift his character back into the light. What follows is a story that levels the field between him and MacArthur. It is the true tale of two World War II generals who received the same medal but found honor on very different paths. The choices these men made at the start of the conflict would drive them thousands of miles apart as if their stories had diverged along the lines of an ever-widening V. But there would be a second act, and another V, one whose lines would bring them back together at the fighting's end. And as with the Vs that General Grant had spied on the steep sides of Missionary Ridge, each would be essential to producing the most important V: victory.

PART I

Above and Beyond

CHAPTER ONE

Fatherland

Mary Pinkney Hardy MacArthur begged the army to send her husband somewhere closer. "Anything else but this," she wrote in June 1898. Twenty-three years had passed since she had married Arthur MacArthur near her family home in Norfolk, Virginia. The wedding had proceeded over the objections of two of her brothers, who had served in the Confederate army and did not want her to hitch her fate to a Union war hero. In the years after, she had followed Arthur far away from the comfortable life she had known to remote army posts such as Fort Wingate, New Mexico, where she had journeyed through scorching heat just months after giving birth on January 26, 1880, to her third and final son, Douglas. Now the army wanted to send Arthur to the other side of the world, to a place called Manila in the Philippines, which the president himself, William McKinley, reportedly joked he could not find on a map. McKinley could not even articulate what he wanted the soldiers to do in this foreign land.

Nevertheless, the War Department would not alter her husband's orders. Arthur himself seemed oddly pleased with the opportunity to join the five thousand men squeezing aboard the six converted cargo ships the War Department had chartered for the seven-thousand-mile voyage across the Pacific. Perhaps because "Pinky," as the family called

Mary, discovered that he had undermined her wish to keep him in a staff position in the adjutant general's office, she refused to join the other women seeing their sweethearts off from the harbor in San Francisco. Instead, she stayed with Douglas, who was busy preparing for West Point, where he would soon commence his own army career at the United States Military Academy. He was eighteen, the same age his father had been when he had picked up the fallen flag in Chattanooga.

Now a fifty-three-year-old brigadier general, Arthur had long ago lost the boyish looks that had made him ripe for ribbing on the parade ground. At five feet ten inches and 185 pounds, he had developed a barrel chest that filled out his uniform. Free of the ringlets that had formerly framed his face, his features had puffed out. The thick mustache he had grown gave him an air of maturity. But through the pince-nez he wore as he sat on one of the wicker chairs reserved for officers on the decks of the ships, his eyes searched the vast Pacific for what they had found all those years before on Missionary Ridge: a chance for glory and a new mountain to climb.

On July 29, 1898, it suddenly appeared—an island that, as one soldier put it, "took the form of a mountain rising abruptly from the ocean and towering skyward." A closer inspection revealed not just one mountain but many, running as far as the men could see down the east side of what they learned was Luzon, the most important island in the Philippine archipelago. On the crude maps they carried, Luzon had the look of a dragon with its massive wings outstretched before them to the northeast, its tail spiraling down to the southeast, and its head jutting out to the northwest. Navigating around the island's northern coast and then turning south into the choppy waters of the South China Sea, the soldiers saw more and more mountains leading them down the island's western side, past a peninsula called Bataan, which extended downward as if the dragon had stuck out its front legs. Tucked behind them was Manila Bay with its namesake city lying eastward along the belly of the beast, where its hind legs descended before wrapping back around toward Bataan without ever reaching it. In the twelve miles of water between lay a tiny island called Corregidor, which dominated the entrance to the bay but, as Arthur's son would one day discover, also lay in the clutches of the dragon.

It was a little before noon on the last day of July when the convoy pulled into formation, steamed past the lighthouse crowning Corregidor, and ventured into Manila Bay. A blinding rain greeted the ships. But when it ceased and the clouds parted, a panoramic view unfolded of the land receding around a rapidly widening body of water filled with canoes balanced on either side by bamboo outriggers bobbing on the glistening waves. Out of the water to one side poked the masts and smashed-up smokestacks of a Spanish fleet that the United States Navy had sent to the bottom weeks earlier. British, German, French, Russian, and Japanese warships had sailed into the bay in the aftermath and now waited in the harbor on the far shore as if curious to see what the Americans would do next. Behind the foreign vessels, the spires and domes of Manila peeked out above the thick stone walls that had once safeguarded the old city but no longer could. The first General MacArthur had arrived and, with him, a new age of American empire.

* * *

The American soldiers' entrance into Manila Bay marked a new era for their country. But their arrival represented more of the same for the Philippines. Foreigners had been coming to the islands since before the dawn of history. Even many of the people whom the Americans would refer to as "natives" had descended from peoples who had come as interlopers in their own time—many aboard boats with outriggers not dissimilar from the ones MacArthur and his men found in Manila Bay. Long before the United States became known as a melting pot capable of absorbing ideas and people from around the world—long before the country had even existed—this melting was already happening under the scorching tropical sun of the Philippines, with the Chinese integrating the islands into their empire of trade and with Muslims sending their missionaries to a culture already tinged with Buddhism and Hinduism. Nonetheless, it seems fitting that the recorded history of a place as culturally diverse as the Philippines should largely begin with its star-crossed role in the first expedition to circumnavigate the globe.

Of the more than two hundred crew members who set off from Spain with Ferdinand Magellan in 1519, only eighteen returned in 1522, and their captain was not among them. The survivors told of the land where they had lost him—an archipelago of palm-filled islands with gold jewelry, porcelain dishes, and houses built on stilts and covered with thatched roofs made of a native leaf called nipa. There were said to be bats the size of foxes and beautiful women whose black hair swept the ground and whose clothes left little to a sailor's imagination. Magellan had begun converting the people on an island called Cebu to Catholicism before deciding to impress them by sailing off to battle their enemies on a neighboring island. But his landing did not have the intended effect. Wading ashore to find a force thirty times as large as his own, he was hit by a poisoned arrow and hacked to death while nobly covering the retreat of his men back to their boats.

Having not made it past the middle group of islands (known today as the Visayas), Magellan never grasped the extent of an archipelago anchored to the north and south by its two largest islands. Toward the top, near Taiwan, lies the dragon-shaped island of Luzon. Toward the bottom lies the slightly smaller island of Mindanao, which dips as far south as Borneo. In all, the islands of the chain number more than seven thousand. Had Magellan's suicidal landing represented the high-water mark of Spanish conquest, the islands might have remained separate entities or drifted into different empires. Certainly, they would not have been christened in honor of Crown Prince Philip, who later as king of Spain made the decision to keep the islands as a colony. In 1570, Spanish soldiers sailed into Manila Bay and razed a Muslim settlement there. Upon its ruins rose the great city awaiting MacArthur and his men.

By the time the Americans arrived, the Spanish grip on the Philippines had already loosened. Once part of the world's mightiest colonial

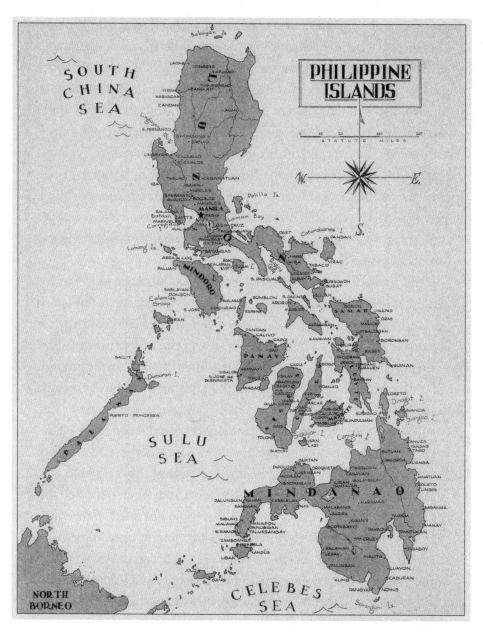

An army map showing the Philippine archipelago. Toward the top lies the dragon-shaped island of Luzon with its head facing westward, one of its wings outstretched to the northeast, and its tail spiraling off to the southeast. The Bataan peninsula juts downward as if the dragon has extended its claws toward Corregidor, the little island guarding the entrance to Manila Bay.

empire, most of Spain's overseas possessions had long ago broken free. The lucrative trade the Spanish had operated between the Philippines and Mexico had ceased even before the latter won its independence in 1821 as part of a revolutionary tide sweeping Latin America. In the late 1890s, the revolution of greatest interest to the United States was the one occurring closest to its shores, in Cuba. The concentration camps, torture, and other cruel tactics that the Spanish deployed against the Cuban people appalled Americans. Many began to expect that the conflict would eventually entangle their own country. What few expected was that far more of America's sons would lose their lives not in the Spanish colony ninety miles away but in the one halfway around the world.

Not for lack of warning signs did the revolution erupting in the Philippines concurrently with the Cuban struggle go largely unnoticed in the United States. More than three centuries of colonial rule had made the Philippines a mountain of Catholicism in Asia but one filled with pent-up fury over the abuses of the friars. In 1896, on the grounds of the iconic Manila park known as the Luneta, the Spanish executed a writer named José Rizal, whose books and social commentary had made him a symbol of the insurgency, never mind that he himself did not completely support it. The next year, Spain negotiated a sort of truce with Emilio Aguinaldo y Famy, the twenty-eight-year-old who had leaped to the front of the independence movement. The Spanish offered Aguinaldo political reforms at some point in the future if he agreed to leave the islands in exchange for money. He accepted and set off for Hong Kong, where his fate as well as his country's would get wrapped up in the American flags flying at half-mast in the harbor.

It so happened that Admiral George Dewey had his fleet, the United States Navy's Asiatic Squadron, in Hong Kong when he received news of an explosion on February 15, 1898, of an American warship docked in Havana, Cuba. Rather than wait for proof of Spanish involvement, American newspapers demanded revenge. In Washington, a thirty-nine-year-old assistant secretary of the navy named Theodore

Roosevelt, who liked nothing more than running the department when his boss was out, as happened to be the case on February 25, sent Dewey a telegraph message reading, "In the event of declaration of war [with] Spain, your duty will be to see that the Spanish squadron does not leave the Asiatic coast, and then offensive operations in Philippine Islands." When war came in April, Dewey saw to that and more. The Spanish squadron he located in Manila Bay would never again sail out of its mouth. The masts and smokestacks that MacArthur and his men saw rising out of the water upon their arrival marked the final resting place of the ships Dewey had sunk on May 1.

The enormity of the victory settled control of Manila Bay but left the fate of the Philippines itself undecided. The days of Spanish rule looked numbered. Little more than Manila remained under Spain's control. Around the city formed a Filipino army under the command of Aguinaldo, who had returned from Hong Kong aboard an American warship in the hope that the United States, which had declared its own independence barely a century before, would support the declaration of independence he issued on June 12, 1898. The other foreign powers whose ships had breached the bay knew no more about America's intentions but had no doubt about one another's. One of their countries would seize the Philippines if the United States did not.

What the United States would do was a mystery even to Americans. Not for mere show had the United States Congress attached an amendment forswearing annexation of Cuba to its resolution authorizing force against Spain. The Philippines, however, had appeared nowhere in the amendment. Where the islands had begun to appear was in the plans of a clique of Washington policymakers led by the irrepressible Roosevelt and immersed in the historian Alfred Thayer Mahan's theories of sea power. Great powers required great fleets, went the thinking, and great fleets required overseas bases for projecting their great power. If Roosevelt and his crew could carry along William McKinley, who seemed determined to keep everyone guessing as long as possible, the United States would plant its flag in the Philippines.

No one would have mistaken Arthur MacArthur for a member of Roosevelt's clique, even though someone might have mistaken Mac-Arthur for Roosevelt himself given the way both men thrust out their chests and hid their faces behind mustaches and spectacles. Both men had also seen enough of their country's western frontier to know that the railroads would soon tame it and that a people as adventurous as Americans would need to go in search of new horizons. At the far-flung forts to which the army had sent him after the Civil War, MacArthur had found few Indians and bandits to fight and, instead, endless hours to read books about the world and refine the idea that would animate the rest of his life: a conviction that America's future lay even farther to the west. At a time when seeing the world for most Americans meant crossing the Atlantic to Europe, MacArthur had set his mind the other way, across the Pacific to Asia. In 1883, his thinking came together, in his usual long-winded way, in a forty-four-page report, written as part of a campaign to secure a position as military attaché to China. Nothing came of the plan despite MacArthur sending his manifesto to his old general, Ulysses S. Grant, now a former president who had recently seen Asia for himself as part of a global tour. "The heated imagination," MacArthur wrote of Asia, "can indulge the boldest assumptions, since it is essentially an unknown country." Passing off one's own ignorance of a place as a qualification for writing about it may not seem an auspicious start for a report, but it led MacArthur to genuinely prescient insights. He envisioned Asia as the future battleground of empires whose "collision . . . would resound on the shores of the Pacific and affect the commerce of the world." As a growing country in need of new markets, the United States could not afford to stay on the sidelines. "Self-interest, sound economy, and pure morals," MacArthur wrote, "point us to the Orient as the field of our future labors."

Now, finally, fifteen years later, those very same forces had brought not just the United States but Arthur MacArthur himself to the Philippines. Here was a mission aligned not only with the tide of history, as he understood it, but also with his own pursuit of glory. The opportunity came on August 13, 1898, when Major General Wesley Merritt, America's top commander in the Philippines, ordered his forces to seize Manila. Although MacArthur had his brigade in the trenches that Aguinaldo's men had dug, the Americans were not to share their victory with the Filipinos. The orders Merritt issued required MacArthur to hold back his supposed allies while advancing against the Spanish. Only afterward did MacArthur learn why. Merritt had struck a deal with his Spanish counterpart. The Spanish would resist the attack only to the extent needed to satisfy their honor in exchange for assurances they could surrender Manila not to the Filipinos but to the Americans.

MacArthur would later take offense to hearing politicians describe the battle for Manila as a "simple feint." By the time he entered the city, more than thirty of his soldiers had fallen. He had stood with them at the front against the Spanish, even as fire had also come from the rear, where furious Filipinos realized that it would not be their flag replacing the huge Spanish one flying over Manila at the day's end. As the Spanish gave way, MacArthur led his men across a deep moat full of foul-smelling water. On the other side stood the colossal stone walls the soldiers had seen from the bay and, inside them, the old part of the city known as Intramuros, literally meaning "within the walls." In places, the masonry stood twenty-five feet high and almost twice as thick. Through one of the gates and down slender streets hemmed in by houses with windows made not of glass but of tantalizing mother of pearl—and past the Spanish-looking churches and government buildings that would have looked ancient even on the continent that inspired their architecture—MacArthur and his men marched. Ahead lay Fort Santiago, where cheers rang out as the American flag went up over the old walls.

For the next four decades, the Stars and Stripes would fly over Manila. How much of the rest of the Philippines would come under the American flag would depend on forces far from the islands: on what instructions the American diplomats set to sail to Paris for negotiations with the Spanish would receive from the tight-lipped McKinley in

Washington. In the meantime, General Merritt named MacArthur as Manila's provost marshal general and placed him in charge of its occupation. In no way had MacArthur's career prepared him for overseeing a sprawling city of three hundred thousand. Of the many books he had read about Asia, few of them offered any insights on the Philippines. He had tried to obtain more information before leaving San Francisco but without much success. For briefing materials, the War Department could provide little more than encyclopedia clippings. One article that MacArthur had found elsewhere advised those headed to Manila, he recalled, "to carry coffins, as few returned alive."

That description seemed dead-on for the conditions confronting MacArthur during the first days of the American occupation. It was the rainy season, and the soldiers were drenched and muddy and yet, maddeningly, short of water because Aguinaldo had shut off the supply, which came from outside the American lines. The moist hot air spread the stench of the excrement and trash that had accumulated on the streets during the months of siege as more and more of Manila's people had crowded into the walls, which the city had long outgrown. Soon, however, life reemerged beyond Intramuros. To the north lay the Pasig River and, above it, the city's commercial center, where shops and merchant houses began to do business, as they had before, in the mornings after their keepers finished sipping their chocolate. In the afternoon, men began once again to take their families to the Luneta, the park just south of Intramuros, for carriage rides and concerts. It was a place where people came to behold the view and be viewed. As a man who knew the value of both, Arthur MacArthur put in his time.

Junior officers remembered MacArthur always dressed up because, as he explained, "neatness in dress of a soldier . . . has much to do in estimating his worth." They also remembered the systematic way MacArthur plunged into what he called a "year of observation and absorption" intended to remedy the "absolute ignorance," in which he and every other American had arrived. The unfamiliarity made his mind, as he put it, "especially sensitive and receptive" to learning. Though still not finding as many books as he wished on the Philippines, he obtained as many as he could from a bookdealer in Hong Kong.

More important were the moments MacArthur found as Manila's provost marshal—and soon after as a major general charged with command of American troops north of the Pasig River—to learn from the Filipino people themselves. "I became very much attached to them. I appreciated them, I think, perhaps, as much as any other American," he would say. "My opportunity for observation . . . was, perhaps, equal to any that entered the islands." He opened his table to prominent Filipinos, and they opened theirs to him. To one, he said, "The thought of social distinction between the Filipinos and Americans in this island has never entered my head." The thought had certainly entered the minds of fellow officers who referred to Filipinos with racial slurs and deemed them unworthy of American-style government. MacArthur disagreed, describing Filipinos as "intelligent" and "generous." He believed that the democratic ideals that had grown in the United States could take root in the Philippines and, from there, spread across Asia. The islands could govern themselves, he said, sooner than most Americans imagined but not as quickly, as he would discover, as many Filipinos wished.

The reasons Americans give for fighting wars have a way of sounding very different at the start of conflicts than at the end, and the Spanish-American War was no exception. A struggle that had begun with outrage over events in Cuba would culminate in the fall of 1898 with American negotiators insisting that Spain surrender the Philippines. President McKinley had finally made up his mind: The United States would annex all the islands. The Americans and the Spanish denied the Filipinos a seat at the negotiating table in Paris, but there was no denying that Aguinaldo's men in the field held a far stronger position—all but surrounding the American forces in Manila. It was while playing cards on the evening of February 4, 1899, two days before the United States Senate approved the treaty, that MacArthur learned the inevitable had happened. The usual nightly exchange of insults between the American and Filipino lines had exploded into an open exchange of fire. A new war had begun.

A little past noon the next day, MacArthur ordered a frontal assault against the defensive positions the Filipinos had spent months strengthening. The casualties should have been appalling, and they were, just not for the attackers, as the textbooks would have predicted. With MacArthur on horseback, his soldiers raced into and over trenches filled with dead Filipinos. So lopsided were the casualty numbers—about ten Filipinos for every American—that even politicians in the United States would later ask for an explanation. MacArthur, as usual, had a lengthy one. In brief, the Filipinos had all the courage that a general could want, just none of the rifle practice. They overshot their targets the same way the Confederate cannoneers at Chattanooga had. MacArthur's troops in the Philippines soon discovered what his troops at Missionary Ridge had: Safety lay not in skulking in the rear but in surging to the front.

Again and again in the weeks that followed, MacArthur sent his men charging into enemy works with similar results. North of Manila, up the island's lone railway, went MacArthur, sometimes traveling in an armored train equipped with machine guns while his men pushed through jungles, swamps, and rice fields on foot. By now, MacArthur's advance had begun to win him space in newspapers back in the United States. A *Harper's Weekly* correspondent wrote that watching MacArthur direct his troops in the line of fire would make any American "gulp a little and feel proud." That praise did not go far enough to satisfy MacArthur's wife, who could finally see the potential in his posting to the Philippines if only he would receive the credit he deserved. Part of the problem lay with MacArthur himself. He was not averse to self-promotion, as even a cursory look at his army file reveals, but he had a stiff formality that kept reporters at a distance. More concerning was that Aguinaldo managed to keep his own distance despite MacArthur's success in the battlefield.

Determined to end the conflict in the fall of 1899, Elwell Stephen Otis, who had replaced Merritt as commanding general, organized an elaborate plan that previewed the landing grounds to which warriors would return in World War II. With MacArthur still moving his army up the railroad from the south, Otis had an amphibious force land to the north on the beaches where the tracks from Manila terminated at Lingayen Gulf, the body of water filling the space between the back of the dragon-like island's head to the northwest and its soaring wing to the northeast. With his men suddenly surrounded, Aguinaldo had no choice but to scatter them. Never again would he ask them to face the Americans head on. Future resistance would take the form of guerrilla warfare. Aguinaldo himself escaped into the mountains. Nevertheless, Otis declared the war over when he returned to the United States in the spring of 1900. It was a presidential election year, and that was the message the politicians wished to hear. They would not appreciate Otis's successor, Arthur MacArthur, informing them otherwise.

Now in command of the more than seventy thousand Americans occupying the islands, MacArthur enjoyed perks he could not have imagined during his days on the frontier: the lofty title of military governor of the Philippines and an official residence at Malacañan, the palatial Spanish house whose veranda opened onto the north bank of the Pasig, just upriver from Manila's commercial district. MacArthur moved into the house in May. One month later, he received for lunch the members of a new commission charged by McKinley with overseeing the transition to civilian rule. At the head of the commission sat William Howard Taft, a 325-pound federal judge who had set his sights on a seat on the United States Supreme Court. Historians have made much of the combined weight of the five commissioners and their secretary—reported to total 1,326 pounds—but however much these men consumed at lunch does not explain MacArthur's decision to bar them from most future meals at Malacañan. The true explanation lies instead in MacArthur's insistence on drawing a rigid line where only a fuzzy one existed between the domain of professional soldiers and political appointees.

Finding that line would topple MacArthur, just as it one day would his son, from the height of power. And because the first General

MacArthur's personal papers burned during the war that the second fought in the Philippines, accounts of the family's first such feud have drawn mostly from Taft's letters, much to Arthur's disadvantage. "The more I have to do with [MacArthur], the smaller the man of affairs I think he is," Taft wrote in July 1900. "His experience and his ability as a statesman or politician are nothing. He has all the angularity of military etiquette and discipline, and he takes himself with great seriousness." When Taft proposed the creation of a "native constabulary" reporting to his commission instead of the army, MacArthur resisted. The United States Army already had what would become an elite group of pro-American Filipino troops known as Scouts. As long as the Philippines remained under military rule, he as military governor should command all forces in the country. He considered Taft's attempts to transform his commission into a quasi-legislative body to be unconstitutional. Only the United States Congress, MacArthur claimed, could set up a civil government for the Philippines. Until then, all authority remained with him as military governor, never mind that his commander in chief, McKinley, had signed off on Taft's idea. As an actual constitutional lawyer, Taft bristled. "It has always been a curious phase of political human nature to me to observe that men who have not had the slightest knowledge of legal principles . . . feel entirely at home in the construction of the Constitution and in using its limitations to support their views."

What Taft found most maddening about MacArthur was his ability—or willingness, anyway—to expound on subjects as if he were "a profound and philosophical thinker," a pretense he kept up with the annoying habit of stacking suffixes upon suffixes onto the end of words for no seeming purpose except padding his own ego. For Arthur, even the most academic question was an important "academical" one. When asked about America's military situation in the Philippines, he might preface his response by discussing the influences of the French Revolution. Taft seethed while listening to MacArthur lecture about how his experience had allowed him to observe the Filipino people more closely than any other American and given him powerful insights into their "psychological conditions." No doubt, MacArthur was condescending, but he was also sometimes right. While Taft informed Washington that the "great majority" of Filipinos supported American rule, MacArthur had realized the opposite: The guerrillas had proved popular with the Filipinos and, even worse, effective against the Americans.

Casualties had begun to climb. Facing an enemy who wore no uniform, American field officers grumbled that MacArthur forced their troops to fight in "white suits and collars." The gloves needed to come off. MacArthur knew it, too. But conceding the need for a change of strategy before the presidential election could have hurt the Republican McKinley's chances of winning a second term, especially given the well-known imperialist ideology of his new running mate, Theodore Roosevelt. Only after the Republican ticket triumphed in November did MacArthur announce plans for a new offensive that would take the battle not just to the guerrillas but to the communities that supported them. He had always believed the army needed to show the benefits of American rule by opening schools and providing the educational opportunities the Filipino people craved—by winning "hearts and minds," as the expression goes. But now he would also ensure the Filipinos learned the other side of the equation: the consequences of not submitting, the destruction of crops and villages.

In the early hours of March 28, 1901, the most amazing news awoke MacArthur at Malacañan. Emilio Aguinaldo was at the door as a result of a wild-sounding plan MacArthur had approved weeks earlier. Colonel Frederick Funston, who had received a Medal of Honor for his courage earlier in the war, had gained access to Aguinaldo's hideaway by pretending to be a prisoner of war and had succeeded in capturing the nationalist leader. Delighted, MacArthur dined with Aguinaldo that morning and many times afterward in the hope that kindness would convince him to do what destroying his army on the plains of Luzon had not: accept American rule and urge his followers to do the same. Among those followers was a young man named Manuel

Quezon, whom MacArthur allowed to visit Aguinaldo. The quiet courtesy MacArthur showed would remain a vivid memory that Quezon
would recall many years later when, as president of the Philippines,
he would welcome MacArthur's son to the same palace.

For now, however, the future of Malacañan belonged to William
Howard Taft. On July 4, 1901, the judge replaced the general as governor.
Arthur MacArthur had triumphed in the Philippines but lost where it
mattered more, in Washington. In some sense, he had fallen victim to
his own success, which had allowed Taft to persuade members of the
McKinley administration that the Philippines no longer required a military governor. Tens of thousands of guerrillas had begun laying down
their arms, even before Aguinaldo finally agreed to issue a proclamation
calling on them to do so. Three years had passed since MacArthur had
last seen the United States. He was ready to return, even if bitter about
the way the War Department had arranged the transition behind his
back. People heard him speak of "the humiliation" he had endured and
how "he would be glad to have an end brought to it."

One last humiliation awaited MacArthur upon reaching San Francisco harbor on August 18, 1901. Dewey and Otis had returned to
adoring crowds. As MacArthur bounded down the gangplank, he saw
nothing of the sort. The army had delegated his reception to a junior
officer. The McKinley administration had sent no one. "MacArthur
Is Slighted," read a headline in his hometown Milwaukee newspaper.
The general did not even see his family. No member had come. Taft
would have his wife, Helen, with him at Malacañan. The evidence suggests Pinky never considered doing the same for her husband. She had
accompanied her son Douglas to West Point and chosen to stay there.
The two of them would meet Arthur halfway across the country in
Chicago. Before heading east for the reunion, Arthur, looking a little
skinnier than he had in 1898, offered a reminder of why Taft had been
so eager to do away with him. The fight in the Philippines was not over,
MacArthur told reporters. More American soldiers would die on the
islands. One of them would be Major Robert Powell Page Wainwright.

*   *   *

Robert Powell Page Wainwright, who relatives called "Robbie," did not go to the Philippines in June 1902 with any illusions about war. He had learned the reality early in life as a result of two deaths, both involving naval officers named Jonathan Mayhew Wainwright. At the start of 1863, when Robbie was ten, Confederate forces boarding the USS *Harriet Lane* had fired a musket ball into the head of his father, Commander Jonathan Mayhew Wainwright II. Seven years later, just as Robbie was beginning his own military career at West Point, the newspapers had brought word of an incident off the coast of Mexico. Pirates had ambushed his oldest brother, Ensign Jonathan Wainwright III. Both the older and younger Jonathan Mayhews, it was said, had died much the same way: with their fingers clutched around their swords. To the end, Robbie learned, Wainwrights performed their duty. The best measure of how their deaths shaped his outlook lies in the choice he and his wife, Josephine Serrell, the New York girl he had begun courting at West Point, made at his post at Fort Walla Walla in the Washington Territory on August 23, 1883, when they named their third child and only son Jonathan Mayhew Wainwright IV, not in spite of the name's history, but because of it.

In the Philippines, Major Robbie Wainwright found himself in a desk job instead of in the saddle, where friends had always thought him happiest. His twenty-seven years in the cavalry had taken him out west, where he had fought in the last of the Indian wars, and then to Cuba, where he had impressed none other than Theodore Roosevelt, who had joined the fight against the Spanish with a volunteer cavalry regiment known as the Rough Riders. Upon returning to Washington as vice president, Roosevelt would take with him memories of Robbie Wainwright's "gallantry," "modesty," and "fine and high sense of honor." Wainwright had not asked for a transfer to the adjutant general's office in Manila, but he had received it, anyway. Just as he arrived, Roosevelt, who had become president upon the assassination of William McKinley, declared the war over, even though it was not really so. True, growing support for American rule had made it harder for guerrilla forces to disappear into the jungles. But malaria, dysentery, cholera, and other microscopic illnesses endemic to the islands remained invisible and far more prolific killers capable of incapacitating entire regiments. Even the great stone walls of Intramuros could not protect against the bite of a mosquito or a sip of contaminated water—or the blockage of an artery, as Major Wainwright's family discovered when he died suddenly in the wee hours of November 19, 1902. "Cardiac embolism" was said to be the cause.

In what was becoming a pattern for the family, Jonathan Mayhew Wainwright IV received the news at West Point, where he had enrolled only months earlier. If the young Wainwright went in search of solace, as he surely must have, he would have found it in the father of an older and especially distinguished cadet named Douglas MacArthur, then in his final months at the academy. At a high-profile Senate hearing, Arthur MacArthur had recently testified that the men who had died in the Philippines had died for the noblest and most important cause imaginable. The world had no position more important or "strategical," as he characteristically put it, than the Philippines. Whoever controlled the islands would determine the future of Asia. By withdrawing from them, the United States would doom the future of democracy in the Far East and set off a great power struggle that would eventually claim the lives of far more of America's sons. By staying in the islands, however, the United States could deter the enemies of democracy with, Arthur assured, "the very least output of physical power." But as Arthur's son would discover forty years later, it would take far more. Everything Robbie Wainwright's son had would not be enough.

CHAPTER TWO

The Call of History

B ehind Arthur MacArthur, Robbie Wainwright, and their fellow soldiers had come a second wave of Americans: lofty-minded teachers
determined to turn their "little brown brothers," as Governor Taft had
dubbed the Filipinos, into English-speakers, build them schools, and
show them the blessings of democracy and the American way. The
newcomers described Manila as the "Pearl of the Orient," even as they
made it, in the words of one newspaperman, "the most thoroughly
typical American city." Soon, it had multiple English newspapers, where
readers could find advertisements for the same brand names beloved
in the United States. Many were for sale in the fancy shops along the
commercial strip north of the Pasig River. The walls of Intramuros still
stood below the river but no longer behind the old medieval-looking
moat. Over the once-stinking water had grown the most American of
remedies: a golf course.

The neoclassical government buildings that had gone up on stately
columns on the east end of the Luneta—and the memorial to the mar-
tyred poet José Rizal that had gone up on the west end—made the
grounds reminiscent of the National Mall in Washington, DC, only
with palm trees instead of elms. Little impressed the Americans gathering at the Luneta late in the day more than the view across the bay

as the sun descended toward the water at an astonishing speed not seen at more northerly latitudes. As the sky flushed orange and red, the dark outlines of Corregidor and Mount Mariveles at the bottom of the Bataan peninsula would come into sharp relief only to fade away as the sun sank behind them.

In the darkness on Sunday, December 7, 1941, English echoed late into the night in the splendid Manila Hotel, which the Americans had built for themselves by the Luneta with luxurious guest rooms and a marble-floor lobby ringed with pillars and arches in the Spanish-mission style. At wicker tables under the pseudo shade of potted palm trees, reporters sharing iced drinks bet on when war might come to the Philippines without knowing that Japanese aircraft carriers were only hours away from bringing it to the shores of Hawaii on the other side of the international dateline, where the United States had its Pacific fleet at Pearl Harbor and where December 7 was still just beginning. One reporter predicted war within the week. Another said never. They had all heard the rhetoric from Japan about ridding Asia of white imperialists and seen the recent headline about the country's militant new prime minister: "TOJO DECLARES JAPAN 'ONE BALL OF FIERY RESOLUTION' AGAINST DEMOCRACIES." But the reporters had also read other headlines suggesting Japan might shirk from committing what seemed to be certain national suicide: "U.S. ADMIRAL SAYS NAVY CAN SINK JAP FLEET IN THREE WEEKS." The reporters knew Japan had a history of surprise attacks, but refused to believe an Asian navy could surprise America's.

The city of Manila itself offered arguments on both sides of the bet. Blackout curtains had gone up over the windows, but the neon lights in the clubs still blazed and beckoned to American soldiers. They had received orders to be ready for war, but they still had time to sneak off that Sunday night for a showing of *Sergeant York*, the new American film about the most storied Medal of Honor recipient from what the newspapers now referred to as World War I, as if a sequel were inevitable. The army wives who had come with their husbands to the islands had taken their children back to the United States on orders from the War Department, but there were still plenty of women—"attractive" Filipina ones, as the word went—to be found.

Some danced near the reporters that Sunday night for a party thrown in the hotel's pavilion by a group of American airmen. Having prepped hours earlier at the bar, the airmen appeared on what they called their "very best drunken behavior." They had gathered in honor of their new chief, Brigadier General Lewis Brereton, who had taken command of the growing air force on the islands. The bespectacled Brereton did not look like the prototypical airman but could certainly act like one with a taste for alcohol and an eye for women. Tonight, however, he seemed surprisingly sober. As his airmen belted out tunes, he listened to a fellow brigadier general, Richard Sutherland, say the war could begin at any hour. Brereton's eyes widened. Sutherland was in a position to know. He served as chief of staff to the commanding general sleeping upstairs in the air-conditioned, gilt-furnished apartment on the hotel's top floor.

No American alive, it was said, knew more about war and the geopolitics of the Pacific than the man in the penthouse. Among the suite's rooms was one with silver frames standing on a large glossy table made of narra, the famed Philippine hardwood, and holding signed photographs of the great generals of the age safely behind glass. On the walls around the table, floor-to-ceiling shelves, also made of narra, showcased books about Asia as well as some of the thousands of other volumes that had belonged to Arthur MacArthur and passed to his sole surviving son, Douglas. For this General MacArthur, the hotel was home.

Since arriving in Manila in November, Brereton had often gone upstairs to listen to Douglas MacArthur talk as he paced around his penthouse in his peculiar way: jaw out in front of him, body almost unnaturally erect as if to make it that last inch and a half to six feet, clothes crisp as if resistant to the tropical humidity, baggy pleated pants pulled up over a small paunch, small and sometimes-trembling hands pocketed except when fidgeting with a cigarette or pencil, and shoes always polished but never near each other as a result of a massive stride. "The more clearly he enunciates his ideas, the more vigorous his walking becomes," Brereton had noticed. And as to when the war would begin, MacArthur could not have been clearer, at least, early on. Nothing would happen until 1942 and probably not until April, by which time he would have his army ready for any force the Japanese could send. He had said it more times than anyone could remember, but he had begun to do so with a little less certainty, Brereton thought.

Nonetheless, MacArthur did not let the racket below from the reporters and the airmen trouble him. He had gone to bed, as he usually did, before midnight in the apartment's smallest bedroom. He left the bigger ones for his wife, Jean, and their three-year-old son, neither of whom had been subject to the evacuation order. The party downstairs finally ended at two in the morning. Not long after, the penthouse phone began to ring. Everything MacArthur had done in his nearly sixty-two years of life should have prepared him to answer the call.

*   *   *

Douglas had received his first lesson in soldiering in 1884 as a four-year-old toddling alongside a company of infantrymen in the American southwest to yet another of those remote forts to which the army kept assigning his father. The three hundred miles of dusty roads that young Douglas covered with the company would serve as the starting point for his memory in later years. The soldiers went down the Rio Grande from Albuquerque and then across a barren land where, however far they trekked, the next watering hole was always said to be ten miles farther. As the company's commanding officer, Douglas's father rode on horseback. Almost everyone else marched. Douglas recalled himself trudging "at the head of the column" in front of a recruit begging for a seat on one of the wagons. "Growl you may," Douglas heard his father quip, "but march you must." Ahead lay Fort Selden, New Mexico, a group of adobe buildings in the middle of a treeless desert more suited to tarantulas and snakes than children.

Douglas's mother, Pinky, described Selden as "lonely." No doubt, she was. Besides Douglas, she had her husband and their firstborn son, a seven-year-old named Arthur III. The four of them had only three rooms, yet they never seemed filled. Months before setting out for Selden, the middle of Pinky's three sons had died from the measles. The loss, Douglas would say, "seemed only to increase her devotion to Arthur and myself. This tie was to become one of the dominant factors of my life." Pinky put four-year-old Douglas in skirts and fussed over the curls in his hair. A two-year-old boy named Franklin Delano Roosevelt could have commiserated that his overbearing mother did no less. But what seemed normal in Hyde Park, New York, seemed less so at Fort Selden. Nevertheless, Douglas never doubted what his mother expected him to become. Every night before bed, she reminded him he must become "a great man" in the image of his father or Robert E. Lee, the general her brothers had served during the Civil War.

There was another bedtime ritual Douglas cherished. As the sun went down, he would stand as straight as he could and watch the flag come down as the buglers played retreat. The sound would echo in his mind ever after, along with the lessons his parents hoped he would draw from the scene. "We were to do what was right no matter what the personal sacrifice might be," Douglas remembered. "Our country was always to come first. Two things we must never do: never lie, never tattle." With no schools, he had to look to his parents for instruction in the basics of reading, writing, and arithmetic. They did their best, but the boy took to riding and shooting far quicker. Those skills seemed more important. His father had declared the frontier all but settled the year before setting out for Selden, but it seemed perfectly wild to young Douglas. Geronimo was on the loose, and the army was on the Apache leader's trail. But Douglas's father was not among the glorious cavalrymen able to give chase on horseback. He was in the infantry and pining for an assignment elsewhere. It finally came in 1886 with orders to go to Fort Leavenworth, Kansas, where Douglas would see his first schoolhouse. Never again would he see the American frontier, but always would he see himself as a child of the west.

Less to his liking, he claimed many years later after politicians there had wrecked his career, was Washington, DC, where he went when his father received his promotion to the adjutant general's office and, soon after, his Medal of Honor. "Washington was different from anything I had ever known. It was my first glimpse at the whirlpool of glitter and pomp, of politics and diplomacy, of statesmanship and intrigue. I found it no substitute for the color and excitement of the frontier," Douglas wrote. He attended a public school on Massachusetts Avenue but did not excel. Not until age thirteen, when the army sent his father to Fort Sam Houston in San Antonio, did Douglas begin to set himself apart. The "transformation," as he called it, took place at the West Texas Military Academy, a school dedicated to the belief that competition brings out the best. It certainly did in Douglas. In 1897, he graduated first in his class and medaled in subjects including "competitive speaking," which would have surprised no one awed into silence in later years by his ability to declaim for hours without pause. His classmates would remember him also as their tennis champion, starting quarterback, and speedy shortstop. "Many of the school medals came my way," Douglas wrote in his autobiography years afterward. "But I also learned how little such honors mean after one wins them," a fact hard to reconcile with the many mentions those honors would receive in the memoir.

Douglas always knew what his parents expected him to do next, and never questioned it save once at the start of the Spanish-American War, when he wished to join a regiment as a teenager, as his father had done. The MacArthurs would not hear of it. They had sent their oldest son to the Naval Academy at Annapolis. They would send their youngest son to West Point, that is, if they could secure an appointment for him. After a first attempt at using their political connections failed, they settled on a more radical plan. For their son's future, they would go separate ways: Arthur to a new post in St. Paul; Pinky and Douglas to Milwaukee, where the family name carried the most political sway and where a congressman had promised to appoint whichever young man scored the highest on a test. Mother and son moved into a hotel, where she oversaw his preparation: his classes at a local high school, his lessons with tutors, and his treatment with a doctor able to remedy a bend in his spine that would have otherwise prevented his admission. "I never worked harder in my life," Douglas recalled. But it would not have been enough, he admitted, without his mother. It was she who comforted him on the morning of the test when he awoke, as he often would when under pressure, feeling nauseated. "Doug," she said, "you'll win if you don't lose your nerve. You must believe in yourself, my son, or no one else will believe in you." The words made an impression. When the newspapers published the scores, MacArthur's 93.3 percent stood double digits ahead of anyone else's. "It was a lesson I never forgot," he said. "Preparedness is the key to success and victory."

Another key was having your mother nearby. When Douglas went to West Point in June 1899, he did not go alone. Pinky came, too. She moved into another hotel, he into the so-called beast barracks where new cadets, called plebes, underwent an initiation at the hands of the upperclassmen. They set their sights on the five-foot-ten-inch, 133-pound MacArthur, whom they noted had "flashing dark eyes" and, despite being on the slender side, a "fine body." But it was not his good looks that made him their top target. It was the proximity of his mother as well as the prominence his father had achieved by that time in the Philippines. "We always prepared a warm reception for the sons of well-known men," said one upperclassman. After a night of particularly strenuous hazing, MacArthur's body went into convulsions. Determined to earn the respect of the upperclassmen and to not get them in trouble, he considered stuffing his mouth so as to stifle his screams. But keeping quiet would only get harder. After a plebe died the next year, a military court called MacArthur as a witness on December 28, 1900, and demanded he name his hazers. "Is it absolutely necessary," he asked, "that I give the names?" Yes, he was told. Refusing could lead to his expulsion. Complying would violate his parents' rule against tattling. The nausea he had felt before his West Point exam suddenly returned, and so did his mother to the rescue, this time by slipping him a poem that ended this way:

> *Like mother, like son, is saying so true*
> *The world will judge largely of mother by you.*
> *Be this then your task, if task it shall be*
> *To force this proud world to do homage to me.*
> *Be sure it will say, when its verdict you've won*
> *She reaps as she sowed: "This man is her son!"*

MacArthur later claimed these lines, which his mother had probably copied from a magazine, gave him the confidence to be, as he put it, "no tattletale." Yet records show he did, when pressed, give names, first to the court, and then again to a congressional committee.

Even so, Douglas made his mother proud. At the end of his four years at West Point, he had the admiration of his fellow cadets, served as their leader in his capacity as the so-called first captain, ranked first among them academically, and built an overall record that would draw comparisons to his mother's beloved Robert E. Lee. "This rating has always astonished me and I have never understood it," MacArthur wrote. "There were a number of my classmates who were smarter than I. . . . I studied no longer nor harder than others, and can only account for such a result by my having, perhaps, a somewhat clearer perspective of events—a better realization that first things come first." As important was having a near-photographic memory well suited to a curriculum that rewarded memorization. When Douglas graduated in June 1903, he had the joy of giving his diploma to his father, who had returned from the Philippines.

It would be Douglas who went to the islands next. Commissioned a second lieutenant in the Army Corps of Engineers, he received orders to head to the Philippines. "The Philippines charmed me," he noted upon arriving after thirty-eight days at sea. It was not just "the moonbeam delicacy of its lovely women," though they were certainly of interest to a twenty-three-year-old single officer. It was also what he called "the amazingly attractive result of a mixture of Spanish culture and American industry" and "the languorous laze that seemed to glamorize even the most routine chores of life." The alliteration "languorous laze" had the sound of Arthur MacArthur, and no doubt Douglas heard echoes of his father's name across the islands. It allowed Douglas to pass through doors not open to most second lieutenants. One evening, he found himself at dinner with two future presidents of the Philippines: Sergio Osmeña and Manuel Quezon, who had visited Aguinaldo in prison only two years earlier. Such men now seemed eager to ingratiate themselves with the Americans, but not everyone was. While MacArthur was working on a harbor in the Visayas, two bandits, as the holdout guerrillas had become known, ambushed him and fired a shot that passed straight through his hat. "Like all frontiersmen, I was expert with a pistol . . . [and] dropped them both dead in their tracks," he remembered. His years on the frontier, however, did him less good when he returned to Luzon with orders to explore the peninsula on the other side of Manila Bay and survey the mountain behind which the sun sank each evening. Like many of the young men later sent on his orders to Bataan, he came down with malaria. Unlike those soldiers, he would be able to go home and recover.

Back in the United States, Douglas's father had once again gotten his name into the newspapers, this time with a pair of predictions: that a future war would pit the United States against Germany and that Hawaii would lie in the line of fire. Neither prediction pleased Arthur's bosses, who happily obliged when he proposed a new assignment that would banish him to the other side of the world in 1905. He would observe the war that had begun the previous year when Japanese ships had launched a surprise attack on Russian ones at Port Arthur in Manchuria, a northern Chinese province. In the half century since the American commodore Matthew C. Perry had brought his warships into Tokyo Bay and forced Japan to cease its centuries of self-imposed isolation, the country had become a burgeoning military power, whose might Arthur witnessed firsthand during the final months of the Russo-Japanese War. When the fighting ended, the War Department agreed not only to let Arthur and his wife, who had joined him for once, continue their travels across Asia but also to take with them as an aide their son Douglas.

In the fall of 1905, Douglas reunited with his parents at a hotel in Yokohama, Japan. From there, they would travel nearly twenty thousand miles across the fiefdoms the European empires had carved in Asia. They would see the Dutch in the East Indies*; the French in Indochina; the British in Hong Kong, Singapore, Burma, and India; and seemingly everyone fighting for a piece of China. Along the way, Douglas observed poverty the likes of which few Americans could imagine, met the emperor of Japan, and attended a dinner held by the king of Siam. It was this dinner that has given historians their only known example of a MacArthur turning down a medal, when the king offered to decorate Douglas for repairing a broken fuse box. He was, after all, a young engineer, albeit one seeing the world through the eyes of his father, the general. Douglas would call the Asian tour "the most important factor of preparation in my entire life." But at the end of eight months of travel, it was time to return to a more typical lieutenant's life.

The officers to whom Douglas reported in the United States, however, sensed he believed his time too precious for the usual duties of an engineer. "I was of [the] opinion that he exhibited less interest in and put in less time upon the drafting room, the plans, and specifications . . . than seemed consistent with my instructions," wrote an officer who supervised MacArthur during a stint in Milwaukee. "He was absent from the office during office hours more than I thought proper." His excuses often involved needing to see his parents, who had settled in the city after learning that William Howard Taft, now the secretary of war, had conspired to assure that Arthur would never achieve his ultimate goal of leading the army as chief of staff. No more mountains

---

* Indonesia

remained for Arthur MacArthur to climb. There were only memories of the ridges of long ago. To those grounds his thoughts had returned on September 5, 1912, when he dropped dead at sixty-seven years old in the middle of a speech to fellow veterans of the 24th Wisconsin.

"My whole world changed that night," Douglas recalled. "Never have I been able to heal the wound in my heart." Pinky really would need her son nearby now, Douglas told his superiors. He suggested Washington, DC, as a spot that would benefit her health, to say nothing of his career. The army brass agreed. Douglas received orders to report to the chief of staff, who happened to be his father's old friend General Leonard Wood.

The order put Douglas and his mother close to power at an auspicious time. First came an opportunity in April 1914 to serve as General Wood's eyes on the ground in Veracruz, Mexico, which American forces under the command of Arthur MacArthur's famous protégé, Frederick Funston, had occupied as a result of a spat between the two countries. Once in the city, Douglas took the opportunity to conduct a daring but unauthorized reconnaissance mission that exposed him, as in the Philippines, to the bullets of bandits. Once again, the bullets left holes in his uniform but not in his body. Once again, his aim proved more accurate and dropped more than one of his assailants. Once again, the only eyewitness testimony to the incident would come from Douglas himself. More evidence than that was needed for the Medal of Honor, as Douglas learned much to his chagrin upon returning to Washington in August 1914. More upsetting to him—and more damning in the opinion of the board making the decision—was the suggestion, which even Funston seemed to share, that MacArthur had shown true courage but also a recklessness that the army should not elevate into an example for others to emulate. MacArthur responded, as his father would have, with an outraged four-page letter declaring himself a "victim" of "rankling injustice." Few other captains—and Douglas ranked no higher at this point—would have used such words, but serving on the general staff in Washington had only reinforced his sense of self-importance.

By 1916, he found himself a major serving as the army's press censor, a position tailor-made to his talent for shaping news coverage of the military and cultivating the reporters who would soon transform him into a household name.

It happened in Europe, when the United States fulfilled part of Arthur MacArthur's prediction by joining the Great War against Germany. As the story goes, Woodrow Wilson's secretary of war, Newton Baker, asked how he could deploy national guard units to the war's western front without showing preferences to forces from any one state. MacArthur, whose duties as press censor had made him close with the secretary, suggested forming a division that would include units from various states so it would "stretch over the whole country like a rainbow." The idea won over the secretary and so did the metaphor. The Rainbow Division was born. Promoted to colonel and transferred from the engineers to the infantry, where his father had served, Douglas went to France in the fall of 1917 as the new division's chief of staff and would rise to become one of its brigade commanders. He would experience the exhilaration of seeing his men follow him like "a roaring avalanche of glittering steel" over the top of a trench into no-man's-land, as well as the indelible horror of seeing "writhing bodies hanging from the barbed wire." In a war where all men lay equal before the randomness of death, MacArthur found ways to stand apart. There was his unusual uniform: the usually stiff cap that he had broken in by taking out its metal frame, the turtleneck sweater he wrapped in the muffler that his mother had made for him, and the riding crop that he carried out of what he called "long habit on the plains." There was also what he refused to wear: the steel helmet he found uncomfortable, the gas mask that would have spared him from the mustard gas he would inhale, and the pistol that he claimed he would have carried only if he had intended to "engage in personal combat."

MacArthur might not have cared to fire a gun, but he certainly seemed to relish being in the middle of gunfire. The commander of his division called MacArthur "the bloodiest fighting man in this army" and added, "I'm afraid we're going to lose him sometime, for there's no risk of battle that any soldier is called upon to take that he is not liable to look up and see MacArthur at his side." The risks he took often seemed to serve no purpose but to force Washington to finally give him the Medal of Honor. He had other explanations, of course. "I cannot fight them if I cannot see them," he once said. If he actually said, as has been claimed, that "all of Germany cannot fabricate a shell that will kill MacArthur," he certainly knew otherwise. "There are times when even general officers have to be expendable," MacArthur responded when asked why he had ignored a bullet that had just nipped his sweater. When ordered soon afterward to deliver either an enemy position or "a list of five thousand casualties," MacArthur answered that he would carry the ground or his name would be atop the list.

This sort of talk did not go unnoticed. Fellow soldiers dubbed MacArthur their very own "d'Artagnan," "the fighting dude," and "the bravest of the brave." The mystique made its way back to the United States, where readers of *The New York Times* learned that MacArthur was "considered the most brilliant young officer in the army" in an article about his promotion to brigadier general in the summer of 1918. Without his knowledge—or so his mother claimed—she had sent a letter a few weeks earlier to the American commander, General John J. Pershing, who had once served under Douglas's father. Pinky reminded Pershing of the connection while petitioning him to promote her son. "I am free to confess to you that my hope and ambition in this life is to live long enough to see this son made a general officer." Pershing approved MacArthur's promotion but then made a point of vetoing his nomination for a Medal of Honor. When MacArthur returned from France, he had earned every medal he could desire save for the one his father had received. But he had also earned powerful enemies, who gave him a new nickname: "the show-off."

Orders to return to West Point in 1919 as superintendent—an office Robert E. Lee had once held—would make MacArthur more enemies. Young for the job, he antagonized the crusty faculty by trying to modernize the curriculum. It was what happened outside the classroom, however, that may have cut short his tenure. He had begun courting a wealthy divorcée named Louise Cromwell Brooks. She was not the first woman who had captivated him. There was a girl he seemed almost proud of being caught kissing at West Point, and the Milwaukee woman whom he regaled with poems including a fictional 26-page one culminating with his desire to see his beloved's face one last time as he lay dying after having performed a feat reminiscent of his father's at Missionary Ridge. More dangerous was the woman who had followed him home from a short visit to the Panama Canal in 1911 in the mistaken belief that he intended to marry her. "Careless" was the word he used to describe that relationship, but he could not have been too much so because when he married Louise on Valentine's Day 1922—a month after his forty-second birthday—he struck her as a virgin, which must have made her only more alluring to him. She was a decade younger than he was but more experienced in such ways. Destined to be remembered as a "flapper," Louise had two children from an earlier marriage and a penchant for making herself the subject of gossip in connection with powerful men, including Douglas's boss: the army's new chief of staff, Pershing. He ensured the newlyweds would not enjoy the pleasant superintendent's house on the banks of the Hudson for long. For reasons that Pershing assured the newspapers had nothing to do with jealousy, he sent MacArthur off to a new posting that his socialite bride might not relish: the Philippines.

For all the time Louise had spent with soldiers, being an army wife did not come easy to her. After she had the satisfaction of seeing all her trunks and suitcases loaded onto the ship to the Philippines, space remained for the other officers' wives to bring only one bag each. As the ship entered Manila Bay in October 1922, Douglas saw "new roads" and "new buildings" all around. Only "the lean gray grimness" of Corregidor in the bay's mouth and Bataan's "massive bluff" running down its side looked the same in what he called "their unchanging cocoon of tropical heat." Once on the islands, Louise devoted herself to redecorating the house her husband received at 1 Calle Victoria on the walls of Intramuros and hectoring the drivers of the two-wheeled calesas passing by for supposedly mistreating their ponies.

For his part, MacArthur found himself at home outside the house with the Filipinos he had befriended eighteen years earlier. These relationships seemed to offend some of his fellow Americans, who accused him of supporting Filipinos in their demands for "equal social status." As far as he could see, the Filipinos deserved it. Of the little more than twelve thousand troops the United States Army had on the islands, only about four thousand hailed from America itself. From the islands arose the rest—members of the elite Philippine Scouts, tracing their lineage back to the days of Arthur MacArthur and proving the crack shots he had predicted they would become when given a fair shot at the firing range. In 1924, as an apparent concession to Scouts angry over the discrimination they faced in the United States Army, Arthur's son was promoted to lead the division that included their units. Some blamed the Scouts' discontent on the fiery rhetoric of Manuel Quezon, who had won over the Filipino people with the same charisma and ideological flexibility that had charmed two generations of MacArthurs. Like the younger MacArthur, Quezon had developed his own dramatic style of speech and dress, including shirts made of the finest silk and showy hats. By this time, he had surpassed his rival Osmeña as the leader of the new bicameral legislature that the United States Congress had given the islands as part of legislation granting them independence "as soon as," it was said, they could achieve a "stable government." Quezon pushed publicly for America to honor its promise even as he fretted privately over how the islands could defend themselves without American support.

In truth, the leaders of America's military had their own concerns over how to defend the Philippines. In the wake of Japan's rout of Russia, American strategists had begun imagining their own future war with the Pacific's new powerhouse. Far from serving as a shield, as Arthur MacArthur had claimed, the Philippines would serve, as Theodore Roosevelt himself came to concede, "[as] our heel of Achilles." Within weeks of the start of a war, the Japanese could land hundreds of thousands of troops in the Philippines while American reinforcements, even if they set off from the new naval base being developed at Pearl Harbor on the Hawaiian island of Oahu, would take months. Between these reinforcements and the Philippines lay five thousand miles of ocean, as well as several Japanese-controlled island chains: the Marshalls, the Marianas (save for Guam, which the United States had taken from Spain), and the Carolines. Faced with these realities, a joint board representing the United States Army and Navy formulated War Plan Orange. Rather than attempting to hold all of Luzon, to say nothing of the other seven thousand Philippine islands, War Plan Orange called for American forces to defend only the area around Manila Bay. In later iterations of the plan, the defensive zone would shrink to just the two places commanding the bay's entrance: Corregidor and Bataan. If American forces could withdraw into those two spots—and somehow hold out as long as half a year—the navy could steam into the bay to their rescue. MacArthur did not relish the plan, even as its preparation required him to make yet another trip to Bataan, this time to scout out defensive positions. "I covered every foot of rugged terrain, over its trails, up and down its steep mountainous slopes, and through its bamboo thickets," he wrote. Nevertheless, when he returned to America in 1925, the question of how American and Filipino soldiers could hold out on Bataan for so long with so little still defied any realistic answer—and always would.

The new command MacArthur took in Baltimore, near where Louise had a house, should have made her happier. Yet it could not save their marriage. Nor could the glamorous promotion that made him the army's youngest major general. In fact, the promotion served as a reminder of what Louise later claimed was the marriage's central problem: interference by Douglas's mother. Prior to the promotion, Pinky had once again written to Pershing on behalf of her son. Louise wrote to Pershing, too, and suggested she wished she had married someone else. Others would hear her poke fun at MacArthur's skills in the bedroom.

The comment she supposedly made after her wedding night ("he may be a general in the army, but he's a buck private in the boudoir") was open to interpretation, but the reenactments people saw her perform with a limp pinkie finger left less to the imagination. When MacArthur received an assignment to serve as the president of the United States Olympic Committee—a post combining his lifelong passion for sports with his love of medals—Louise did not accompany him to the 1928 games in Amsterdam. When later that same year he set off for the Philippines as America's newly appointed top army commander on the islands, she set off for Reno, Nevada, for a divorce. And when orders brought him back from the Philippines in September 1930, he arranged for a new and younger lover, a Filipina actress named Isabel Rosario Cooper, to follow him to his new posting in Washington. Once in the capital, he put her up in a secret apartment. As for himself, he would live with his mother across the Potomac in a house at Fort Myer, behind Arlington Cemetery, where her idol Robert E. Lee had once lived and her husband now lay in the ground. "If only your father could see you now," Pinky said to Douglas. "You're everything he wanted to be." President Herbert Hoover had made Douglas the army chief of staff.

The same month that MacArthur returned from the Philippines for America's top army command, 107 seats in Germany's Reichstag went to members of a national socialist party loyal to a former lance corporal named Adolf Hitler, who had seen the Great War from the losing side and lusted for revenge. Almost exactly a year later, a suspicious explosion on one of the railways that Japanese forces had controlled in Manchuria since the Russo-Japanese War served as a pretext for them to seize the entire province. In the United States, meanwhile, the new chief of staff found the army locked in an existential battle not against foreign foes but against domestic ones. Awaking to the reality of an economic depression that had burdened the country with a deficit the likes of which it had never known outside wartime, politicians began slashing the army. Cheering their every slice were the pacifists born out of the disillusionment of the First World War and convinced that their country could avoid a second by disarming. No idea could have incensed MacArthur more. "No one takes seriously the equally illogical plan of disbanding our fire department to stop fires or disbanding our police departments to stop crime," he said.

The police, however, seemed inadequate to the threat MacArthur saw cresting in 1932: World War I veterans coming by the hundreds and then thousands and camping on the banks of Washington, DC, as part of a campaign to persuade Congress to advance payment of a bonus they had been promised. Even after Congress rejected their demands, some of the men would not disperse. MacArthur no longer saw the faces of the men who had followed him in France. He saw Communists bent on revolution. They, in turn, would see the chief of staff, with his medals and decorations gleaming, take to the streets with his troops when orders came to clear the protesters. By the end of the night, the bonus marchers' camp had gone up in flames. That they themselves had set the fire did not matter. Nor did it matter that stories of MacArthur mounting his horse for a charge were fiction. The newspapers seared the image of MacArthur as a dangerous "man on horseback" into the nation's memory. MacArthur sued a pair of columnists for depicting him as a dictator, even though Governor Franklin Roosevelt of New York had done no less in private. He said MacArthur ranked among the "most dangerous men in the country."

Upon replacing MacArthur's political hero, Herbert Hoover, as president the next year, however, Roosevelt did not go along with his friends who favored replacing the army chief of staff. MacArthur kept his job, even after he lashed out at Roosevelt in a White House meeting about the cuts the administration had proposed for the army. "When we lost the next war, and an American boy, lying in the mud with an enemy bayonet through his belly and an enemy foot on his dying throat, spat out his last curse, I wanted the name not to be MacArthur, but Roosevelt," MacArthur remembered saying. "You must not talk that way to the president!" Roosevelt responded. Then he composed himself in a way that amazed MacArthur, and ordered the army chief of staff to work out a compromise with the budget office. MacArthur would do so but not before succumbing to the old nausea and vomiting outside the White House.

The army's budget also lay in the crosshairs of a new force: the acolytes of Brigadier General Billy Mitchell, who had fought in the skies over France during the Great War and spent the years afterward accusing superiors in the military of failing to develop the airpower capabilities needed to win the next war. A court-marital conviction in 1925 led to Mitchell's resignation but not before he predicted that Americans stationed at military facilities on the Hawaiian island of Oahu would wake up one morning to find Japanese planes overhead. MacArthur later claimed, when it was convenient to do so, that he had tried to save Mitchell when assigned to serve on his court-martial and even shared his views. But opposing evidence comes from the budget battles MacArthur waged as chief of staff against congressmen who saw investing in airpower as a license to enact deep cuts to the military's overall manpower, including the officer corps that MacArthur viewed as the army's nucleus. "An army can live on short rations, it can be insufficiently clothed and housed, it can even be poorly armed and equipped, but in action it is doomed to destruction without the trained and adequate leadership of officers," he said. Events would test this theory, but for now, it served only to turn certain congressmen into enemies.

In 1934, one of those congressmen tipped off the columnists whom MacArthur had sued for libel to the secret apartment he kept for his lover, Isabel Cooper. That MacArthur had already broken up with her made matters worse. She had saved the racy letters he had sent her under the name "Daddy," and shared them with the reporters, who, in turn, would share them with the world, he knew, unless he ended his lawsuit. He did. Why had he not just said, "So what?" some in the know asked. Then they remembered—his mother.

With his days as chief of staff numbered, MacArthur needed a way out of Washington. The Philippines offered one. The old question of how to defend the islands America had secured at the cost of blood and treasure a generation earlier had begun to mutate in the minds of some politicians into a new question: How to wash their hands of all responsibility for the islands as quickly as possible? In 1934, Congress passed legislation putting the Philippines on track for independence in ten years' time. In the meantime, the islands would enjoy self-government as a commonwealth under the protection of the United States military. Little suspense surrounded who the Filipinos would choose as their commonwealth's first president, Manuel Quezon. He had ensured he would receive the credit in the islands for the independence legislation by being in Washington for its passage. Only in the privacy of his friend MacArthur's office did Quezon dare to express the doubt that had long disturbed him. "Do you think that the Philippines can be defended after they shall have become independent ten years hence?"

"I don't *think* that the Philippines can defend themselves," MacArthur answered. "I *know* they can." His confidence did not come from envisioning a large standing army or a traditional navy. A new commonwealth, he realized, could afford neither. Its defense, he argued, should draw instead on what the islands did have in abundance: the courage that his father had seen all those years ago in the eyes of the Philippine people. To Quezon, the younger MacArthur proposed a Philippine army modeled after Switzerland's: a small standing force of about a thousand officers and ten times as many enlisted men who would see their ranks swell in time of war thanks to the compulsory military training civilians would receive at camps established across the archipelago. If forty thousand men passed through these camps each year, the Philippines would reach its full independence in ten years' time with four hundred thousand men ready to bear arms. Rather than simply hold Corregidor and Bataan, as War Plan Orange envisioned, the Philippine army that MacArthur proposed would have the skill and numbers to bludgeon an enemy force on the landing beaches.

Quezon had one more question: Would MacArthur himself agree to oversee the creation and command of this army? He would. In exchange, he would receive $33,000 a year from the commonwealth, not to mention the $7,500 he would continue to collect for his service in the United States Army. He would also receive housing—not Malacañan palace, which Quezon had reserved for himself, but the next-best location, the Manila Hotel's spacious penthouse. All of this would have made MacArthur perhaps the best-compensated army officer in American history, and it did not even include the bonus he had negotiated with the Philippine government. For every year the Philippines followed his military advice, he would receive a commission of nearly half a percent of whatever the commonwealth spent on defense. Only later would the full benefit of this unusual arrangement become clear.

In late 1935, a few months shy of his fifty-sixth birthday, MacArthur set off for the Philippines and what he assumed would be the final posting of his career. For certain, he knew it would be the final posting for his eighty-three-year-old mother, whom he let come after hearing doctors say they could do no more for her failing heart. When her husband had set off for the islands a generation before, she had imagined them as the ruin of her family. Now she would make it there and no farther. She had no need to see the United States again. Douglas was the only child she had left. His oldest brother, Arthur III, had died by this time of appendicitis. Weeks after arriving in the Philippines, Pinky MacArthur passed away in the Manila Hotel.

Pinky had been too sick to meet the thirty-six-year-old woman with whom Douglas had begun having breakfast on the ship. When together, he always occupied the high ground, standing nearly a foot taller than she did. They both had dark hair: his combed over and retreating in the face of a rising forehead; hers wrapping over her ears. He was said to have twenty-three suits, all custom-made by a Chinese tailor. Perfectly proportioned, she could find an outfit in a store and wear it off the rack. He spoke in a deep patrician voice, she with a charming southern accent. At a cocktail party aboard the ship, she was introduced as Jean Marie Faircloth, he as the general. In time, she would call him "my general." He would tell her the story about his father's charge up Missionary Ridge. Her grandfather had also been there, she would say, only he had started the day with the Confederates at the top. A child of a divorced Tennessee couple, she had found romance at a young age in the stories of those bygone days and in the sound of the bugle, just as Douglas had. Long before falling in love with a general, she had fallen in love with the idea of the army. She made visits whenever she could to forts and had found excuses to stay longer than she planned. She had embarked across the Pacific because she had not found a soldier she could call her own in America. He had also not found what he sought: a woman capable of adoring those strange poems he had written long ago. Jean would. In the Philippines, he saw how close she drew to his staff until she seemed like one of its members. At night, she would accompany him to the movies. He liked musicals and westerns that dispensed with moral ambiguity. She enjoyed the Manila social scene, including the parties at Malacañan Palace, where huge blocks of ice cooled the entrance to an outdoor dance floor bordering the Pasig River. He himself did not dance but would pretend to sip an iced drink of lime juice and gin until a quarter to nine, when he would say, "Ready, Jean?" and lead her to a car waiting to take them to the theater.

She did not accompany him on a trip he made to the United States in 1937 but made her own, suspiciously, at the same time. After burying his mother beside his father at Arlington Cemetery, Douglas went to New York City and met Jean at the Municipal Building on the last day of April. There and then, they wed. The next day, he spirited her off for a tour of West Point for what classified as a honeymoon. Just over nine months later, a son arrived in Manila. They named him Arthur MacArthur IV. Quezon would serve as godfather.

Back in the Philippines, people noticed that MacArthur spent less time in his office at 1 Calle Victoria, the old house he had shared with his first wife on the walls of Intramuros. In the mornings at the Manila Hotel, Arthur as a toddler would rouse the general from his bed at half past seven for a march that would end with singing duets in the bathroom. Douglas would then get his papers in order before going into the office. No one expected to see him there before eleven in the morning. At two o'clock, he would return home for lunch with Jean, who prided herself on always being home when he was. After eating, he would take a siesta and then do some reading. He would finish in time to be out on the balcony so he could pace back and forth as the sun set behind the dormant volcano at the tip of Bataan.

In the fading light, MacArthur increasingly seemed to see only what he wanted as if blinded by the reflection of his own rank. For his chief of staff, MacArthur had insisted on the service of a major ten years his junior named Dwight D. Eisenhower. Having missed out on the opportunity to make a name as a fighter during World War I, Eisenhower had done so subsequently as a staff officer thanks to a nifty pen and an affable nature that had made him indispensable to every higher-up he had served. MacArthur was no exception. Eisenhower closely studied MacArthur's style, including his peculiar habit of referring to himself in the third person and his ability to dominate discussion. "On any subject he chose to discuss, his knowledge poured out in a great torrent of words," Eisenhower remembered. "'Discuss' is hardly the correct word; discussion suggests dialogue and the general's conversations were usually monologues." Only occasionally would MacArthur pause for the answer to a yes-no question. But increasingly Eisenhower found MacArthur willing to have these questions answered only in the affirmative. MacArthur, Eisenhower wrote in his diary, "[is] indulging in a habit of damning everybody who disagrees with him over any detail, in extravagant, sometimes almost hysterical fashion."

Others noticed, too. More and more, Quezon began turning to Eisenhower instead of MacArthur for advice. Maybe it was because MacArthur, after seeing some poll numbers, had told Quezon that Roosevelt would lose the 1936 election instead of winning, as he did, in a landslide. Maybe it was because MacArthur, who had assumed the distinctly un-American and much-mocked title of field marshal, had begun dreaming up a military parade where he could sport his custom black-and-white sharkskin uniform as well as the cap he had richly embroidered with gold, even though Eisenhower argued the Philippines could not afford such pomp when its training camps had fallen short of supplies, to say nothing of enrollees. Maybe it was because MacArthur had forfeited his real power on the last day of 1937, when he retired from the United States Army. No longer did MacArthur represent a connection to Washington. And no longer did Quezon have time to meet with MacArthur, even though he had not retired from serving the Philippine government. When brushed off by Quezon's secretary, MacArthur said, "Some day your boss is going to want to see me more than I want to see him."

That day would come sooner than even MacArthur knew. In July 1937, an exchange of fire between Japanese and Chinese forces at the Marco Polo Bridge outside the city of Peking sparked war. As the fighting spread to Shanghai and Nanking, a bloody tide carried refugees ashore to the Philippines with stories of Japanese warriors raping and killing their way through China, the land whose markets had always lain behind America's real interest in Asia. Little resistance could come from the old colonial powers; they were too busy trading away land closer to home in Europe to a rearmed Germany, now under Hitler's absolute control, in the hope of avoiding war. It came anyway in September 1939, after the German invasion of Poland finally backed Britain and France into declaring war. The European powers that had drawn the borders of Asia suddenly looked unable to maintain their own. In May 1940, the Netherlands, whose colonies still included the Dutch East Indies, fell to the German war machine. France, still in charge of Indochina, fell soon afterward, as the British, still colonial masters of India, Burma, Hong Kong, and Singapore, evacuated troops from the European continent.

As the battle in Western Europe moved to the skies over Britain, Japanese leaders speaking of a "new order in Greater East Asia" eyed the semi-orphaned, resource-rich colonies to their south. When the United States tried its hand at deterrence by placing its Pacific fleet at the naval base it had built at Pearl Harbor and by issuing an embargo on some of the raw materials essential to the Japanese military, Japan tried its own policy of deterrence by signing a defensive pact with Germany and Italy. America answered with additional sanctions, Japan with additional aggressions. When the Japanese occupied French Indochina in July 1941, the United States made it impossible for the Japanese to buy the one commodity their military needed most: oil. Both powers now felt under siege: the Japanese economically, the United States geographically with hostile forces on the verge of encircling the Philippines.

It was at this moment that Roosevelt called America's most famous general out of retirement. The appointment to command United States Army Forces in the Far East came as no surprise to MacArthur. He had suggested it months earlier. With the new Philippine army to be annexed to the American one, all the forces in the archipelago would be his, and so once again would the ear of the mercurial Quezon. For the newspapers, MacArthur declared, "This action of the American government in establishing this new command can only mean that it intends to maintain, at any cost and effort, its full rights in the Far East."

In private, however, the situation appeared otherwise. During MacArthur's retirement, army and navy strategists faced with the reality that Congress had not given them enough resources to prevail in a one-front war coalesced around a plan called Rainbow Five for the dreaded but increasingly likely prospect of a two-front war. Under the plan, American forces would assume the defensive against Japan while focusing first on the more feared German adversary. As one of the colors in the "rainbow," War Plan Orange still set the strategy against Japan but with a change: The reinforcements supposed to sail to the rescue of the Philippines would now have other places to go. The men withdrawing into Bataan and Corregidor would have to do so with no timetable for their relief. Rather than months, it might take years.

The defend-the-beaches plan that MacArthur had based on the Swiss example had not impressed his fellow American generals at the time of his retirement for the manifest reason that the landlocked Swiss had no beaches to defend. "Unlike Switzerland, the Philippines are not a compact land unit, but an archipelago. The intervening water areas will be controlled in war by the naval forces of the enemy," read a report endorsed by MacArthur's immediate successor as chief of staff, Malin Craig. But now there was a new chief of staff, George C. Marshall, and a new secretary of war, Henry L. Stimson, and it was to them that MacArthur protested. True, American forces in the Philippines had totaled little more than twenty thousand men, including Philippine Scouts, when MacArthur had taken command in July. But he would have more than one hundred thousand once he fully mobilized the Philippine Army reserves who had passed through his training camps. And by the spring of 1942, he said that number would be two hundred thousand. No wonder Marshall and Stimson came down with what the latter would later diagnose as a case of "contagious optimism." They found another reason for optimism in the new bomber that Boeing had developed. Designed to fly at high speeds in excess of 250 miles per hour and at high altitudes above antiaircraft defenses, the four-engine B-17 boasted a range that would allow it to strike targets hundreds of miles away. The Flying Fortress, as the plane became known, appeared able to fulfill the old prophecy Billy Mitchell had made of dominating the seas from the skies and sending an invading force to the watery depths before it could near the shore. By stockpiling Flying Fortresses, the Philippines could become what Stimson called a "self-sustaining fortress." By November 1941, he would see to it that the Philippines had thirty-five of these planes, more than double the number in Hawaii.

With these bombers came Lewis Brereton, the general whom MacArthur had handpicked to lead his air force. Brereton would have to wait until the night of December 7 for the rowdy reception thrown in his honor at the Manila Hotel's pavilion, but he did not have to wait for an invitation to the hotel's penthouse. That came immediately upon his arrival on November 3. Ready to slap his back and throw one arm around him was his new commander wearing only a dressing robe over his underwear. A full embrace followed the next day after MacArthur had read the secret letter Marshall had asked Brereton to carry in his luggage. MacArthur, Brereton remembered, "acted like a small boy who has been told that he is going to get a holiday from school. He jumped up from his desk and threw his arms around me." Marshall had agreed to dispense with the decades of thinking that had gone into War Plan Orange. MacArthur's plan was now America's. "They are going to give us everything we have asked for," MacArthur exclaimed to his chief of staff, Richard Sutherland, the successor to Eisenhower, who had happily accepted orders taking him back to the United States. In fact, the army had earmarked so much equipment—more than a million tons—for the Philippines that the orders created a shipping backlog.

Whether these supplies would arrive on time depended on how one interpreted the signs that began appearing in the sky in early December. There was the mysterious aircraft spotted around the same time each morning north of Manila, in the vicinity of Clark Airfield, the only place in Luzon capable of housing the B-17. To the west at the smaller Iba airstrip, technicians staring at the screen of a newly installed radar system in an otherwise dark hut began following strange blips. B-17 crews conducting reconnaissance over the waters north of Luzon, meanwhile, encountered unidentified bombers flying south from Formosa, as Taiwan was then called, only to see them reverse direction and head back toward the island, said to be a Japanese staging ground. By this time, MacArthur knew that a last attempt at negotiations with Japanese diplomats had collapsed in Washington. "Japanese future action unpredictable but hostile action possible at any moment," the War Department had warned him on November 27. He still said that the conflict would not begin until the spring of 1942, but newsmen on December 5 heard him concede it could come at any time after the new year. To admit war might come any earlier would be to open himself to the unthinkable: that his buildup had come too late to avert disaster yet early enough to make that disaster even more costly for the United States.

Part of MacArthur must have pondered that possibility, because he ordered the B-17s sent to the bottom of the archipelago, to a field on the island of Mindanao, where they would be beyond the range of any

Japanese attack from Formosa. In fact, twelve more Flying Fortresses were on the way to Mindanao from California. They would have to refuel a few times along the way. As MacArthur went to bed on the night of December 7, he had every reason to expect that the planes would make their scheduled stop by the shores of Pearl Harbor while he slept.

*   *   *

Several minutes after seven in the morning Hawaii time, radar operators stationed on the northern edge of the island of Oahu reported "a large number of planes coming in from the north." They were told not to fret; it was the B-17s bound for the Philippines. The whole world would soon know otherwise but only after hundreds of Japanese bombers and fighters had delivered death and destruction upon America's Pacific fleet, the ships that War Plan Orange strategists had once envisioned battling their way across the ocean to rescue the Philippines. MacArthur could not believe it when he picked up the phone in the predawn darkness of Manila on December 8. "Pearl Harbor?" he exclaimed. "Why, that should be our strongest point!" For hours afterward, even after reporting to his office in the house where he had once lived on the walls of Intramuros, he would continue to believe that American fighter planes and antiaircraft defenses had repulsed the Japanese attack.

At five in the morning Philippine time, Brereton arrived at the headquarters and headed toward MacArthur's office but found the path blocked by Sutherland. A forty-eight-year-old Yale man described as "sound" and "productive" but also as "brusque, short-tempered, autocratic, and of a generally antagonizing nature," Sutherland relished his role as gatekeeper and would not admit the air force chief even after hearing the urgent matter at stake: Brereton had not yet fully carried out MacArthur's earlier orders to move all thirty-five of the B-17s to Mindanao. More than half remained at Clark in range of the Japanese bombers on Formosa. In this peril lay opportunity. If the B-17s took off at daylight, they could strike the Japanese on Formosa. If the B-17s tarried on the ground, however, the opposite might happen: a repeat of Pearl Harbor, where the Japanese had found hundreds of American planes parked in perfect rows as if arranged to facilitate their destruction. The best way to prevent another such disaster was to go on the offense. The pilots just needed targets on Formosa, but Sutherland remembered Brereton being unable to provide any specific ones and admitting the need for additional reconnaissance, which MacArthur had refused permission to conduct days earlier. For his part, Brereton remembered urging—and Sutherland endorsing—preparations for a raid as soon as the sun rose, without further reconnaissance. The attack just needed MacArthur's approval.

By sunrise, no word had come. Time was running out. At 7:15 in the morning, Brereton once again showed up outside MacArthur's office and once again asked Sutherland for a definitive answer. MacArthur would later claim the proposal never reached his desk. But a witness saw Sutherland go into MacArthur's office and come back with an answer. "The general says no. Don't make the first overt act." The words echoed the instructions attached to the final warning MacArthur had received from Washington on November 27. "If hostilities cannot, repeat cannot, be avoided the United States desires that Japan commit the first overt act." Surely, by any standard, the attack on Pearl Harbor classified as an "overt act." How could MacArthur think otherwise? The question confounded Brereton and his airmen. Historians trying to piece together the many conflicting accounts of that morning have struggled, too.

The secret lies behind the doors of MacArthur's office. The journalist John Hersey, who had gained admission months earlier for an interview with the general, described the space as "more like a formal drawing-room than a soldier's office." In fact, the room had served as MacArthur's bedroom during his first marriage. Hersey found "old books and pictures, inlaid cabinets dating back to the Spanish occupation, a deep sofa and comfortable chairs, a beautiful Chinese screen, a huge Chippendale desk, and, for the military touch, regimental flags and the Stars and Stripes." In the collection of flags stood one for every command MacArthur had ever held. Although they now formed a line behind his desk, the path from one to the next had been far from straight. Nonetheless, it had led him back here to 1 Calle Victoria. MacArthur liked to tell stories of first-time visitors who had "turned away from the entrance" to the headquarters of the U.S. Army Forces in the Far East on the assumption that they had come to a "private dwelling" instead. But if "private" meant personal, then the visitors were right. For the son of a soldier convinced that America's future faced west toward the Philippines, the mission of the headquarters was personal. "Personally—I must not fail," readers of *Life* magazine had recently seen Douglas MacArthur quoted as saying. "Too much of the world's future depends upon success here. These islands may not be the door to the control of the Pacific, they may not be even the lock to the door. But they are surely the key to the lock that opens the door—for America. I dare not allow that key to be lost." At this moment, MacArthur was where he belonged—straddling the same two worlds as the house perched atop the thick stone walls running between the centuries-old buildings of Intramuros and the American-made golf course.

The position gave MacArthur a perspective that no one as new to the islands as Brereton could understand. "The Philippines, while a possession of the U.S., had so far as war was concerned, a somewhat indeterminate international position in many minds, especially the Filipinos and their government," MacArthur explained years later. The Japanese had attacked the United States. As far as he knew, they had not yet attacked the Philippines.* He had "not the slightest doubt" they soon would. But he also knew, as he later put it, "[that] great local hope existed that this would not be the case." If it appeared that American rather than Japanese forces had taken the first step toward involving the Philippines in a war that MacArthur recognized would inflict a fearful

---

* Unbeknownst to MacArthur, the Japanese had already bombed sites in the far north and far south of the islands.

toll upon the islands, he would risk what he had always considered the centerpiece of his defense strategy: the support of the Filipino people themselves. He had never really believed that thirty-five bombers could defeat Japan. Had he thought so, he would never have ordered the planes to Mindanao, where they would be out of range of the Japanese planes on Formosa but also unable to carry out an immediate strike against them. To prevail in what he had come to believe would be a "glorious land war," he would need hundreds of thousands of Filipinos willing to meet the enemy on the beaches and plains—and to wage "a people's contest" like the one Abraham Lincoln had declared after he allowed the Confederates to fire the first shots of the Civil War. And to command this Filipino army in what he believed would be its most pivotal field of battle, MacArthur looked back into American history and found a weathered cavalryman reminiscent of the frontier's final days at Fort Selden. MacArthur's mighty air force would not make it into the sky in time. But the horseman of his boyhood dreams would make a last stand for the ages.

CHAPTER THREE

First Steps to a Last Stand

It was not fair to say, as critics later would, that the B-17s never got off the ground on December 8. They had taken off earlier that morning after receiving reports of Japanese planes from Formosa on a path for Clark Field. The B-17s stayed close to Clark while their crews awaited a decision from MacArthur's office. They flew just to the east of the field around a solitary mountain named Arayat after the biblical peak where Noah had received God's promise never again to destroy the earth. A haze obscured the top of the mountain, but not a cloud blocked the view the other way, to the west, of the Zambales Mountains, including Mount Pinatubo, a dormant but dangerous volcano that seemed to contradict the peaceful assurances of Arayat. Between these mountains ran a great plain of rice paddies and sugar fields stretching all the way north to Lingayen Gulf, where Japanese bombers were reported. Around ten in the morning came an update: The Japanese planes spotted over the water had turned back toward Formosa but before doing so had turned east and dropped their bombs on northern Luzon. Any hopes that the Philippines could stay out of the war had now exploded. For the B-17s came new orders: return to Clark, and prepare for an attack on Formosa. No one showed much haste, however. As the B-17s landed to have their bombs loaded, the crews went off for lunch.

Lunch had also begun next door, a step closer to the Zambales, at Fort Stotsenburg, which resembled not so much an army post as a country club complete with a dance hall, tennis courts, and an eighteen-hole golf course. The white gates and buildings—barracks for the soldiers and bungalows with porches for the officers—formed a quadrangle, which served as the post's parade ground. At the far end lay a polo field for Stotsenburg's most iconic regiment: the 26th Cavalry. A highly selective and trained group of Philippine Scouts led by American officers, these soldiers endured as an endangered breed—fighting men on mounts. The stories of Hitler's tanks driving across Europe—and made-up propaganda about Polish horse soldiers fighting back with nothing more than sabers—made the cavalry seem a relic of America's long-gone frontier. But there were still some who believed that the horse soldier had not yet ridden his last mile, and among them was Stotsenburg's newly arrived commander, Major General Jonathan Mayhew Wainwright IV.

Toward the end of lunch, a hush came over a group of soldiers huddled around a radio broadcasting supposedly breaking news: Japanese planes had begun bombing Clark Field. The silence gave way to smirks. If the report were true, the soldiers would have heard an explosion. Then, a moment later, they did. A look of terror came across their faces as they raced outside. Men already out had seen the bombers coming from the northwest, from the clear skies over the mountains north of Pinatubo. The planes had come in two flawless-looking Vs and totaled fifty-four in all. Almost everyone assumed them to be United States Navy planes until the bombs began falling on Clark. The hangars and other buildings around the field disappeared behind plumes of smoke. The vibrations shook Stotsenburg.

As soldiers searched for cover, they saw a tall man stepping down from the commander's house and running out alone onto the lawn, where his long neck seemed to hold up his bright blue eyes as an unmistakable target. It was the fifty-eight-year-old Wainwright. Everyone called him "Skinny," and he was, but, as one admirer put it, of the "lean, tough" sort. He moved with a slight limp as a result of an old fall that had injured his lower back, but made good time nonetheless as he set off toward his headquarters on the west end of the parade ground. After him ran a young Filipino servant struggling to catch up while inexplicably wearing the steel helmet meant to cover the gray hairs exposed on the general's head. "Mother of God, General," the young man yelled, as if on behalf of a generation new to war. "What shall I do?"

"Go get me a bottle of beer," Wainwright said. The young man could use a laugh, Wainwright thought, and he himself could use the beer. He was not on much sleep. He had worked the previous day before taking off to umpire a polo match, which the 26th Cavalry had lost. As he had stood on the reviewing stand, he had kept his face, one of the players remembered, "imperturbable." Only after everyone had changed into their white dress uniforms and gathered for dinner and drinks had a bourbon relaxed his expression. Conversation had turned to a new movie called *They Died with Their Boots On* about the colorful nineteenth-century cavalryman George Armstrong Custer and the doomed stand he and his men had made in 1876 on a river called the Little Bighorn. It had been late at night when Wainwright finally turned off the lights in his bedroom and well before dawn when the phone woke him. He suspected something bad, and it was. He summed it up for an aide afterward. "The cat has jumped," he said of the Japanese. He knew that he would soon have to meet them on the shores of Luzon.

Before the Japanese bombers had even reached Clark, Wainwright had finished packing his field equipment. The cavalry officers who had fought long ago on the western plains of America would have recognized the contents. There was the saddle patterned on the design that the future Union general George McClellan had drawn up before the Civil War; the iconic 1873 Colt .45 revolver known as the Peacemaker; and the silver pocket watch that Wainwright had seen his father carry while serving at Fort Custer, not far from where the real Custer had died and not long afterward either. The Battle of the Little Bighorn was not the stuff of Hollywood lore for Wainwright. He had grown up just downriver from the Last Stand and soon would have his own.

*   *   *

The train back in those days had not gone as far as Fort Custer in the
Montana Territory. The final thirty-six miles took six hours by mule-
pulled wagon or even longer by a stagecoach known as a "jerky," which
rode as it sounded up the valley of the Bighorn River to the point where
it met the Little Bighorn. Over the confluence stood a plateau and, upon
it, a parade ground that would have looked rougher but still familiar
to the soldiers at Stotsenburg, with housing for the enlisted men on
one side and fourteen cottages for officers on another. In 1886, upon
completing the trip to Fort Custer, Lieutenant Robbie Wainwright of
the 1st Cavalry moved into one of the cottages, which proved much
too small for the family he had brought with him. There was his wife,
Josephine, affectionately called "Dodo," and their three children: a
five-year-old daughter named Helen, a four-year-old daughter named
Jennie, and the baby boy—three-year-old Jonathan, who would go by
his middle name, Mayhew. The girls would have their own room while
Mayhew and his beloved stuffed rabbit would have only a roll-away
trundle bed in his parents' room.

The cottage was a place to sleep, but it was not a place the family
would call home. Wainwright would later remember his childhood as
one without a home, as a succession of moves from one cavalry post to
another. Between his birthplace in Walla Walla, Washington, and the
move to Fort Custer three years later had come stops at Fort Bidwell,
California, and Fort Maginnis, Montana. Over and over again, relatives
would hear Mayhew's mother, Dodo, say, "Home is where the husband
is." Over and over again, she would pack up her three children. On a
wintry day several months after Mayhew's birth, family lore says she
bundled her children and their nurse into a horse-drawn sleigh and
set off over the snow and ice, when a sudden jolt threw baby Mayhew
from his blankets and over the side. Moments passed. Incredibly, no
one noticed. Finally, with a scream, Dodo did. She ordered the driver
to turn around so she could search the snow for her boy. By the time

she found him, a snowbank had almost swallowed his little body. If he held a grudge for being left behind, no one could see it by his face. It looked a little red, but his mother remembered him giving her a smile.

Mayhew, of course, would remember nothing of the episode. His "first distinct" memories, as he put it, would date to Fort Custer. He would have seen the cavalrymen mounting their horses for the thirteen-mile ride across the Little Bighorn and up a hill crowned by a stone monument bearing the names of Custer and the more than two hundred men who had perished by his side. Responsibility for tending the grounds of the battlefield had fallen to the soldiers of Fort Custer. Occasionally, they would still find unburied human remains. There had been no white survivors, but there were Indians nearby who could recall how Custer and his men had made their hopeless stand on that hill, where they had heaped their dead horses into a wall against an overwhelming force of Cheyenne and Lakota warriors. One day, when Mayhew was about four, his father returned home with a mysterious Winchester rifle that he had seized after shooting an Indian warrior who had supposedly found it on the battlefield days after Custer's death. A boy growing up in such a place could not help but imagine himself in Custer's place. For the rest of his life, Mayhew would cherish a photograph of himself and his sisters as children by the Custer monument and read every book he could about the Battle of the Little Bighorn.

The Montana sky seemed to stretch forever, but young Mayhew could see no way of life beyond the cavalry. He watched how the men handled their horses and did not flinch at age six when hoisted atop an Indian pony for the first time. He listened to the gruffness in the troopers' voices and learned to speak as they did. He heard their songs and jokes, too, and joined in. As he grew older, he would call pretty young women "fillies" and say they were "foaling" when they gave birth. His parents made sure he also saw the more civilized side of life. They dressed him in kilts, made sure he saw them wearing white gloves to parties, sang him old Scottish songs, and started him on the violin at age seven. Horses, however, had claimed his heart.

Even heading east to Fort Sheridan around Chicago in 1896 after moves to Arizona and Kansas could not break the bond the boy had forged with horses. Fellow students remembered him riding a spotted pony to school. "He was a likable chap," remembered a female classmate who would see him at parties and kept a photograph she took of him at age fourteen with his hair parted back across a tall forehead. He had sprouted since his years at Fort Custer and turned tall and thin. A male classmate remembered Wainwright as "studious." He must have been, for in 1902 he gained admission to West Point, though surely his grades mattered less than the letter of recommendation he received from his father's friend Vice President Theodore Roosevelt, who had written it just days before becoming president. The letter unsurprisingly said more about the older Wainwright, whom Roosevelt had seen fighting in Cuba, than it did about the younger. As to why Mayhew wanted to go to West Point, friends heard him quip that "he came to West Point because he did not know any better." Probably that was true. He had always assumed he would follow his father into the cavalry, and that trail hugged the banks of the Hudson River to West Point.

Wainwright arrived at the academy in the summer of 1902, just as a first classman, or senior, named Douglas MacArthur assumed his place as first captain on the parade ground and stood a year away from the "rare" feat of pairing that military honor with an academic one by graduating at the top of his class. If Wainwright saw any of himself in MacArthur, few others did. MacArthur's appearance served as a source of awe, Wainwright's as a source of guffaws. Six feet two inches tall but only 125 pounds, Wainwright had legs so long and a neck so goose-like that the other cadets assigned him the nickname "Skinny" almost by default. "The only person in the world," he would later say, who addressed him as Jonathan was MacArthur, and even he usually referred to Wainwright by a nickname, albeit a more puzzling one: "Jim," perhaps because of the way the plebe signed his name, J. M. Wainwright.

In the classroom, the difference between Wainwright and MacArthur looked starker. In English and French, Skinny ranked seventy-fifth and seventy-fourth, respectively, in a class of eighty-four at the end of his first year. His twenty-sixth-place finish in mathematics, the subject West Point valued most, reflected greater promise but still no sign of greatness. Overall, he ranked thirty-eighth in his class. In fairness, few of the thirty-seven cadets ahead of him confronted adversity the likes of which he had. Family tradition says he had learned the news of his father's death in the Philippines in the cruelest way imaginable: by reading it in *The New York Times* on November 21, 1902. His mother and sisters had gone to the Philippines with his father, so there was no one with whom to share the grief until they returned with the body for its burial at Arlington Cemetery. The academy granted Wainwright leave to attend the funeral and no more. Upon returning, he faced the same discipline as his fellow cadets, and perhaps it was this unbending structure that saved him from falling into despair.

In fact, by looking at where Wainwright stood at the end of his first year in the military disciplines of drilling (eighth in his class) and conduct (fourth in his class), one could see the beginnings of a path that would lead him not to the academic position MacArthur had achieved but to the military one. By the time Wainwright graduated in 1906, he would stand first and second, respectively, in military efficiency and soldierly deportment. And despite being caught swearing and smoking—both of which would become lifelong habits—he would stand an excellent eighth in his class in conduct. Overall, he finished a respectable twenty-fifth.

More important to Wainwright was that he would stand where MacArthur had on the parade ground as first captain. "Who would have thought . . . such as he would ever be first captain?" read a caption in the academy's 1906 yearbook. "Many honors have been heaped upon his head—so many that it's a wonder his slender frame has withstood their bending moment without any more damage than giving to his knees a permanent set." In truth, no one begrudged the honors Skinny had accumulated. He had won the respect of his classmates, not to mention their wagers during target practice, where one cadet learned only after losing a pound of cigarettes not to bet against a boy who had learned to shoot with the cavalry. In addition to qualifying as one of the six best marksmen in his class, Wainwright played on the academy's polo team and organized dances as hop manager.

His classmates would remember him serenading them with songs such as "Shenandoah" and making them laugh. The yearbook would capture his humor. Writing a piece on how a first captain should bring the cadet battalion to attention, he advised employing a "stony stare" and a "fiery glance" while "chopping the 'shone' off as short as you can" at the end of bellowing "ten-shone!" When asked if he had gotten enough sleep at the academy, he quipped, "Not enough to press my trousers properly." Jokes about his weight aside, his fellow cadets thought he could hold up against whatever the future brought. "Don't be afraid, Skinny," they wrote in the yearbook. "You could get through most anything." They had no idea.

At graduation, Dodo presented her son, the newly minted second lieutenant, with a sword inscribed with his name. Never did he need to consider what he would say when asked which branch of the army he wished to enter. His heart had always yearned for the cavalry. The army obliged and ordered him to his father's old regiment, the 1st Cavalry, which was then in Texas but soon to head to the Philippines, where American troops continued to face resistance from the Muslim Moros in the south. How much Wainwright participated in those operations remains uncertain, but there is no doubt he spent most of his time at a malaria-infested camp that the army already called Stotsenburg but that in no way yet resembled the country club it would become. Fed up with the bugs, lizards, and rats infesting the officers' crude houses, the wife of a colonel in Wainwright's regiment insisted she would have preferred a tent in a field.

It was perhaps for the best, then, that Wainwright waited to take a wife until coming back to the United States in early 1910. He had met Adele Holley in 1897, when he had been fourteen and she ten and the army had sent both their fathers to the Chicago area. They had gone their separate ways: he to West Point, she to schools in upstate New York, Massachusetts, Virginia, and Pennsylvania. On occasion, they had seen each other, as when he had invited her to be his date to a West Point hop, but she never imagined a future with him. Evidently, however, he had begun imagining one with her while he was in the Philippines, because within weeks of his return, he proposed. As to how he did it, she would say only that his line of attack carried her heart.

The wedding took place on February 18, 1911, in an army chapel made lovely with mountain laurel and palm leaves at the Utah fort where Adele's father was stationed. A color guard carrying the Stars and Stripes as well as the flags of all the regiments represented stood on either side of the bride and groom. He wore his dress uniform, she a dress of white satin with a long veil and a wreath of orange blossoms. A newspaper correspondent would later describe her hair as "brown" and "wavy," her eyes as "fine," and her body as "plumpish," which her new husband liked. She had "good looks and figure and plenty of the latter," he would say. When they went to dances together, he would brag that she "quite took the shine out of the other 'femmes.'" No other "femme," he might have added, could have adjusted so easily to the far from conventional life of a cavalry wife. Born into the army, she had traveled with her father across the United States as a girl and even to the Philippines as a young woman. She now looked forward to a nomadic life hitched to her husband and the horses he loved. Home would be where he was.

After a honeymoon in California, the newlyweds made the first of their many moves together to a house with leaking pipes at Fort Yellowstone, where they toured the famous geyser Old Faithful and camped under a mosquito net in the park. Wainwright's interest in history had not waned. He brought so many boxes of books with him that she had no choice but to surrender her pantry to his library. Nevertheless, they seemed happy. They would play cards and chess and go on rides. He would call her "Kitty" and "Skipper." She would call him "Mayhew" or "Skinny." His superiors, meanwhile, called him a "remarkably energetic and tireless horseman." In December 1912, however, not quite two years into his marriage, while training at the Cavalry School, as it became known, at Fort Riley, Kansas, Wainwright snapped one of his slender legs, just as his West Point classmates had predicted. The timing could not have pleased Adele, who was pregnant. Her husband wanted a boy, and she gave him one. On April 6, 1913, at a post in Monterey, California, they welcomed Jonathan Mayhew Wainwright V. They would call him "Jack," as the boy himself would later explain, because that was the name of the beloved horse his father would ride to a ribbon two years later at the San Francisco world's fair.

The west had not lost all its adventure. In 1916, in search of a bandit in Arizona, Wainwright took his troopers on a seventy-mile trek over a twenty-one-hour period through rain, darkness, and mountainous terrain. He filed away a letter crediting the operation's success to his "good judgment," but opportunities to show it in the field of battle remained rare. Most of the praise he received on horseback still came from the field of sport, for which he often coordinated entries for his regiment. When the United States began sending its boys to the western front of World War I, the cavalry largely stayed home to patrol America's southern border.

Although strategists struggled to find a place for fast-moving cavalry in a war of stagnant trenches, they found one for Wainwright in February 1918: in a classroom in France, where American officers learned how to serve on the general staff. By June, Wainwright had the training he needed to serve as the assistant chief of staff to the 82nd Division. With several American companies of the so-called Lost Battalion trapped behind German lines in October, the job of drafting orders for a dangerous rescue fell to Wainwright. The operation required an audacious flanking maneuver that would ultimately succeed in saving more than a third of the trapped men and lead to the Medal of Honor for the man who would inspire the film *Sergeant York*. At some point in the fighting, Wainwright took what he called a "snoot full of gas" when he had to rip off his mask while trying to make himself heard on a phone call with a general. Wainwright himself would have trouble hearing afterward in his left ear. By the time the final gun of the war fell silent, Wainwright had achieved the temporary rank of lieutenant colonel and a reputation as a soldier of "exceptional ability." A Distinguished Service Medal followed.

As soon as the army allowed wives to join their husbands in Europe, Adele remembered, she and young Jack were on the "first boat." They would live in occupied Germany. It was a "grand time," she remembered. The three of them toured the continent, and Wainwright did what he loved: organizing horse shows and winning polo cups. Jack revered his father. It was hard not to, given how others hailed him as "the bravest man." One general told Adele that her husband knew only two commands: "forward" and "commence firing." She heard others, however, describe her husband in different terms. "Softie," they called him because, as Adele put it, "he felt sympathy for the defeated people." He urged his soldiers to learn the language of the land they occupied, and even brought in a professor to teach a class. The story goes that Wainwright did not exempt himself from taking the final exam. But after seeing his own score, he made sure no one else saw theirs. German evidently came no easier to him than French had at West Point.

By the time Wainwright left Germany in the fall of 1920, he had also left behind his wartime rank and reverted to a mere major. Not until 1929 would he achieve a lieutenant colonelcy again. By contrast, Douglas MacArthur had managed to keep his general's star and had already made his name famous. Wainwright's name had also become known but only in a smaller circle of influential military men. One was a cousin also, confusingly, named Jonathan Mayhew Wainwright, who would become assistant secretary of war when Warren G. Harding replaced Woodrow Wilson as president in 1921. Another was Malin Craig, the general who would one day succeed MacArthur as chief of staff. Craig had served with Wainwright in the 1st Cavalry and then in France and would make sure the younger man stayed on the path to becoming a general officer himself. That path went through Washington, DC. It was there that Wainwright briefed Congress on the ceremonies for the burial of the unknown soldier at Arlington Cemetery in 1921 and earned the thanks of the White House for his role in the funeral procession for Harding, who died in office in 1923. Upon seeing Wainwright's cavalrymen the next year, General Craig said he had never seen riders better dressed, horses better groomed, and a squadron better trained. They were, said Craig, "entirely up to the high standard of everything undertaken by this officer."

It was also in Washington that Wainwright received his first real look at War Plan Orange during a stint serving on the army's general staff. "I could do a good job when we have the Jap war," a fellow officer remembered hearing Wainwright say. Whatever illusions he harbored about the plan vanished when he commenced what would be the capstone of his military education at the Army War College in Washington in 1933. A report Wainwright helped write at the college took a dim view of Orange. Over a period of years, the United States would defeat Japan, the report found. But in the first months of a war, Japan would overrun the Philippines. The American garrison on the islands faced annihilation.

After graduating from the college in 1934, Wainwright went back to the Cavalry School at Fort Riley with the official title of assistant commandant and the less official one of "Mastership of the Cavalry School Hunt," which entitled him to a fox horn while donning his red jacket and leading his fellow hunters on horseback. The young officers attending the school looked up to Wainwright. He would tell them, "Cavalry leaders are born and seldom made." Though his list of great ones included only a handful more names than the Union generals Philip Sheridan and George Armstrong Custer and Confederate generals J. E. B. Stuart and Nathan Bedford Forrest, the students at Riley would have added Wainwright's own name—and, unintentionally, made him seem a relic of the previous century to which the others belonged.

During Douglas MacArthur's reign as chief of staff, the army had begun to mechanize more of the cavalry. Soon Wainwright's old regiment, the 1st Cavalry, would have tanks instead of horses. "Modern firearms have eliminated the horse as a weapon, and as a means of transportation," MacArthur wrote. When Wainwright heard the news, friends joked, it "broke his heart" as his bowlegs fit "a horse much better than a tank." He never doubted the need for tanks but insisted that some missions would always require horses. A commencement address he delivered in 1935 hailed the horse as "the fastest and most reliable means of movement yet produced, considering all types of terrain, all conditions of weather and all of the many difficulties that may arise because of failure of supply and of the intricacies of automotive power." In sum, he told the graduates, "Mobility must still remain our watchword." They had heard him strike the same theme in more colorful language around the campfires they would share at night. "When you young gentlemen get orders," he would say, "you should be able to move out at once. Just piss in the fire, call your dog, and get going."

In 1936 came orders putting Wainwright in command of the country's most high-profile cavalry post: Fort Myer, where the army chief of staff had his residence across the river from Washington. The politicians in the city had outraged MacArthur, who had already left for the Philippines, by appointing a soon-to-be critic of his plan to defend the islands as the army's new chief of staff: Wainwright's mentor, Malin Craig. It was Craig who arranged for Wainwright to come to Fort Myer and, in two years, to become a brigadier general. As a colonel, Wainwright already had two horses; as a general, he could now ask for a third. Color did not matter to him as long as the animal proved "quick footed" with "some jumping ability." The army would also give him a new aide: Lieutenant John "Johnny" Ramsey Pugh, a twenty-nine-year-old West Point graduate who had used his time at the academy to become, as his yearbook recorded, "an omnivorous reader and riding enthusiast." It was a good match for Wainwright, who everyone knew loved horses but loved reading, too. With him to Fort Myer had come 2,508 pounds of books, including a popular four-volume Robert E. Lee biography by Douglas Southall Freeman, who argued that the Confederate commander had surrendered his army but not his honor.

The proximity of Fort Myer to Washington meant no escape from politics and politicians. On Fridays during the winter months, the cavalrymen would stage riding maneuvers for the hundreds of people who would cross the Potomac and pack into the fort's riding hall. In spring 1937 at the fort's annual Society Circus, President Roosevelt himself watched the cavalrymen stage a show featuring an old-time charge against Indians. The social life at the fort made the newspapers, and so did its commander and his wife. "They have been charming hosts at many delightful social functions. And under the general's direction . . . the Friday afternoon exhibition drills have become among the most popular events of the year," one reporter wrote. Another declared that "there has never been a more popular couple at Fort Myer." Adele was said to be "gentle and gracious with a deep and delicious sense of humor," her husband to be the best sort of "strict disciplinarian," the kind whom men universally "adore."

Thankfully, not all the words said about Wainwright made the newspapers. There were whispers about his drinking. Cavalrymen did not usually attract notice for drinking, not because it was rare but because it was so common. People remembered Wainwright telling an old joke about it. "Gentlemen," a colonel tells his men after seeing them on a spree, "I don't mind an eye-opener in the morning. Everybody needs that. I can understand the need for a pick-me-up around 10:30 and nobody's gonna hold a couple of drinks before lunch against you. I know you need something to keep you awake around mid-afternoon and of course you're entitled to a few drinks before dinner and a brandy or two afterwards. But, gentlemen, this constant sip, sip, sip all day long has got to stop." Wainwright made no secret of his love for bourbon. Perhaps there was a shade of truth in the fictional account a fellow officer wrote of Wainwright appearing at the gates of heaven. Asked to explain his love for liquor, the fictional Wainwright answered, "I guess I did drink a little too much sometimes. But Your Honor, there is one question the answer to which I have always wanted to know. Begging your pardon, Sir, but if God didn't intend for us poor mortals to enjoy it, why did He permit such wonderful stuff as good scotch and bourbon to be made?" To drink for breakfast, the real Wainwright would surely have quipped.

That sense of humor—the same Wainwright would show in the opening minutes of the raid on Clark Field—made it hard for even those closest to him to judge the seriousness of the problem. One of his nieces insisted there was no problem. However much he drank, he held his liquor, she wrote, "like an officer and a gentleman." His aide, Johnny Pugh, agreed. Accounts of Wainwright's drinking sprees did not square with the general Pugh remembered serving. Another soon-to-be aide named Thomas Dooley, however, had a different explanation. When his boss drank, he became "a completely different person," Dooley wrote. Alcohol seemed to augment Wainwright's courage but not necessarily his wisdom. And soon he would need both.

In September 1939, as World War II erupted in Europe, Malin Craig, who had done so much to advance Wainwright's career, gave way to George Marshall, who was determined to sack old officers stuck in "outmoded patterns," ill-equipped for war against Germany's fast-moving Blitzkrieg tactics. At fifty-six years old, Wainwright might have found himself among the "deadwood" Marshall vowed to clear away. The newspapers described Wainwright as "a sideburned, old time cavalryman." Fortunately, commanding officers over the years had described him as an especially talented one. "Natural leader, magnetic personality, clipped speech, good disciplinarian, popular with officers and men, alert, forceful" were the words they used. Having left Fort Myer for a brigade command in Texas, Wainwright hoped to position himself to fight the war he was certain the United States would soon join across the Atlantic. Instead, he received a choice of three posts vital to the Pacific: the Philippines, Panama, or Hawaii. He chose Panama. For some reason, the army sent him to the Philippines, anyway. Before leaving, he participated in a massive war game being held in Louisiana. The army inserted him mid-action into command of a group of horsemen about to be overrun by tanks. It was too late to save the cavalry. All he could do was save himself. Wainwright, newspapers reported, "dodged behind a station pump. Being thin all he had to do was stand quietly to avoid capture." It was an easy decision in a war game. It would not be so simple in a real war.

On September 18, 1940, with the skyscrapers of New York in the background, the army transport ship *Grant* raised a one-star pennant in honor of Wainwright, the one-star general boarding with his wife and his mother-in-law, now a widow. Wainwright's own mother, Dodo, had died the previous year and left a sadness that had not subsided. The traveling party also included Johnny Pugh, who brought his wife and their baby boy, about to take his first steps. The Philippines remained a place where officers brought their children, but the Wainwrights' only son was no longer a child. Jack was now twenty-seven years old. Despite the family's hopes that he would go to West Point, he had found his calling at sea as a sailor aboard an ocean liner. He had also found love with a young woman named Elfrida to whom he had proposed. Wainwright had begged his son to go on a few more voyages before going to the altar. Only by spending time apart could a man and woman know how much they wished to be together. If their love endured upon reuniting, they could marry then. When the couple rejected this advice and married in April 1940, Wainwright had no choice but to fall on his sword. On another point, however, he would not do so. If war came, he expected his son to leave commercial shipping for a berth in the United States Navy. "Our family is always in every war. Don't be an exception," read the letter Wainwright wrote en route to the Philippines during a stop in San Francisco after passing through the Panama Canal. Secretly, he worried that being in the Philippines would mean he himself would "miss the war," the real one, that is, in Europe. The army, he joked, had sent him "out to pasture." If so, he would go out as a major general. The one-star pennant atop the ship switched to a two-star pennant upon word that he had received yet another promotion.

After a trip made memorable with bridge tournaments, movie screenings, dances, and occasional seasickness, the ship arrived in

Manila on November 1, 1940. For the first time in his career, Wainwright found himself in command of a division. Ten thousand men strong, the so-called Philippine Division represented the largest American army unit on the islands, yet only two thousand of the troops were actually American. The rest were Philippine Scouts. Though some of the troops occupied barracks in Manila and some at Fort Stotsenburg to the north, Wainwright would make his home for now at the division's headquarters at Fort McKinley, slightly south of the city. The house awaiting him was so large that he joked about moving his horses into the parlor when they finished their own voyage, as all three of them did, the next month.

Much has been written about the many ways Americans in the Philippines found to amuse themselves in the years leading up to the war, but the diary Wainwright kept tells a lesser-known story: one of intense preparation to carry out War Plan Orange. Back in 1899, Arthur MacArthur and other American officers had seen that the beaches along Lingayen Gulf offered an ideal landing site for depositing troops at the top of Luzon's central plain, which pointed the way southward between the mountains to Manila. If the Japanese attacked, Wainwright expected them to make the most of this geography and to do so in December or January when the weather would most favor a landing. It was those months, then, that Wainwright devoted to a series of war games shortly after his arrival. "Orange [Japan] has landed at Lingayen," Wainwright wrote in his diary on January 12, 1941. "Withdraw to Bataan," the peninsula where American forces would make their last stand. The years he had spent studying the plan had made his opinion of it only more pessimistic. Like MacArthur, Wainwright believed the best defense against an attack required counterattacking, not retreating. "A defense must be active, damn it, not passive," Wainwright would later write. "[Orange] was a defeatist plan, but our feeling in the matter didn't change it." His men needed to be ready to execute it, and he would see to it that they were. "Sometimes I feel as if my life was a continuous string of never-ending war games," Pugh wrote.

This is not to say that there was no time for leisure. Friends had heard Wainwright call golf a "namby-pamby" game and tease the men he saw "wasting their time chasing a little pill." But after arriving in the Philippines, he took up the sport not because he learned to like it but because it passed the hours. To his new daughter-in-law, who would become a confidante, Wainwright described a normal day at Fort McKinley this way: "I ride every morning at 6:00 AM for about 1-1/4 to 1-1/2 hours, come home, clean up, change clothes, eat breakfast, and go to work usually driving around first to see the troops at training and inspect the post, then go to my office and home at 1:00 for lunch. In the afternoons, play a little golf and go back to the office to clean up what has been left over." The next cocktail hour never seemed far away, and a wise officer always kept his dress whites close by. In the evenings, there were dances and dinners at the many Manila clubs, including the University Club, where Wainwright would return the next year under very different circumstances. Though he could not foresee the humiliations in store for him there, he began to see a change in Manila. It began to lose, as he put it, "the sparkle."

By spring 1941, husbands and wives had been living for months with the knowledge that their days together were numbered. Wainwright had informed his officers of the army's evacuation order. "Like most of the other wives, Mrs. Wainwright did not want to go," Wainwright later wrote. "Like most of the other husbands, I guess, I lied to her and told her it would be just a short separation; that the trouble would blow over soon." In his bones, however, he had begun to feel otherwise. The dreaded day came on May 14, 1941. At noon, Adele and her mother headed off to sea. "There were sudden tears along the rails of the ship and all of us on the dock, waving with frozen smiles, felt mighty bad," Wainwright remembered. His diary entry for the day captured the emotions best: "Oh! How lonesome but I must hold up. Adele is gone." His health had been good. But in the weeks afterward, his eyes would struggle with reading, and his teeth would hurt. Pugh remembered feeling a similar "ache" after his wife and young son sailed away. So did almost every married American officer not named Douglas MacArthur. It could be argued that the order in May had no effect on MacArthur's family because he had officially retired from the United States Army. But even when the army called MacArthur back into active service in July 1941, his wife and son still did not go back to America. Wainwright never felt the need to ask why. The possibility that as a general Wainwright might spare himself from the awful farewells forced upon more junior officers never occurred to him.

In some ways, the relationship between MacArthur and Wainwright had changed little since their days at West Point. MacArthur persisted in addressing Wainwright as "Jim," even though almost no one else did. In front of others, Wainwright addressed MacArthur as general but privately sometimes dared to be among the few who called him Douglas. That liberty, however, in no way made them equals. Outside an inner circle that never included Wainwright, MacArthur kept himself a distant figure. He did not relish going out to share cocktails with fellow officers, as Wainwright so often did. When MacArthur saw Wainwright for dinner or in some other social setting, it was usually because protocol required it.

Before MacArthur assumed command of United States Army Forces in the Far East, his conversations with Wainwright almost never touched on fighting Japan. Afterward, they touched on little else. MacArthur explained that he envisioned dividing his force in Luzon into two corps—a northern and a southern force—and offered Wainwright, as the highest-ranking field commander, his pick. "Which do you consider the most important point in the Philippines to defend?" Wainwright asked. "Where do you think the main danger is—the place where some distinction can be gained?" Only after MacArthur answered the north did Wainwright say, "I'd like that." In truth, he had already known the answer—the north included the beaches of Lingayen—but it was better to defer to MacArthur even if it would not always be so easy to do.

The newly organized North Luzon Force would have its head-quarters at Fort Stotsenburg, which fittingly gave the old cavalryman

Wainwright command of the famous 26th Cavalry but also meant he would retain only a sliver of the polished Philippine Division, most of which MacArthur planned to keep as part of a reserve force around Manila between the two corps. The bulk of both the North and South Luzon Forces would come instead from the so-called Philippine Army, which MacArthur would form out of the conscripts who had passed through the training camps he had run since 1937. Of the ten Philippine Army divisions, which began being inducted into the United States Army in September 1941, Wainwright would command four.

In these conscripts, MacArthur saw a way out of the years of strategic struggle behind War Plan Orange, an alternative to retreating to Bataan. But as the first regiments arrived at their camps, Wainwright saw something else: an organizational challenge familiar perhaps to generals from long-standing colonial powers such as Britain but completely foreign to any American general. Attired in canvas shoes and short pants and lacking steel helmets, the conscripts did not look like soldiers. They did not act like them either. "A paper army," Wainwright would call them, by which he meant a fighting force that existed in the memos generals passed back and forth but not in the barracks. "The Philippine Army troops are not well trained so I will have a big job getting them ready to fight," Wainwright wrote to his son and daughter-in-law. It was not the troops' fault. For all the work American teachers had done to spread English—and the recent steps the Philippine government had taken to make a national language out of the dominant Luzon dialect known as Tagalog—the conscripts from the countryside could often understand neither. Even the simplest order regarding basic sanitation required time-consuming translations into six different dialects before all the members of one company could understand it. And even if more time could have gone to combat training, the camps did not have enough ammunition to spare for practice with the rifles the United States had furnished from stock left over from World War I. Some of the artillery units had never fired their guns. Had they, they would have discovered that some of the decade-old shells no longer worked.

Not until November 28 did Wainwright move to Fort Stotsenburg and officially assume command of the North Luzon Force. MacArthur had said not to rush. "You'll probably have until about April to train those troops," he had told Wainwright during a meeting in Manila. At Stotsenburg, Wainwright found a headquarters in name only. He had little more than Johnny Pugh, on the verge of becoming a major, and the young sociable new aide, Thomas Dooley, on the verge of becoming a captain. A corps commander needed a far larger staff, and Wainwright would need to build his from scratch. An even more daunting challenge awaited to the north at the camps housing the Philippine Army divisions. After visiting these camps including one called O'Donnell in early December, Wainwright left disgusted with the "filthy" and "poor" conditions he saw.

More and more, Wainwright found himself reflecting on what MacArthur had said during their last meeting. Even if the older man was right that the Japanese would wait till April—even if the warnings from Washington of imminent attack were wrong—Wainwright did not see how the Philippine Army would be ready. He could not imagine the troops under his command holding the beaches "at all costs," as MacArthur's orders on December 3 stated. For so many untrained men dispersed over so long a coastline, there were not enough good officers, not enough good means of transportation, and basically no means of communication beyond unsecured telephone lines. MacArthur had deluded the War Department, to say nothing of himself, into believing his command to be "ready for any eventuality." He needed to know the truth. Before waking to the news of Pearl Harbor on December 8, Wainwright had planned to deliver the message in person to Manila. By the time he had packed his field bag and stepped outside to the roar of bombers, however, his travel plans had changed. Rather than heading south for a meeting with MacArthur, he knew he would be heading north for a meeting with the Japanese.

As the Japanese bombers continued pounding Clark Field, a car drove up beside Wainwright. Out stepped his aide Tom Dooley, who had been visiting a girl he liked in Manila. Dooley had expected to see Wainwright in the city for breakfast but had set off for Stotsenburg after the general had not shown, as he usually did, fifteen minutes early. Realizing that the road back to Stotsenburg had taken Dooley through the fires consuming Clark Field, Wainwright called his aide a "damned fool" and then made plans to award him a Silver Star for his courage. Dooley, like Pugh already, would become like a son to Wainwright. He would celebrate his aides' birthdays and fret for their safety. But for now, he could think only about how much he longed for his wife as he made his way over to the wreckage of the airfield.

Low-flying Japanese fighter planes had finished the job the bombers had begun. Bits of the B-17s that General Brereton had left behind on Luzon lay in ruins beneath the smoke. So did the hope of stopping a Japanese invading force before it reached the islands. Dooley was certain the United States would reassert air supremacy soon. But Wainwright knew otherwise. In the days ahead, Brereton would request permission to remove the remaining B-17s on the archipelago to Australia. And with the skies surrendered, so would be the seas. Japanese bombers would blow up the naval base the Americans had maintained in Manila Bay by the ruins of the Spanish fleet, and almost all the ships that America had left would sail away. For the foreseeable future, the skies and seas would belong to the Japanese. They would land soon, and to oppose them Wainwright had Philippine Army divisions that he could not trust and only one regiment of Philippine Scouts that he could: the eight hundred horsemen of the 26th Cavalry.

*   *   *

On the night of December 10, the Philippine troops manning the beaches along Lingayen Gulf saw shadows in the water. One of the Philippine Army batteries opened fire. Then all the batteries began spewing out the shells the army had so carefully rationed over the preceding months. The old machine guns joined the firing spree. So only the 26th Cavalry. The horsemen made their stand on a hill, even as the American tanks fell behind it—a move that created confusion when Japanese tanks came up the rear at nightfall and took aim at the horses. Had not the Scouts led their steeds across a bridge that a quick-thinking officer stayed behind to set ablaze, the Japanese would have routed the regiment. As it was, it had suffered 150 casualties and lost many of its best horses, including one of Wainwright's own. A bullet had struck his beloved Little Boy in the brain. "It is hard to see a man die," Wainwright wrote. "But for a cavalryman it is almost equally hard to see a gallant horse die."

With the Japanese in control of Lingayen, Wainwright had no choice but to begin pulling his forces back from the beaches, toward the headquarters he had established below the nearby Agno River. There, in a camouflaged metal trailer surrounded by a few tents and a bamboo shack covered with coconut leaves, he began plotting the counterattack he hoped to deliver with the aid of what he had learned from the fighting so far. MacArthur had proven both farsighted and naïve: farsighted that Filipinos could make outstanding soldiers; naïve that rapidly mobilized conscripts could. Only with a full division of Philippine Scouts like the men of the 26th Cavalry did Wainwright have any hope of throwing the Japanese back upon the beaches. MacArthur had such men in reserve: the Philippine Division that Wainwright had formerly commanded. If MacArthur would send it north now, Wainwright saw possibilities. "Give me an answer now on whether I get the Philippine Division," he said on a call to MacArthur's office on the afternoon of December 23. A long silence followed, then came an answer: "It's highly improbable."

That night, someone from 1 Calle Victoria called back. There was to be no counterattack at all, Wainwright was told. "WPO-3 is in effect." Now it was Wainwright who went silent. "You understand?" the voice on the other end asked.

"Yes," Wainwright said, "I understand." He did understand, all too well. WPO-3 meant War Plan Orange. There were many close to

did the vintage rifles. "It was like dropping a match in a wareho
of Fourth of July fireworks," said an American officer who witne:
the display. "Instantly Lingayen Gulf was ablaze." In the morn
MacArthur's office released a statement declaring that the Philip
troops had proven their mettle by repulsing an enemy landing. In tr
the troops had unleashed against a single reconnaissance motorl
whose operators now knew the location of virtually every Amer
gun. Nevertheless, MacArthur's assurances that his forces had be
"mopping up" the remnants of the invasion filled American newspa
with banner headlines. As late as December 14, *The New York Ti*
proclaimed, "JAPANESE FORCES WIPED OUT IN WESTE
LUZON," never mind that they had not even landed there yet.

To the east, however, there was no denying that the Japanese
landed. They had established three advance bases. One lay on the ta
the dragon-shaped island, south of Wainwright's sector. The other
lay in it, north of Lingayen Gulf on the dragon's wing, where Wainw1
could offer little opposition. So he had opted to give none. To l
defended every inch of a coastline as long as Luzon's, as MacAr
had previously ordered, would have left Lingayen Gulf open to
main landing, which Wainwright still expected shortly.

It came in the early hours of December 22 but with a twist: Ins
of landing on the bottom of the gulf where the Philippine guns
put on their firework display twelve days earlier, some 43,000 Japai
troops began splashing ashore on the more sparsely defended eas
side where they could link up with the earlier expeditionary la
ings now marching down the side of the dragon's wing along a coa
highway called Route 3. The road would eventually take them, if
stopped, straight down the central plain, around the side of Ma
Bay, and into the capital. They would come with air support and tar
Wainwright begged for tanks of his own but received only five. So
would later say there was a feeling the old cavalryman could no
trusted with more. What Philippine Army forces he had in the vicir
quickly gave way. To slow down the Japanese on their D-Day, he l

Wainwright who thought MacArthur had been mad for having abandoned the plan in the first place. A lower-ranking general who served under Wainwright would say, "MacArthur and Sutherland were trying to draw up a plan in a few days after discarding the one that had been worked on for twenty-five years.... To discard a plan like that, I thought was a terrible thing." An aide later claimed that he heard Wainwright himself describe the switch to MacArthur's plan as a "major" mistake. If so, Wainwright kept that opinion secret from even members of his own family. In fact, years after, they would credit him with having urged MacArthur to "scrap" Orange. The secret to reconciling these seemingly contradictory accounts lies in Wainwright's own memoirs, where he made a point of saying he shared MacArthur's preference for offensive action but also added that War Plan Orange was the only plan the army had. That was a diplomatic way of saying what Wainwright had realized as soon as he had seen the Philippine Army troops: MacArthur's strategy had never been a realistic alternative. The months spent shifting to it, Wainwright recognized, would now make War Plan Orange all the much harder to implement. On the first day of fighting under Orange, the army should have begun readying Bataan's defenses for the stand the troops would eventually make on the peninsula. Under MacArthur's plan, however, the food, medicine, and other supplies that the men would need in the jungles of Bataan had instead moved farther away, to depots as dispersed as the forces MacArthur had stretched upon the shores of Luzon.

Wainwright estimated he had 28,000 troops whom he would have to corral from points across North Luzon for a journey that would require soldiers to go an average of 150 miles. He had rehearsed a similar maneuver the year before, albeit with professional soldiers, and would fall back now on the same series of parallel defensive lines he had used then—the first traversing the central plain just below Lingayen and each subsequent one lying one night's march farther south, closer to Manila Bay. The timing worried Wainwright the most. If he held any line too long, the Japanese would turn his retreat into a rout. But if he abandoned his lines too soon, he would doom the South Luzon Force making its own retreat from Japanese troops landing on the tail of the island. A look at the dragon-shaped island reveals why. To reach Bataan, the members of the South Luzon Force would first have to move up the hind legs of the island past Manila and then curve around the belly of the bay. As they did, they would find themselves traveling up Route 3, the same road that Wainwright's North Luzon Force would be withdrawing down. In fact, the two forces would pick up Route 7, the highway to Bataan, in the same place, a city called San Fernando, ten miles below Wainwright's fifth and final defensive line. His men needed to hold that position as a shield as long as it took for the South Luzon Force to pass behind. The additional time could benefit Wainwright's own men, too. If they made it too quickly to Bataan, they would find it unfortified, undersupplied, and unready to receive them.

In times of trial, history often serves as comfort. In search of it, Wainwright looked to the Civil War stories he loved for a precedent for the challenge he faced. He could find none on either the Union or Confederate side. "It was unlike any of the textbook retreats I had studied," he wrote. "In these classic retreats the object was to get away from the enemy by speed of movement. Moving down toward Bataan, we had the definitive mission of delaying the enemy as long as practicable." MacArthur hoped it would be "practicable" until January 8.

What Wainwright saw on the morning of December 24, however, made him wonder if it would be practicable till even Christmas. Driving in his Packard sedan with Tom Dooley to a town called Binalonan on the far-right side of the first defensive line, where the depleted 26th Cavalry had gone into reserve behind a Philippine Army division, Wainwright spotted Japanese tanks pouring down Route 3 unopposed. In fact, had he not chosen to take an old road running parallel to the highway, his sedan would have met the tanks head-on. The Philippine Army division supposedly standing in the way had vanished and left the 26th Cavalry to once again stand alone against the Japanese onslaught. Mistaking the explosives the cavalrymen had fashioned out of soda bottles and gasoline

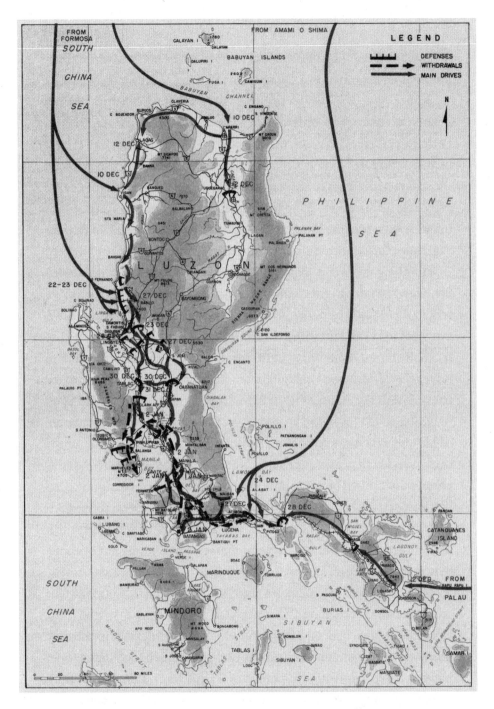

A map made for MacArthur's reports showing the Japanese offensive on Luzon in December 1941 and early January 1942, as well as the retreats the North Luzon Force had to make from the shores of Lingayen Gulf and the South Luzon Force had to make from the tail of the island.

for antitank weaponry, the Japanese stopped their tanks and sent in their infantry. Dismounted in a ditch, the crack-shot cavalrymen beat back wave after wave of soldiers screaming "Banzai!" The intensity of the fire made it no place for a general, but Wainwright insisted on having his Packard parked. "I'm going on," he said and gave instructions in case he did not return. Major William Chandler of the 26th Cavalry noted the "characteristic coolness" with which Wainwright stepped out of the car a little before noon. "Word of his presence," Chandler wrote, "spread up and down the line like wildfire, and the men settled down to their sharpshooting of incautiously exposed Japs with renewed confidence."

How long the cavalrymen could keep it up was what worried Dooley. He begged Wainwright to look out for his own safety. The drink of scotch that Wainwright happily shared with the cavalry officers, however, seemed to fill him with a determination to share whatever fate they faced. Not until around 1:30 in the afternoon did he finally consent to leave. The cavalrymen held out for another two hours, while he moved back behind the Agno River, where the rest of the army would soon make its second defensive line. "A bleak Christmas," Wainwright noted in his diary the next day before adding this: "I am more proud of the cavalry today than ever in my life." There would be little other holiday cheer, only canned beans, a little scotch, and memories of family celebrations past: "[the] Christmas tree, the arrangement of our boy's toys, the carefully wrapped packages for my wife," Wainwright wrote. This year, he could send her only a radio message, which was not nothing, he would soon learn.

A pattern began to emerge. Wainwright would take up a new defensive line, which was never so straight or solidly held as to merit the word, see it breached, and then order his men to fall back to the next position to the south under the cover of night. Even though Wainwright had approved requisitioning buses and cars, he could not round up enough to compensate for the shortage arising from the sudden switch to War Plan Orange. "Buses," Wainwright wrote, "[were] loaded to the ceilings." Philippine Army soldiers left to walk saw signs of disaster wherever they looked: down below at the bare feet poking through their canvas shoes, up above at the Japanese planes flying unopposed. "Our troops are under continual bombing and strafing by the enemy," Johnny Pugh wrote. "The best trained troops in the world would not hold under such circumstances, and these are green raw Filipinos." Casualties and desertions thinned divisions already short of full strength. As they fell back, depots containing enormous quantities of food and other supplies that the soldiers would need on Bataan fell behind enemy lines.

By December 30, the eastern end of Wainwright's fourth defensive line had completely collapsed at a place called Cabanatuan and left the Japanese free to race down Route 5, a highway running south parallel to Route 3 before merging with it near Manila Bay but not before offering a shortcut to a critical river crossing that the South Luzon Force would need to make at a town called Calumpit. If the Japanese seized the bridges there, the members of the South Luzon Force would have no way to cross the yawning Pampanga River as they rounded the bay.

Seeking to head off disaster, Wainwright gave orders to form the fifth and final defensive line and headed to a place called Plaridel just east of Calumpit. It was here that the Japanese forces advancing down Route 5 would face a choice: take the shortcut to Calumpit or continue south toward Manila. On December 31, Wainwright found Brigadier General Albert Jones, the commander of the South Luzon Force, in a Plaridel schoolhouse. His men had begun crossing the Pampanga before dawn, and Wainwright now ordered Jones's covering force to fall back closer to the bridgehead. Jones refused. "I'm giving you a direct order," responded Wainwright, believing that both sides of the bridges lay within his sector and that he outranked any general in the Philippines not named MacArthur. Only then did Jones reveal what MacArthur had done: His headquarters had changed the dividing line between the North and South Luzon Forces to the Pampanga itself. The shift made sense as the two armies reached their nexus, but the failure to inform Wainwright was inexcusable. So humiliated was Wainwright afterward that he misrepresented the incident in his own diary.

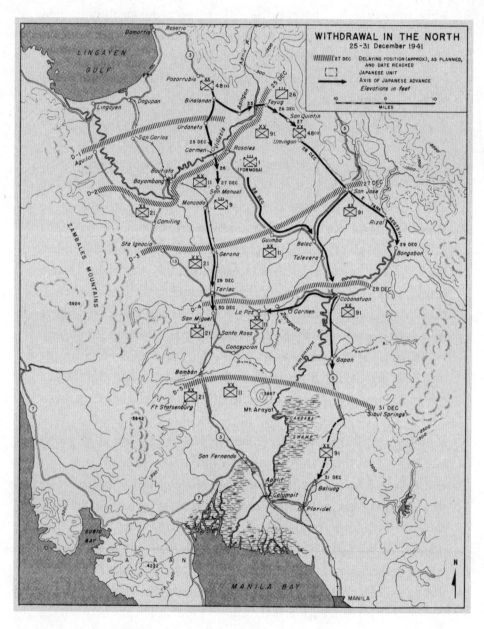

The successive defensive lines where Wainwright and his men made their stands during the retreat from Lingayen. The routes of the North and South Luzon Forces could converge at San Fernando only after the latter had made it across the Pampanga River at Calumpit, near where Route 3 and Route 5 meet.

But instead of holding a grudge, Wainwright would hold the other side of the bridges. He waited there until Jones crossed with the last of his men during the predawn hours of the first day of the new year. The two generals found some alcohol and drank to 1942. Sometime after five in the morning, Wainwright ordered the bridges blown. His chief engineer had rigged them with dynamite but protested that he still had crews working on the other side. Wainwright agreed to delay but soon spied Japanese soldiers approaching. "We cannot wait any longer," he said. "Blow it now." He would never forget the "deafening roar" as the spans crashed down at 6:15 a.m. into the river that now stood between the bulk of the Japanese army and the South and North Luzon Forces set to converge in San Fernando and then down into Bataan.

In truth, the Japanese stranded on the other side of the Pampanga worried little about the pathetic parade vanishing across the river. The road ahead for the Americans and Filipinos would be neither easy nor clear. Cars and buses and trucks would clog the highway as soldiers and civilian refugees carrying what they could filed alongside and as bombs and bullets rained from planes flying overhead. At the top of the peninsula where Bataan began lay another major river crossing. Of the 28,000 men Wainwright had led from the shores of Lingayen, only 16,000 would cross this final bridge. In all, however, thanks to the time he had won with his skilled withdrawal, more than 80,000 soldiers would. Last among them would be Wainwright himself. This time, he insisted on being the final man across the steel span his engineers then blew into the water. "The general's sentimentality gripes me at times," Dooley would say afterward. The Japanese would vastly underestimate the number of soldiers Wainwright would succeed in leading into Bataan but would not underestimate the amount of food awaiting them there. As the Japanese soldiers watched Wainwright escape across the Pampanga River, they had every reason to believe that what remained of his ragged force could not hold out long in a hostile jungle poorly prepared for a last stand. Indeed, his escape had cleared the path to the prize the Japanese coveted most: the city Arthur

MacArthur had entered in 1898. There had been no all-out battle for Manila then, and Arthur's son would make sure there was none now. To spare the capital, Douglas MacArthur had declared it an open city. The Japanese would not find him there. He had fled across the water to Corregidor, the rock at the entrance to the bay, in the clutches of the dragon.

CHAPTER FOUR

Tunnel View

Around the same time Wainwright learned that War Plan Orange had gone into effect, Jean MacArthur did, too. On the evening of December 23, her husband came home from his office on the walls of Intramuros and sat down to dinner in the penthouse dining room framed by windows on three sides. During the day, she had seen Japanese planes fly by and drop their bombs on targets around the bay. There was nothing to see at night with the curtains drawn and the city blacked out except for occasional mysterious flares, which were said to be the work of Japanese collaborators. The strange sounds that residents heard in the darkness added to their paranoia. Air raid alarms and scattered gunfire mixed with the music still emanating from the Manila Hotel's dance floor. In spite of the revelry happening below, Jean had sent little Arthur and his nanny—the Chinese woman named Loh Chiu but always called Ah Cheu in the family—to sleep downstairs in the belief that the penthouse would take the worst of a bomb. Alone with the general in the dining room, Jean remembered the "spooky" light that the dim lamp by the table cast on his face as he began telling her that he had aborted his plan to hold the beaches and that Manila would fall as the North and South Luzon forces made their way to Bataan. MacArthur would not meet them there. He would move his headquarters to Corregidor. Jean, Arthur, and Ah Cheu would come, too. They would leave the next afternoon.

The news did not astonish Jean. She had sensed it coming. Her husband had known for some time that his plan to defend the beaches had failed, even if he refused to admit it to anyone beyond his most trusted advisers. One day earlier, he had invited his personal aide, Lieutenant Colonel Sid Huff, over to the penthouse and told Jean and Arthur to sit around the Christmas tree and open their presents while they still could. Some boys might have found the timing alarming but not Arthur. Rarely had he known a day when he had not received some gift from his father. On this day, the boy found a red tricycle. Jean unwrapped box after box of clothes, including some lingerie. "Sir Boss," she said using a pet name for her husband as she held up the outfits, "they are beautiful. Thank you so much." She might have thanked Huff instead because MacArthur had ordered his aide to pick out Jean's presents. MacArthur had no time to visit stores, and Jean now knew that she would have no space to carry any of these new garments with her. She wrapped them back up and hid them in a closet.

Each of them could take only one suitcase to Corregidor. Jean filled hers mostly with canned food and other supplies Arthur might need. She also packed her marriage certificate, as if worried someone somewhere might doubt that she had really married Douglas MacArthur. At four o'clock on December 24, Sid Huff arrived and began carrying the suitcases downstairs. Jean convinced him to take Arthur's new tricycle, too. As Huff loaded the baggage onto a truck, Jean took a last look around the drawing room decorated with gold furniture, red drapes, and satin walls. Her eyes stopped at a glass-door cabinet that she had custom built for the medals and decorations her husband had won during his four decades in the army. Grabbing a towel, she swiped it across the shelf until she had wrapped up all the awards. There were two more items to move: a pair of vases the emperor of Japan—the current emperor's grandfather—had presented to General Arthur MacArthur during his travels. Jean could not take the vases with her. Instead, she placed them on a stand near the entrance. "Maybe when the Japanese see it, they will respect our home," she said. Then she looked down at Arthur and said, "Ready to go to Corregidor?"

At the pier, however, the ship *Don Esteban* was not ready. Already once that day, Japanese bombers had struck around the port. The ship would wait for night, when darkness would provide cover. In the meantime, workers loaded the commonwealth's currency reserves and bank deposits onto the ship. Arthur played on the steel deck until an air raid siren forced him below. When Jean brought him back up, he said, "Mummy, I've seen enough of Corregidor." Her efforts to explain that they had not even left the pier made no headway. The boy set his eyes toward the Manila Hotel. "I want to go home," he said. As the sun set, Jean brought Arthur back below deck and comforted him with Old Friend, the stuffed rabbit she had packed for him. It was dark now, but the boat still did not move. The hundred or so passengers waited for one more. Jean's husband had given orders not to leave without him.

At his office at 1 Calle Victoria, General MacArthur still had business to do. First was a farewell to General Brereton, the head of the Far East Air Force. MacArthur had ordered Brereton to Australia with the remaining B-17s. For what had happened to the other bombers, both men knew they would have to answer to history. "I hope that you will tell the people outside what we have done and protect my reputation as a fighter," MacArthur said.

"General, your reputation will never need any protection," Brereton responded. He had asked to stay on MacArthur's staff, but the old man saw no role for the air chief now. They had lost the battle for the skies on that first day. So dangerous was the situation afterward that aides had urged MacArthur to take down the American flag atop his headquarters for fear it would draw Japanese bombers. "Take every normal precaution," MacArthur had said, "but let's keep the flag flying." He had insisted on standing without a helmet atop the walls of Intramuros as the bombers would fly past. When they had gone, he would return inside to his office, where he would pace back and forth, as he did now upon Brereton's departure.

MacArthur's eyes scanned the row of flags behind his desk before stopping at one in the corner: the red four-star flag he had used during his days as the army chief of staff. Now a four-star general again, he wondered if the flag might come in handy. "Rogers," MacArthur bellowed at an enlisted man named Paul Rogers, "cut off that flag for me." A clerk most valued for his skills as a stenographer, Rogers had no scissors and no clue how to cut a flag without one. "Cut it off," MacArthur repeated. So, with his boss glaring, Rogers began untying the banner. When done, he handed it to MacArthur, who tucked it under his arm. "Well," he said, "I guess it's time to go. There isn't anything left to do here." He put on the gold-braided field cap he had worn throughout his time as the field marshal of the Philippines. "I'll be back," people heard him say as he headed out to the limousine ready to take him to the *Don Esteban*.

One last disagreeable duty awaited at the pier: a meeting with Admiral Thomas C. Hart, the navy's top Asiatic commander, who had stayed in Manila despite ordering almost all his ships away from the Philippines. He had infuriated MacArthur by refusing to indulge the notion that the ships could assist with bringing relief to the islands through the blockade the Japanese had begun to establish. The navy, MacArthur believed, had betrayed the army.

Not until past eight o'clock did MacArthur board the *Don Esteban* and set off for Corregidor. The munitions and supplies the Americans had set ablaze rather than leave for the Japanese illuminated the sky and silhouetted the weeping men lowering the American flag over Intramuros, where MacArthur's father had first seen it rise to the sound of cheers in 1898. In a warehouse near the pier, the books that had belonged to Arthur MacArthur but that had not found a place on the shelves of the penthouse library went up in flames. The sound of the explosions followed the passengers out into the darkness of the bay as the city receded behind them into the distance. Only the stars lit the sky ahead. Some of the soldiers started singing Christmas carols, which filled them with such a longing for home that they switched to off-color songs they would have never sung in front of their families. Fortunately, little Arthur heard not a word as he slept below deck with Old Friend. His father sat alone above with his head cradled in his hands.

*   *   *

If Luzon looks like a dragon with its claws wrapping around Manila Bay, then Corregidor looks like a tadpole in danger. Widest to the west where its mountainous head faces the South China Sea, the island trails off three and half miles to the east with a tail leading into the bay whose entrance it divides into two. Just a few miles to the north across the narrow upper channel lies the tip of the Bataan peninsula. Out of the larger lower channel to the south rise three other islands, little cousins to Corregidor. Americans seeing the lay of the land for the first time in 1898 marveled that the Spanish had allowed Admiral Dewey to steam his fleet into the bay, and vowed never to let anyone repeat the feat. Around the head of Corregidor, work began on building batteries powerful enough to repel invasion from the South China Sea. But the batteries when done had two weaknesses: all lacked turrets and lay open to attack from above, and many could direct their fire only toward vessels attempting to enter the bay via the South China Sea. If an enemy landing at Lingayen Gulf approached Manila Bay from the rear and succeeded in gaining control of the mountains at the bottom of the Bataan peninsula, it would control elevations commanding the highest peaks on Corregidor. In other words, to retain Corregidor, American forces would need to retain Bataan. And even if they could, the designers of Corregidor's defenses had failed to account for the dawn of the age of airpower.

Americans posted on Corregidor in the years leading up to World War II recognized these shortcomings but could do little about them because of a 1922 disarmament treaty the United States and Japan had signed. In exchange for agreeing to limits on shipbuilding, Japan had insisted the United States halt further fortification of the Philippine coastline. The treaty, however, said nothing about building a tunnel for a road. If it so happened that such a tunnel could double as a bomb-proof shelter, then the officers overseeing its construction would feel no obligation to say so. As it turned out, Corregidor was in need of such a tunnel. Between the mountainous head of the tadpole and the tail stood Malinta Hill. In 1931, engineers using prisoners for workers began mining their way through the hard rock of the hill and carving out a semicircular-shaped opening about twenty-five feet wide. The tunnel would stretch eight hundred feet from one end of the hill to the other, and the digging did not stop there. Off the main east-west tunnel, workers built a couple dozen lateral lines as well as other branch-offs and annexes that could provide living quarters, office space, storage facilities, and even a hospital. Concrete reinforced the rock walls and made the entire complex a bomb shelter capable of housing thousands of people. By the time MacArthur set off for Corregidor on Christmas Eve, the tunnel already did. Among the new residents were President Manuel Quezon, his family, and much of his government.

It was an hour before midnight by the time the *Don Esteban* docked at a narrow, low-lying strip of the island known as "Bottomside" between the entrance to the Malinta Tunnel and "Topside," as the high ground crowning the island's head was known. George Moore, the general in charge of the harbor defenses, led the MacArthurs into the tunnel to their sleeping quarters with an apology. "We have never had women around here and things may be a little crude," Moore said. Jean, Arthur, and Ah Cheu would sleep with Quezon's wife and daughters in one lateral. MacArthur and his staff would sleep with Quezon and his aides in another. All of the men would have their own bunks but would have to share a bathroom. Each lateral had only one of those. On one side of the bathroom, separated by nothing more than a piece of cloth, was the room where Quezon would sleep. On the other side was the room where he and other Catholic Filipinos had set up a little chapel and

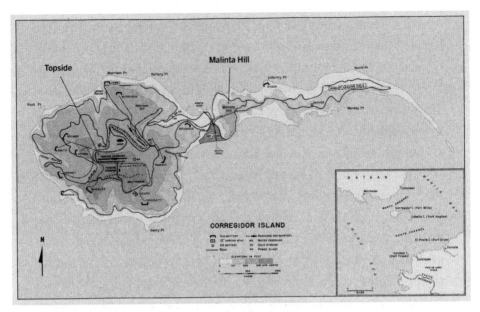

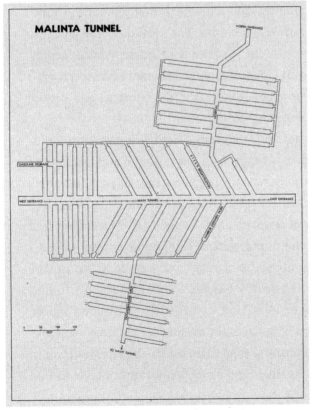

A map showing the tadpole-shaped island of Corregidor in the mouth of Manila Bay, as well as a diagram of the Malinta Tunnel, cutting through its namesake hill. Nominally built for other purposes, the main tunnel, laterals, and annexes could serve as a bomb shelter.

would observe a midnight Christmas mass. Even far away from the latrines, the musty air had a sickening smell that the abundant use of disinfectant somehow made worse. Already suffering from tuberculosis, the once energetic and now emaciated Quezon struggled to breathe. The sound of his coughing echoed through the darkness. Never again would MacArthur spend a night in the tunnel.

Despite being warned that Topside was an easy target for bombers, MacArthur moved his family and his headquarters there the next morning. In prewar days, the pleasant quality of life on Topside surprised new arrivals who knew Corregidor only by its nickname, "the Rock." In truth, rich vegetation, including blooms of hibiscus and bougainvillea, covered the island while sea breezes kept the temperature several degrees cooler than Manila. By the old Spanish lighthouse on Topside, the army had built houses of white stucco for officers, as well as barracks for enlisted men, a club, a movie theater, a parade ground, and the obligatory nine-hole golf course. For a few days, the Japanese allowed MacArthur to enjoy the new home he made with his family. He had a turkey dinner for Christmas and celebrated Jean's forty-third birthday. His staff set up a headquarters in the barracks and posted marines to guard the corner office for him.

Then, on December 29, came the air raid siren. Jean had been standing on the porch of her new house with her husband and his chief of staff, Sutherland, when she heard the noise and saw Japanese bombers approaching in a V formation across the clear sky over Topside. "You better get Arthur and get down as quick as you can," MacArthur told her, as a bomb struck the movie theater. She found Arthur with Ah Cheu inside the house and led them, as fast as she could in the sandals and dress she had on, to a nearby bunker. She barged in only to find a soldier showering naked inside but immediately confronted a more serious problem: the iron doors to the bunker would not latch no matter how hard she pushed. For more than three hours, the boy would sit in his nanny's lap and make no sound as the explosions outside rattled the doors open and shut.

During lulls in the attack, Jean would send her driver, a Filipino sergeant by the name of Benny, to check on her husband. He had insisted on standing outside and counting the planes, even after one of their bombs crashed through the room where he had slept the previous night and another through the roof of the barracks where he had his office. As usual, he refused to wear a helmet, so his Filipino orderly, Sergeant Domingo Adversario, tried to hold his own over both their heads. "One half [in] front my face, one half in front general's face," a reporter heard Adversario explain afterward. It was his hand, not his helmet, that blocked a shard of steel whirling at MacArthur's head. The orderly could feel MacArthur's knees quaking, but others watching from farther away saw only the general's courage. "MacArthur did not take cover even when the entire Topside area was disintegrating and burning around him," one awestruck aide wrote afterward. "He was still standing erect in the shambles as the last planes droned away."

That was the end of life on Topside. The process of packing up what remained of MacArthur's headquarters began immediately. From then on, his staff would work inside the Malinta Tunnel. In a meeting there, Quezon demanded MacArthur explain his recklessness. "The Japs have not as yet fabricated the bomb with my name on it," MacArthur kidded, even though Advesario had already told Quezon otherwise. "I also know that I have no right to gamble with my life," said MacArthur, turning earnest. "But it is absolutely necessary that at the right time the supreme commander should take these chances because of the effect all down the line, for when they see the man at the top risking his life, the man at the bottom says, 'I guess if the old man can take it, I can take it, too.'" MacArthur's office issued a curious press release afterward. "General MacArthur narrowly escaped serious injury in a recent bombing raid in Bataan," it read, never mind that he had been nowhere near Bataan and that none of the frontline troops heading there had seen the example he hoped to set.

The next day on a platform erected just outside the Malinta Tunnel and decorated with Philippine and American flags, MacArthur staged another moment rich in symbolism: an inauguration ceremony for Quezon. An election held just weeks before Pearl Harbor had given him a second term in office. When he had taken the oath for the first time six years earlier, MacArthur had brooded that the American president, Franklin Roosevelt, had authorized his soldiers on the islands to give the commonwealth's first president only a nineteen-gun salute instead of the twenty-one reserved for truly independent heads of state. MacArthur called the gesture an "insult." Now, in the distance as Quezon prepared to commence his second term, there was the sound of more fire than MacArthur could have ever wished. Chief Justice Jose Abad Santos, whom the Japanese would soon capture and make a martyr, administered the oath. Like the American president, the ailing Philippine one now relied on a wheelchair but hid it for his inauguration. Standing on his own, Quezon said, "At the present time we have but one task—to fight with America for America and the Philippines."

MacArthur spoke next. Like his father, he believed the future of democracy depended on the Philippines. Unlike his father, he had a gift for words as lofty as such ideas, even if sometimes he would have been better off dropping his rhetorical flourishes and, as the expression goes, just getting on with it. The speech he delivered this day found the right balance with echoes of the man he remembered as his father's hero, Abraham Lincoln.

Never before in all history has there been a more solemn and significant inauguration. An act, symbolical of democratic processes, is placed against the background of a sudden, merciless war.

The thunder of death and destruction, dropped from the skies, can be heard in the distance. Our ears almost catch the roar of battle as our soldiers close on the firing line. The horizon is blackened by the smoke of destructive fire. The air reverberates to the dull roar of exploding bombs.

Such is the bed of birth of this government, of this new nation. For four hundred years the Philippines has struggled upward toward self government. Just at the end of its tuitionary period, just on the threshold of independence, came the great hour of decision. The whole country followed its great leader in choosing the side of freedom against the side of slavery.

A few more sentences, and then MacArthur finished and looked to the sky. "Oh merciful God," he said, "preserve this noble race." Only a few dozen people had witnessed his performance; none of them would forget how his voice had broken and his eyes had moistened.

Although his staff had set up headquarters in Lateral 3 of the tunnel, MacArthur continued to insist on living with his family beyond its walls, albeit in a less conspicuous position than Topside. He picked a small gray cottage on the tail of the island, not far from the tunnel's eastern entrance. He would start his days there by putting on khaki pants and a khaki shirt with four bright stars that he would then conceal under a jacket. At first, he wore a leather jacket, but, as the mercury rose, the island's Chinese tailor made him a khaki one that he would wear for much of the rest of the war. Though he tried his best to keep up appearances, his clothes began to lose their usual crispness. He still shaved daily but no longer with fresh water. The bombs had damaged the island's water system and, even when fixed, made drinking water a cherished commodity. After hearing an enlisted man ask why officers could shave with fresh water but he could not, MacArthur ordered that everyone, himself included, shave with salt. His skin grew tougher, its creases more pronounced. The distinctive curve of his nose had always seemed beak-like. Now an aide noted that he looked "like a tired hawk."

After breakfast and a morning cigarette—he had not yet taken to pipes—MacArthur would head off for the first of several daily visits to Lateral 3 of the Malinta Tunnel. He would carry a wooden walking stick and grin as he strolled down the aisle his aides had formed with desks on either side. "Good morning, Dick," MacArthur would say as he passed Sutherland, who had the final desk before his own at the end of the aisle. No matter how many times aides had swept MacArthur's desk before he arrived, the walls of the tunnel would always have a fresh coat of dust and moisture ready for him. Nevertheless, he would lay his cap down and go to work. "MacArthur sat, sometimes bent over dispatches or reports, sometimes leaning back, foot propped against a desk drawer, talking to Sutherland," remembered the clerk Paul Rogers. The light lessened so much toward the back of the lateral that the staff had set up a sleeping area just behind MacArthur's desk. Here, between the bunk beds, MacArthur would do his pacing with Sutherland in tow. They worked so closely that Sutherland could sometimes give orders on behalf of MacArthur without consulting him. In the event of his death, MacArthur let it be known that Sutherland should take over, never mind that there were generals on Bataan who outranked him. When those generals received orders from Corregidor, they heard Sutherland's voice rather than MacArthur's. Sutherland's specialty, the headquarters team learned, was delivering bad news. "Somebody around here has got to be the S.O.B. General MacArthur is not going to be . . . so I guess I'm it," Sutherland said. He expected his fellow staff members to man their desks for long hours. MacArthur himself did not take Sundays off.

Neither did the Japanese. When the air siren would go off—and the roar of the bombers loudened—people lurking outside the tunnel would race past the sandbags into the entrance and huddle against the walls even as they began to convulse and crack and leak dust. Everyone had learned to leave the middle of the tunnel open for the ambulances that would arrive with men bleeding from where they once had limbs. Out of Lateral 3 would suddenly emerge MacArthur, walking against the flow of incoming traffic and heading toward the entrance with a scowl on his face and with a tail of aides begging him to reconsider and turn around. He never listened. He would venture out to watch the battle between the island's antiaircraft guns and the Japanese bombers as if he were, as one aide put it, "keeping a baseball score." When one of the bombers would disappear with a puff of smoke and a flash, the others would simply close the gap in the V formation. If the planes caught MacArthur at home rather than at the office, he would step outside while Sergeant Benny loaded Jean, Ah Cheu, and Arthur into a car and drove them to the tunnel ninety seconds away. Jean would then return to the house, where she would ride out the raid with her husband and, if she could find it, a glass of sherry.

No one knew what impact the terror would have on Arthur. Never in history had so many bombs fallen within a small radius of a boy so young and so far from any peers. At first, the air raids made his stomach hurt. Then, as tends to happen with children about to turn four, he became an expert. He would reassure his nanny when she saw a small Japanese plane crisscrossing the island in the mornings. "No bombers," he would say. "Oblivation plane," by which he meant observation plane. When the bombers showed up a few hours later, he would recognize them, too, and scream, "Air raid! Air raid!" When the skies cleared, he would stand guard outside the entrance to the tunnel while sporting a military-looking cap. "Good morning, General," soldiers would say as they passed him. "I'm not a general," Arthur would respond. "I'm a sergeant." Asked why, he would pause, then say, "It's because sergeants drive automobiles." Much as he liked cars, he liked nurses more. They liked him, too. And when not covered in blood, they would meet him at their mess for lunch. If bored later in the afternoon, he would inform his mother, "I'm hawngry. I've got to go to the tunnel."

The boy sergeant never went without food, but other soldiers had less. General MacArthur began to lose weight. Japanese bombers permitting, he and Jean made a point of eating once a day at the mess the officers had set up outside the tunnel entrance. MacArthur would line up with the others "cafeteria fashion" and, when his turn came, hold out a white china plate to the Chinese chef dishing out whatever stew he had. The men knew not to ask what was in it. The meat often came from carabao, the water buffalo Filipinos hitched to carts. "Is good for you," the chef would say. In the early days, an abundance of canned fruits and jams would supplement the chef's concoctions. After the meal, as men sipped brackish-tasting coffee and flies swarmed, the general would linger and would hold court with the reporters who had found their way onto the Rock. He would opine on subjects such as the quality of Japanese infantrymen—"first-class," he would call them—while tipping back his chair and puffing on the second of the three cigarettes he allowed himself each day.

One day in January, people on Corregidor learned that henceforth they would have only two meals a day, though many officers still found a way to obtain a third. MacArthur had ordered all his troops on Corregidor and Bataan on half rations after receiving a distressing report about the food shortage on the peninsula. In fifty days the soldiers on Bataan would run out of canned meat and fish, in forty days canned milk, in thirty days flour and canned vegetables, and in twenty days rice. "As things stood," the quartermaster said, the troops on Bataan would make it no longer than "two months on a most unbalanced one-half ration" diet.

None of these numbers should have come as a surprise. When War Plan Orange had gone into effect, the first barges carrying food from Manila had not gone to Bataan but rather to Corregidor with the *Don Esteban*. Not until sometime on Christmas, once the quartermaster had succeeded in stocking the Rock with enough food to feed ten thousand men for six months, did MacArthur's headquarters allow shipments to proceed to Bataan. The quartermaster had warned that stocking Bataan with enough food for a six-month stand by 43,000 men would take two weeks under the best of circumstances, and these were to be the worst of circumstances: twice as many men to supply and only half as much time to do so, with railroads closed, roads jammed, and red tape everywhere. Millions of pounds of rice that could have filled eighty thousand stomachs for a year were left behind in a warehouse along the retreat route from Lingayen because Quezon's government barred transporting food between provinces. Only the barges crossing the bay from Manila had much success delivering supplies to Bataan, but no more of them could make the trip now. Using field glasses similar to the pair MacArthur wore around his neck while inspecting different positions on the island, the men on Corregidor could see the ruins of the piers that the Japanese had continued to bomb despite MacArthur's pleas to spare the city from further destruction. The hotel he had called home still stood. But easily visible with the glasses was the new colossal Japanese flag on the building's roof. When the Japanese had entered the city on January 2, the last supply line to Bataan had collapsed.

So had morale on the peninsula, according to reports reaching Corregidor. "How are the boys?" MacArthur liked to ask officers who had taken the short boat trip over from Bataan. "Sagging," he heard. Around sunrise on January 10, he set off to see for himself in a boat with Sutherland and a few other officers. After crossing the supposedly shark-filled channel separating Corregidor from Bataan, the men split up into four cars that drove them in tandem up the east side of the peninsula. MacArthur had divided his forces on Bataan into two. Under the command of General George M. Parker, the II Philippine Corps had command of the east side. Under the command of Wainwright, the I Philippine Corps had command of the west side. Both generals had received notice to have top officers ready to greet MacArthur. He first visited Parker and then headed west on the one road running across the width of the peninsula, about halfway up it. At some point, Japanese guns finding the range of the road from afar forced the officers to stop and get out of the cars. Everyone took cover—everyone except MacArthur, who insisted on standing next to his Ford in the open. "There is no Jap shell with MacArthur's name on it," he said, lapsing, as he often did, into the third person. When the shelling stopped, the officers climbed back into the cars and set off westward again, across the peninsula, until reaching the clearing where Wainwright had his officers waiting.

The word Wainwright used to describe the way MacArthur looked when he popped out of his car was "fit." He wore his leather jacket, which looked out of place in a sweltering jungle where even Filipinos accustomed to heat sweated through their clothes. "Jonathan," Mac-Arthur said, using Wainwright's given name, "I'm glad to see you back from the north. The execution of your withdrawal and of your mission in covering the withdrawal of the South Luzon force were as fine as anything in history." Mindful of MacArthur's penchant for sweeping statements about history, Wainwright did not dwell on the praise. More meaningful was MacArthur's promise to have Wainwright promoted and to give him the army's second-highest military decoration, the Distinguished Service Cross. MacArthur then asked Wainwright where he had positioned his 155-mm artillery guns. As it turned out, Wainwright had a pair of them in walking distance. He offered to escort MacArthur over to them. "Jonathan, I don't want to *see* them. I want to *hear* them," MacArthur said, as if unaware that the men manning the guns might want to see him. In fairness, he had lunch plans on the bottom of the peninsula. By around four in the afternoon, he had returned to Corregidor in higher spirits than when he had left. His staff in the Malinta Tunnel heard him say, "Our 155s were music to my ears."

For a time, stories of the visit also lifted spirits on Bataan. MacArthur had not seen as many men as he could have, but word of what he had said spread. Wainwright's senior aide, Johnny Pugh, had begged for the opportunity to accompany his boss to the speech, and it did not disappoint. According to the notes Pugh took and shared with others, MacArthur proclaimed that the "enemy's temporary superiority of the air would soon be a thing of the past, and if events proceeded as he expected, a counter attack was in the offing." Most amazingly, he announced he would soon reoccupy Manila. "He was so optimistic about the whole situation, and so enthusiastic that I suddenly found myself feeling a part of momentous events," Pugh wrote. The struggle on Bataan, MacArthur said, "had caught the imagination of the American people."

That last part, at least, was true. In January 1942, Americans looking at the globe could find few other spots of hope. In the hours and days after Pearl Harbor, Japanese forces had fanned out across the Pacific, all around the Philippines. To the east, the other islands that the United States had annexed after the Spanish-American War and that had served as stops for planes traveling between the Philippines and Hawaii fell one by one: first, Guam in the Marianas, and then, Wake Island even farther to the east. With the loss of those two islands and the destruction inflicted on America's Pacific fleet, the Japanese had severed America's line of communication across the world's largest ocean. The Philippines stood alone on the other side. To the west of the archipelago, the British had surrendered Hong Kong and watched as the Japanese advanced down the Malay peninsula toward Singapore. To the south of the Philippines, operations had begun that would make the Japanese masters of the resource-rich Dutch East Indies and draw even the future of Australia into question. The situation looked as grim in the Atlantic. Still committed to a Europe-first strategy, President Roosevelt requested Congress return the favor after Germany and Italy declared war on the United States in the wake of Pearl Harbor. But with German submarines emerging on its eastern shore, the United States seemed far from taking the fight to the fascists.

Only in the Philippines could Americans find what they so desperately craved: evidence they were fighting back. MacArthur gave it to them. He had control of the radio transmitters that served as the only reliable means of communication between the Philippines and the United States, and he was not afraid to use that power to his advantage. The public relations machine that his aides Major LeGrande Diller and Major Carlos Romulo, a former Filipino newspaper publisher, operated out of Lateral 3 of the Malinta Tunnel flooded the press with communiqués. None of these press releases went out without Mac-Arthur's edits. Sometimes he simply cut out the middleman and drafted the communiqués himself, "always with an eye on their effect on the MacArthur legend," as Sutherland would put it. If one believed these accounts, MacArthur's army had retreated in the face of the 80,000 or possibly even 100,000 Japanese soldiers who had landed at Lingayen, not the 43,000 who actually had. Despite being "greatly outnumbered," the Americans and Filipinos on Bataan and Corregidor were said to have forced the enemy to bring in "heavy" reinforcements, never mind the Japanese had actually felt free to release their best troops for operations elsewhere in the Pacific. So much exaggerated information had gone out that it seemed believable when MacArthur's press aides passed along the absurd story that the Japanese commander in the Philippines, Lieutenant General Masaharu Homma, had committed ritual suicide in MacArthur's old penthouse. MacArthur had the ability, as Johnny Pugh witnessed on Bataan, to make soldiers—and also reporters— feel as if they were part of something larger than themselves, but too often that something got lost in the aura around MacArthur himself. "Of 142 such communiqués issued between December 8, 1941, and March 11, 1942," one biographer found, "109 mentioned only one individual, MacArthur." Even when separated by a shark-filled channel from their commander and his press machine in the Malinta Tunnel, the soldiers on Bataan heard themselves labeled over and over again as "MacArthur's."

Newspapers in the United States picked up the theme. In January alone, MacArthur appeared in six banner headlines running across the top of the front page of *The New York Times*. They sounded almost monotonous. "M'ARTHUR FIGHTS ON," "M'ARTHUR UNITES HIS LINES FOR CRUCIAL STAND," "M'ARTHUR REPELS ATTACK," "M'ARTHUR REPELS FOE," "M'ARTHUR REPULSES FOE," "M'ARTHUR ROUTS FOE." *Time* magazine put his picture in gold tint on the cover above the heady caption, "MACARTHUR OF THE PHILIPPINES," and the even headier quotation, "By God, it was Destiny that brought me here." Even little anecdotes, such as the one about him admonishing an aide afraid to fly the American flag, had a way of sneaking above the fold of front pages. Some leaders claim not to read their own press. MacArthur demanded a daily summary of his.

Historians have questioned what MacArthur achieved with his public relations campaign, but leaders in Washington saw immediately. He had emerged from the first month of the war as America's highest-ranking hero, a voice that policymakers could not ignore. Instead of having to answer to them for the loss of his air force or his whiplash-like shift back to War Plan Orange, they would have to answer to him for failing to meet his demands for reinforcements. This was the real struggle he waged inside the Malinta Tunnel. The maps around his desk may have shown Bataan, but he aimed the cables he wrote at Washington. "All you have to do is fight the enemy," staff members heard him say. "I have to fight the War Department [and] the navy."

MacArthur had not accepted the navy's unwillingness to send ships to the rescue, never mind that even the most optimistic versions of War Plan Orange had said that it would take six months—and that was without the destruction wrought at Pearl Harbor and without the priority the United States had given to the war in Europe. The latter was another principle MacArthur had never accepted. "The Philippine theater," he believed, remained the "locus of victory or defeat." Even as Roosevelt welcomed Prime Minister Winston Churchill of Britain to Washington for talks renewing their commitment to a Germany-first strategy, MacArthur fired off messages insisting the European theater could wait till after the winter and calling for an "immediate combined effort of all resources of the United States and her allies by land, sea, and air" in the Philippines. It had been no small miracle that the wreckage at Pearl Harbor had included none of the four aircraft carriers in America's Pacific fleet, and it would now take an even bigger miracle for the navy to agree to bring any of those vessels anywhere near the Philippines. But a miracle was what MacArthur expected the War Department in Washington to deliver. "Time is ripe for brilliant thrust with aircraft carriers," MacArthur wrote. The Philippines presented the United States with what he described as a stark choice. "Move strongly to their support . . . or withdraw in shame from the Orient."

On the other end of these messages, which MacArthur sent in code via radio, was Chief of Staff George C. Marshall. Both born in 1880, Marshall and MacArthur had a long history. When MacArthur had held the title of chief of staff, there had been those who believed he had tried to sabotage Marshall's career by assigning him to a post with the Illinois National Guard. Nonetheless, Marshall would call rumors of any hostility between the men "damn nonsense," even if MacArthur could be "very, very difficult." For help dealing with his demands, Marshall summoned an expert: MacArthur's former chief of staff, Dwight D. Eisenhower, now a general himself. Asked how the army could best support MacArthur, Eisenhower responded, "It will be a long time before major reinforcements can go to the Philippines, longer than the garrison can hold out with any driblet of assistance, if the enemy commits major forces to their reduction. The people of China, of the Philippines, of the Dutch East Indies will be watching us. They may excuse failure but they will not excuse abandonment. We must do what we can." Marshall liked what he heard and put Eisenhower to work on it immediately. Much-needed supplies would begin accumulating in Australia, but how to get them the rest of the way to the Philippines remained a vexing question. With the navy rejecting MacArthur's demands for carriers, Eisenhower would have to rely on blockade runners. Very few would make it through.

Nevertheless, Marshall assured MacArthur that "every day" he could hold out brought the army closer to an answer. In the meantime, MacArthur could take pride that his defense of the Philippines had become, as Marshall put it, "an epic of this war." Still astonished at how fast the fight-them-on-the-beaches strategy had collapsed, Eisenhower found the praise sickening but saw its purpose. "MacArthur is as big a baby as ever," Eisenhower wrote in his diary. "But we've got to keep him fighting."

MacArthur should have understood the game in Washington because he was playing a similar one with his troops on Bataan, most of whom, he reminded Marshall (lest he forget), were Filipinos. While they risked their lives, homes, and families, it seemed the United States would not risk even a single ship for them. "Unquestionably ships can get through," MacArthur wrote to Marshall on January 17. "I am having increasing difficulty in appeasing Philippine thought along this line. They cannot understand the apparent lack of effort to bring something in. I cannot over emphasize the psychological reaction that will take place here . . . unless something tangible is done." All that mere words could do, MacArthur had already tried. In a message to the troops on Bataan two days earlier, he had doubled down on what he had told their general officers during his visit. "Help is on the way from the United States, thousands of troops and hundreds of planes are being dispatched. The exact time of arrival of reinforcements is unknown as they will have to fight their way through Japanese attempts against them. It is imperative that our troops hold until these reinforcements arrive," he wrote. "If we fight we will win; if we retreat we will be destroyed." He would later claim, after history had made a mockery of these words, that he himself had believed them. But his actions raise doubts. Barely a week after promising that help was on the way, he ordered subordinates not to increase Bataan's food supply but rather to ship some of it to Corregidor in preparation for the eventual loss of the peninsula.

* * *

By the start of February, Corregidor resembled a construction site stuck in the demolition phase. Those emerging from the Malinta Tunnel in search of fresh air could find it nowhere. The once pleasant sea breeze now served only to circulate dust from the ruins of the buildings in the dry season. The Philippine sun grew stronger every day. It beat down on the craters pocking the ground and through the holes torn in the forest canopy. Although the bombers no longer flew over the island as frequently, the Japanese would soon begin lobbing shells from the guns they had hidden more than ten miles away in the hills on the south side of Manila Bay.

For weeks, calls for MacArthur to surrender had come from the Japanese. On February 1, they found a voice he could not ignore. More than forty years had passed since Emilio Aguinaldo had surrendered to Arthur MacArthur. Now the old insurgent broadcast a message calling on Arthur's son, as a friend of the Philippines, to surrender to the Japanese. They had promised the islands independence just as America had. Filipinos, Aguinaldo said, had no stake in the war.

Much as the Japanese propaganda upset MacArthur, he actually worried more about the effect of tone-deaf American propaganda on his friend Quezon. Everyone could see the Philippine president did not have long to live. His temperature would sometimes run as high as 105 degrees in the tunnel. He could do little more than park his wheelchair and rage while listening to radio broadcasts featuring members of the Roosevelt administration bragging about the volume of supplies headed to Britain without saying a word about the Philippines. Family members would try to calm Quezon. When they could not, MacArthur would send over a member of his staff. One day, it happened that no one could placate the president. "Listen to what the shameless ones are saying in Washington," he yelled. "I cannot stand this constant reference to England, to Europe. . . . How typically American to writhe in anguish at the fate of a distant cousin while a daughter is being raped in the back room." In his anger, he asked MacArthur to forward a letter to Roosevelt. "My people entered the war with the confidence that the United States would bring such assistance to us as would make it possible to sustain the conflict with some chance of success. All our soldiers in the field were animated by the belief that help would be forthcoming. This help has not and evidently will not be realized." Given that the United States could not defend the Philippines, Quezon asked permission to seek a separate peace by which both American and Japanese forces would vacate the islands and agree to the archipelago's immediate independence and status as a neutral power in the war.

When the full letter reached Washington on February 9, Eisenhower remembered it landing like a "bombshell." In a meeting at the White House, Roosevelt said, "We can't do this at all." Aside from the absurdity of expecting Japan to honor the borders of the Philippines as Japanese soldiers violated borders everywhere else in the Pacific, the proposal asked the impossible of Roosevelt: to cede American territory and to agree to a deal reminiscent of the attempts to appease the Nazis on the eve of war in Europe. MacArthur would later say that he had tried to talk Quezon out of sending the proposal. But a letter MacArthur sent under his own name with it convinced some in the War Department that he was sympathetic to the idea. Secretary of War Henry Stimson called MacArthur's letter "worse" than Quezon's because—however myopic the view from the Malinta Tunnel—MacArthur should have known better.

Surely, MacArthur did know better. If he seemed eager to share the neutrality proposal, it was almost certainly because he realized the outrage it would cause in Washington. Having failed through all conventional means to change America's overall strategy, he had decided to wield against Washington the last and most desperate weapon at his disposal: the threat of complete humiliation. "The temper of the Filipinos is one of almost violent resentment against the United States," he wrote. "In spite of my great prestige with them, I have had the utmost difficulty during the last ten days in keeping them in line. If help does not arrive shortly, nothing, in my opinion, can prevent their utter collapse and their complete absorption by the enemy."

The reply that Marshall, Eisenhower, and Stimson drafted for Roosevelt gave MacArthur, if necessary, permission to surrender the Filipino troops under his command but not the American ones—never mind that the latter stood no chance without the former. "It is mandatory that there be established once and for all in the minds of all peoples complete evidence that the American determination and indomitable will to win carries on down to the last unit," Roosevelt wrote to MacArthur. "I therefore give you this most difficult mission in full understanding of the desperate situation to which you may shortly be reduced." In private, Stimson summed up the message this way: "There are times when men have to die."

MacArthur began to believe his own time near. Once Bataan fell, he knew Corregidor could not stand much longer. "This type of fortress, built prior to the days of air power, when isolated is impossible of prolonged defense," he said. "There is no denying the fact that we are near done." Although he did not usually like to carry a gun, he began to make an exception in his jacket pocket for a small pistol. The gun had belonged to his father and had a double barrel. After much searching, Sid Huff found two bullets that would fit. "Thanks," MacArthur said, as he loaded them. "They will never take *me* alive." Another man might have forced his wife and young son to evacuate, but MacArthur would not. He asked Jean if she wanted to sneak away with Arthur in one of the submarines that occasionally delivered small shipments of supplies to the Rock. "I'm just not going," she said. "Arthur and I stay with you." MacArthur accepted her decision. "My son is a soldier's son," he would say, and "will share the fate of the garrison."

One who would not share the garrison's fate was Quezon. In the wake of his neutrality proposal and concerns that he might open negotiations with the Japanese in Manila, leaders in Washington wanted him off Corregidor, far away from the fighting. MacArthur had resisted the idea before but now accepted it and arranged a submarine to carry Quezon, his family, and members of his government away on February 20. MacArthur and Sutherland drove down to the dock with the Philippine president and his wife. "Manuel," MacArthur said as he helped Quezon out of the car and embraced him. "You will see it through. You are the Father of your Country, and God will preserve you." Quezon could scarcely speak. He pulled off the ring he used as his seal, slid it on MacArthur's finger, and said, "When they find your body, I want them to know you fought for my country." There were times when men had to die.

But Douglas MacArthur was no longer just a man. The headlines had turned him into something more: a symbol of hope that the United States could not let die. A debate had begun within the War Department over whether to order the entire MacArthur family out of the Philippines. Eisenhower worried that the discussions reflected not "military logic" but rather "public opinion." There was no denying that. Politicians had rushed to tie their names to MacArthur's. The Republican Wendell Willkie, who had lost the 1940 election to Roosevelt, called on the president to "bring Douglas MacArthur home" and "put him in supreme command of our armed forces." Even Democrats joined in. The majority leader of the House called MacArthur "one of the outstanding Americans of all time." According to *The Washington Post*, voters agreed, too. A front-page article said that by "fighting his last-ditch fight in the bamboo jungles of Bataan," MacArthur had inspired "millions of humble Americans." By their will, his name would soon grace parks, schools, dams, and roads, including a prominent boulevard running into Maryland along the Washington side of the Potomac River. Eisenhower could call MacArthur a baby all he liked, but other parents preferred to call their own newborns after Douglas MacArthur. There would even be a proposal to add his face to Mount Rushmore.

MacArthur's face seemed to be everywhere—everywhere except Bataan, the place where people needed to see him most. For all his talk about the need for soldiers to see their commander taking risks, the soldiers on Bataan had not seen him since January 10. He had not repeated the short trip across the channel. In the eyes of the men on the other side, he had not returned. Perhaps he could not stand to see them rotting away, the same way his aides remembered he never could stand a movie with a hospital scene. Perhaps he could not stand to tell them the terrible truth—that help was not on the way. Perhaps he had heard that some of the soldiers, especially the American ones, had begun calling him a new nickname, "Dugout Doug," and mocking him to the tune of "The Battle Hymn of the Republic." Their song went like this:

> *Dugout Doug MacArthur lies a shaking on the Rock*
> *Safe from all the bombers and from any sudden shock*
> *Dugout Doug is eating of the best food on Bataan*
> *And his troops go starving on.*

> *Dugout Doug's not timid, he's just cautious, not afraid*
> *He's protecting carefully the stars that Franklin made*
> *Four-star generals are rare as good food on Bataan*
> *And his troops go starving on.*

> *Dugout Doug is ready in his Kris Craft for the flee*
> *Over bounding billows and the wildly raging sea*

For the Japs are pounding on the gates of Old Bataan
And his troops go starving on.

We've fought the war the hard way since they said the fight was on
All the way from Lingayen to the hills of Old Bataan
And we'll continue fighting after Dugout Doug is gone
And still go starving on.

After each verse came the chorus:

Dugout Doug, come out from hiding
Dugout Doug, come out from hiding
Send to Franklin the glad tidings
That his troops go starving on!

The soldiers singing this song had not seen MacArthur crossing no-man's-land during World War I. They had not seen him strolling out of the Malinta Tunnel during air raids on Corregidor. What they had seen were the reports crediting their courage to his leadership. But they did not fight for him. Readers back home might hear the term "fighting general" and picture MacArthur. But the boys on Bataan would say they had seen a real fighting general—the two-starred one on their side of the channel—and his name was Wainwright.

CHAPTER FIVE

Battling Bastards

There was another reason Douglas MacArthur's communiqués dominated newspaper coverage. Not until a few weeks into January did his censors allow correspondents on Bataan to file their own dispatches. And even then, correspondents found themselves at the whim, as they put it, "[of] the powers that be" on Corregidor. Some of the rules seemed reasonable. Nothing more than five hundred words. Nothing about specific military operations. Other restrictions seemed capricious. A magazine writer discovered that some official had determined that General Wainwright's beloved 26th Cavalry had already received too much attention for its heroics during the retreat from Lingayen and that articles about the fighting on Bataan needed to avoid mention of not only the regiment but also horses in general.

By this time, serious reporting about the men of the 26th or their mounts would have astonished readers accustomed to MacArthur's upbeat headlines. Only about half the cavalrymen who had started the war—and far fewer of their horses—had reached Bataan in fighting shape. The men's skin peeked out from the holes in their uniforms; the horses' ribs stuck out from their emaciated sides. The men nodded off in the saddle as the heads of their horses sagged. On the trails that the men hacked while riding along the edge of ravines and down the steep sides, the horses struggled to raise their hooves over the vines lining the ground.

This was the fighting force that Wainwright sought out on January 16 after learning that a Philippine Army division had withdrawn in spite of orders to the contrary from the village of Moron—a key point at the end of his line toward the top of Bataan, right below where the final river standing in the way of the Japanese met the South China Sea. The cavalry would have to move into Moron and keep the Japanese on the opposite bank until Wainwright could move the infantry back into position.

Lieutenant Edwin Ramsey of the 26th had just returned from a reconnaissance mission when he saw Wainwright driving up in his Packard and looking skinnier and more impatient than usual. Wainwright saw Ramsey, too, and remembered having watched him play in the polo match the day before the war began. "Ramsey," Wainwright said, "you take the advance guard." When another officer objected that Ramsey needed rest, Wainwright growled, "Never mind! Ramsey, move out!" Always be ready to "piss in the fire" and "get going"—that was what Wainwright had preached at the Cavalry School in Kansas. That was how he had seen his father send off his riders onto the plains of the Old West. And that was how the Philippine Scouts and their American officers carrying on this tradition in the jungles of the Far East would ride off for what would become the last charge in the history of the United States Cavalry.

Ramsey led his platoon up to Moron in two columns along what passed for a road. "It was scarcely more than a jungle track, deeply rutted and thick with dry-season dust, a gray powder that irritated the eyes, clogged the nostrils, and coated the throat," Ramsey remembered. "The underbrush tangled up closely on either side, so dense that one could not see three feet within it. It was a dark, dangerous place, virtually an invitation to an ambush." In the village, he and his men found abandoned-looking nipa huts built on stilts of bamboo around a square containing a stone cathedral. Running above the town was the river Wainwright needed the cavalrymen to hold until he could bring up the infantry. As the riders neared the village square, there was a silence, then the sound of fire from the direction of the water. The first Japanese troops had already crossed. If not turned back immediately, they would win control of the town. Seeing Japanese reinforcements splashing across the muddy water, Ramsey had only seconds to act but more than a century of tradition to follow. "Charge," he ordered. "Bent nearly prone across the horses' necks, we flung ourselves at the Japanese advance, pistols firing full into their startled faces," Ramsey recalled. "We must have seemed a vision from another century, wild-eyed horses pounding headlong; cheering, whooping men firing from the saddles." The Japanese soldiers still in the river turned around and ran back to the other side. At the edge of the brown water, the cavalrymen stopped, dismounted, and formed a line before going back to clear the village of the Japanese who had made it across the water.

When the infantry finally arrived at the front, Wainwright surveyed the field and ordered the 26th Cavalry to the rear. He did so despite the sadness he saw in the men who had dismounted by the river. Sniper fire from the opposite bank made it impossible for them to reclaim their horses. Perhaps it was as he watched the cavalrymen pull out on foot that he made a decision: They would never again mount their horses in battle. Before the war, he had insisted that horses remained the "fastest and most reliable means of movement yet produced, considering all types of terrain, all conditions of weather, and all of the many difficulties that may arise because of failure of supply." But those same three factors—terrain, weather, and supply—had forced a reevaluation. "The jungle terrain of Bataan in a defensive situation was no place for horse cavalry," wrote a fellow officer privy to Wainwright's thinking. A few days later in a thick patch of jungle that served to conceal his battered trailer from Japanese airplanes but not from the angry monkeys throwing fruit down from the trees, Wainwright ordered the horses of the 26th Cavalry sent far from the front, to the peninsula's bottom, where the quartermaster would put them out to pasture. If the men on

Bataan could not procure more food—if the promise of help being on the way did not come to fruition—Wainwright knew that the horses would have one last heartrending service to perform.

*   *   *

If Wainwright had overestimated the ability of horses to maneuver, he had underestimated the ability of the Japanese to do so. The Americans had chosen Bataan for their final stand partly because the peninsula seemed to offer so little room for offensive maneuver. Stretching only twenty-five miles southward to its tip, Bataan places only twenty miles between the South China Sea to the west and Manila Bay to the east. Into this stubby piece of land crowded eighty thousand Philippine and American soldiers, as well as more than twenty thousand refugees. They had all come to Bataan via Route 110, which ran down the east side of the peninsula to the port of Mariveles at the bottom before snaking back up the other side as high as Moron, which Wainwright had ordered the 26th Cavalry to hold as the far western point of the line that he and General Parker formed across Bataan's width. Between Wainwright's half of the line on the western side and Parker's half on the eastern side lay a five-mile gap supposedly filled by the impassable peaks around a dormant volcano named Mount Natib. Wainwright believed Natib uncrossable. When MacArthur had made his one visit, however, his chief of staff, Sutherland, had looked at the mountain and disagreed with Wainwright. So, evidently, had the Japanese, who sent their soldiers over the slopes and, as a result, forced the Americans and Filipinos to begin withdrawing on January 23 to a second line of resistance farther south.

By January 26, Wainwright and Parker had their men in the reserve position on what then became known as the main line of resistance. The line ran right below the peninsula's only east-west road, which the troops could no longer use, and through the valley formed by Mount Natib to the north and the peninsula's larger dormant volcano, Mount Mariveles, to the south. As before, Wainwright commanded

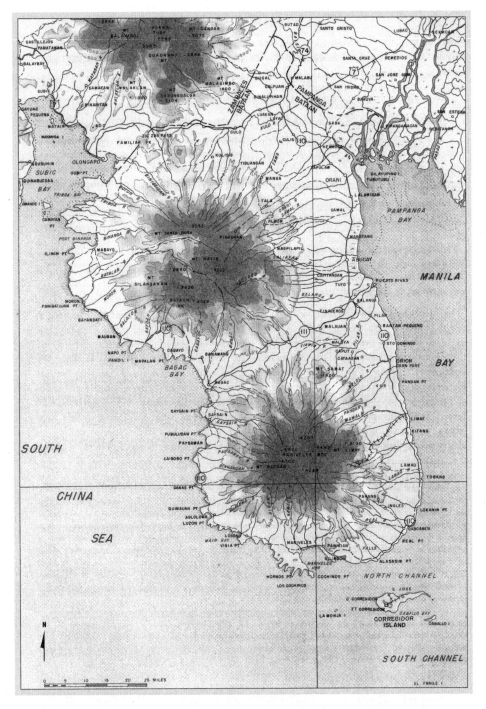

A map made for MacArthur's reports showing the terrain of Bataan. Moron, the site of the cavalry's last charge, lies on the coast of the South China Sea, west of Mount Natib. After the Japanese surprised Wainwright by making it over Natib, American and Filipino forces had no choice but to drop back to a second defensive line running between Orion on Manila Bay and Bagac on the South China Sea.

the western side, Parker the eastern. Though there was no longer a gap between them, the geography changed dramatically from east to west. Where Parker's side began with rice paddies and sugar fields growing in the low-lying land off Manila Bay, the jungle on Wainwright's side stretched to the end of the cliffs jutting out over the cove-lined seacoast. So dense and opaque was this unmappable jungle that even veteran soldiers confused the names of geographic features and struggled to maintain contact with neighboring units. Incredibly, a thousand Japanese soldiers pursuing Wainwright during his retreat infiltrated his lines before his troops had dug all their trenches, and then managed to disappear into the jungle. By the time Wainwright's men figured out what had happened, the Japanese had divided into two so-called pockets: a "little pocket" four hundred yards behind the trenches and a "big pocket" about a mile behind.

Wainwright had warned that he did not have enough troops to stop such incursions while also guarding his long flank along the sea. Already the Japanese had begun staging landings well behind the main line—at places such as Quinauan Point, far down the coast where Wainwright had little more to offer for opposition than airmen who had lost their planes but had not yet learned to use a rifle. If these Japanese landing forces managed to move even just a little inland—if they received additional reinforcements from the sea—Wainwright foresaw they would capture the only supply road left to his army: the stretch of Route 110 that the men called the West Road. Wainwright proposed moving the main line farther south so he could shorten his flank. But MacArthur would not hear of it. He had told the War Department that he had "personally selected and prepared" the line Wainwright now inhabited for a "final stand." There was to be no more arguing. In the secrecy of his diary, Wainwright confided his fear: "It will not be long before we are surrounded."

It was at this time that Wainwright requested that navy officers on Corregidor send him an aide who could coordinate land-based defenses with what few vessels the United States had left in the waters around Bataan. The navy dispatched Lieutenant Malcolm Champlin, a thirty-year-old Naval Academy graduate known as "Champ." At the start of February, he set off across the channel to Mariveles, where a smashed-up-looking sedan waited to take him up the West Road, around the slope of the mountain, along the cliffs, and over bridges spanning the many streams flowing into the South China Sea. Just three hundred yards before Champlin reached one such crossing, three Japanese planes dropped bombs near the bridge but, fortunately for him, failed to destroy it.

On went Champlin up the coast. Under the pressure of ceaseless tires and tank treads, the surface of the single-lane road had disappeared under inches of dust that kicked up whenever traffic passed. Only occasionally did the blue water of the South China Sea glimmer through the thorny underbrush, bamboo thickets, and vines filling the gaps between the massive trees lining either side of the road and covering it in a canopy of branches. Only a little sunlight could come through, and no sea breeze at all. The walls of this wooded enclosure trapped the hot humid air inside them together with the stench of rotting flesh from both man and beast.

Only after an hour and a half of driving did Champlin reach a hill off a trail where guards halted traffic. The rest of the way, he would have to walk. It was not far. On a ridge about three hundred yards away stood a grove of especially tall trees that Wainwright had chosen to house his new command post after pulling back to the second line. The monkeys from the trees around the old post had not followed, but the Japanese planes flying above had. Thankfully, through the thick foliage, their pilots could see neither Wainwright's old trailer, now covered in vines, nor the group of tents erected near it. In the middle were tables that staff members had built out of bamboo poles. By one stood Wainwright quizzing aides while pointing out locations on a map pinned to a tree. When someone introduced Champlin, Wainwright feigned an unhappy look. "What do I have to do, go through God Almighty before I can talk to the navy?" Then, with a smile that put Champlin at ease, Wainwright said, "I'm glad to have you here, son. Come over for a chat in the trailer as soon as you are settled." An admiral on Corregidor had advised Champlin to bring a present that he walked over to the trailer later that day. "To cement some army-navy relations," said Champlin, unwrapping a towel around a bottle of alcohol and handing it to Wainwright.

"Young man," Wainwright said, visibly excited as he analyzed the bottle, "do you realize . . . I haven't had a drink for three months?" Longer-serving aides could have pointed out other occasions when Wainwright had found a drink but would not have quibbled with the spirit of his remark. They had seen their commander hesitate before accepting gifts as unremarkable as a little ham. Only the pleading expression on the face of his aide Tom Dooley had prodded Wainwright into finally saying yes. "Imagine hesitation at the sound of ham," Dooley wrote afterward even though he knew exactly why: the guilt of leading men who made do with so little.

Under normal fighting conditions, Wainwright would have ensured his soldiers had at least four thousand calories a day. In Bataan, he struggled to provide them with two thousand. Theoretically, MacArthur had put the troops on Corregidor on the same half rations. In reality, the troops on Bataan always received less even though they needed more for the obvious reason that fighting in foxholes expends more energy than being holed up in a tunnel. Even within Bataan, soldiers found disparities. Those on the front lines received less food than those closer to the slaughterhouses and storage facilities in the rear because of the lack of roads, gasoline, and refrigeration, as well as the willingness of hungry soldiers to steal from trucks. If meat made it to the front line at all, it often arrived with a side of maggots. By the start of February, the quartermaster could no longer deliver anywhere near the six ounces of meat and six ounces of flour the average American soldier expected as part of his half rations or the six ounces of fish and ten ounces of rice the average Filipino soldier expected as part of his. In vain would either search for coffee or tea. Not even five days' worth of canned fruits and vegetables remained.

Like others on Bataan, Wainwright and his aides ate only twice a day. If their food tasted better, it owed to a Filipino cook named Francisco, who seemed able to produce pastries, as Dooley put it, "from nothing." The aides discovered Francisco made a good carabao steak as long as he started with meat from a younger animal. Unfortunately, they also discovered that most of the carabao on Bataan were, as Wainwright joked, "veterans" with meat so tough that Francisco would have to soak it and pound it for hours before cooking. "Even then," Wainwright said, "it was a test for the strongest teeth." And yet that never deterred flies from swarming the table. Nonetheless, Dooley called meals a "nice time" when the general would usually have a party of ten. Sometimes he would recite old army poems for his messmates. With censorship rules loosened, wire service reporters began taking a seat around the bamboo table. Frank Hewlett of the United Press became a regular. He found Wainwright reticent but with a "dry humor" and "a story for every occasion." Clark Lee of the Associated Press came for dinner one evening with questions for Wainwright about his retreat from Lingayen but found him willing to discuss only one topic: going on the offensive. "If the United States will send me two divisions of American troops, or provide me with two trained Filipino divisions, and just enough airplanes to keep the Jap planes off our heads, I will guarantee to drive the Japs off Luzon in short order," Wainwright said.

After dinner, conversation would carry on in the darkness as the air turned surprisingly cool. There was never any escape from the jungle. "You can't retire from this battlefield to some dive or nightclub," explained Lieutenant Thomas Gerrity, who joined Wainwright's staff for a time as a liaison to the air corps. The aides looked for distraction where they could. They played game after game of rummy, wrote playful verses, traded a copy of the journalist William Shirer's *Berlin Diary* about the rise of Nazi Germany, marveled that their own country could be so unready for war, and talked about when it would deliver the aid MacArthur had promised. In search of clues, they would tune in to the "Voice of Freedom," the nightly program that MacArthur's

Filipino press aide, Carlos Romulo, broadcast from Corregidor. If lucky, Wainwright's staff members would find a signal from a station in San Francisco. More often they received the propaganda that the Japanese broadcast.

On the rare days when an American submarine would make it through the blockade, Wainwright would dash off a letter for the vessel to carry out to Adele. Most nights he would settle for making a short entry in his diary. Most of his staff members followed his example and kept one. Johnny Pugh dedicated his to his wife. "I live not with the expectancy for the new day, but for the comparatively quiet night which follows the day," Pugh wrote. "It is then that I am able to think of the happy days which we have had together; it is then—when I am permitted to sleep—that my dreams bring us together. Sleep has become my only pleasure." Quiet was not easy to find. The artillery guns that MacArthur called music to his ears would fire over the tents and blankets covering Wainwright's aides as they tried to sleep. The sound of the howitzers, Dooley wrote, "practically dumps you out of bed when they fire a salvo."

In the morning, the aides would sometimes take baths in the mountain streams and joke about how they had gone "native." The knowledge of how high the mercury would rise—almost always over ninety degrees—made the shock of the cold water endurable. "Hard to get started, but a wonderful feeling when you get in. Better still when you get out," Dooley recorded. Other days, the aides would have what they called a "bucket bath." Whatever the source of the water, soap was in short supply. A razor passed as a present worthy of a general. At some point, Wainwright arranged to have his head shaved. The dust made hair unmanageable.

If Wainwright had his way, every day would have started with a plan to see the troops. "Let's go visiting," he would tell his aides. If he had to stay at the command post, he would turn, they found, "nervous and impatient." He needed to be on the front lines. They were not hard to find. Traveling a short distance in almost any direction would take him there. There was the main line of resistance a few miles north, the pockets just behind it, and the landing sites lower down the peninsula. In truth, the ability of Japanese snipers to move undetected in the jungle and take up positions in trees made nowhere safe. Because American officers made prized targets, even generals had to come armed and ready. Hewlett described Wainwright "carrying his .30 caliber sporting rifle, with its elaborately carved stock, and wearing a big .45 pistol in cowboy style, hanging low from his belt." While Wainwright's Filipino driver, Sergeant Centimo, readied the car, Wainwright's orderly, Sergeant Hubert Carroll, notified the aides about which of them would come along. Carroll himself almost always did.

One morning shortly after arriving, Champlin received his first invitation to ride in the Packard. He found it parked outside camp and riddled with bullet holes. If he wondered why, he soon learned. He piled into the car with Wainwright, Pugh, and Dooley while Carroll and another sergeant stood on boards alongside the doors, with their heads turned upward in search of Japanese planes. As they drove, Champlin learned that Wainwright liked to pass the time by discussing cavalry tactics with his aides and quizzing them as if to ensure they would keep the tradition alive. Just a mile past the command post, a major stopped them and warned that a bend in the road ahead would expose their car to artillery fire. Proceeding nevertheless, they forgot about the warning until taking the bend a second time on the way back to the command post later that day. This time, they heard shells whistling overhead and saw them exploding just in front of the car. As Centimo pulled off the road into the underbrush, Champlin followed the other aides into the woods, where they dove into the first foxholes they found. Only then did Champlin notice Wainwright standing in the open, talking with a stranger, and leading him over to some sandbags where they sat together twenty yards from where the shells were landing. After the artillery had quieted, Champlin learned that Wainwright had remembered the stranger from the old days at the Cavalry School. That explanation did not seem sufficient to excuse the risk Wainwright had taken. "General Wainwright," Champlin said, "why is it that you, a major general and commander of half the troops on Bataan peninsula, risk your life the way you just did a few minutes ago? It seemed to me that you were doing a very foolish thing."

Wainwright grinned as if he had heard the question before. "Champ," he said, "think it over for a minute. What have we to offer these troops? Can we give them more food? No. We haven't any more food. Can we give them ammunition? No. That also is running low. Can we give them supplies or equipment or tanks or medicine? No. Everything is running low. But we can give them morale and that is one of my primary duties. That is why I go to the front every day. Now do you understand why it is important for me to sit on sandbags in the line of fire while the rest of you seek shelter?" Champlin never doubted Wainwright again.

As for Wainwright, he did not even note the story in his diary. Nor did any of the other aides with him. They had all seen him have closer calls with death. Dooley had seen Wainwright when a Japanese plane had plunged down upon him with its machine guns firing, and when a bullet from a Japanese sniper rifle had barely missed his head only because he had ducked a moment before when Carroll had screamed, "God damn it, General, get down." Pugh had seen Wainwright on the front lines in a close-range rifle shootout against five Japanese soldiers hiding in a haystack. Gerrity, the air corps liaison, had seen Wainwright get out of his car and personally supervise engineers clearing a blocked stretch of road for tanks headed to the front when one had struck a mine. "Dead generals don't make good generals," Gerrity felt obliged to tell Wainwright afterward.

By early February, the outlines of the two enemy pockets behind Wainwright's main line had come into focus. So had the challenge they posed. The Japanese had dug in and could move unseen through tunnels running between their foxholes and trenches. Artillery could not root them out. Nor could tanks operating alone. The jungle-lined paths would require infantrymen operating in concert, slashing through the vines and bamboo, and willing to fight foxhole by foxhole if necessary.

"We had to go up and practically breathe in the faces of the dug-in Japs," Wainwright wrote. "It was fighting that would be considered fantastically improbable if seen on a movie screen." On the morning of February 5, Wainwright summoned his generals. He told them that he would commit every reserve he had against the pockets and asked for ideas for how best to do so. General Albert Jones, who had crossed paths with Wainwright during the confusion at Calumpit, proposed, first, cordoning off the two pockets individually so they could not reinforce each other and, then, destroying them one by one. "All right, Honus," Wainwright said, using a nickname for Jones, "you take charge."

That morning would mark a turning point in the fight on Bataan not only because of the new strategy against the pockets but also because of events transpiring down the coast of the peninsula where the six hundred Japanese soldiers who had landed at Quinauan Point in January faced increasingly desperate odds against the Philippine Scouts whom Wainwright had dispatched to take over the battle. The attempts that he had feared the Japanese would make to reinforce Quinauan by sea had succeeded only in scattering their troops elsewhere on the coast and left the position isolated and untenable. Nonetheless, the Japanese had fought on, even as their foxholes filled with bodies and the air filled with the stench of death and swarms of flies. Rather than surrender when backed to the edge of a cliff overlooking the beach on February 4, some of the Japanese jumped. The calmer among them had scaled down the steep side and taken refuge in a cave cut into the rocks. "When this was reported to me, it was hard to believe," Wainwright said. "I ordered another proffer of honorable surrender." As he met with his generals about the fighting in the pockets, his troops at Quinauan Point would present his offer at the entrance to the cave.

During World War I, Wainwright's fellow officers had teased him for the sympathy he had shown for vanquished foes. Perhaps this compassion had taken root as a result of a childhood spent in fields fertilized with the blood of Custer's cavalrymen. The ideals of the 1929 Geneva Convention, which the United States had ratified for the humane treatment of prisoners of war, came naturally to Wainwright, and this made what happened at the entrance to the cave on February 5 even more stunning to him. Instead of receiving a surrender, as he was certain would happen, his soldiers received a barrage of bullets. "The old rules of war began to undergo a swift change," he wrote afterward. "What had at first seemed a barbarous thought in the back of my mind now became less unsavory." Remembering how Union soldiers had exploded a mine under the Confederate trenches around Petersburg, Virginia, he went to work on a plan for the cave at Quinauan Point. He had engineers drop dynamite from the cliff above the cave while boats fired into it. "There were no survivors," he wrote. "It had at last dawned on me, as it was to dawn on so many commanders who followed me in the Pacific war, that the Jap usually prefers death to surrender." More worrisome for Wainwright's own future was word that some of his own troops had come to prefer death to becoming prisoners of the Japanese. In time, he would learn why. For now, however, he tried to set an example of magnanimity. Seeing that his men had tied up a Japanese prisoner with telephone wire, Wainwright ordered the man unbound and then gave him perhaps the most sought-after item on all of Bataan: a cigarette.

By February 17, Wainwright could declare his forces victorious in the Battle of the Pockets as well as the Battle of the Points and in full control of the western sector as far north as the main line of resistance. For days afterward, he saw no Japanese soldiers within three kilometers of his lines. Except for the daily artillery duels and bombings, he described Bataan as "quiet" in his diary. By some accounts, the American and Filipino troops could have retaken the ground they had surrendered when they had fallen back from their first line. The Japanese had suffered enormous casualties. Yet Wainwright never doubted that they would reinforce and return. He needed to have his troops ready. The success they had found in the field had lifted their morale. But there was no denying that their bodies had begun to break down.

With almost no wheat left, the Americans on Bataan could only dream of their old bread rations as they joined the Filipinos living mainly on rice. With the last of the canned meat almost gone and with carabao having become an endangered species, everyone knew that the cavalry horses would have to go to the slaughterhouses next. There would be no choice. The so-called half rations the army provided soldiers on Bataan had shrunk from two thousand calories a day to fifteen hundred. Consumed by hunger, men scoured the jungle for ways to supplement their diet. Some tried monkey and iguana, which was said to taste like chicken. Others took their chances with various plants and wild berries, many of which proved poisonous.

At his command post at night, Wainwright could hear soldiers sharing what they called "food stories" about what they would eat if back home. Short of vitamin A, they struggled to see in the dark because of a condition called night blindness even as they conjured memories of meals past. Their mouths would water as their gums bled and their teeth became loose because of the lack of vitamin C. Men who had lost twenty pounds would suddenly find their limbs swelling with fluid in bizarre ways. Known as wet beriberi and caused by a lack of vitamin B_1, the disease was rarely seen in the United States but would become a familiar sight to Wainwright.

"Rotten" was the word he used to describe sanitation everywhere he looked. His chief engineer warned that one could find the front lines by the smell. Too weak or too frightened to make the trip to the latrines at night, men would simply relieve themselves where they lay in their foxholes or trenches. Dysentery spread. Even a soldier like Wainwright, schooled in proper hygiene, suffered from diarrhea. The lack of toilet paper made the affliction more miserable.

No longer were the Japanese the chief enemy on Bataan. Wainwright's soldiers at Quinauan Point had taken to calling it "Quinine Point," a cruel pun on the name of the medicine they so desperately needed to control malaria because they could not control the mosquitos spreading the disease. By the end of February, the supply of quinine had fallen so low that the number of men being hospitalized with the chills, sweats, and high fevers characteristic of malaria rose to almost five hundred a day.

The two hospitals set up toward the bottom of the peninsula struggled to maintain any semblance of order. Despite the best efforts of doctors and nurses, the hospitals never had much order from the start. The buildings at one originally had nipa roofs. The wards at the other hospital never had any roofs at all, only the branches hanging over the clearing that bulldozers and Filipinos hacking with long knives had made in the jungle. In beds made with bamboo frames, the patients lay exposed not only to the usual pathogens that all hospitals battle but also to rats and snakes. As admissions to the hospitals rose, nurses began stacking patients in bunks three high. Some men found space only on top of the same dirt that would go over the dead at the cemeteries established nearby.

Wainwright did what he could for morale. Supposedly, in a meeting one day, he held up a medical report for his corps and declared it "the finest damn record I've ever seen." Asked why, he explained that only one soldier that month had contracted a venereal disease. "I wonder how that joker found himself a woman out here in the jungle," he laughed. "I bet you he was a cavalryman." By the end of February, however, the humor had become harder to find. An urgent meeting he called on the health crisis on February 26 brought only more misery when a Japanese bomb hit the command post and wounded four. "Bataan was a hopeless hell," he wrote long afterward, "where everything was bad except the will to live, the memories of home (as torturous as they sometimes could be), and the ever-dimming hope that the great country we represented would somehow find a way to help us." One day around this time, Dooley found Wainwright deep into a bottle of scotch at an hour that seemed earlier than proper.

There were still stories of convoys on the way, but they had become harder to believe. The victories the Americans and Filipinos had won on Bataan had not reversed the reality that the Japanese ruled the sky and sea. As if to leave no doubt whom the tides of war still favored, the British surrendered Singapore on February 15. "Hope of reinforcements here is slowly dying," Johnny Pugh wrote in his diary in early March. In his opinion, MacArthur had made the situation worse with promises that never came true. "The fact remains that truth (no matter how it hurts) is best," Pugh wrote in his diary. "Jap propaganda to our troops now includes such statements as these: 'Don't be fooled any more by the lies which the USAFFE [United States Army Forces in the Far East] officers are telling you. Surrender yourselves at once or else you will be completely annihilated.'" As the soldiers gave less credence to the promises coming from Corregidor, they gave more to fantastic accounts of the luxuries afforded to their counterparts living on that little island. Frank Hewlett, the wire correspondent, decided to put the mood on Bataan into verse. To everyone's astonishment, the poem made it past the censors.

> *We're the battling Bastards of Bataan*
> *No mama, no papa, no Uncle Sam*
> *No aunts, no uncles, no nephews, no nieces*
> *No pills, no planes, no artillery pieces.*
> *. . . And nobody gives a damn.*

Perhaps nobody did give a damn, at least when it came to the cavalry. "Out of a clear sky," one of Wainwright's fellow old-time cavalry officers recalled, "the ax fell." On the last day of February, as part of George Marshall's reorganization of the army, Franklin Roosevelt signed an executive order abolishing the office of chief of cavalry. It was a cruel coincidence that the announcement came almost to the day the slaughtering of the horses of the 26th Cavalry began. "The horses had eaten all the rice straw stacks remaining in that tip of Bataan since the last harvest," Wainwright wrote. "There was no forage for them . . . and their tough meat became eagerly sought slivers in our rice." There is a much-repeated story that Wainwright insisted that one of his own horses be shot first. The story, however, did not originate with Wainwright. Of his three horses, he said that only one—a brownish red, prizewinning thoroughbred named Melhap—made it alive to Bataan, where he went out to pasture with the horses of the 26th Cavalry. When food ran out there, Pugh found a small patch of grass off the West Road, where he moved Melhap along with his own horse, Sir Conrad. "They are slowly starving," Pugh wrote his wife. "I try not to think of them. With men facing slow starvation, it is unworthy of me to think of private possessions. However, knowing you love Sir Conrad, I do not think of him as a possession or an animal but a person just as you and I." Surely, Wainwright felt the same. What happened to the two horses afterward remains uncertain. If, as some say, soldiers finally did receive an order to shoot Melhap, Wainwright never admitted to giving it. He would later claim that the Japanese had taken his horse prisoner. By then, death may have seemed preferable.

*   *   *

Early on the morning of March 10, a summons from Corregidor arrived at the command post. A phone call followed from Sutherland, saying MacArthur wished to see Wainwright. A boat would take him to Corregidor at noon. Pugh, Dooley, and Champlin would come, too. As they drove down the West Road to the docks at the bottom of the peninsula, Sergeant Carroll looked through the openings the battle had left in the tree canopy. When they had driven this way the day before, Champlin had looked into the sun and seen a silhouetted speck growing larger until he could see it had wings and guns bearing down on them. "Get the hell out of this car," had shouted Champlin, tearing off Wainwright's seat belt and jumping out. Dooley admitted to feeling "scared stiff" afterward. Wainwright, in matter-of-fact fashion, simply recorded "strafed by Jap plane" in his diary entry for the day. As they climbed into a weather-beaten boat, Pugh asked if Wainwright knew what MacArthur wanted. Two months to the day had passed since Wainwright had last seen MacArthur—since MacArthur had last seen Bataan. "Wish to God I knew," Wainwright said. Fatigue had made him forget to ask.

At Corregidor, soldiers immediately escorted Wainwright into the Malinta Tunnel and then into the headquarters lateral. MacArthur was not at his desk, but Sutherland was at his and rose to address Wainwright. "General MacArthur is going to leave here and go to Australia," Sutherland said. "The president has been trying to get him to leave Corregidor for days but until yesterday the general kept refusing. He plans to leave tomorrow evening around six thirty by motor torpedo boat for Mindanao. A plane will pick him and his party up there and fly us the rest of the way." Although MacArthur would keep overall command of the Philippines, Wainwright would take charge of all forces on Luzon, including both sides of the Bataan peninsula but not including Corregidor, which would remain part of a separate harbor command. Sutherland stopped as if he suddenly realized he had launched into the details without exchanging any pleasantries, without asking how Wainwright was. In fairness, there was no need to ask. Anyone could see. Already thin before the war, Wainwright had managed to lose 20 of his usual 172 pounds. "You look hungry, Skinny," Sutherland said. "Have some lunch and then we'll go up to the house," by which he meant MacArthur's place outside the tunnel. Wainwright thought about the rice he had scooped out of his mess kit that morning, then shook his head. "Nope, I think not," he said and cast his gaze toward Bataan. "We eat only twice a day over there."

There was no more to say. Sutherland took Wainwright out the opposite end of the tunnel and brought him to a slate-colored cottage. Wainwright could hear MacArthur talking inside to his wife before he appeared on the porch. He looked tired but smiled as he grasped Wainwright's hand. "I want you to make it known throughout all elements of your command that I'm leaving over my repeated protests," MacArthur said. "If I get through to Australia, you know I'll come back as soon as I can with as much as I can. In the meantime, you've got to hold."

Wainwright replied that he and his men had made the defense of Bataan "our aim in life." That answer did not seem to satisfy MacArthur. "Yes, yes, I know," he said. "But I want to be sure that you're defending in as great depth as you can. You're an old cavalryman, Jonathan, and your training has been along thin, light, quick-hitting lines. The defense of Bataan must be deep. For any prolonged defense you must have depth."

"I know that," Wainwright said. He also knew he had warned about how long his front and flank had become—and, yes, how thin, too—because his troops lacked the training needed to fill the trenches and the food needed to fill their stomachs. Had MacArthur been to Bataan since January, he would have seen for himself. Wainwright could have said any of that. Yet he said none of it. "You do not speak of such things when a man knows the situation as well as you yourself do," Wainwright later wrote. He did not even mention how little ammunition his men had left as he listened to MacArthur go on about making good use of the artillery. There was a silence as Wainwright pondered what to say in response. "You'll get through," he said.

" . . . and back," MacArthur said without pause. The words had a resolve to them. In Australia, MacArthur would have the opportunity to do what he could not on Corregidor: accumulate the men, airplanes, and supplies needed to defeat the Japanese and free the Philippines. Wainwright had already said he understood, but MacArthur seemed to want to hear it again. Why else did MacArthur start repeating all the reasons he had to go? "I told him again that I understood, because I did," Wainwright wrote. "He was going because he is a soldier, and a soldier obeys orders from his commander regardless of his own emotions, ambitions, hopes." Wainwright could have said the same about himself. When the news became known to the public—when the newspaper reporters came asking Wainwright for comment—he would describe himself as among MacArthur's greatest admirers and say his escape meant "not only relief for Bataan but also Japan's obliteration." Aides might hear Wainwright hint at the "major military errors [that] had been committed by the high command," but the world never would. MacArthur had asked that his reputation be defended. Wainwright would see it done because he was a soldier, "and a soldier obeys orders from his commander regardless of his own emotions, ambitions, hopes."

Across the channel, Wainwright could hear the sound of guns calling him back to Bataan. He walked back through the tunnel with MacArthur, who stopped to shake hands with Wainwright's aides and left them amazed that he recalled their names. Out of the other side of the tunnel, the two generals stood alone again. "Good-bye, Jonathan," MacArthur said as he handed Wainwright some cigars and shaving cream and shook his hand. "When I get back, if you're still on Bataan, I will make you a lieutenant general."

The most vital point had gone undiscussed. Wainwright had not asked—and MacArthur had not offered—when he would return. Both knew that the answer would make all the difference to soldiers running out of food and yet no difference at all to a duty that would carry on however long it took. "I'll be on Bataan if I'm alive," Wainwright said as he stared into MacArthur's dark eyes one more time and then headed down to the boat. "Many times in the days and months and years that followed our last meeting on Corregidor," Wainwright would write, "I thought of my parting promise—a promise I could not keep."

CHAPTER SIX

The Trough

Wainwright had been led to believe that MacArthur had decided to leave the Philippines only the day before their meeting on Corregidor. But in truth, MacArthur had known his fate for more than two weeks. "Where's Jean?" was all he could say when he first saw the orders on February 23. Once he had found her, they shut themselves in their cottage with Sutherland. In the lengthy discussion that followed, neither Jean nor Sutherland would remember hearing MacArthur threaten to resign in protest. Only MacArthur himself would recall that detail. He would also remember his "entire staff" having to talk him out of heading to Bataan and offering himself to the commanders there as a "simple volunteer," as he put it, willing to die beside the soldiers whom leaders in Washington had ordered him to leave behind. "Where in the hell did you get this?" MacArthur's chief engineer, Hugh Casey, asked upon being presented with MacArthur's version of events long after the war. When told that the information had come from MacArthur's own memoirs, Casey responded, "I still don't believe it. He never would have resigned his commission." And given he never did, it is hard to argue.

Nevertheless, MacArthur would maintain that he would have refused to leave the Philippines if not for one specific argument: that he could return almost immediately. In his memoirs, he recalled aides assuring him that the "men, arms, and transport which they believed were being massed in Australia would enable me almost at once to return at the head of an effective rescue operation." But his letters at the time reveal that he knew that "a great deal of organizational work" would have to be done first. Just weeks earlier, he had warned that the boys on Bataan would run out of food before the army could accumulate enough force in Australia. Even if the buildup down under now proceeded faster than he had previously assumed possible, how would he bring the men and arms back with him to the Philippines? The number of times the navy had rejected his pleas to run the Japanese blockade should have made him skeptical.

There was another argument that should have made MacArthur skeptical: that he would have faced a court-martial had he refused to leave the Philippines. In theory, he could have. The order came in the name of the president himself. In reality, however, the political considerations that Eisenhower remembered being very much on the minds of the top brass in Washington would not have allowed a court-martial. After the Republican Wendell Willkie had raised the idea of rescuing MacArthur in early February, *The New York Times* had run an analysis piece warning that "many observers" believed that it "would be a psychological blow to the enlisted men's morale and to the morale of the Filipinos and would shatter a basic tradition upon which much of the structure of military elan has been reared—the tradition that a commander shares the fate of his men." If ordering out a general looked bad, court-martialing an extremely popular one for refusing to go would have looked worse, and appearances were not inconsequential to Franklin Roosevelt. For such reasons, he had initially opposed removing MacArthur altogether. "It would mean that the whites would absolutely lose all face in the Far East," the president was heard to say. "White men can go down fighting, but they can't run away."

In vain had the author of *The New York Times* analysis searched for a good precedent for a commander abandoning his men. In fact, the military history that Americans at the time knew best—their civil war—offered a few. There were the Confederate generals who had abandoned their army and fled in 1862 after Ulysses S. Grant had surrounded their garrison at Fort Donelson in Tennessee. But their flight to freedom had ended in everlasting ignominy. A newspaper columnist who had attended West Point with MacArthur could not imagine that Roosevelt, with all his "humanity and affection," would condemn any general to have to choose between deserting his men or disobeying an order. But if the choice did come, the columnist had little doubt what MacArthur would do. He would remember the doomed stand the Texans had made at the Alamo and, if need be, go down with his men at Corregidor. "These men are MacArthur's own men, who have shown their willingness to die for him," the column read. "They have lifted him to a pinnacle of glory. Would he desert them? I think not." It was not the American way.

In later years, Prime Minister Winston Churchill of Britain wondered if he had helped his American cousins warm to a new way by offering a more recent precedent—one from Europe, where he had ordered the commander of a British army surrounded at Dunkirk to escape by sea to England for fear that his capture would hand the Germans a "needless triumph." The situation was hardly analogous given the British had already evacuated most, though not all, of their soldiers. Nonetheless, Churchill recalled his Dunkirk orders making such an impression on American officials that they requested copies. "It may be (for I do not know) that this influenced them in the right decision which they took in ordering General MacArthur to hand over his command to one of his subordinate generals, and thus saved for all his future glorious services the great commander who would otherwise have perished or passed the war as a Japanese captive," Churchill wrote afterward. "I should like to think this was true."

For his part, MacArthur liked to believe that another prime minister had more to do with the decision. With Japanese bombs starting to fall on the northern part of his country, John Curtin, the Australian prime minister, requested an American take charge of the Southwest Pacific. Perhaps it was this plea that overcame Roosevelt's resistance to removing "the captain," as one of his advisers put it, "[from] the sinking ship." Certainly, the president preferred to have MacArthur in Australia than to have him, as Willkie had proposed, in Washington.

On February 24, the day after receiving Roosevelt's order, MacArthur accepted with the caveat that the timing be left to his discretion. "A sudden collapse," he warned, might ensue if he went too soon given the "peculiar confidence" the Filipinos had in him. "Rightly or wrongly these people are depending upon me now not only militarily but civically, and any idea that might develop in their minds that I was being withdrawn for any other purpose than to bring them immediate relief could not be explained to their simple intelligence," he wrote. Roosevelt agreed.

It was assumed that MacArthur would take his family with him. As MacArthur defined the word, family included a nanny, so there was no thought of leaving behind Ah Cheu. His aide Sid Huff remembered MacArthur also receiving permission to take the "nucleus of his staff," but the War Department had signed off only on his chief of staff, Sutherland. The decision to make a list of sixteen other officers, including Huff, Casey, the deputy chief of staff Richard Marshall, and the intelligence chief Charles Willoughby, was MacArthur's. The decision to leave space for a press aide (LeGrande Diller) and a stenographer (Paul Rogers) seems strange given MacArthur's insistence that he and Sutherland selected the men based solely on their "anticipated contribution" to the liberation force that would return with them to the Philippines. Apparently almost no thought was given to the inverse question: Which men should stay because of their "anticipated contribution" to the garrison that would have to hold out in the meantime?

Most of the men on MacArthur's list assumed they would leave Corregidor, as President Quezon had, by submarine. Huff had made his career in the navy before joining MacArthur's staff and could imagine no other way of going until one night in the cottage when he saw

MacArthur pacing back and forth, puffing a cigar, and launching into one of those phony conversations where he would occasionally pause for an answer that would make no difference to whatever he said next. Huff realized he should have seen it coming. He had noticed how the general hated confined spaces. "It was almost as if he suffered a touch of claustrophobia," Huff wrote. "[MacArthur] wanted room to move about and to see what the enemy was doing," even if that meant allowing the enemy to see what he was doing. For the same reason MacArthur hated hiding beneath the rock of the Malinta Tunnel, he could not make peace with days spent traveling beneath the waves. He wanted to ride above them, he told Huff. That no one else liked the idea made no difference. MacArthur had made up his mind. They would go by PT boat.

*   *   *

Short for patrol torpedo boat, the PT boat had a longtime fan in Mac-Arthur. One day in 1936, he had summoned Huff to the headquarters straddling the walls of Intramuros and asked him to jump-start the construction of a Filipino navy. MacArthur did not have battleships and aircraft carriers in mind; the fledgling commonwealth could not afford those. Instead, he conceived a navy of torpedo boats. With a fleet of such boats, he could repel whatever force the Japanese brought. "General," Huff replied, "never in my life have I even seen a torpedo boat." Except for bootleggers who had used an early version of the vessel for bringing their spirits ashore during Prohibition, few Americans at the time had. Only recently had the United States Navy begun testing its own designs. Less than eighty feet long with three 1,200-horsepower engines and built out of mahogany and plywood rather than the steel used on the standard ships of the time, the design that MacArthur would eventually see sacrificed size for speed and traded protective armor for being well armed with torpedoes and turreted machine guns. Huff's building program in the Philippines would not amount to much.

But before the outbreak of the war, the United States Navy had brought six of its own PT boats to the archipelago, and they would stay with the soldiers there even as most of the fleet sailed to safety.

Like MacArthur himself, these PT boats provided American newspapers with irrationally optimistic copy at a time when the United States Navy's conventional warships had taken a beating. Nicknamed "mighty midgets" and "sea mosquitoes," the PTs were said to be "the deadliest thing afloat," even though their torpedoes often misfired. The PTs were said to travel an outrageous eighty miles per hour, even though few sailors had ever seen one exceed a still-swift fifty miles per hour. The boats could not reach even that without proper maintenance, which the fighting and supply shortages in the Philippines made impossible. The gasoline fed into the boats on Bataan had a strange waxy substance, which crews attributed to Japanese sabotage. Over time, the engines would clog up and then, without warning, break down.

One day MacArthur brought Jean down to Corregidor's north dock to see the boats for herself and make sure she could handle the trip. For all the positive press the mosquito boats had attracted, no one claimed they provided a smooth ride. As the boats sped up, their fronts would rise up, as if bucking out of the water. "When you ride one of these floating bronchos at top speed down the slope of a fifteen-foot wave and smack head-on into that green wall of water on the other side—well, this is no place for a weak pair of legs or an uncertain stomach," read an article from 1941. "No wonder the sailors of the mosquito fleet have to be tough. Some navy veterans who volunteered for the service had to quit and go back to the broad decks of the battleship, quiet as country lanes in comparison with the fast little torpedo boats."

Waiting for MacArthur and Jean at the dock was the PT squadron commander, Lieutenant John Bulkeley, with his own boat, PT-41. Without explaining why, MacArthur asked Bulkeley to take Jean on a half-hour ride so she could "get a feel for the boat." Bulkeley responded as he usually did when asked if his boats could do a mission. "No problem at all." Despite being only thirty years old and only a

Union forces storming Missionary Ridge in Chattanooga, Tennessee, on November 25, 1863. Having saved his regimental flag from falling, Lieutenant Arthur MacArthur carried it to the crest. Only many years later, when his son Douglas was ten, would Arthur win the Medal of Honor for the feat.

General Arthur MacArthur as he looked around the time he fought in the Philippines. His mustache and pince-nez would remind some of Theodore Roosevelt, who as assistant secretary of the navy gave orders sending American ships to Manila Bay.

Robert Powell Page Wainwright as he looked during the Spanish-American War. He died in the Philippines in 1902, shortly after his son, Jonathan Mayhew Wainwright IV, started at West Point.

Fort Custer in the Montana Territory around the time Robert Powell Page Wainwright brought his family there in 1886. Not far from where the cavalry commander George Armstrong Custer had made his last stand ten years earlier at the Little Bighorn, life at the fort would leave Robbie's son with a deep curiosity about the battle as well as an undying love for horses.

A sketch of the American flag being raised over Manila's Fort Santiago on August 13, 1898, after Arthur MacArthur led his troops into the walled part of the city known as Intramuros. A secret arrangement between the American and Spanish high commands spared the city from a more destructive battle.

Douglas MacArthur as he looked in 1918 during the final months of World War I, where he earned a reputation not only for his unusual uniform but also for the eagerness with which he exposed himself to enemy fire. "There are times when even general officers have to be expendable," MacArthur explained.

Jonathan Mayhew Wainwright IV receiving his first general star in 1938 while on horseback at Fort Myer near Arlington Cemetery. "Cavalry leaders are born and seldom made," he liked to say. His fellow cavalrymen would have numbered him among those born to the role.

MacArthur (seated) at a lunch in Manila in 1939. On the far right is the younger Dwight D. Eisenhower, who grew frustrated with his role on MacArthur's staff. In the middle is Philippine president Manuel Quezon chatting with Eisenhower's wife, Mamie.

Manila as it looked in the years before World War II. By the water, in the foreground on the right, is the Manila Hotel, where MacArthur and his family made their home, and behind it, to the left, the walls of Intramuros. Cut off on the right is the Luneta, where people would watch the sun set over the bay.

Philippine Scouts of the 26th Cavalry performing tricks on their horses before the war. Based out of Fort Stotsenburg, the 26th Cavalry would provide Wainwright with his most reliable fighters during the retreat from Lingayen. He would later describe its members as among the finest troops in American history.

MacArthur (right) speaking to Wainwright in 1941 as they prepared for a Japanese invasion of the Philippines. Wainwright said he wanted command of the North Luzon Force after asking MacArthur, "Where do you think the main danger is—the place where some distinction can be gained?"

MacArthur (left) sitting with his chief of staff, Richard Sutherland, in the headquarters lateral of the Malinta Tunnel on Corregidor. MacArthur refused to live in the tunnel but agreed to move his headquarters there after the Japanese air raid on the island on December 29, 1941.

A photograph taken by the Japanese of their bombers flying over Corregidor during the early months of 1942. When the planes appeared, sirens on the island would sound and send people racing into the Malinta Tunnel.

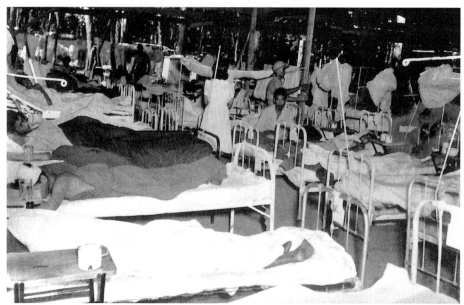

A hospital on Bataan. By late February, hospitals on the peninsula received almost five hundred malnourished men a day as a result of malaria alone. "Bataan was a hopeless hell," Wainwright later wrote.

A navy recruiting poster showing a patrol torpedo (PT) boat and Lieutenant John Bulkeley, minus the beard many remembered him having in the Philippines. On March 11, 1942, MacArthur and his family boarded Bulkeley's boat, PT-41, for the first leg of their daring escape from Corregidor.

Jean MacArthur, her four-year-old son, Arthur, and his stuffed rabbit, Old Friend, recuperating in March 1942 on Mindanao after their perilous journey from Corregidor aboard PT-41. Although the layover gave them an opportunity to clean up, it did not reduce fears for their safety as word of their whereabouts spread. A B-17 would take them the rest of the way to Australia.

17

A Japanese photograph showing the beginning of the Bataan Death March in April 1942. Hundreds of American soldiers and thousands of Filipino ones would not make it to the end. Those who survived the march would discover the horrors of Camp O'Donnell.

18

A Japanese photograph showing Wainwright sitting directly across a long table from General Masaharu Homma while attempting to negotiate Corregidor's surrender on May 6, 1942. John Pugh, Wainwright's most trusted aide, appears next to the general on the far left side of the photograph. Sitting on the other side of Wainwright are his chief of staff, Lewis Beebe, and his other aide, Thomas Dooley.

19

Japanese soldiers leading the defeated American garrison out of the Malinta Tunnel on Corregidor. Wainwright worried the Japanese would carry out a massacre inside the tunnel if he did not agree to their terms.

20

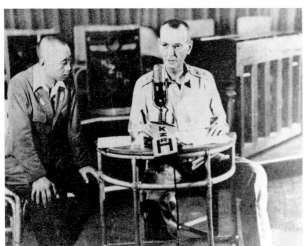

Wainwright in the Manila studio where he made the broadcast ordering all forces in the Philippines to surrender. "I believe General Wainwright has temporarily become unbalanced and his condition renders him susceptible of enemy use," MacArthur said afterward.

lieutenant, Bulkeley answered only to admirals and generals, and even they hesitated before questioning his command of the six PT boats in the Philippines. Wainwright's naval liaison, Malcolm Champlin, described Bulkeley as "one of the most colorful" characters of the war. "He reminded one, on first glance, of a swashbuckling pirate in modern dress. He wore a long, unruly beard and carried two ominous looking pistols at his side. His eyes were bloodshot and red-rimmed from constant night patrols and lack of sleep, but his nervous energy was tremendous and never seemed to give out."

The ride Bulkeley gave Jean around the bay could not give a true sense of what she and her family would face at sea, which experienced sailors said was like "tobogganing through a boulder field." Nonetheless, Jean assured her husband she could handle it. Only then did he fill Bulkeley in on the plan. Bulkeley could scarcely believe its audacity. The Japanese had around two dozen ships patrolling Manila Bay, not to mention mines. MacArthur would stand a better chance going by submarine, Bulkeley said. "No," MacArthur responded. "The PT boat is the safest way because the enemy would never suspect I would do it that way." Bulkeley thought about it and agreed. From that moment on, he would regard MacArthur as "a sheer genius" and went to work charting a course from Corregidor's north dock more than five hundred miles south to the island of Mindanao, which lay within flying range of Australia for the B-17s that would be waiting to take MacArthur and his fellow passengers the rest of the way. Four PT boats, traveling in a diamond formation, would make the trip. Bulkeley himself would carry MacArthur's family, as well as Sutherland, Huff, and a few others. They would travel over the course of two nights and spend the day between in hiding on an island named Tagauayan in the Sulu Sea. MacArthur wanted to depart on the Ides of March. But the moon had its own schedule. They would go when only a slender slice showed in the night sky on March 11.

At 7:15 that evening, Jean was sitting on the front porch of the cottage when her husband whispered, "It is time to go." Into a car they went with Arthur and Ah Cheu. Each of them could bring one suitcase. In hers, Jean remembered packing only a pair of slippers, a robe, a coat, and a spare dress that would give her two outfits counting the one she had on. Arthur could not bring his tricycle from Christmas, but he did have Old Friend, the plush rabbit. In later years, MacArthur would battle rumors that he could have taken more men with him on the boats had he not insisted on filling them with all sorts of unnecessary belongings, most ludicrously a piano. In truth, he had forgone the one suitcase allotted to him. He carried almost nothing, not even a razor. In the days ahead, he would borrow someone else's. At the last moment, he looked at the car he had used on the island, and asked that the license plates with the four general stars be taken off and placed in the boat. He had already sent home via submarine the medals, press clippings, marriage certificate, and other documents Jean had saved from the penthouse.

Via Chase National Bank, where the Philippine government kept funds, MacArthur had sent home something far more valuable: a $500,000 payment that Quezon had approved before leaving Corregidor. Equal eighty years later to $9 million and unlike any transaction in the history of American arms, the payment perplexed the members of the Roosevelt administration who had to sign off on it. One cabinet secretary thought General Wainwright also received a payment. He had not. But Richard Sutherland, Richard Marshall, and Sid Huff had: to the amount of $75,000, $40,000, and $20,000, respectively. The money they received continues to defy good explanation, but historians have found one for MacArthur's sum: It was fulfillment of the deal he had negotiated upon agreeing to serve as the father of the Philippine Army: the percentage promised him of the annual Philippine defense budget, plus outstanding salary payments. Rogers, the headquarters stenographer, heard MacArthur tell Sutherland, "The amounts hardly compensated for income they had lost during their service with the military mission." That sounds suspiciously like the excuse poorly paid public officials always make for accepting money they should

not. MacArthur should have known how the payment would make
him look. His former chief of staff, Eisenhower, did. When offered
a similar—albeit smaller—payment from Quezon upon his arrival
in Washington, Eisenhower turned it down not because he deemed
it illegal but because he realized how it could tarnish his reputation.
Somewhere inside himself, MacArthur must have shared this fear, for
he kept the payment secret for the rest of his life. When the historian
Carol Morris Petillo uncovered the transaction in 1979, she wondered
if the money might explain MacArthur's fixation with returning to the
islands he was about to leave. Had Quezon enriched MacArthur as a
way of indebting him to the Philippines?

It is no defense of the transaction to note that the bond between
MacArthur and the Philippines was already strong enough. In the
absence of any financial incentive, the force of history, the ties of
family, and the call of honor all would have conspired together to
draw him back. These were the islands where his father had fought
and found the key to America's destiny as a Pacific power. These were
the islands where Douglas had lost his mother, proposed to his wife,
welcomed a son, and made a home. These were the islands whose
people and culture had charmed him as a young officer and whose
beaches he had committed himself to defending as a general officer.
On these islands, without so much as a goodbye, he would leave the
tens of thousands of starving soldiers who had retreated to Bataan
on his whim and found what hope they could in the promises he had
made but could not make true.

At the dock waited some of the few who had learned about his plans.
As he helped his wife and son onto PT-41, he looked back at Corregidor and how much it had changed. "My eyes roamed that warped and
twisted face of scorched rock," he remembered. "Through the shattered
ruins, my eyes sought 'Topside,' where the deep roar of the heavy guns
still growled defiance, with their red blasts tearing the growing darkness
asunder." There, amid the ruins where he had spent his first days on
the Rock, he saw the Stars and Stripes still waving from the flagpole.

He looked at George Moore, who would stay at his post in command of Corregidor's defenses. "George," MacArthur said, "keep the flag flying. I'm coming back." For the first of what would be many times, Huff heard MacArthur say, "I shall return."

Before he could return, he would have to make it out. The Japanese guns that had been shelling the island fell quiet as he climbed aboard the boat. "What's his chance, Sarge, of getting through?" MacArthur heard someone in the small crowd ask.

"Dunno. He's lucky. Maybe one in five," came the answer.

MacArthur did not feel lucky. He had lost weight. His grimy uniform no longer fit. "I could feel my face go white, feel a sudden, convulsive twitch in the muscles of my face," he wrote. He had tried to hide it, but his wife could see it. "He was just heartbroken," she remembered. He raised his gold-braided cap and waved farewell. It was time. The men traveling on the three other boats had already boarded and waited for him off the coast of Bataan. "You may cast off, Buck," MacArthur instructed Bulkeley, "when you are ready."

Once the four boats had rendezvoused in the bay, Bulkeley brought PT-41 to the front. The others carried higher-ranking naval officers, but MacArthur told Bulkeley not to take orders from them. "I was in command of the expedition, and MacArthur made perfectly clear that no army general and certainly no navy rear admiral was going to tell me how to do it." In a line, Bulkeley led the boats through the American mines. He knew these, he said, "like the back of my hand." The Japanese ones worried him more. "We had to go through the business there of very quietly, at the same time slowly . . . spotting those mines and fending them off," he remembered. Finally, the boats reached the South China Sea but not safety. Japanese ships patrolled just beyond the bay. "Sinister outlines," MacArthur remembered, appeared "against the curiously peaceful formations of lazily drifting cloud." Then, on a nearby island, they saw fires illuminating the sky. Had someone seen the PT boats and set the blaze as a warning to the blockading ships? Bulkeley would not wait to find out. "There," he said, "we cranked on high speed," which in the current state of the boats meant a mere thirty-eight miles per hour.

Inside the boat, only the roar of the three engines could be heard. Little light could be seen. The gathering clouds had smothered the last trace of moonlight and stirred the waters over which the boat skimmed. In the lower cockpit, MacArthur sat on one side of an old mattress Huff had laid. Jean sat on the other. In the nearby corridor where the officers had their bunks, Ah Cheu and little Arthur lay. Both of them had fallen seasick immediately. MacArthur soon did, too. Among the family, only Jean could stomach the waves. "We would fall off into a trough, then climb up near the slope of a steep water peak, only to slide down the other side," MacArthur wrote. He likened the experience to taking a "trip in a concrete mixer." The spray from the sea stung their skin even when below deck. The engines became so drenched at one point that the crew had to pause them. By 3:30 a.m., PT-41 was alone. The other boats had disappeared.

As it turned out, PT-32 had suffered mechanical problems of its own. Two of its three engines had stopped working. With no hope of reaching the meeting place at Tagauayan before dawn, the passengers pulled into a cove off the coast of another island in the Sulu Sea. As first light appeared over the horizon, so did a dark shape that the sailors aboard PT-32 assumed to be a Japanese destroyer headed toward them. Unable to speed away as they would have preferred, they waited with torpedoes ready. Just before firing them, someone cried out, "That's not a Jap destroyer. It's one of our boats." The approaching PT boat had looked larger than it was thanks to two men standing on its deck and braving the waves. One of them was a drenched Douglas MacArthur. His bravado had almost gotten his own boat sunk.

Anchored side by side, the passengers on the two boats ate hotcakes while little Arthur befriended a pet monkey that PT-32's cook had named after the Japanese prime minister. Huff could see MacArthur growing impatient. Tagauayan was not much farther. The other two boats might already be there. MacArthur did not want to fall more behind. Bulkeley reiterated the risks of meeting a Japanese ship in the daylight, but MacArthur deemed them worth taking.

As they set off and found the waves cresting even higher than before, MacArthur began to change his mind. "That's the wettest bunch of generals I have ever seen," Bulkeley joked, as the spray washed over the boat. MacArthur did not laugh. For the first time since Pearl Harbor, people heard him question his own judgment. Perhaps he should have listened to his advisers and taken a submarine. How much more time on one of these boats could his family endure? Finding only one of the two missing PT boats waiting at Tagauayan gave MacArthur his answer. No more, he said, as they anchored on the island. He and his family would wait for a submarine that was supposed to reach Tagauayan the next day. Now it was the navy brass that urged MacArthur to stay the course. Rear Admiral Francis Rockwell, the party's top naval officer, warned that delaying the journey at this juncture would only prolong the peril. Besides, Rockwell said, the worst of the voyage was surely over. Bulkeley bet otherwise. "I warned," he said, "there was going to be very, very rough seas." MacArthur looked at Rockwell and then at Dick Sutherland. "Dick, I can't do anything to Rockwell. But if it's rough tonight, I'll boil you in oil."

With PT-32 no longer seaworthy, PT-41 and PT-34 took on additional passengers and set off southward for Mindanao just shy of sunset. As to the bet between the naval admiral and the lieutenant, the sea had the final say. "It was rougher than hell out there," Bulkeley remembered. MacArthur quickly became too sick to boil anyone. His hands seemed to lose circulation. He could barely move them, let alone lift himself off the mattress, as he surely would have done, upon hearing the chatter above deck about an enemy ship drawing near. Jean, taking a break from massaging her husband's hands, popped her head above deck, saw the outline of a Japanese cruiser, and then went back below without a word. "Not one bit of panic crossed her face," Bulkeley remembered. "It could have been the death of us all at that time if they had sighted us." Salvation came from the speed with which the tropical sun goes down. Within fifteen minutes, it had slipped below the horizon and let the boats slip away into the darkness.

No one aboard had slept since leaving Corregidor. Huff had rested a thermos filled with hot coffee on a ledge over the mattress where Jean tended to her husband. "That's going to fall off, Sid," she warned. Too exhausted to move, Sid said not to worry only to have a wave send the thermos crashing to the ground with hot coffee and broken glass flying into the air. When Jean turned on a flashlight to clean up, she heard Bulkeley shout, "Put out that damn light." Japanese searchlights from a nearby island appeared in the sky. Perhaps the Japanese had heard that MacArthur had fled Corregidor; perhaps they had mistaken the roar of the PT boats for airplanes. Either way, even the faint glow of a flashlight made the boat stand out in the sea of blackness.

Huff had finally fallen asleep when he heard someone calling, "Sid? Sid?" The voice belonged to MacArthur. "I can't sleep." And since MacArthur could not, Huff would not either. MacArthur started talking. In the darkness, his mind had been replaying the events that had sent him, like the boat he now rode, up the cresting wave to the Philippines and then crashing down away from the islands. "He was in the trough of the wave at the moment," Huff wrote. "What had happened, I soon realized, was that he had had time to think back over our defeat in the Philippines and he was now trying to analyze it and get it all straight in his mind. And to do that, he wanted to think out loud . . . his voice slow and deliberate and barely distinguishable above the high whine of the engines." He remembered how Filipino politicians had underfunded his army from the outset, how the military establishment in Washington had undermined his authority, and how the White House had completed his humiliation by forcing him to flee. There was blame for everyone save for himself. No wonder Huff struggled to separate his boss's voice from the whine of the engines. Huff hardly added a word. He listened as MacArthur went on for hours. Not until two in the morning did the monologue end with a good night and a promise to promote Huff to colonel, as if he had just performed the greatest service of his career.

First light on March 13 brought the first view of Mindanao. The Japanese had landed on the southern side of the island, and MacArthur's fellow passengers did not know what reception to expect when they docked on the northern side. "Everybody was alert and craning his neck as we rounded the last bend," Huff wrote. As the harbor came into view, so did a welcoming party of American army officers. One of them remembered seeing MacArthur stand on the bow of the boat and thought at that moment he could have stood in for George Washington in the famous painting of him crossing the Delaware River. Nearby stood Jean, her body hurting the way she imagined a football player must feel after a scrimmage, her dress the same she had worn thirty-six hours earlier. She looked, Huff thought, "a bit like an old-time gypsy carrying her provisions in a red bandana." At some point during the voyage, her handbag had gone overboard. But her son still had his stuffed rabbit, and her husband still had his cap. Stepping ashore, he wrung it out and put it on. The salt water had shrunk its size. But the gold lace still shimmered. With only a compass and a map, Bulkeley had managed to deliver MacArthur to Mindanao on schedule. The missing PT boat arrived a few hours afterward. Bulkeley and his team would all receive silver stars, MacArthur promised. "You have taken me out of the jaws of death, and I shall not forget it." MacArthur would later nominate Bulkeley for the Medal of Honor.

The danger was not done. When MacArthur arrived at the nearby Del Monte airfield, he did not find the four B-17s he expected. One of them had crashed en route from Australia. Two of them had turned around because of mechanical problems. The fourth had made it but looked, in MacArthur's words, "not fit to carry passengers," especially not his wife and only child. He sent a letter demanding that "the best three planes . . . be made available." As he waited for the new bombers to come, he saw Japanese fighters flying back and forth overhead. Whether the pilots knew of his whereabouts, he could not know. What he did know was that word of his arrival on Mindanao had begun to spread. A desperate Filipino woman looking for information about her family back in Luzon had wandered into the airfield and demanded to see Mrs. MacArthur. Jean had no information about the family, but the woman seemed to possess a surprising amount of information about the MacArthurs' supposedly secret travel plans.

There was no choice but to detain the woman until after the night of March 16, when two of the three new B-17s arrived from Australia. Engine troubles had caused the third plane to abort its flight and given Jean, who had flown over the Pacific before and not liked it, more reason to worry about the safety of these planes. Watching one of the junior-looking pilots promptly down eight cups of coffee upon reaching Del Monte did not reassure her. Nor did hearing the same pilot describe the two planes as in bad shape—held together, as he put it, "with chewing gum and baling wire." Nevertheless, MacArthur insisted that all the members of his party could fit aboard. Taking only the coffee-stained mattress for little Arthur to lie on, the MacArthurs shed most of the rest of their baggage and boarded one of the bombers. Sometime after midnight, MacArthur remembered the plane, as he put it, "rattling down the runway with one engine sparking and missing." Little more than a pair of flares lit the way. But unlike the B-17s at Clark, these two bombers made it off the runway.

As they flew through the night, the darkness masked the islands and waters the Japanese had turned into a vast empire that MacArthur would have to recross if he were to return to the Philippines. With the rising sun came a clear view of Japanese ships around an island in the Dutch East Indies—and then news of an air raid where the B-17s planned to land in Darwin on the northern coast of Australia. Instead, they would have to proceed a little farther south to a place called Batchelor Field. "Never, never again will anybody get me into an airplane," Jean told Huff as she climbed off the plane at 9:30 in the morning "Not for any reason! Sid, please find some other way we can get to Melbourne without getting off the ground." Huff returned with bad news. They needed to get back on the plane at once. "Don't ask any questions," he told her. The pilot took off so quickly that MacArthur did not even have time to take his seat. "Get that pilot's name!" he barked after almost falling over, only to learn that the pilot might have saved his life. Japanese bombers were said to be incoming.

When the plane landed a few hours later, the doors let in the scorched air of Alice Springs, a little town in the middle of the Australian outback. Huff called it "the end of the world." But to MacArthur, it must have seemed like the beginning, a return to that barren landscape where he had made his first memories at Fort Selden. Perhaps that was why he was so eager to see the western playing that night at the town's outdoor movie theater. But he did not enjoy himself, as he usually did, and left early. If he had hoped to recover the romance of Selden, it was not there. He now had the body of a sixty-two-year-old, a dangerously dehydrated son, and a wife as resilient as any in the annals of the army but nonetheless repulsed by the gigantic flies infesting the town's sole hotel and the thought of sharing the one bathroom on her floor with all the men staying on it. For Jean, Alice Springs had but one virtue: the railway line leading out of it. Some of MacArthur's aides would fly ahead to Melbourne and set up his headquarters. But she and her family would take the train, even though that meant beginning a rail journey of well more than a thousand miles on the old locomotive that pulled into the station with a smokestack and cowcatcher in front and old cars with wooden benches in tow. The journey, Jean said, would do her husband good. As she looked at kangaroos out the window, he put his head in her lap and fell asleep. "That's the first time he's really slept since Pearl Harbor," she said.

By March 20, 1942, newspapermen in Australia knew where to find MacArthur. In the town of Terowie, they waited in the station where he would transfer from the uncomfortable train to one more suitable for the man the president of the United States had sent to lead allied forces in the Southwest Pacific. When MacArthur stepped off the old train, he looked surprised by how large a crowd had gathered to greet him. "Welcome to Australia," came the cries. He had prepared a statement on a spare envelope and asked the reporters if the words he said now would make their way to the Philippines as well as the United States. Yes, said the newspapermen, one of whom described MacArthur as looking "lean" and "tall" and wearing a "loose hanging jacket and slacks and no insignia except a laurel wreathed peak on his cap." As Jean and little Arthur gazed with manifest admiration, MacArthur began to speak.

The president of the United States ordered me to break through the Japanese lines and proceed from Corregidor to Australia for the purpose, as I understand it, of organizing an American offensive against Japan, the primary purpose of which is the relief of the Philippines. I came through and I shall return.

As to when the day of return would come—the question that neither MacArthur nor Wainwright had dared ask at their parting—a clue lay a little farther down the tracks at Adelaide, where MacArthur's deputy chief of staff, Richard Marshall, waited. Marshall had flown ahead to Melbourne and brought a preview of what his boss could expect to find upon his arrival there. When the train reached Adelaide and Marshall climbed aboard, MacArthur began asking about plans for the offensive. Marshall shook his head. "The horrible truth," Huff remembered Marshall saying, "was that there was no allied army in Australia worthy of the name. There was no navy. No air power, other than a token force." Worse, there was no definitive timetable for when the buildup would take place. Marshall's information could not answer when MacArthur would return. But it did answer the only question that really mattered to the boys MacArthur had left behind on Bataan. He would not arrive in time.

MacArthur would later call the news "the greatest shock and sur-prise of the whole damn war." In truth, he had known it all before. If, as he later claimed, his staff members had deluded him into believing otherwise, he would have himself to blame for letting them and little excuse for having deluded others. Before flying off from Mindanao, MacArthur had written President Quezon a letter assuring him, "I understand the forces are rapidly being accumulated [in Australia] and hope that the drive can be undertaken before the Bataan-Corregidor situation reaches a climax." But before dismissing these words as deceitful, it is worth asking from where else MacArthur's hope could have sprung. If he really came to believe he could return at once to the Philippines, it sprang from the same source that made him believe he could find a way out of the conundrum that had stumped a generation of military planners saddled with War Plan Orange. It sprang from what his mother had planted inside him before the first test of his military career, the entrance exam to West Point. "You must believe in yourself, my son, or no one else will believe in you." He had found the hope then—and ever since—in himself. It had survived the battering his body had taken across thousands of miles of sea and sky and rail but not the last leg of the trip. Reality had caught up. When Marshall finished his report, MacArthur could not speak. "God have mercy on us," he finally said.

The world would long remember his words outside the train. But in a shockingly short span, MacArthur and his aides would forget where exactly he had delivered his famous statement. They would remember only the heartache he felt afterward as he paced inside the train with Jean with the knowledge that his faith in himself would not suffice. He wondered whether he should return at once to Corregidor before concluding that the sacrifice would achieve nothing. "I shall return," he had said. But he would not do it alone. He could not do it alone. He was not enough. And if he alone was not enough, would he not have been the wiser to say, "We shall return"? His many critics would later argue so. But unless he meant to include his family and staff, the first-person plural pronoun would have made no sense at the time. American forces had not left the Philippines. MacArthur had left without them, and, as he would soon see, it would not be so easy to speak for Wainwright and the others who had stayed behind.

*   *   *

In an Oval Office decorated with shamrocks for St. Patrick's Day, reporters heard Franklin Roosevelt predict that Americans would rally around his decision to rescue MacArthur, and largely they did. "I know that every man and woman in the United States admires with me General Mac-Arthur's determination to fight to the finish with his men in the Philippines," Roosevelt said. "But I also know that every man and woman is in agreement that all important decisions must be made with a view toward the successful termination of the war. . . . In other words, he [MacArthur] will be more useful in supreme command of the whole Southwest Pacific than if he had stayed in Bataan peninsula." What the soldiers on Bataan—the men who had seen MacArthur on the peninsula only once—would think of their own usefulness when they heard these sentences seemed not to concern the president. What concerned him was what had worried him before: whether the decision would make the United States look weak in the eyes of its enemies. Indeed, the Japanese press wasted no time in calling MacArthur a "deserter" who had revealed "the futility of further resisting Japanese pressure." But the enemy propaganda did not catch the army chief of staff, George C. Marshall, unprepared. He had readied an unprecedented response. To defend MacArthur's honor, the president would award the general the one military honor his father had received but he never had: the Medal of Honor.

Planning for the award had begun in January. "Secretary of War extremely anxious no opportunity be overlooked [to] recognize General MacArthur's gallant and conspicuous leadership by award [of] Medal of Honor," read a secret message that Marshall had sent Sutherland. "Desire you transmit [at the] proper time your recommendations and supporting statement with appropriate description any act believed sufficient [to] warrant this award." Not until his last night in the Philippines—hours before boarding the B-17 out of Mindanao—did Sutherland send his recommendation: Give MacArthur the medal upon his arrival in Australia for the "utter contempt" he had shown for "danger under terrific aerial bombardments" and the "tremendous effect" such acts of courage had "upon the morale of his troops."

As MacArthur had learned earlier in his career, the medal required "incontestable proof." Sutherland tried his best to supply it. He recounted for Marshall the story of MacArthur standing in the open as Japanese bombers had leveled his house on Topside. The Filipino orderly sacrificing his hand for MacArthur's head went unmentioned. Unimpressed, Marshall admitted to the secretary of war, "There is no specific act of General MacArthur's to justify the award of the Medal of Honor under a literal interpretation of the statutes." In the past, such shortcomings would have ended MacArthur's chances. This time, it did not even pause the process. Some opposition to the award came from Eisenhower, who later likened it to saluting a soldier "for sitting in a hole," by which he surely and somewhat unfairly meant the Malinta Tunnel given how often MacArthur had ventured outside it. Not caring one way or the other, Marshall set aside time out of his own schedule to write a citation crediting MacArthur with "gallantry and intrepidity above and beyond the call of duty . . . for the heroic conduct of defensive and offensive operations on Bataan peninsula." The award was necessary, Marshall informed the president, "to offset any propaganda by the enemy." Roosevelt agreed. So paranoid were both men about enemy propaganda that they turned America's most sacred medal into its own form of propaganda. In fairness, had they not awarded MacArthur the medal, Republicans in Congress had threatened to do so through legislation circumventing the usual process.

For the first time, a father and son would share America's highest military award. Plans were made for an official presentation in a few months' time on June 30, 1942, fifty-two years to the day that the first General MacArthur had received his medal. If the second General MacArthur had secured one part of his family legacy, he knew he had forsaken another: the islands so associated with his family's name. MacArthur learned about the medal headed his way before giving a speech on the evening of March 26 to members of the Australian Parliament. "We shall win or we shall die," he said, never mind that he himself had left the Philippines without doing either.

A few days more would pass before MacArthur could find the right words to thank Roosevelt and Marshall for the medal. "I feel that this award is intended not so much for me personally as it is a recognition of the indomitable courage of the gallant army which it *was* my high honor to command," MacArthur finally wrote on March 29. Emphasis on "was" because no longer was he in direct command as he had planned. To his surprise, Washington had changed the orders he had given upon leaving the Philippines, and it was evident in the message Wainwright had sent on March 28. "Just announced that you have been awarded Congressional Medal of Honor. Please accept my warmest congratulations. None was ever more deserved. I am truly happy." The message came not from the large island of Luzon, where MacArthur had assigned Wainwright, but from the little one of Corregidor, where Washington had moved him into command of all forces in the Philippines.

CHAPTER SEVEN

A Dreadful Step

Wainwright had tried to keep his word. He had remembered that MacArthur wanted the officers on Bataan to understand why he had left. So on March 11, 1942, the night the PT boats set out, Wainwright had gathered his fellow generals around his trailer at his command post on Bataan and told them the news. "They were all at first depressed," Wainwright remembered. "But I soon saw that they understood, just as I understood. They realized as well as I what the score was." The next day, after transferring command of his half of Bataan to Albert "Honus" Jones, Wainwright set off with his trailer to establish a new headquarters in a comparatively quiet clearing farther down the peninsula, away from the front lines where he had spent so much time. "It was not a very ideal set up," he wrote. For one, the new command post lacked adequate communication equipment. For another, Wainwright lacked the staff needed to command forces across Luzon. Unlike MacArthur, who had taken most of his staff with him, Wainwright did not want to poach from his successor. Among officers, he brought only Johnny Pugh and Tom Dooley. Wainwright's orderly, Sergeant Carroll, came, too. So did the driver Centimo and the cook Francisco, who now performed his twice-daily miracles with only rice, a little meat, and a coffee substitute.

Dooley did his best to dress up a new mess with a nipa roof and clean utensils, but there was no hiding the reality. Rations for soldiers on Bataan had fallen again, now to one thousand calories a day. That amounted to half of a half ration. A surgeon said it was "barely sufficient to sustain life without physical activity." Even at these levels—even with another one-third cut to the rice that now served as the staple of everyone's diet—the food would last only another thirty days. In search of more time, Wainwright looked across the channel to Corregidor, which still housed the rations MacArthur had taken away from Bataan in January. If returned, they could provide another fifteen days of sustenance, which would mean fifteen more days for MacArthur to deliver a miracle.

Under MacArthur's command structure, however, the stores on Corregidor still lay beyond Wainwright's grasp. Before leaving the Philippines, MacArthur had divided the islands into four commands: Wainwright on Luzon, including Bataan; Major General George Moore on Corregidor and the other harbor islands; Brigadier General William Sharp on Mindanao at the bottom of the archipelago; and Brigadier General Bradford Chynoweth on the Visayas in the middle. Although Wainwright outranked the others, the arrangement gave him no power over them. For reasons MacArthur had not explained, he wanted no one left behind in the Philippines to have such broad power. If disputes arose among the four commands, as inevitably would happen, MacArthur had left behind a member of his staff to serve, in effect, as his mouthpiece: Brigadier General Lewis Beebe on Corregidor. The arrangement, Wainwright admitted, "irked me a bit." Having previously advised MacArthur on supply issues, including the January food transfer, Beebe had little to recommend himself to the soldiers starving on Bataan.

Nonetheless, on March 18, Wainwright set off across the channel for Corregidor in the hope of reasoning with Beebe. "It was, as I knew it would be, a fruitless visit," Wainwright wrote. Beebe would not budge. He simply repeated the orders MacArthur had given before leaving: Do not raid Corregidor's stores for Bataan. The logic baffled Wainwright. If the Japanese starved Bataan into submission, they would move their guns atop Mount Mariveles at the tip of the peninsula, and then no amount of food would save Corregidor. "I came back to Bataan with a heart made heavier," Wainwright wrote. To have command over all men on Bataan but no control over the supplies they needed across the channel had put him in a humiliating position.

Unbeknownst to Wainwright, Beebe was in an even more humiliating position. Corregidor had begun receiving messages from George Marshall addressing Wainwright as commander of all United States forces in the Philippines. Somehow MacArthur had forgotten to tell the War Department that he had divided the command before leaving the islands. Beebe urged MacArthur, now in Australia, to rectify the mistake at once and resolved, in the meantime, not to inform Wainwright about the messages from the War Department. After Wainwright's visit to Corregidor, days passed with no response from MacArthur but more communications from Washington—most notably a message from Roosevelt congratulating Wainwright on a career milestone: his advancement to lieutenant general because, as the president put it, "of the confidence I have in your leadership and in the superb gallantry of the devoted band of American and Filipino soldiers under your command." What MacArthur wanted no longer mattered. Beebe could not disobey his commander in chief. "Thank goodness some of my worries are taken off my shoulders," Beebe wrote in his diary. On the morning of March 21, he called Wainwright's headquarters with the news.

Wainwright already knew half of it. The previous day, a radio on Bataan had picked up a San Francisco broadcast mentioning his promotion to lieutenant general. To celebrate, aides had laid a tablecloth for dinner, set up candles, and made cocktails out of a drink they called "native gin." Now, over the phone, Beebe said he had some more good news, but the line cut out. "Yes, yes," Wainwright implored. "Go ahead." The ear injury he had sustained during World War I made it hard to hear the voice on the other end of the lousy connection to Corregidor. He asked Pugh to join the call. Then Beebe's voice came back through. "The troops in the Philippines are to be called hereafter the United States Forces in the Philippines, and you're designated as commander in chief," Beebe said. "Can you come over?"

For the second time in scarcely a week, Wainwright and his aides packed up their belongings. He put on the best shirt he had left and added a third star made of tin to the two already embroidered on either shoulder. "A soldier could wish for a little more ceremony when he gets another star, I guess," Wainwright wrote. "Yet it was still a thrill." Then he set off for the tip of Bataan and the boat awaiting him there. Never again would he live in the trailer that had served as his home since departing Stotsenburg in December. He would make a new home across the channel. Arriving at Corregidor's north dock, where Mac-Arthur had left, Wainwright proceeded to the Malinta Tunnel, where he issued his first order assuming command of all forces—army and navy—in the Philippines. Beebe would become Wainwright's chief of staff.

Evidently, the messages Beebe had sent earlier had not made it to MacArthur as he traveled by train to Melbourne, because around the time of his arrival, the sight of Wainwright's order from Corregidor caused a shock. Sutherland was heard to pronounce Wainwright unqualified. As to why, he and his boss would have more to say later. For now, however, MacArthur did not make his objection personal. After sending a message demanding Wainwright explain himself, Mac-Arthur realized that it was he who needed to explain himself to the War Department. "Special problems," he wrote, "with the intangibles of the situation in the Philippine Islands" required dividing the Philippine command. Only hearing this idea now, George Marshall swiftly rejected it. The distance between Australia and the Philippines made the arrangement, he wrote, "impracticable." The Philippines would still technically fall under MacArthur as supreme commander of the South-west Pacific. But day-to-day command needed to rest with an officer on the archipelago. Logical as that sounded, Marshall's arrangements failed to reckon with the most important of the "special problems": If one man had command of all the Philippine Islands, one man could be forced to surrender them all.

The Japanese had already sent Wainwright a demand to surrender. As if to tease the American and Filipino soldiers desperate for a drink, Japanese airplanes had dropped copies of the ultimatum in empty beer cans. "At the least the Japs might have sent a couple of full cans," Wainwright was said to have quipped upon fishing out the message. "Your Excellency," it read, "you have already fought to the best of your ability. What dishonor is there in avoiding needless bloodshed? What disgrace is there in following the defenders of Hong Kong, Singapore, and the Netherlands East Indies in the acceptance of honorable defeat?" If he surrendered, the Japanese vowed to adhere to "international law" in their treatment of his officers and men. If he did not respond before noon on March 22, however, the Japanese would consider themselves "at liberty to take any action whatsoever." MacArthur had never dignified such messages with a reply. Neither would Wainwright. "No answer was needed," he said, "and none was sent."

The fight remained far from over, Wainwright assured his aides. Between soldiers and sailors—between military personnel and civilian staff—his force numbered ninety thousand on Bataan with eleven thousand more on Corregidor. "Lee marched on Gettysburg with less men than I have here," aides heard Wainwright say. "We're not licked by a damned sight." The obvious went unsaid: Lee had lost at Gettysburg. And more men would not save Wainwright. Only more food could.

*　　　*　　　*

In leaving the Philippines, MacArthur left an opening in the newspaper coverage. During the first months of the war, his name had so dominated the headlines that almost no other had found space. The war correspondents had gotten to know Wainwright, but few of their readers had. If Americans back home had heard of him at all, they knew him only as MacArthur's second in command. "He was the . . . Unknown General," explained one correspondent before adding that MacArthur's move had "changed all that." Indeed, it had, and Pugh thought it about time. "I am glad for he has done much to enhance the prestige of General MacArthur," Pugh wrote. "It is now time to heap a little glory upon his own head." By the end of March, Wainwright was on his way to becoming a household name. Newspapers fleshed out the portrait of an "old-time hard-boiled cavalryman" with colorful details about his reputation as "one of the worst" golfers in the army and "one of the best single-handed cussers you ever heard." They hailed him as a "master strategist," as the "most front going general," and as a "modern warrior with enough horse soldier tradition to hold that thin line if it could be held." He was, in one writer's opinion, "the spiritual inheritor of Custer" but also, in the opinion of a *Washington Post* cartoonist, a worthy heir to MacArthur. "Looks like a perfect fit," declared the caption over a sketch of Wainwright's legs sticking out of an enormous pair of shoes labeled MacArthur's.

If one believed the newspapers, Wainwright's appointment had given the soldiers on Bataan confidence that they could hold out until MacArthur's return. "We still have plenty of generals left but Mac-Arthur's the one the Nips fear most. And they should, because he will get us enough planes and other reinforcements to chase the Japanese all the way back to Tokyo," a sergeant told the United Press correspondent Frank Hewlett. The resulting article described Wainwright as "second in their [the soldiers'] affection and admiration only to MacArthur himself." It was a strange sentiment coming from Hewlett, who had spent enough time in Wainwright's camp to know otherwise, but one that testified to Wainwright's own determination to defend MacArthur's reputation. Nonetheless, the "Dugout Doug" chorus sang on. The only good that its members could find in MacArthur's vow to return was comic relief. When nature called, they would tell their buddies, "I am going to the latrine, but I shall return." For all Wainwright's efforts to explain the command change, most American soldiers on Bataan took it as proof of what they had suspected: Help was not on the way and would not be anytime soon.

To Corregidor, Wainwright and his aides brought some of the resentments that soldiers suffering on Bataan had developed against the so-called tunnel rats living in the Malinta Tunnel. Wainwright's first days on Corregidor did nothing to disabuse him of these prejudices. There was champagne and ice cream for dinner that first night. No wonder the men on the Rock seemed healthier and better fed. Even their skin looked different. Life in the tunnel had turned them a pasty color that contrasted with the rich brown hue Wainwright had earned on Bataan. "Here's where I get some sleep," he joked. For a few days, it seemed he might. He and his aides settled into a house near where MacArthur had lived outside the tunnel's eastern entrance. In his diary, Wainwright noted that the deadline the Japanese had given in their ultimatum had passed, and "nothing has happened."

Then, on March 24, something did happen. The Japanese gave Wainwright what Beebe called "a royal welcome" to Corregidor. Wainwright had gone to inspect one of the island's batteries when planes appeared overhead. "We field soldiers don't hit the dirt every time a Jap plane comes in sight," someone heard him say. Only after some back-and-forth did the Corregidor veterans persuade him to join them in a shelter—and not a moment too soon. One bomb fell fifteen yards to one side of the shelter, another fell twenty-five yards to the other side.

The bombs kept falling. The planes kept coming. The Japanese had moved their pilots to Clark Field, which put them close enough to hit Corregidor day and night and put the island under an around-the-clock bombardment. After a night of it, Wainwright accepted the inevitable, picked up a walking stick that MacArthur had left behind in his cottage, and moved into the Malinta Tunnel. Had Wainwright waited any longer, he and his aides would surely have died in the explosion that collapsed their house. "After taking these bombings in open foxholes for three months," Pugh wrote, "we have finally become tunnel rats. However, the area of Corregidor is so small that it's sure suicide to take no cover during these heavy raids." It was enough to almost make Wainwright long for Bataan. At least there, he said, "you can move around a little."

Bataan was never far from Wainwright's thoughts. When the planes did not fly as far as Corregidor, he would venture out of the tunnel and watch them drop their bombs over the peninsula. He would see the dust rise over the tree cover, over men he knew were incapable of rising from their foxholes. Despite having promised to continue MacArthur's policy of not depleting Corregidor's stockpiles for the sake of Bataan, Wainwright began to send back some of the food taken from the peninsula in January. And rather than stretch it out for fifteen additional days, as he had previously planned, he decided to distribute it immediately. The soldiers could not wait. Not by much but for the first time in a long time, some would see their calories increase. Wainwright also embarked on a more ambitious plan. Attempts to run the Japanese blockade had succeeded in bringing some supplies to the southern Philippines, but only a small amount had made it beyond a depot on the island of Cebu in the Visayas. To get these supplies the rest of the way to Manila Bay, Wainwright proposed that MacArthur dispatch some bombers like the ones that had taken him to Australia. If they could carry out a surprise raid on Clark and the other Japanese airfields in Luzon, the diversion might provide the opening needed to run the blockade and deliver a month's worth of food to Bataan and Corregidor. Bombers were in short supply, MacArthur responded. He would see what he could do.

Time was running out. On March 28, Wainwright made his first trip back to Bataan. He would not repeat MacArthur's mistake of staying away, even though there was no good news to share with the generals who gathered to greet him. All of them could see the enemy had brought in reinforcements for an offensive that seemed imminent. None of them could see how their troops could resist. Dooley, who accompanied Wainwright across the channel, had his first panic attack of the war upon returning that evening to Corregidor. Wainwright did something more constructive. The Japanese had sent him an ultimatum. Now he sent the War Department one—not as a threat but rather to be, as he put it, "utterly frank." His predecessor had never been so. Perhaps because MacArthur had been so eager to depict his forces as outmanned, he had lowballed how many mouths he had to feed on Bataan. Wainwright had to explain that the force there did not add up to the mere forty thousand Secretary of War Stimson had come to believe, but to a number twice as high. If more food did not arrive on Bataan before April 15, wrote Wainwright, "the troops there will be starved into submission."

There was much else Wainwright could have written. There was the question he dared not ask aloud but needed to answer in his own mind. If Bataan fell—if Corregidor followed, as he expected—must he go down with it? There was still a way out. His command encompassed all the islands in the Philippines. If he moved his headquarters to Mindanao, he could escape with his staff and leave someone else to surrender. If he considered the idea seriously, the first entry of a new diary he began on April 2 reveals he did not consider it for long.

> On this date, I hereby pledge myself, that, unless ordered by higher authority to do so, I will not move my headquarters to the south, in the event that the fall of Corregidor is imminent, but will, if necessary surrender myself with my troops. No other course of action would be honorable.

The rides he had taken as a boy to the site of the Little Bighorn— the Civil War stories he had read as an army officer lugging his books from post to post—pointed the way. Custer had died with his cavalrymen. Lee had surrendered with his army at Appomattox Court House. MacArthur had left his post. Wainwright would not leave his. Below the words, he signed his name. The full diary entry took up only a page. But from that one page, he could already foresee the others to follow.

When the sun came up the next morning, April 3, the Japanese observed the anniversary of their earliest emperor's death with the beginning of an offensive they hoped would bring the Philippines into their empire. For the Catholic Filipinos and many of their American brethren, it was a holiday, too: Good Friday, when they believed their savior had died for their sins. They remembered his sacrifice and prepared to make their own in the foul-smelling trenches and foxholes cutting across the width of the peninsula. Between the I Corps Wainwright had led on the west side of the peninsula and the II Corps on the east side was the Pantingan River and to its east Mount Samat, a lonely peak between Natib to the north and Mariveles to the south. It was just north of Samat at ten in the morning that the Japanese guns unleashed an artillery bombardment so fierce that it reminded the older American officers of the western front of the Great War. Worries as to how their men would survive the soon-to-come rainy season went up in flames as incendiaries rained down on the still-parched trees and the Americans and Filipinos living beneath. They had cursed the jungle but would miss its dense cover. Now there would be nowhere to hide, nowhere to go but backward, no way to stop the Japanese advance. The division guarding the front of Samat had, according to reports reaching Corregidor, "disintegrated."

It was happening much as Wainwright had anticipated but not, as he discovered on April 4, as MacArthur did. From Australia came a rebuke. The War Department had sent MacArthur a copy of Wainwright's prediction that the troops on Bataan would be "starved into submission" if not resupplied before April 15. MacArthur thought more food would arrive before then. But even if it never came at all, he would permit no thought of submission—never mind that holdovers from his time on Corregidor reminisced about how he himself had countenanced such scenarios in January when he had begun sending Bataan's food reserves to Corregidor and again in February when he had passed along Quezon's neutrality proposal. None of that seemed to matter to MacArthur now. "Under no conditions," he radioed, "should this command be surrendered. If food fails, you will prepare and execute an attack upon the enemy." Specific instructions followed. A feint by the

I Corps on the west side would allow the II Corps to spring a surprise attack on the east side and push upward out of Bataan. If the operation succeeded, the troops might seize a Japanese supply base and then live off the fields of Luzon's central plain. Even if the operation failed, some soldiers would make it out alive and could fight on as guerrillas in the mountains.

MacArthur had planned it all out on paper. But once again, he had not seen the faces of the troops. If he had, he would have seen the "hollow-eyed," defeatist expressions Wainwright and Dooley saw when they crossed the channel again on the morning of Easter Sunday, April 5. At the II Corps headquarters, they found Major General George Parker drawing up a plan to regain the lost ground, which he did not yet realize included the summit of Samat that morning. And while the "Voice of Freedom" broadcasting from Corregidor claimed that Filipinos would rise again like Christ, the soldiers running down the back slopes of Samat saw no way back up. So worried for Wainwright's safety was Dooley that he broke the axle of a jeep speeding back to their boat. Returning to Corregidor, Wainwright responded to MacArthur. "The troops have been on half rations for three months and are now on less than that amount which results in much loss of physical vigor and sickness. Nevertheless, before allowing a capitulation, the operation you suggest will be attempted," Wainwright wrote, as if he viewed MacArthur's plan not as an alternative to surrender but as a precursor to it. "Very bad" was how Wainwright summed up the situation in his diary for the second day in a row.

The only good news that evening came from the radio. A station in San Francisco, near where Adele had moved with her mother in Monterey, had invited her to broadcast Easter greetings to her husband. She had insisted on bringing their dog to the studio, so Wainwright could hear the familiar bark in addition to her voice. "I would travel many a mile and endure many a hardship if necessary to send my love to my husband [and] to each and every brave lad fighting by his side in the Philippine Islands," she said before sharing some news she knew would cheer Wainwright. Per his instructions, his son, Jack, had gotten himself into the war. He would serve in the merchant marine. The family name would be upheld "on both land and sea."

Wainwright could not respond immediately. But the next day NBC arranged for him to broadcast a message to all his countrymen back home. "Fellow Americans: It is an unusual privilege to address you from this far-off outpost of democracy," he began. "Recently, I was entrusted with the command of the United States Forces in the Philippines. The responsibility is tremendous, but I am proud of this opportunity to give the best that is in me to the defense of my country. With the unfailing patriotism of our American soldiers, the unswerving loyalty of our Filipino troops, and the unlimited assistance of the United States, we will win."

As to what would happen if "unlimited assistance" did not come, Wainwright did not say but could plainly see on the maps covering his desk. Parker's plan to retake the ground lost by the II Corps had ended with it losing even more. Having cracked the main line of resistance in the middle, the Japanese had begun swinging the eastern half of it open like a door toward the southeast and Manila Bay until only the trees themselves blocked the way to Mariveles. The circles under Wainwright's eyes grew blacker as they searched for some way to save Bataan. His gray hair had begun to grow back; the short spiky strands sticking up, as observers put it, "like a brush." Carlos Romulo, whom MacArthur had left behind to carry on the "Voice of Freedom" broadcast, described Wainwright as aging years in days. On Bataan, Wainwright had found solace on the front lines. Now he found himself tied to the telephone lines.

It was a purgatory partly of Wainwright's own making. Upon assuming command of all forces in the Philippines, he could have dispensed with the Luzon command he had founded only days earlier and ordered the corps commanders on Bataan to report directly to him, just as he had previously done to MacArthur. But Wainwright chose not to. At this moment, the army's "most front going general" made the odd decision to lengthen the chain of command between himself and the front. He gave the Luzon command to a major general named Edward "Ned" King and, with it, control of the two corps on Bataan. Born in Georgia in 1884 on the Fourth of July and raised to revere his Confederate ancestors, King had married the daughter of one of Robert E. Lee's division commanders and unofficially launched his own military career as a nineteen-year-old cannoneer at a funeral for a Confederate general who had surrendered with Lee at Appomattox. To the Philippines in 1940, King had come on the same boat as Wainwright.

On April 7, 1942, Wainwright sent King a plan for saving Bataan. Much to the pride of Wainwright's aides, their old I Corps had held its ground on the west side of Bataan. What if its new commander, General Jones, swung it eastward and flanked the Japanese soldiers pouring through the hole in the II Corps? General King did not like the idea but agreed to pass it on to Jones, who liked it even less. It was "asinine," Jones said. His men were too feeble. The banks of the river between the two corps were too steep. And the time required to mount the operation was too great. Only after those objections had gone back up the chain of command did the three generals arrange to have a telephone call, which ended with Wainwright only more frustrated. The other generals had rejected his plan without offering one of their own.

King never did say what he had in mind. But Wainwright knew. He knew it as soon as King's chief of staff, Arnold Funk, came across the channel to Corregidor later that afternoon and stepped into the Malinta Tunnel—"his face," Wainwright remembered, "a map of the hopelessness" taking hold on Bataan. "General," Funk said to Wainwright, "General King has sent me here to tell you that he might have to surrender."

Wainwright knew what Funk wanted to hear. He wanted Wainwright's approval. But Wainwright could not give it. Back in February, Roosevelt had ordered MacArthur to "keep our flag flying in the Philippines so long as there remains any possibility of resistance." Those orders remained in effect. So did the instructions MacArthur had sent. Wainwright had them lying right there on his desk. "You go back and tell General King that he will not surrender. Tell him he will attack," Wainwright said. "Those are my orders."

Tears filled Funk's eyes. "General, you know, of course, what the situation is over there. You know what the outcome will be."

"I do," Wainwright said. There was no more he could say, no more he could do. He had orders. So did the men on Bataan. Funk would carry the message back to King.

Wainwright struggled to conceal his feelings afterward. Soldiers seeing him in the Malinta Tunnel could tell he had wept. "I have had to closely guard General W.," Pugh wrote in his diary. Against what, Pugh did not say. But others assumed the worst—that only Pugh and Dooley stood between the general and alcohol. Wainwright still spoke of the II Corps finding some line it could hold behind a river. But Pugh could see his boss was "hoping against hope." Wainwright knew what would happen on Bataan. He knew what it would mean for Corregidor, too. He knew MacArthur wanted his press aide Carlos Romulo, the "Voice of Freedom," spared from that fate. Romulo received orders to report to Wainwright the next day in the back of the headquarters lateral. "He was sitting at his table tieless, his collar open," Romulo recalled. "As I saluted, he stood up and pushed back the reports piled before him."

"I'm ordering you out of Corregidor," Wainwright said.

"What do you mean?" Romulo asked, surprised.

A plane would take off from Bataan that evening, Wainwright said, and Romulo was to be on it. He would go to Mindanao and then to MacArthur in Australia. "Bataan is hopeless," Wainwright said. He knew by the reports of soldiers crowding the docks at the bottom of the peninsula in the hope of escaping and the message he received from their officers saying, "If any troops were to be withdrawn from Bataan, they should be withdrawn on the night of April 8–9 as it would be too late thereafter." He knew by the hodgepodge of soldiers who washed ashore on Corregidor in lieu of the cohesive unit of Philippine Scouts he had requested and believed necessary to fend off a future invasion of the Rock. He knew by the arrival of a barge carrying grime-covered women who had refused until the final hours to abandon the patients they had nursed in the Bataan hospitals, which the Japanese had bombed with disregard for the rules of war. He knew by the sounds of explosions in the dark as the troops on Bataan blew up their ammunition and by the earthquake that shook the Malinta Tunnel as if to show how little he could control. "The troops on Bataan are fast folding up," he wrote MacArthur.

At 11:30 on the night of April 8, Wainwright sent King new orders, more in line with MacArthur's instructions. Instead of striking to the east, the I Corps should fight its way northward and attempt to break out of Bataan. Wainwright knew the maneuver had no chance of success. He knew before he even received the final call from King at three the next morning. The connection between Corregidor and Bataan, always bad, had grown worse. Wainwright struggled to hear and put Beebe on the phone. Oddly, it seemed King had no questions about the new orders. He wanted to know only this: Would all the soldiers on Bataan remain under his command, as he put it, "regardless of what action I may take?" Yes, Wainwright assured.

At six in the morning, an officer brought a message for Wainwright. That he should have known what it said made it no less of a shock. King was surrendering his soldiers on Bataan. "Go back and tell him not to do it," Wainwright exclaimed. But there was no going back. The white flag had already crossed the front. Realizing that Wainwright had orders from MacArthur forbidding surrender, King had made the decision on his own. It was April 9, seventy-seven years to the day since the surrender at Appomattox Court House. Fewer than thirty thousand soldiers had surrendered there. Nearly eighty thousand would on Bataan. The history weighed on Wainwright. "He has taken this new blow very hard, for he is thinking of it in the light of history," Pugh wrote. "Never has a general officer been given a more difficult assignment."

Wainwright never blamed King. "The decision which he was forced to make required unusual courage and strength of character," Wainwright wrote MacArthur. "Physical exhaustion and sickness due to a

long period of insufficient food is the real cause of this terrible disaster."
True, King had broken an order, but only because Wainwright had
refused to break one himself. As he later explained, "I had my orders
from MacArthur not to surrender on Bataan, and therefore I could not
authorize King to do it. But King was on the ground and confronted
by a situation in which he had either to surrender or have his people
captured or killed piecemeal. This would most certainly have happened
to him within two or three days." Someone had to end the charade
MacArthur had perpetuated, as Dooley put it, "[by] conveying the
wrong idea . . . to [the] War Department and press." MacArthur had
made them all believe that the Philippine Army could hold out, that
food would, too, and that surrender was a choice. But, as Pugh wrote
in his diary that night, "King had no other choice. The enemy twice
bombed our main Bataan hospital, were shelling into the area of the
only other. Troops were no longer under control." Organized resistance
had already ceased. Only bloodshed would have continued.

In spite of all the misleading accounts that Washington had received
about conditions on Bataan, leaders there were not as deluded about
the situation as Wainwright and his aides feared. In fact, Roosevelt
had thought better of his order to fight to the last American in the
Philippines. At some point in the early hours of April 9 Melbourne
time, he sent MacArthur a message to share at his own discretion with
Wainwright, for whom it was written.

> [I] am keenly aware of the tremendous difficulties under which you
> are waging your great battle. The physical exhaustion of your troops
> obviously precludes the possibility of a major counter stroke unless our
> efforts to rush food to you should quickly prove successful. Because of
> the state to which your forces have been reduced by circumstances over
> which you have had no control, I am modifying my orders to you. . . .
> I feel it proper and necessary that you should be assured of complete
> freedom of action and of my full confidence in the wisdom of whatever
> decision you may be forced to make.

Perhaps MacArthur never considered what the president's words would mean to Wainwright at this sad juncture. Perhaps MacArthur deemed Wainwright undeserving of the consolation they would bring. Either way, MacArthur opted not to pass along the message because he had received it, as he told the War Department, "simultaneously" with word of Bataan's surrender. "As the action taken on Bataan anticipated the authority conveyed in the message, I do not—repeat, not—believe it advisable to transmit now its contents to General Wainwright."

Unfortunately for MacArthur, Roosevelt decided to send the message to Corregidor on his own. As it turned out, Wainwright already had a copy. The Corregidor radio station had intercepted the version sent to MacArthur, whom Wainwright as a result knew had chosen not to pass it along. In the wound of the surrender, that knowledge stung. So as not to let it fester, Wainwright would later claim that MacArthur apologized, but contemporary records show only a more awkward exchange between the two: Wainwright passive-aggressively inquiring if MacArthur did "not concur" with Roosevelt's message and MacArthur choosing to merely confirm that it gave Wainwright "complete authority to use your own judgment."

For Bataan, the revised orders had come too late. For Corregidor, they had come just in time. Hours after King's surrender, the Japanese already had some guns in place on the bottom of Bataan and began firing on Corregidor, just as the strategists behind War Plan Orange had feared. As the Rock's batteries prepared to return fire, Wainwright ordered them to desist. "You can't fire on those artillery positions because four thousand of our soldiers are hospitalized there! I want you to hold off for three days and give the Japs time to evacuate the patients." The artillerymen objected. If the batteries did not respond now while still operational, they might not have the opportunity later. But Wainwright would not waver. From lookouts on Corregidor, observers could see Japanese soldiers marching American and Filipino prisoners. To what end, Wainwright would have to wait to learn. The Japanese had severed the phone lines to Bataan. Wainwright could only stare out at the thick jungle canopy and wonder what horrors it concealed. He could think of little else those first few days after the fall of Bataan.

The lead headline in *The New York Times* credited Wainwright with having saved many from captivity. The luckiest had found boats on Bataan. The less fortunate had swum for Corregidor. It had taken days to sort out all the new arrivals. When fully counted, they totaled more than two thousand. In the cruel math of a military siege, Wainwright could not celebrate all their escapes. Some of them, such as the few 26th Cavalry members who made it over, had something to contribute and joined the fifteen hundred marines manning the beaches. But for the most part, the newcomers made it to a bed in the hospital wing of the Malinta Tunnel and no farther, and the tunnel already had too many people consuming calories with no way of expending them toward the defense of the island. Of the thirteen thousand souls on Corregidor, civilians accounted for a few thousand. Wainwright tried his best to rally them. In a proclamation, he called on them all to view themselves as part of a team. "Bataan has fallen, but Corregidor will carry on. On this mighty fortress—a pearl of great price on which the enemy has set his covetous eyes—the spirit of Bataan will continue to live," he wrote. "Corregidor can and will be held. There can be no question of surrendering this mighty fortress to the enemy."

The younger men seemed to believe it. "Morale of this spot is going up. All think we can hold out here and trust that the united effort will eventually wipe the Japs from this area," Dooley wrote. In the knowing looks that veteran officers exchanged, Wainwright could tell they knew otherwise. So did MacArthur, it seemed, based on the messages coming from Australia. On April 12, he sent orders to "prepare a careful plan of demolition for the harbor forts to be applied in case of necessity," by which he meant defeat. He also finally sent some bombers on the air raid that Wainwright had long begged them to carry out on Japanese targets, but the operation came too late to make any difference except in the headlines. The day after Bataan's surrender, the Japanese had taken possession of Cebu, where supplies had been stockpiled, and forced the American commander there, Brigadier General Chynoweth, to flee into the mountains with a few hundred men. With the provisions on Cebu now lost, MacArthur seemed less interested in how the bombers could help the Philippines and more interested in who else they could carry back to Australia. Two of the officers he requested, Wainwright protested, could not be spared. One was Corregidor's "only experienced code officer remaining," and the other was the only man who could fix the island's frequently damaged telephone lines.

By this time, the Japanese had most of the 18 batteries and 116 artillery guns they would place on Bataan in action. Wainwright began to relax his rules against returning fire but not fast enough to please the artillerymen, who would never forgive him for having put them at a disadvantage. In truth, the guns on Corregidor never stood a chance. "The Bataan peninsula is covered with a dense, tropical growth whose trees often stand more than a hundred feet high. Enemy batteries under those trees employed smokeless powder and were therefore almost impossible for our range-finders to locate," Wainwright wrote. "On the other hand, Jap observation posts atop the 4,700-foot Mariveles Mountains near the tip of Bataan, as well as Jap observation balloons and prowling aircraft, made it easy for their gunners to correct their fire on our batteries and other critical targets." Within days, the Japanese had put half of Corregidor's guns out of action. "The Japs are gradually taking this place apart," Wainwright's chief of staff, Lew Beebe, wrote in his diary on April 16. "It is rather amazing that with all the bombing we had, more damage has been done by artillery in the past few days than was done in previous months. If it keeps up, we will have all our guns knocked out." So accurate was the fire that leaving a searchlight on for more than a few seconds would mean it being put out for good.

Inside the Malinta Tunnel, the lights would flicker. Occasionally, they would go out and plunge everyone into what Wainwright called "the most Stygian blackness imaginable." In the hours after an attack, people would sometimes have to go without water as crews raced to fix leaks in the pipes and restore power to the pumps. Although the boxes lining the tunnel contained a couple months' worth of food, only once in April could the garrison operate the pumps needed to replenish the Rock's reservoirs, which had begun the month with only three million gallons—enough to fill about four and a half Olympic swimming pools but not very much at all when one imagines thirteen thousand thirsty, dust-covered bathers sharing the water. Left to dream of showers, men learned to reuse the same cup of water several times, first to sponge their skin, and then to wash their clothes. With the air blowers turned off during attacks so as to avoid sucking in the dust from the explosions outside, the smell intensified. The sweat and heat did, too. At night, the tunnel would cool off, but sleep did not come easily. Many in search of a bed found nothing more than a crate or the concrete floor. "I don't see how some of the men get any sleep . . . with people talking and walking all around them and cars passing within a foot of their heads," Beebe wrote in his diary. "It would be something like sleeping on the curb at 42nd and Broadway in New York." In the hospital wing, nurses stacked the wounded, as they had on Bataan, in beds three high.

Wainwright was one of the lucky few with any privacy. At the back of Lateral 10 where a ventilation shaft created a welcome draft, he set up living quarters in a pair of seven-by-nine-foot rooms, both splashed with leftover white paint from the hospital. One room served as his bedroom. He called the other his "living room" but only in jest. In reality, the cot he unfolded for Pugh filled the space. Beebe had a room nearby, and he and Wainwright grew close despite the awkwardness that had marred their first days together on Corregidor. "I liked the way he did business. He doesn't hem and haw when he is called upon to make a decision," Beebe wrote of Wainwright. "When an officer asks General Wainwright for anything, he had better be prepared for quick action, because it gets it. Likewise, when General Wainwright asks for anything, one had better be prepared to deliver the goods with equal speed. He thinks like lightning and he can't tolerate people among his close associates who are mentally slow."

Wainwright had made his career in the cavalry on speed. But time inside the Malinta Tunnel passed slowly. His days would begin at six in the morning. Once dressed, he would go for a morning stroll. Stepping out of Lateral 10, he would find himself about equidistant from the main tunnel's eastern and western ends. Whichever direction he would turn, he would reach an entrance where he could survey the destruction from the blasts he had felt overnight.

Next came breakfast, which Wainwright would usually eat with those convalescing in the hospital. The men on Bataan would have envied the coffee and toast and sometimes the bit of bacon the patients had. He would have lingered with the wounded in the hospital longer if not for the stack of paperwork awaiting him in the headquarters lateral.

After putting in a couple hours at the office, Wainwright would find an excuse to tour the island's defenses. Some days he would go on foot. Other days he would take a beat-up Chevrolet. Both the Buick and Chrysler he had inherited from MacArthur had already become casualties of the Japanese gunners ready to fire at the first moving object they could find.

Wainwright would return to headquarters around noon. When he had first come over, he had made a point of refusing to eat around this time in solidarity with Bataan, where his men had eaten only breakfast and dinner. Technically, there should have been no lunch on Corregidor either, but, in practice, most men found something. Wainwright himself began having soup.

If his workload and the Japanese bombload allowed, Wainwright would break up his afternoon office time with a second tour of the island. Around eight o'clock, he would have dinner, which, as the siege wore on, turned into a reprise of earlier meals. Beebe complained that he once had corned beef hash three times in a day. In the evening, Wainwright would finish the daily reports that both MacArthur and Marshall expected to receive.

Before climbing into his cot, Wainwright would venture outside, just beyond the tunnel entrance, for a cigarette and a chat, as he put it, "with anybody who came along." On the night of April 25, two shells did. They killed fifteen and wounded thirty-five others but missed Wainwright. On the morning of April 28, however, the Japanese got him as he walked toward the entrance with one of MacArthur's cigars in hand. "My head suddenly felt as if someone had rammed a red-hot pipe through one ear and out the other. But a cigar is a cigar, especially one of MacArthur's. I continued out . . . to view the damage and take my smoke. I noticed that every sound, from voices to shelling, was quieter than before." The blast had ruptured his left ear drum and damaged the right one, too. Hard of hearing before, he would now struggle to hear at all.

He did not need to hear the blasts the next day. He could feel them. Everybody could. It was Emperor Hirohito's birthday. The Japanese bombers kicked off the celebration around 7:30 in the morning. Then the artillery took over. Inside the tunnel, the generals tried to guess how many shells fell before agreeing on a number north of two thousand. "The Japs are really beginning to get rough," Beebe recorded, "and it appears that they have settled down in earnest to pounding this island until it is a total wreck." Reports of the Japanese assembling boats and rehearsing landings left little doubt that the fire would not stay at long range for much longer.

As Wainwright looked around the tunnel, he still saw faces he hoped to save: the nurses he deemed as brave as any of America's female pioneers, the older officers he deemed too weak to weather the captivity he expected for himself, and, of course, the officers MacArthur deemed essential to his operations in Australia. That night, two seaplanes landing off the coast of the Rock provided an opportunity to save fifty souls. One nurse whom Wainwright helped out to the plane embraced and kissed him. He never expected to see her again. "Wish you were coming with us," said a man.

"I couldn't," Wainwright responded. "I have been with my men from the start, and if captured, I will share their lot. We have been through so much together that my conscience would not let me leave before the final curtain." Wainwright's favorite wire service reporter, Frank Hewlett, had made it out weeks earlier, but the words he had coined stayed with Wainwright. "I have been one of the 'battling bastards of Bataan,'" Wainwright would tell some of the lucky ones leaving Corregidor, "and I'll play the same role on the Rock as long as it is humanly possible."

It was what Wainwright's closest advisers feared. For the same "special" reason MacArthur had not wanted to give Wainwright command over all the Philippines, Johnny Pugh and Lew Beebe argued that their boss now needed to avoid capture. If Wainwright tried to surrender himself, the Japanese would "blackmail him into surrendering" not just the island where he had his headquarters but all the islands in the archipelago. Pugh begged his boss to relocate to Mindanao. Wainwright refused. He had foreseen these arguments weeks earlier when he had scribbled his vow in his diary and would not let them sway him now. "This was General MacArthur's headquarters," he said in Lateral 3, "and this is where I will stay."

To Australia, Beebe sent a radio message imploring MacArthur to overrule the decision not only for Wainwright's sake but also for his staff members'. "I am making this statement in the hope that you will not misunderstand my motives," Beebe wrote. "If I could accomplish anything by remaining here, with the ultimate probability of becoming a Japanese prisoner of war, I can say in all sincerity that I would be only too glad to remain." Even staying in Mindanao at this point would serve little purpose, Beebe argued. The Japanese had begun staging new landings on the island that would soon give them control of the Del Monte airfield, which MacArthur had used to escape. If Wainwright did not fly from there to Australia soon, there would be no going.

Wainwright did not approve the message, and he need not have worried about MacArthur doing so either. Beebe had said that Wainwright's "experience and knowledge of Jap tactics" made him "too valuable to the government to be lost," but Wainwright had reason to question whether MacArthur shared that view. As the siege of Corregidor entered its final days, MacArthur sent an icy letter demanding Wainwright busy himself answering specific questions about his conduct during Bataan's last days. It was in this context that Beebe received a response from MacArthur's chief of staff. Only the War Department, Sutherland wrote, could order Wainwright out of Corregidor because it alone had made the decision to post him there. As for Beebe himself, Sutherland added that "it was the hope of General MacArthur and myself" that Wainwright would send his staff members to Australia when he no longer needed them.

Wainwright did try to send out one of his most trusted staff members on May 3 when the submarine *Spearfish* surfaced alongside Corregidor. It was to be the last boat out. Worried what MacArthur and others would say when Corregidor eventually fell, Wainwright wanted someone he could trust to escort the records of the campaign back to the United States and explain them in person to George Marshall at the War Department. For the mission, Wainwright selected his long-serving aide, Johnny Pugh, and promised, if he accepted, to have him promoted from his current rank of lieutenant colonel to full colonel. But Pugh would not accept. Wainwright had set an example by staying with his men, and Pugh would honor it by staying with his general. "That was just your devotion and loyalty to me," Wainwright would write many years later as he thought about the wife and young son whom Pugh could have gone home to see.

Wainwright had his own son to consider. To Fort Stotsenburg before the war, Wainwright had brought part of a large and valuable firearms collection that he owned and hoped to leave to his son one day. Many of the guns Wainwright knew by now had fallen into Japanese hands, but a few of them including his old Colt revolver and a newer Smith & Wesson had made it to Corregidor. He had given the Colt revolver to one of the men departing the Rock on the seaplanes a few days earlier with instructions to deliver it to General MacArthur as a gift, but it never made it to MacArthur because the passengers never made it to Australia. They had to abandon the plane on Mindanao, where they made the decision to conceal the gun in a tree. The Smith & Wesson had spent more time by Wainwright's side during the fighting. He did not want the Japanese to have it. The *Spearfish* would spirit it to Jack. He also included a letter to his wife. "It will probably be my last to you for a long time," he wrote.

Between seven in the morning and noon the next day, no five-second period passed without a shell falling on Corregidor. It was equivalent to the Japanese dumping on the island, according to Wainwright's calculations, six hundred trucks loaded to the brim with shells weighing a total of 1.8 million pounds. "It took no mental giant to figure out . . . that the enemy was ready to come against Corregidor," Wainwright wrote. From Washington, George Marshall asked what chances the garrison stood. Worse than one in two, Wainwright answered. Few of Corregidor's field batteries and machine guns had survived. Ditto for the trenches, barbed wire, machine-gun nests, and the other defenses erected on the beaches. The shelling, he wrote, "[had] literally pulverized" them all. The once lush island hardly had any plants or trees left to provide cover. Not even in the trenches of World War I had Wainwright seen such a barren landscape. No wonder the morale of the men had begun to plummet. Since the Bataan surrender, the Corregidor garrison had suffered six hundred casualties. Even if the men somehow fought off a landing, they would have to surrender for lack of water within days unless they could find a way to get the island's pipes and pumps operating again.

The strategists behind War Plan Orange had imagined that the United States could hold the entrance to Manila Bay for a maximum of six months. Even with all the mistakes and miscalculations that had marred the execution of Orange—none greater than MacArthur's decision to run away from the plan only to retreat back to it—Wainwright and his men had made it just short of five months. Time had run out. It was time to prepare for the inevitable. Wainwright worked with his staff on a surrender message so the men and women under his charge would know what to do lest he not live to see the hour. A submarine had already carried away most of the gold in the Philippine treasury. But there were still banknotes to burn and wooden chests of silver coins to sink at a secret spot in the water off Corregidor.

Now it was around eight o'clock on the evening of May 5. At the east entrance of the tunnel, Wainwright stared into the night and wondered if it concealed the boats the Japanese had ready. Their shells had left Corregidor with almost no searchlights, and the moon would not rise until around eleven, which meant the Japanese had time to approach in the darkness before landing in the moonlight. For now, only the embers of Wainwright's cigarette and the explosions from the Japanese artillery illuminated the night. Eventually, the shells forced him back inside. In his bedroom in Lateral 10, he sat back in a chair with Beebe but could not relax as the firing outside intensified. "I don't like the sound of that, Lew," Wainwright said, jolting upright, as if alarmed his ears could hear anything. He strained to hear more and liked what he heard even less. "I'm afraid we're in for it. This sounds to me just like artillery preparation before an attack."

Fifteen minutes past eleven o'clock came the call Wainwright had anticipated. "The Nips are landing out near North Point," on the island's tail to the east. Inside the tunnel, men began flipping over their desks, dumping out the drawers, ripping down the maps adorning the tunnel walls, and shredding every piece of paper they could find. Outside the tunnel, the marines fought to hold their ground. For a time, Wainwright dared to hope they might drive the Japanese back into the sea. But before long, the Japanese established a beachhead on the northern shore and then drove south as if to form a line severing the tail of the island in two. By two in the morning, they had succeeded in doing so and moved west toward the eastern entrance of the tunnel.

As Wainwright took in the news, someone slipped him a message. In the blizzard of shredded paper accumulating in the tunnel, the operator decoding the words had simply copied them down on a piece of lined paper. It was from President Roosevelt.

During recent weeks we have been following with growing admiration the day-by-day accounts of your heroic stand against the mounting intensity of bombardment by enemy planes and heavy siege guns.

In spite of all the handicaps of complete isolation, lack of food and ammunition, you have given the world a shining example of patriotic fortitude and self-sacrifice.

The American people ask no finer example of tenacity, resourcefulness, and steadfast courage. The calm determination of your personal leadership in a desperate situation sets a standard of duty for our soldiers throughout the world.

In every camp and on every naval vessel, soldiers, sailors, and marines are inspired by the gallant struggle of their comrades in the Philippines. The workmen in our shipyards and munitions plants redouble their efforts because of your example.

You and your devoted followers have become the living symbols of our war aims and the guarantee of victory.

The thousands of troops and hundreds of planes MacArthur had promised had never arrived. Only words had. Marshall had commended Wainwright for "the continued demonstration that you and all members of your command are giving to the world of hardihood, courage, and devotion to duty." The British commander on the besieged and heavily bombed island of Malta in the Mediterranean had sent a message telling Wainwright that his "magnificent" stand had been "a great inspiration to us all." But no words meant more to Wainwright than these from Roosevelt at this moment when the Japanese line had pushed west to a ridge not even a mile away from the eastern entrance to the tunnel. At 3:30 that morning, Wainwright radioed back. "All done our best to carry out your former instructions and keep our flag flying here as long as humanly possible," he told Roosevelt. "I will counterattack at dawn."

As the sun rose, it seemed to some as if the prehistoric volcano that had shaped the contours of Corregidor had erupted again. Into the thick plumes of yellow dust rising where the shells fell by the entrance of the tunnel, Wainwright sent the last of his reinforcements: five hundred sailors unfamiliar with the infantry tactics they would need to fend off the enemy now only five hundred yards from the tunnel entrance. Backward, at first, went the Japanese. Then forward came their tanks. The old bowlegged cavalryman had held them off as long as he could. He had fallen back from one defensive line to the next on the journey from the shores of Lingayen to the jungles of Bataan and into the rock of the Malinta Tunnel. But there was nowhere to go now but from one side of the tunnel to the other: from the shells exploding at the western entrance to the shells exploding at the eastern entrance and, over and over again, past the entrance to the hospital, where more than a hundred women, including the fifty-four remaining American army nurses and the twenty-six Filipino ones, still tended to the thousand sick and wounded patients stacked in beds. As Wainwright paced through the aisle that the tunnel rats had learned to leave for ambulances, he imagined what it would look like when Japanese tanks rolled in—what would happen to the women. He knew what he had to do. "This thing has got to be stopped during daylight hours," he said. "We are going to have to surrender sooner or later, and we might as well face the facts now." Beebe and Moore, the harbor commander, agreed.

There were messages to send. The men on Corregidor needed to know they should begin destroying their large-caliber weapons, as well as other military equipment. General Sharp, the Mindanao commander who had also now assumed charge of the units still fighting in the mountains of the Visayas, needed to know that Wainwright would renounce his command over all forces outside Manila Bay in the hope that they would not have to surrender with him. Roosevelt needed to know that there was "a limit of human endurance and that limit has long since been past" and that Wainwright had made this decision "with broken heart and head bowed in sadness but not in shame." MacArthur needed to know that Wainwright had "fought for you to the best of my ability from Lingayen Gulf to Bataan to Corregidor, always hoping relief was on the way." General Homma, the Japanese commander, needed to know that Wainwright had decided to surrender Corregidor and the outposts he still had on the three smaller fortified islands in Manila Bay so as "to put a stop to further sacrifice of human life." At 10:30 in the morning, over the radio frequency that MacArthur and Romulo had used for the "Voice of Freedom," Beebe read the message he had prepared with Wainwright. "At twelve noon, local Daylight Saving Time, May 6, 1942, a white flag will be displayed in a prominent position on Corregidor."

Twice over the last month, Japanese fire had brought down the American flag atop the hundred-foot pole on Topside. Both times, courageous men had risked their lives to put it back up. They had done it for the same reason Arthur MacArthur had picked up the flag on the way up Missionary Ridge. None of them could bear to see their emblem fall. But now they had orders from Wainwright to let it do so. At noon, Colonel Paul Bunker, who had graduated from West Point in 1903 thirty-two spots behind Douglas MacArthur, brought down Old Glory and burned it. Up went the white flag Wainwright had promised the Japanese. Into the flames disappeared all the stars and all the stripes save for a small scrap of red Bunker would retain.

*   *   *

The choice of when to surrender had belonged to Wainwright. The choice of when to accept it belonged to the Japanese. Wainwright could only wait on the afternoon of May 6 at the bungalow they had selected, less than a mile up the coastal highway from the dock at a village called Cabcaben on Bataan. Only chips remained of the coat of white paint that had once covered the house. It resembled the stately brick house where Lee had surrendered to Grant at Appomattox Court House only in that both had long elevated porches, this one wrapping around the side facing Manila Bay and having a long wooden table where everyone could have sat had not Wainwright insisted on standing in the corner.

So Beebe, Pugh, Dooley, and Carroll, as well as another member of Wainwright's staff named Major William Lawrence, found their own spots. They could see the porch led into a kitchen. They gestured for water and finally received some but no food. They had not eaten since the previous day.

After an hour of standing, Wainwright found himself marched down the porch and into a yard where the Japanese had their cameramen and photographers waiting to document the moment. For the next half hour, they subjected Wainwright to the indignity of being lined up with his aides and posed for pictures. "It was easy to tell which was the American commander in chief for he was the eldest, tallest and most distinguished looking in the party despite the tired, haggard, frightened look on all their faces," wrote one of the journalists invited by the Japanese.

Overall, the Japanese found none of the Americans particularly impressive looking. It was easy to see why when a convoy of Cadillacs pulled up to the house around 6:30 in the evening. Out of the cars stepped three aides wearing golden sashes and flanking an imposing-looking Japanese man whom Wainwright identified as General Homma. "I think all of us were a little astonished by his size," Wainwright admitted. A Japanese newsman observed that Wainwright looked as "thin as a crane" and "made a pathetic figure against the massive form of General Homma." Indeed, the contrast between the two commanders seemed to overturn the diminutive stereotypes Americans held about the Japanese. Where the months of half rations had made Wainwright's old West Point nickname no laughing matter, Homma stood only a few inches shorter and cut a more strapping figure at almost two hundred pounds. Where Wainwright had only the stars on the drooping shoulders of his khaki uniform, Homma had rows of ribbons pinned to his olive-drab jacket and puffed out by his massive chest. Where Wainwright had left behind his service revolver on his desk in Lateral 3—and carried only the walking stick MacArthur had left—Homma wore a sword. "How they worship those damned swords!" Wainwright thought. For his part, the Japanese general returned the stare from the Americans with what Wainwright deemed "bored contempt" and a half-hearted salute.

With the Japanese leading the way, Wainwright and his party went back up the porch, where Homma seated himself at the center of the long table. Several other officers then bowed to him before taking the chairs on either side of his. Homma's three aides moved into a line standing behind their chief. Only then did someone gesture to Wainwright to take the center seat on the opposite side with Beebe and Dooley sitting to the left and Pugh and Lawrence sitting to the right. Alone behind Wainwright stood Sergeant Carroll with his back to Manila Bay. By this time, the Americans had set their eyes on the carts full of juice, wine, fruit, bread, and meat that the Japanese rolled onto the porch from the kitchen. Homma began to speak in Japanese. "Welcome," someone translated. "You must be very tired and weary."

"Thank you, General Homma," Wainwright responded. "I have come to surrender my men." It was what he had been trying to do all day. Nothing had gone as it should have. The Japanese had continued firing on Corregidor as if they had not seen the white flag that had gone up over the island at noon and as if they had not heard the message Beebe had repeatedly broadcast. Around two o'clock, a marine who had marched out of the Malinta Tunnel with a musician and a flag-bearer an hour earlier returned with a message: The Japanese would receive only Wainwright. So out of the tunnel he had gone. In the Chevrolet with his aides, he had driven as close as he could to the Japanese lines and then walked with a white flag toward the artillery lobbing shells over their heads and the machine guns firing past them. Finally, a Japanese lieutenant able to speak English had come forward to parley. "We will not accept your surrender unless it includes all American and Filipino troops in the whole archipelago," the lieutenant had said. It was exactly what Pugh and Beebe had feared would happen. Wainwright had refused to negotiate with a lieutenant, but a Japanese colonel entering the discussion had responded with "an angry torrent of Japanese" that Wainwright could not understand but whose meaning he could guess. "In that case I will deal only with General Homma," Wainwright had said. The Japanese had agreed to bring Wainwright to Bataan for that purpose. In the meantime, their assault on Corregidor had continued, never mind the inhabitants there had no more defenses. They had already destroyed all their weapons. The only hope for saving the men and women in the tunnel—for averting a massacre far bloodier than the Little Bighorn—lay with Homma.

Wainwright handed Homma a document stating the parameters of the surrender. No one on the Japanese side showed any interest in what Wainwright had written. Homma said something. Would, his translator asked, Wainwright surrender all the forces in the Philippines?

"Tell him," said Wainwright, addressing the translator but staring at Homma, "I command no forces in the Philippines other than the harbor defense troops and small detachments in northern Luzon. Tell him that the troops in the Visayan Islands and on Mindanao are no longer under my command. They are commanded by General Sharp, who in turn is under General MacArthur's high command."

Homma looked astonished. The Japanese whispered furiously to one another. "General Homma says that he does not believe you," the interpreter said. "He says that it has been reported many times by the United States radio that you command all troops in the Philippines. He will not accept any surrender unless it includes all forces."

Wainwright insisted that he had lost his authority over the Visayas and Mindanao.

"Since when?" Homma demanded to know.

"From two to three days ago," Wainwright lied, afraid to admit that he had radioed the message to Mindanao only hours earlier, before he had ordered all the radio equipment on Corregidor obliterated, which meant that even if he could take back control over the other troops, he had no way to revise his instructions to General Sharp. What would happen, Wainwright wanted to know, if they could find no way around the impasse?

Homma grinned as if it were obvious. "Hostilities against the troops in the fortified islands of Manila Bay will be continued," he said. Then he proposed a solution. He would provide a Japanese plane so Wainwright could send a staff officer as a messenger to General Sharp on Mindanao. At this point, the two commanders began repeating themselves: Wainwright insisting he had given up control over the Visayas and Mindanao; Homma asking again and again why a general could not take back what he had given up and growing angrier each time. By this time, Homma had balled one of his hands into a fist. Finally, he smashed it on the table. "At the time of General King's surrender in Bataan, I did not see him. Neither have I any reason to see you if you are only the commander of a unit of the American forces. I wish only to negotiate with my equal, the commander in chief of American forces in the Philippines. Since you are not in supreme command, I see no further necessity for my presence here."

At this moment, one of the newsmen remembered Pugh yelling, "Wait!" and then whispering, as he had done through much of the meeting, into Wainwright's ear with Beebe doing the same. Perhaps something of this nature did happen because Wainwright attempted to make a last-minute accommodation: He would accept the Japanese offer to fly one of his staff officers down to Mindanao not, as Homma hoped, to order Sharp to surrender but to make contact with Australia and "strongly recommend" that MacArthur accede to such a surrender.

Now it was Homma who huddled with his officers in hushed tones. They need not have whispered because none of the Americans knew a word of Japanese. Had they, they might have heard Homma's chief of staff say, "It is useless to continue the meeting." Homma rose from the table. He had held the conference, he said, only to accept the capitulation of the full archipelago. Since the American offer did not encompass all the islands, there was no reason to continue. Within minutes, he and his aides had cleared off the porch and driven away.

The attack on Corregidor would go on. Shock overtook Wainwright. He could scarcely speak. His men had lacked the weapons to stop a tank before and now lacked the weapons to stop even a foot soldier. They had unilaterally disarmed. The image he had conjured before of the Japanese tank edging into the tunnel pushed into his mind again, and he could see no way around it. But, of course, there had been a way around it. Pugh and Beebe had begged Wainwright to go south and, when he had said his honor would not allow it, begged MacArthur to intervene. Even Homma, who had hidden his fluency in English from the Americans, wondered why Wainwright had not gone to Mindanao if he had no intention of surrendering all the forces in the Philippines. People noticed Wainwright putting more of his weight on the walking stick as if he would fall over without it. "General," he heard Dooley say a few minutes after Homma's departure, "you'll have to arrange some way to accept his terms, or the blood of every one of those people on Corregidor will be on your head." Beebe and Pugh whispered the same. Another concession had to be made.

Wainwright would not have hesitated at this moment had he been certain that MacArthur would approve. It was not knowing that made it so hard. It was the suspicion that MacArthur would not approve. At every opportunity, he had stood in the way. He had opted not to transmit Roosevelt's letter giving Wainwright freedom of action, refused to believe the plight of the forces on Bataan, forbade them to surrender, insisted they fight on as guerrillas, and had subsequently left orders for the soldiers in the Visayas and Mindanao to do the same in the event of Corregidor's fall. But Wainwright did not believe the forces in the southern Philippines could hold out long enough or achieve enough, as he put it, "[to] compensate for the massacre of twelve or thirteen thousand people." For nearly a half century, the United States had tried to project its power across the Pacific without bearing the military and financial burdens of a great power. The men and women MacArthur had left behind on Corregidor could not now make up the balance with their lives. But Wainwright could save these lives by trading away the freedom of his fighters in the south. He knew MacArthur might have preferred to die rather than to make such a deal. MacArthur had said the Japanese would never take him alive—and they had not. He had left. He had sent orders for Wainwright to demolish Corregidor's defenses rather than let them fall into the hands of the Japanese but had made no provision for the people left totally defenseless in the tunnel. Had Roosevelt intended to write off all these lives, why had he made his confidence in Wainwright's judgment so clear? For better or worse, Wainwright had received command over the full Philippines, and now he reasoned he must use it to surrender all forces on the islands. The opportunity to do so to Homma had passed. A Japanese officer told Wainwright he could return to Corregidor and surrender to the highest-ranking Japanese officer there.

The sun had long since set under the western sky as Wainwright and his men set off back across the channel on a Japanese barge. "It was a black night, full of blow, and the waters of Manila Bay were wild," Wainwright remembered. The ride was hell. The boat tossed in the tides until finally beaching off a rocky part of Corregidor in chest-deep water. Trying to carry Wainwright and Beebe above the water, Carroll and another enlisted man tripped over their own feet. Beebe, who had already fallen seasick, had his head go under. Wainwright would wade the rest of the way ashore. There would be no pictures of him doing so, and that would be just as well. The men and women who awaited his return outside the tunnel where the Japanese had rounded up their newest hostages would try to reassure him that he had done his best. Nonetheless, he would feel, he said, as if he had "taken a dreadful step." The glory of sloshing ashore through the water was lost on Wainwright. It would be for MacArthur to find.

PART II

The Will to Return

CHAPTER EIGHT

Down Under

The broadcast sounds as if it could have come from a radio station anytime in the 1940s and anywhere in the United States, with one big band song after another. But the voice breaking in to the music informs otherwise. "You are listening to station KZRH, the voice of the Philippines, reaching you from Manila," says the announcer with an American-sounding accent. The day is May 7, 1942. The time is minutes before midnight. "Tonight, as we have previously announced, we have a special presentation to make. We now turn it over to our main studio."

On comes a Filipino host "calling the attention of everyone everywhere." He has a guest to introduce. Music playing in the background and other signals competing for the frequency from around the world make it suddenly hard to hear. "From the bomb-splattered, ill-wrecked sectors of Corregidor and through the hot, dusty roadways of Bataan," the host says of his guest, "he has . . . made his way to this city accompanied by high-ranking officers of the Japanese army. He has come to speak to all of you, to give you his own message, in his own words, from his own lips. Listen now to General Jonathan M. Wainwright."

"This is Lieutenant General J. M. Wainwright," says a deep, almost robotic voice pausing between the J and M as if not recognizing the initials. "Message for General William F. Sharp, commanding the

Mindanao and Visayan forces." The words are drawn out, the tone expressionless as if read from a script. "To put a stop to further useless sacrifice of human life . . . I tendered to Lieutenant General Homma, the commander in chief of the imperial Japanese forces in the Philippines, the surrender of the four harbor defense forts of Manila Bay. General Homma declined to accept my surrender unless it included the forces under your command. . . . After leaving General Homma with no agreement between us, I decided to accept, in the name of humanity, his proposal and tendered at midnight May 6–7, 1942, to the senior Japanese officer on Corregidor the formal surrender of all American and Philippine army troops in the Philippine Islands. You will therefore be guided accordingly and will—repeat, will—surrender all troops under your command to the proper Japanese officer. This decision, on my part, you will realize was forced upon me by means entirely beyond my control."

The message continues for more than half an hour. For long unexplained stretches, the broadcast goes silent but then resumes with more instructions for Sharp, as well as other officers in the archipelago. The voice tells them to share their new orders with General MacArthur but, as if anticipating what he might say, warns in the next sentence not to disregard them. "Failure to fully and honestly carry them out can have only the most disastrous results." In the final minutes, the speaker fights through a fit of coughing and sniffling and then signs off.

Exactly when and how Douglas MacArthur heard the message remains unknown. Certainly, within hours of the conclusion of the broadcast in the wee hours of May 8, he knew of its existence. Less than two days had passed since the newsmen gathering at the headquarters he had established in an insurance building in downtown Melbourne, Australia, had left disappointed. MacArthur had refused to see them. A spokesperson merely read out the news that Wainwright had surrendered. Not until the next day did MacArthur relent and provide a handwritten public statement explaining his silence. "Corregidor needs no comment from me," he wrote. "It has sounded its own story at the mouth of its guns. It has scrolled its own epitaph on enemy tablets. But through the bloody haze of its last reverberating shot I shall always seem to see a vision of grim, gaunt, ghastly men, still unafraid." That was the way MacArthur wanted the world to remember Corregidor—fighting to the last man, preferring death to surrender.

The KZRH broadcast threatened to tarnish that image. Around the world, listeners would hear a man identifying himself as Wainwright pleading with fellow Americans to surrender. General Sharp had received the message in Mindanao. So had employees of NBC San Francisco, who made a recording for analysis in the United States. So then had Wainwright's wife, who said the voice did not sound like the man she knew. Before hearing her opinion, MacArthur had concluded the same. "I place absolutely no credence in the alleged broadcast by General Wainwright," MacArthur wrote. "The enemy in the Philippines has consistently endeavored to attribute spurious statements to prisoners as part of their propaganda campaign."

In the days that followed, evidence began to mount toward a different conclusion. First came the release of a photograph showing a man who was undeniably Wainwright speaking at the KZRH studio. Then came reports of one of Wainwright's staff officers arriving on Mindanao with orders confirming the authenticity of the broadcast. Why would Wainwright have cut Sharp loose before Corregidor's surrender only to rope him back in after? MacArthur would entertain only one explanation, the least charitable one possible. "I believe General Wainwright has temporarily become unbalanced and his condition renders him susceptible of enemy use."

How would General Sharp respond? If MacArthur had his way, the commander on Mindanao would disregard Wainwright's message. "Orders emanating from General Wainwright have no validity. . . . Separate your forces into small elements and initiate guerrilla operations," read the message MacArthur sent to Sharp on May 9 with the perfunctory-sounding preface of "if possible." In truth, MacArthur knew how little was possible. He did not say it now but had admitted it days before Corregidor's surrender, when he had informed the War Department that the guerrillas would not amount to more than "a few scattered bands of desperate men . . . whose effectiveness will be practically negligible." The forces on Mindanao had already lost control of the airfields he had hoped would expedite his return to the Philippines. But even if he privately conceded that he could no longer fly back to the islands, he wanted to keep the flag flying somewhere on them for the public's sake. That was why the news Sharp sent on May 11 came as such a blow. After seeing Wainwright's representative, Sharp announced he had made a decision: Instead of dispersing his men to fight on as guerrillas, he had ordered them all to surrender immediately. "I now have no means of communication with the Philippines," MacArthur informed the War Department. No longer was he connected to the islands he called his second home. The path back would be long and hard. It would begin Down Under.

*   *   *

Members of Douglas MacArthur's staff knew that their boss liked maps. There was one he seemed especially to relish during his days in Australia: an outline of the United States superimposed over a swath of the Southwest Pacific. Even a cursory look at the resulting image reveals the audacity of his vow to return to the Philippines. Between Melbourne, where his quest would begin, and Manila, where he hoped to finish it, is an area vastly larger than the mainland United States. Had MacArthur's cartographers superimposed more of the Americas onto the Southwest Pacific, Melbourne would sit in the vicinity of Colombia and Ecuador, Manila in the middle of Canada. When viewed this way, MacArthur's vow to return sounds as quixotic as a South American general setting off to conquer the upper reaches of North America. Plus, much of the United States, as rendered on his map, had by this time fallen to the Japanese, with Borneo, Java, and Celebes giving the Japanese Seattle, San Francisco, and Salt Lake City; with the better

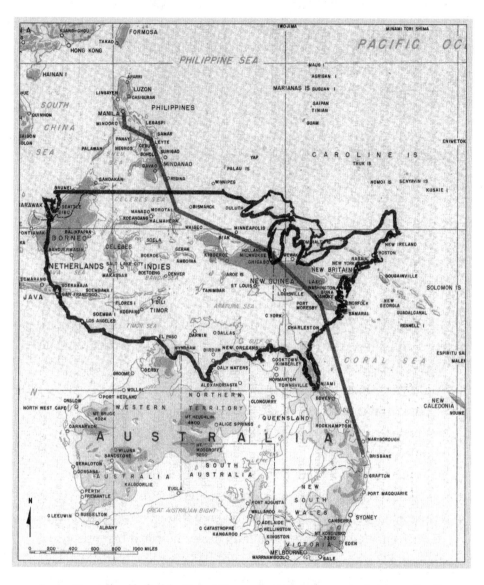

A map MacArthur liked of the United States superimposed over the Southwest Pacific theater. The map put into perspective the vast distance MacArthur would have to cover before fulfilling his vow to return to the Philippines.

part of Timor giving them the southwest of MacArthur's youth; with the northern part of the sprawling island of New Guinea giving them Milwaukee and Chicago; and with a base at Rabaul on the island of New Britain giving them a powerful bastion around New York. Even Texas and Florida, which swoop down into northern Australia on the map, did not look safe.

In secret, the Japanese had decided that they lacked the manpower to occupy a landmass as large as Australia. But in the spring of 1942, MacArthur was not alone in viewing the continent as ripe for the taking. The country had denuded its own defenses by sending the best of its men overseas to fight with the British, and the 25,000 Americans whom MacArthur found upon his arrival could not make up the deficit. According to his recollections, which were characteristically self-serving, matters had become so dire on the eve of his arrival that Australian leaders had forsaken all hope for opposing a landing on their shores. He remembered receiving a plan instead for a scorched-earth defense by which the Australians would cede three-quarters of the continent and retreat behind a line running from Brisbane about midway up the east coast to Adelaide toward the eastern side of the southern coast.

The parallels to the retreat to Bataan haunted MacArthur. He had not forgotten how leaders in Washington, as well as the naval commanders in the Pacific, had disappointed him in the Philippines, and he began to believe there was a conspiracy—maybe by "a New Deal cabal," as he described the Democrats in the executive branch—to do the same to him in Australia. "I cannot too strongly represent that the defensive force here must be built up before hostile direct pressure is applied, for it would then be too late," he wrote to George Marshall. "We must anticipate the future or we will find ourselves once more completely outnumbered."

The Japanese, in reality, had never really outnumbered MacArthur's men in the Philippines, but he had not admitted that before and could not do so now. The sacrifices made on Bataan and Corregidor required rationalization, and his defenders found it in the myth that the five-month stand in the Philippines had held down the best of the Japanese army and slowed its advance toward Australia. George H. Brett, the American air force commander in Australia, wondered if MacArthur felt guilty about "having left his men at the most critical moment of their hopeless fight." Perhaps he did, because Brett was not alone in finding MacArthur, as the journalist Clark Lee put it, "short, sharp, and frequently insulting." But there were other explanations, too, especially in the case of Brett, whom MacArthur blamed for having sent the beat-up B-17s to pick up his family and fellow PT boat passengers from Mindanao. The experience MacArthur had shared with the other officers whirling around in the PT boat like concrete in a mixer, to use his metaphor, had cemented their place in an inner circle that others struggled to penetrate and that made him, if possible, even less approachable than before. Still led by Richard Sutherland, these men would become known as the "Bataan Gang," never mind that most of them had not once slept on Bataan. "To them everyone in the world was either for MacArthur . . . or against him," Clark Lee wrote. "They moved in an atmosphere of unreality. The world centered around MacArthur; nothing else was important."

That was the message MacArthur himself sent about his theater of operations—nothing else mattered. The United States and Britain proceeded with their plans for defeating Germany first. But the European theater remained a distant concern to MacArthur. Advised that intercepted communications showed the Japanese massing their carriers for another surprise attack in the Pacific, he responded that "the Atlantic and Indian oceans should temporarily be stripped in order to concentrate a sufficient force for this special occasion," as if those theaters could simply break for intermission. Frustrated that the British had not returned the nearly fifty thousand Australian troops serving in the Middle East, he hinted that it would be only fair for the British to supply troops of their own for Australia. When the Australian prime minister passed the suggestion along to his British counterpart and attributed it to an American general, it touched off a diplomatic row that President Roosevelt himself had to settle. "I fully appreciate the difficulties of your position," Roosevelt wrote to MacArthur afterward. "They are the same kind of difficulties which I am having with the Russians, British, Canadians, Mexicans, Indians, Persians and others at different points of the compass. Not one of them is wholly satisfied."

It was a gentle way of prodding MacArthur to see the bigger picture. The Atlantic could not be stripped; as it was, German submarines had sent to the sea floor millions of tons of shipping that the Allies would need to win the war in Europe. The Middle East could not do without those Australian troops; as it was, a German general named Rommel had begun an offensive that would lead to the surrender of thirty thousand British troops in North Africa and put the pyramids of Egypt and the Suez Canal in his sights. No front, Roosevelt informed MacArthur, mattered as much at the moment as the one the Soviets held against their onetime ally Germany. A year after launching a surprise attack on the Soviet Union, Hitler had planned a new offensive that would involve more than fifty divisions and climax in a city called Stalingrad. "In the matter of grand strategy," Roosevelt wrote, "I find it difficult this spring and summer to get away from the simple fact that the Russian armies are killing more Axis personnel and destroying more Axis material than all the other twenty-five United Nations put together."

MacArthur agreed, and he told the president he knew just the way to help the Soviets: a rapid buildup against their old nemesis, Japan. Not for the first time, MacArthur went on to imagine that the Soviets might come to his aid by opening a new front in the Far East when, of course, what they really wanted was the United States to open a new front against German forces in Europe. Whatever the argument for sending reinforcements elsewhere, MacArthur always seemed able to turn it into an argument for sending them to him instead. He had gotten more men than he admitted. By mid-summer, America would have a hundred thousand in Australia. But it was not enough to please him. If more was not done soon, he warned, "much more than the fate of

Australia will be jeopardized. The United States itself will face a series of such disasters and a crisis of such proportions as she has never faced in the long years of her existence."

Then came news from Midway, an American-held atoll about eleven hundred miles from Hawaii but considered part of that archipelago. The Japanese had attempted a surprise attack, but it did not come as a surprise to the Americans. The intelligence the War Department had shared with MacArthur had proved accurate. On June 4, 1942, the Japanese sent four aircraft carriers into the fight. None would make it out. MacArthur realized the battle might serve as a turning point in the Pacific. The Japanese defeat, he radioed Marshall, "has brought about a new situation which should be exploited at the earliest possible date through offensive action."

Predictably, MacArthur knew just the place for this offensive action: his theater. He proposed an attack on the base the Japanese had built on the island of New Britain at Rabaul, around New York City on his superimposed map. If allowed to hold this base, the Japanese would use it to strengthen the forces they had established in the Solomon Islands and New Guinea, and cut off Australia. But if forced out of Rabaul, MacArthur argued, the Japanese would have to abandon these other positions and retreat seven hundred miles northward, up to a latitude on par with Mindanao. In one swoop, he could bring himself back to the doorstep of the Philippines. "Speed is vital," he said. He had everything he needed to commence the offensive, he added, so long as the navy could supply him with marines ready for amphibious operations (his soldiers had no such training) and two aircraft carriers (Rabaul sat beyond the range of American fighter planes based in Australia). An ardent football fan, MacArthur should have known he sounded like a coach declaring his team ready for an away game with only backups and no bus to transport them. "Extreme delicacy," he conceded, would be necessary to persuade the navy to go along with the plan.

The admirals had refused to put the Pacific fleet at the disposal of any army officer, let alone MacArthur, whom they remembered as all too eager to risk carriers in the Philippines. The army, for its part, scoffed at serving under the navy. So even though the United States and Britain had agreed that each theater of the war should have a single commander—a principle known as unity of command—the animosity between the two major branches of America's military forced the joint chiefs in Washington to split the Pacific Ocean into four sections. Three of them—the north, central, and south—fell under Admiral Chester W. Nimitz. The fourth section belonged to MacArthur. Known as the Southwest Pacific, it stretched as far south as the bottom of Australia, as far as west as Java, and as far east as the Solomon Islands. For what George Marshall called "psychological reasons," the army had insisted the area also jut northward to take in all the Philippines. MacArthur had to have the entire archipelago. The way back, he argued, went through Rabaul, which also conveniently lay in his theater.

If an operation required aircraft carriers and amphibious landings, however, Admiral Ernest J. King, who served as the navy's counterpart to Marshall in Washington, argued that arbitrarily drawn boundary lines on a map should not determine who had the overall command. Expertise and training should dictate that decision. MacArthur should take a backseat. A naval officer should lead the way. King, as it turned out, already had plans in the works for operations in the Solomon Islands, which he argued the navy would have to make its way up before approaching Rabaul. As usual, MacArthur sensed a conspiracy. In a long letter, he warned Marshall that if the navy had its way, it would take charge over all offensive operations in the Pacific theater. Marines would do the fighting while army soldiers, MacArthur warned, "[would be] relegated merely to base training, garrisoning, and supply purposes." He went on to explain that he had discovered during his time as chief of staff a secret navy plan for "the complete absorption of the national defense function." With good reason, Marshall began to wonder if MacArthur cared more about fighting the navy than the Japanese. "I am engaged in negotiations as to command in the proposed operations and will keep you informed," Marshall wrote. "Regardless of the outcome of these negotiations, which I hope will be as you desire, every available support both army and navy must be given to operations against the enemy."

Not until July 4—a month after Midway—did Marshall inform MacArthur that the army and navy had reached a compromise breaking up the offensive against Rabaul into three tasks. The navy would take the first one: a series of landings in the lower Solomons, which included an island named Guadalcanal. The joint chiefs had removed it from MacArthur's theater by slightly moving his easternmost boundary line westward. Responsibility for the main attack on Rabaul would rest with MacArthur. But before undertaking it, he would have the task of clearing the northeastern coast of New Guinea—the world's second largest non-continental island, stretching above Australia on MacArthur's modified map all the way from his mother's hometown of Norfolk, Virginia, to the Great Plains. The Japanese controlled the western part of New Guinea and much of the northern coast to the east but had failed, as a result of a draw of sorts at the Battle of the Coral Sea in May, to dislodge the Australians holding the important position of Port Moresby on the southeastern coast. In the interior of the island rose a mountainous jungle passable from Port Moresby only by one trail running to a village called Buna, which as of yet sat unoccupied by the Japanese on the northeastern coast. MacArthur recognized Buna as the key to his campaign. If he could move the Australians up the trail and establish an airfield at Buna, he could use it as a base for controlling the skies over New Guinea and eventually Rabaul.

It was a sign of optimism that MacArthur decided to move his headquarters on July 20 hundreds of miles northward, from Melbourne to Brisbane. If he really ever believed, as he later insisted, that the Australians seriously planned a retreat behind the so-called Brisbane line in the event of a Japanese invasion, he no longer did, for the move would have otherwise risked putting his family, which would go with him, back on the front lines. In truth, both he and the Australians had reached the same conclusion: The struggle for Australia would take place not down around Brisbane but above the continent, in New Guinea.

That did not mean that MacArthur did not worry for the safety of his family. He posted armed soldiers on the train taking them from Melbourne to Sydney and then from Sydney to Brisbane. Rumors of a plan to kidnap four-year-old Arthur had spooked the family. Jean could no longer take the boy to the park or the zoo or the dance class he liked unless she had a security detail consisting of an armed driver and Sid Huff. MacArthur told his aide to go wherever Jean and Arthur did, and to bring his pistol. Australians eager to see the family of their American savior gathered wherever Jean went. Seeing her begin to show signs of nervous strain, MacArthur instructed her to stop accepting the social invitations that would otherwise have filled her calendar. Likewise, he ordered his son not to pose for any more photographers, though he made an exception for a *Life* magazine cover story capturing the boy wearing a beret over his chubby face while riding the new tricycle that had replaced the one left behind on Corregidor. "Arthur has evolved a curiously mixed-up accent," the magazine noted, "between his father's perfect enunciation, his mother's Southern drawl, and his amah's pidgin English." The MacArthurs reduced the risk of their son adding much Australian to this mix by pulling him out of a local kindergarten class after he caught a series of colds from the other children. The family would begin the search for a private tutor in Brisbane.

The MacArthurs would have for their home a floor of a wing of Lennon's Hotel, a newly renovated building with air-conditioning. The general and Jean would each have their own suite complete with a sitting room. They would use her kitchen for meal preparation, which she attempted to do herself with limited success, and his kitchen as a place to store the newspaper articles she would clip about him. Arthur would share a smaller suite with Ah Cheu. In the mornings, the boy would report to his father's suite, where the two would resume their tradition of marching. "Boom, boom, boomity, boom," they would chant as they made their way around the room. Arthur would then cover his eyes. And with one final "boom," his father would drop a new toy. Every morning, it would be something and too often two of the same things, so Arthur could share—or rather, not have to share—with a playmate.

Surely in spite of this ritual, MacArthur received a telegram naming him "America's number one father for 1942," per the decree of the National Father's Day Committee. "By profession I am a soldier and take pride in that fact but I am prouder, infinitely prouder, to be a father," MacArthur responded. "It is my hope that my son when I am gone will remember me not from the battle but in the home repeating with him our simple daily prayer, 'Our Father who art in heaven.'" He did not mention that he did not have time to go to church with Jean on Sundays, but he did find time to write similarly affected-sounding acknowledgment letters to the many such honors that associations conferred upon him especially around June 13, when the United States celebrated Douglas MacArthur Day by resolution of Congress.

MacArthur settled into a routine that allowed little time for social functions. "Hostesses used every lure in vain," an Australian reporter noted. "[MacArthur] went nowhere except between his hotel and his headquarters." Weekdays and weekends alike, MacArthur would put on his famous cap, which he continued to wear despite efforts to find him a new one, and set off with tommy-gun-toting guards for his office. He would arrive at ten in the morning, when his staff members had their morning reports ready. He would read them at his desk and then pace as he worked through problems and summon Sutherland when new ones arose. "Dick," he would call out, "come in and let's work this out." At two in the afternoon, MacArthur would go back to the hotel for lunch and a nap. He would return to the office at four and stay often as late as nine.

As in Melbourne, an insurance building would serve as MacArthur's headquarters in Brisbane. Receptionists received instructions to say, "Hello, this is Bataan," when answering the phone. In the eighth-floor office he usurped from the company's president, MacArthur himself had no phone. Aides knew the ringing sound infuriated him, and he struggled to work the contraption, anyway. In addition to the usual

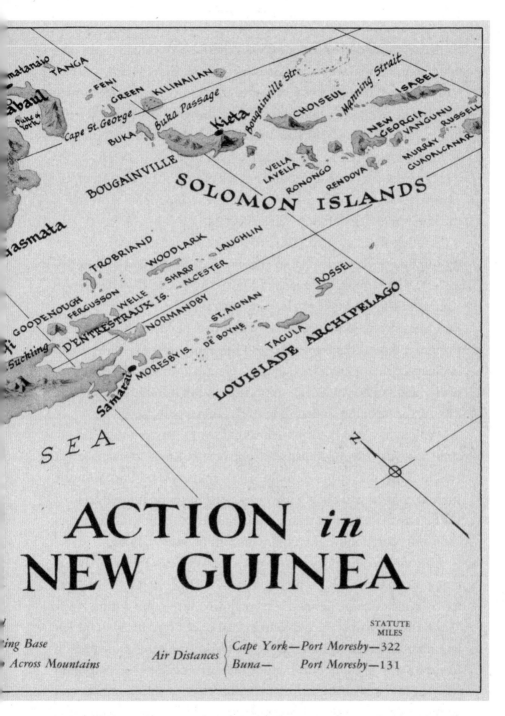

An August 1942 army news map showing the situation in eastern New Guinea and the islands around it. Unshown on this map is the trail running through the mountains between the Japanese landing site at Buna and the base MacArthur's forces had at Port Moresby.

trinkets on his desk, he had a wooden chest for his Cuban cigars on a table against a wall where he had hung a poem about youth. A secretary wondered if MacArthur wanted the poem so as to console himself on what he had lost. Behind his back, fellow generals would refer to him as "the old man." His hair remained black, but some thought it dyed. No longer did it comb over his bald spots as easily. His hands had trembled for some time but attracted more notice now. An officer who saw MacArthur for the first time in years wondered if the fall of the Philippines had left him "shell shocked."

Another shock awaited MacArthur as he opened his new headquarters on July 20. Reports of a Japanese convoy heading toward northeastern New Guinea had reached MacArthur's staff days before. An American officer assigned to lead an Australian force up the trail from Port Moresby to Buna urged MacArthur to expedite the timetable for the move. Busy with his own move to Brisbane, however, MacArthur's intelligence chief, Charles Willoughby, played down the danger. Seizing Buna, he thought, could wait until August. But it would not wait. On July 22, the Japanese landed thousands of men at Buna.

Willoughby said the Japanese would stop there. But they did not stop. Instead of the Australians pushing north up the mountain-jungle trail to Buna, the Japanese would take it south toward Port Moresby. Instead of assuming the offensive, MacArthur found himself back on the defensive. Instead of taking Buna the next month without bloodshed, the operation would require months of bitter fighting.

The only uplifting news came at the end of July with the arrival of a new air commander. To replace Brett, Marshall suggested the five-foot, six-inch George Kenney. Having flown over France during World War I, the fifty-two-year-old Kenney had once heard his idol, the late legendary airman Billy Mitchell, say that MacArthur was more friendly to airpower than commonly known. MacArthur did not seem friendly when he first welcomed Kenney to Brisbane with a half-hour harangue about airmen having no loyalty. Kenney responded that he would give his loyalty so long as MacArthur provided the support needed to do the job. "George," MacArthur said as he wrapped his arm around Kenney, "I think we are going to get along together all right." The test came a few days later as Kenney plotted an air raid only to find that Sutherland had modified the orders. According to one account, "Kenney rushed to the chief of staff's office for an immediate showdown with him: he angrily took a piece of blank paper from the chief of staff's desk, put a tiny penciled dot in the corner, and informed Sutherland that the blank area represented his knowledge of air matters and the dot symbolized Sutherland's." Sutherland backed down after Kenney threatened to do what Lewis Brereton had lacked the guts to do in the hours after Pearl Harbor: storm into MacArthur's office and demand the supreme commander himself settle the dispute. As Midway had turned the tide for the navy, the ascendancy of Kenney would begin to clear the skies for the air force over the Southwest Pacific.

A fog, however, remained around MacArthur. "To make something out of nothing seems to be my military fate in the twilight of my service. I have led one lost cause and am trying desperately not to have it two," he wrote. "The way is long and hard here, and I don't quite see the end of the road." Not for weeks more would he resolve to go to New Guinea and see the way for himself.

*   *   *

No one at the War Department intended the wording as an insult to MacArthur. But the draft that reached him on July 31, just days after the depressing news from Buna, allowed for such an interpretation. It was a citation for an American commander who had "distinguished himself conspicuously by gallantry and intrepidity at the risk of his life above and beyond the call of duty, in action against Japanese forces on the Bataan peninsula and on Corregidor." The citation credited the man for having "frequently visited the extreme forward elements of the troops under enemy fire and on several occasions joined the firing line with a rifle and engaged in fire action" and for providing an example that "was responsible for a high state of morale in the American forces under extremely trying and adverse conditions." Witness statements accompanying the citation testified to how the individual "utterly disregarded his own safety on all occasions" and defied aides trying "to dissuade him from taking the personal risk involved." For all these reasons, the Medal of Honor would go to Lieutenant General Jonathan Mayhew Wainwright, that is, if his former commander agreed. Almost in a pro forma way, as if expecting no objections from a man who had recently received the same medal himself on questionable grounds, George Marshall forwarded the draft citation to MacArthur for "remarks."

MacArthur, as it turned out, had some remarks. He began his response the next day by reminding that he had already given Wainwright the Distinguished Service Cross for his leadership during the retreat from Lingayen. Those actions, however, "fell far short" of the Medal of Honor, MacArthur wrote. "Award of the Medal of Honor to General Wainwright would be a grave injustice to a number of other general officers . . . who not only distinguished themselves by fully as great personal gallantry . . . but who exhibited powers of leadership and inspiration to a degree greatly superior to that of General Wainwright thereby contributing much more than he to the stability of the command." At stake was more than the feelings of these others officers, MacArthur wrote. Awarding the medal to Wainwright would damage Wainwright's record by necessitating the disclosure of "adverse observations" about him. MacArthur said he preferred to keep these facts to himself so as to avoid "embarrassing repercussions." But if Marshall persisted in pursuing the medal for Wainwright, there would be no choice but to put them in writing.

Without saying what these "observations" were, MacArthur now claimed they were what had necessitated dividing the Philippines into four separate commands in the first place. Gone was the explanation about "special problems . . . with the intangibles of the situation in the Philippine Islands." Only the inadequacy of Wainwright remained.

In fairness, the evidence suggests that MacArthur always shared the off-the-record assessment Sutherland later offered of Wainwright as "strategically and tactically . . . not too good." Sutherland, for one, would never forgive Wainwright for the gap separating the two corps on Bataan's first defensive line. But if MacArthur had harbored such strong concerns when he left the Philippines, how had he rationalized expanding Wainwright's command to all forces on Bataan even if not to all forces in the islands? Something had changed. Perhaps it had happened when Marshall forwarded the message from Wainwright predicting that Bataan would be "starved into submission" within weeks (MacArthur had responded that the "rigor" in rationing food might have "relaxed" in his absence). Perhaps the change had happened when Wainwright's prediction on Bataan had come to pass despite Mac-Arthur's orders forbidding surrender. Certainly, it had happened by the time MacArthur learned of Wainwright's broadcast ordering the surrender of all forces in the Philippines.

For MacArthur, the Medal of Honor conjured the image of his father raising the flag under fire. To have the award go to a man who had ordered the colors struck in the Philippines of all places would have struck at what had become Douglas's birthright. To defend the medal, he would destroy a man. He had already laid the foundation by describing Wainwright as sounding "unbalanced" on the radio broad-cast. From that word could rise the charge that Wainwright had let his drinking undermine his judgment. Almost surely, that was what MacArthur meant when he hinted at revelations that would embarrass Wainwright and the army alike.

On the other side of the world, Marshall could feel the fury in MacArthur's words. The threat to Wainwright's reputation as well as the army's stunned the chief of staff. His deputy questioned "General MacArthur's motives." Secretary of War Stimson did, too. He encour-aged Marshall to call MacArthur's bluff. "If the papers showed that Wainwright deserved it, as Marshall thought they would," Stimson wrote, "I favored giving it to him regardless of MacArthur's objection."

Marshall would have done so had he not had a war to win and an army whose prestige he could not afford to squander through what he was warned would lead to a "public airing of the case." A decision on the medal would have to wait until the end of the war. And so would solace for the general doomed to be the war's highest-ranking American prisoner.

CHAPTER NINE

Honor of Another Kind

They had feared the coming of the rainy season on Bataan, and now it found them midway up Luzon's central plain, in the town of Tarlac. They had dreamed of taking showers on Corregidor, and now they struggled to keep their bunks dry. They had cursed the dust blinding their eyes, and now they saw mud and mildew everywhere. They had lain awake through bombardments, and now they tried to sleep through thunder. When the clouds cleared between the storms, they could see Mount Arayat rising to the south beside their old home, Fort Stotsenburg, a few dozen miles to the south. They had surrounded their barracks there with parade and polo grounds. Now a few hundred yards of barbed wire did the job. The Japanese needed no more to hold 179 of their most prized prisoners—American generals, colonels, and their aides and orderlies—in a two-story barracks built to hold half as many Philippine Army trainees. Everyone talked of escape. The Japanese must have known. They divided the prisoners into groups of ten and explained that if any man disappeared, the other nine members of his group would die for his disobedience. So would the camp's senior American officer, the lieutenant general who somehow managed to keep a sense of humor after hearing the news. "If anyone contemplates taking off," Wainwright quipped, "please let me know so I can go too."

His men could see he would not have made it far. "He was in very bad shape," one remembered. His health looked impaired, his limp more pronounced, his spirit depressed. There was nowhere for him to go but backward in his own mind. The Japanese had forced Wainwright to relive his piece of the war many times over: in the interrogation sessions they subjected him to about what he had done with Philippine banknotes and silver; in the hours they forced him to pose for a painting of the failed May 6 negotiation on the porch of the bungalow; in the way they made him partly retrace the route of his initial retreat to Bataan. On May 7, the day after his surrender, they had taken him back across the channel from Corregidor to the peninsula. "We drove up through Bataan, with all its shadowy memories, rounded the bay by way of San Fernando Pampanga and Calumpit, where we had fought for the very right to reach Bataan, and arrived in Manila in about four hours," Wainwright remembered. He had not wanted to read the surrender message on the radio that night, but the Japanese had insisted and rushed him over to KZRH. That part of the city had once reminded him of Times Square but no longer. The neon lights had gone out, and the crowds of theatergoers, diners, and shoppers had disappeared. "Now there was nothing. No one was astir. Only an occasional Jap Army vehicle or a furtive pony cart used the once bustling streets," he wrote. "Manila was dead."

For weeks after the broadcast, the Japanese had confined the general and his staff to rooms at the University Club, where he had often socialized before the war. His captors made certain he would regard himself not as a guest—not even as a prisoner of war—but as a hostage until the messengers he had sent to distant parts of the Philippines completed their missions and secured the surrender of all forces on the islands. For all he had known, even one captain insisting on holding out could have done in thousands of lives. Wainwright's staff member Major Lawrence had already lost his to pneumonia after the Japanese had all but denied him basic medical care at the club. Not long after, Wainwright had looked out his second-floor window and seen the

Japanese parading thousands of prisoners up a boulevard still bearing the name of Dewey, the great American admiral, and then around the Luneta, which his countrymen had remade in the image of their own National Mall. At first, Wainwright could not recognize the beaten-down men passing beneath him. Then he did. "They were the men of Corregidor," he realized, "being marched through the streets in their wretched condition to prove to the silent thousands of natives lining the street that the Jap conquerors were superior in every way."

By this time, Wainwright had heard about a larger march the Japanese had staged. His artillerymen on Corregidor had spied the beginnings of it in the hours after General King's surrender on Bataan. General Homma had needed to shepherd the American and Filipino forces off the peninsula as quickly as possible so he could make room for his own forces—the ones he would need to undertake operations against Corregidor. But instead of the forty or even fifty thousand American and Filipino soldiers he had expected to find on Bataan, he had found himself with about eighty thousand starving prisoners in no condition to go anywhere on foot. How to transport them to prison at Camp O'Donnell, the former Philippine Army training camp not far from Tarlac on Luzon's central plain, had posed a problem that Homma had left to his subordinates. They had solved it through what would become known as the Bataan Death March.

Up the east side of Bataan, the prisoners had come in jumbled columns, a few men abreast. The fighting had turned what was not a bad road before into a terrible one. Dust was everywhere, shelter from the sun seemingly nowhere. If the prisoners needed water—and they all desperately did—they would have to drink from roadside ditches filled with animal waste and the bloated bodies of men beaten for having made the mistake of asking to fill their canteens from the nearby wells or walking too close to the vehicles driving the opposite way full of Japanese soldiers swinging poles and rifles. In many cases, the bodies in the ditches belonged to men who simply did not have the strength or will to carry on to the next stop ten miles northward and sometimes twice that far. The Japanese promised food ahead but never had enough. Alongside the road gathered Filipino civilians risking their lives to deliver food to family members and perfect strangers in the ranks of the sun-burned, blistered bodies. The Japanese rewarded the prisoners who made it the sixty-six miles to the highway junction of San Fernando by stuffing them into train cars that would carry them most of the rest of the way to O'Donnell. Crammed in so tight as to give deadly meaning to the term "standing room only," men with dysentery relieved themselves where they stood. Some breathed in the smell. Others could not breathe at all.

Hundreds of the American marchers—and thousands of the Filipino ones, who had always made up the bulk of the army on Bataan—never reached O'Donnell. Those who did discovered what Wainwright had when he had visited Philippine Army camps shortly before Pearl Harbor: conditions were "filthy" and "poor" and made worse at O'Donnell by there being only a few water spigots for the tens of thousands of troops pouring in. According to reports reaching Wainwright at the University Club, deaths at the camp had reached three hundred a day. In desperation, he had written a plea to General Homma: If the Japanese did not have sufficient supplies for the camp, perhaps they would allow the United States or the Red Cross to send a ship through the blockade with emergency provisions. No real response to the proposal came, only more anxious days of waiting for the Japanese to accept his surrender.

Not until June 9, 1942, did the Japanese give Wainwright a handwritten note, which one of them translated as such: "Your high command is hereby terminated for yourself and the members of your staff, and you now become prisoners of war. You and the members of your staff will be moved to the prisoner of war enclosure at Tarlac at 10 A.M. today." Off they went in a truck, up the ruins of Luzon's central plain to Tarlac for a reunion with General Ned King and the other senior officers who had surrendered on Bataan and passed through Camp O'Donnell.

The fare prepared at Tarlac by boiling a mysterious two-inch fish (head included) in a kettle and pouring the resulting soup over rice seemed not bad by comparison to the pebbles and insects served with the rice at O'Donnell, but Wainwright could not stomach it. At all times of night, friends would have to help him down the stairs, out of the barracks, into the rain, and to the outhouse clogged with diarrhea because the Japanese had shut off the pipes to the toilets.

As the days in his diary passed—he had managed to retain the book he had begun on April 2—his thoughts turned more and more to the past. Over and over again, he read his previous entries, as if searching for how they had led him here. His aides tried to cheer him on July 31 by celebrating the fortieth anniversary of his entrance into the army but could not lift his spirits. He could not have imagined that a letter recommending him for the Medal of Honor had made its way to Australia that very day. Had he, he might have guessed in the more paranoid regions of his mind what MacArthur would write back. Wainwright had begun preparing for it. In his diary, he started drafting an explanation for his actions, as he put it, "while all facts are still fresh in my memory." On August 1, the day MacArthur sent his response to Marshall, Wainwright noted a conversation with a fellow prisoner about how unprepared they had found the conscripts MacArthur had supposedly trained before the war. "The Philippine Army was doomed before it started to fight," Wainwright wrote. Of special interest to him was evidence that MacArthur himself had recognized this reality. Lew Beebe recalled hearing MacArthur describe Bataan as "doomed" as early as January when he had ordered some of the peninsula's food reserves shipped to Corregidor.

Wainwright resisted the urge to take these facts to their logical conclusion. But other officers made it for themselves. "A foul trick of deception has been played on a large group of Americans by a commander in chief and small staff who are now eating steak and eggs in Australia," wrote one prisoner. "God damn them!" If MacArthur played the villain in the story that the prisoners told themselves, they needed him to play the savior, too. The question of when he would fulfill his vow to redeem the Philippines was never far from thoughts at Tarlac.

If he performed as poorly as he had during the opening months of the war, it might be a long time, one officer reckoned. The absence of any sign of an advance from Australia added to the despair.

Then, on August 11, came the first sign of hope. MacArthur's soldiers had not gone anywhere as far as Wainwright had heard, but someone slipped him the news that the navy had landed marines at Guadalcanal in the Solomons. It was a long way from the Philippines, but it was the right direction. MacArthur, Wainwright estimated, might return to the Philippines as early as the end of 1943. But he himself, Wainwright now knew, would not be there. That very day, the Japanese brought the prisoners at Tarlac back to Manila and loaded them on a ship for Formosa. A Japanese officer assured Wainwright he would find Taiwan, as the island was also known, "a very beautiful place." The officer then paused, looked at Wainwright with a smile that would haunt his memory months later, and added, "Yes, you'll like."

*   *   *

There had been clues during the Battle of Bataan as to what lay ahead. Given the choice between surrender and mass death, the Japanese trapped in the cave at Quinauan Point had astonished Wainwright by choosing the latter. It was not just a preference. It was Japanese army policy and said to be a part of a Samurai code known as Bushido, which the Japanese translated for westerners as the "way of the warrior." Schools and popular authors instilled the creed in every Japanese male when young. He grew up knowing his parents would prefer to receive his ashes from the battlefield than a letter from him in a prison camp. In surrendering, he would disgrace not only himself but also his family. If he returned home alive from the experience, he could expect, at best, a life of ostracism. If an officer, however, he could expect no life at all. In this case, Japanese society offered only one recourse—the choice that many of the prison guards Wainwright would meet believed he should have taken—suicide.

That is not to say Wainwright's decision surprised the Japanese. To the contrary, they had expected he would surrender far sooner than he had. They understood that surrender was part of the western way of war. In their eagerness to impress western powers in the late nineteenth and early twentieth centuries, the Japanese had carefully upheld international agreements for the treatment of prisoners, as Arthur MacArthur and other observers had been able to attest during the Russo-Japanese War. By 1929, however, attitudes in Japan had changed. Although Japanese representatives signed a new Geneva Convention that year, their leaders back home refused to ratify it. A country whose soldiers never surrendered had nothing to gain from the protections. Nonetheless, Japan assured the world after Pearl Harbor that it would follow the spirit of the agreement, which required each warring power to treat prisoners consistent with how it would treat its own soldiers of equivalent rank. An American enlisted man who had seen how little the Japanese valued the lives of their own soldiers could take little comfort from this. Nor could an American general aware of what the Japanese expected from their own officers.

The way the Japanese loaded the prison ship for Formosa made the point. The Americans had to stand and wait at the pier for hours. Only after the Japanese had loaded the ashes of their honored dead could the prisoners come aboard. The ship ventured out of Manila Bay, past the little island Wainwright had surrendered in its mouth, up along the jungle-clad western coast of the peninsula he had defended, and across the strait the Japanese bombers had crossed in the hours after Pearl Harbor en route to Clark Field. Into view on August 14 came the southwestern coast of Formosa, which the Japanese had forced China to relinquish a half century before. Worried what diseases Americans might introduce, the Japanese subjected the prisoners to a thorough medical exam, much of which, Wainwright noted, "centered about the rectum." Only after passing it did the prisoners have the privilege of transferring into the suffocating bedbug-infested cargo hold of the small steamer that would take them around the bottom of the island and partway up its east coast to a town called Karenko. On August 17, they filed off the boat to find the locals assembled on the street for yet another Japanese prisoner parade. The faces staring at the Americans as they marched made them feel, Wainwright wrote, "as if we were freaks."

Around three o'clock, the parade passed through a gate into a yard tucked into a river bend and surrounded on every side by 150 yards of barbed wire. The Japanese led the prisoners toward a two-story barracks topped with dark tiles and lined with porches. The back porch opened into a washing area; the front opened out onto a parade ground full of grass. Trees and shrubs lined the gravel paths traversing the yard and leading up a set of terraced stairs to the prison headquarters. Beyond the barbed wire to the east was the ocean and to the west a vista alternating between purplish valleys and iridescent mountains with their peaks touching the clouds. On the other side of the river, the prisoners could hear the sounds of children attending school. The smiling Japanese officer in Manila had been half right. Karenko was charming. But Wainwright immediately knew he would hate it.

Once inside the yard, the Japanese assembled the Americans on the parade ground, ordered them to drop their baggage, and bow. By the rules of the camp, even the highest-ranking American officer had to salute the lowest-ranking Japanese private. The colonel in charge of all prisons on Formosa was there to welcome the Americans and instantly became known to them as "Old Sourpuss" because of his manifest impatience as they struggled to learn the proper way to bow, first to him, and then to the elderly captain in charge of Karenko. Able to speak only Japanese, the captain launched into a speech about how Nippon, as the Japanese called their country, had cleared the seas and skies of American ships and planes and left American soldiers without hope of victory. "It is entirely the gracious gift of His Majesty the Emperor that you have crossed over the death line, being assured of the safety of your life, and can enjoy peaceful living. . . . Anyone who does not observe the Nippon military discipline shall be severely punished, and the life of such prisoner shall NOT be always assured. . . . The Americans and the English are not allowed to hold the haughty attitude over the peoples of Asia or to look them down which has been their common custom for a long time. If there is any such attitude at all on your part, you shall be severely punished." When the captain finished, few of the Americans had understood a word but had received one message nonetheless: They could not rely on English. They would need to learn Nipponese. The interpreter translating the speech struggled to do so as if intimidated by his own officers. The Americans would nickname him "Mickey Mouse."

There was nothing comical about what followed. The Japanese made the Americans strip to their underpants and lay out their clothes and baggage at their feet. "We stood there like human scarecrows," Wainwright remembered, as guards combed through toiletries and unwound rolls of toilet paper as if perpetually certain that the next sheet would be the one containing a secret file. After what seemed like hours under the scorching sun, the Americans received back their clothes save for their shoes. The guards handed out Japanese-style clogs to the prisoners but then started screaming at them when they failed to take off these wooden sandals upon entering the barracks. The Japanese did not allow clogs inside.

Wainwright found he had a room with Ned King at the end of the first floor. Each of them had a metal-framed bed with a straw mattress, a few blankets, and a sack of rice the Japanese called a pillow. At six foot two, Wainwright had to bend his own frame to fit the bed's but could not complain much. In other rooms, lower-ranking general officers and colonels found their bunks pushed so close together that the only way in and out of them was over the foot of the frame.

The days began at six in the morning. The prisoners would put on their old uniforms, now bearing a badge displaying their name in Japanese characters as well as a prison number, and then assemble outside on the parade ground for roll call. The Japanese split the prisoners into squads of twenty and named Wainwright chief of one made up mostly of his fellow generals. He had learned as first captain at West Point how to bring men to attention by yelling, "Ten-shone." Now the Japanese insisted he learn their way: "*kiotsuke*" for attention, "*tenko*" for roll call, and "*bango*" for count off. His men would have to respond with "*ichi*" for one, "*ni*" for two, and so on. Wainwright made a glossary, which he tried to memorize, but his hearing problems made it hard to identify foreign words. Concerned the Japanese would punish his men for his mistakes, he soon ceded the title of squad leader to King. At the end of roll call, the prisoners had to bow even lower than normal to a white post positioned, it was explained, so as to point the way toward the emperor in Japan. Until the prisoners mastered this bow, they had to practice it over and over. Even when they got it right, they knew they would have to do it again at eight in the evening. Roll call happened twice a day.

Between the first and second roll calls, the Americans had three meals at regular intervals in their cramped rooms. If that sounded better than the two meals Wainwright had on Bataan, he learned otherwise when the bearers sent to the kitchen returned with a bucket of rice and a bucket of vegetable soup, which the prisoners universally described as "watery." The fare was almost always the same for breakfast, lunch, and dinner, and it was never enough. When split among the members of a squad, the soup filled two thirds of a bowl and the rice not even a tea cup. "We were as hungry after finishing it as when we began," Wainwright wrote. "We took to counting the two or three beans which sometimes appeared in the bottom of our soup pail, and if a man received a bean in his soup, and another did not, it made for hard feeling."

The only regular protein came either from the bean paste known as miso served occasionally with breakfast or the weevils and worms always available in the rice. Early on, Wainwright would look for the bugs so he could remove them. Within weeks, he began looking for them so he could eat them. Neither was easy for Americans to do with chopsticks. The prisoners resorted to using their hands for one activity: scrounging for snails in the yard. "The snails which did show themselves were far removed from the escargot which French chefs can prepare so tastefully," Wainwright wrote, "but those who found them considered themselves lucky and hobbled quickly over to the kitchen to boil them in hot water and wolf them."

Having survived Bataan and Corregidor, a general nicknamed Skinny could have assumed he had no more weight to lose. But Karenko showed him otherwise. In his diary, which he continued to keep, he started recording his weight. On August 29, twelve days after arriving, it stood at 136.4 pounds. By September 15, it had fallen to 134.2 pounds. By September 26, 132 pounds. The Geneva Conventions guaranteed that prisoners would receive the same calories as their captors. But anyone looking at the fare the guards ate could see that the "systematic starvation," as Wainwright called it, was a one-way affair.

If there was one area where the Americans did not wish for the treatment the Japanese gave their own soldiers, it was discipline. Frequently slapped, Japanese soldiers did not hesitate to hand out the same—and much worse—to westerners who had no idea how to respond. The translator whom the prisoners called Mickey Mouse laughingly advised them to take a page from their Bible and "turn the other cheek." But hunger made it hard for the prisoners to bite their tongues. At one point, an American colonel who had taught at an army quartermaster school in Chicago could not take it any longer and decided to bring the Japanese a suggestion for reducing the food imbalance. For his bravery, he received a beating. Still convinced that he could find a sympathetic Japanese officer, he tried again to make his case and received two more beatings.

The Japanese offered the prisoners one way to increase their food. They could work for more. The Geneva Conventions, Wainwright knew, forbade captors from forcing officers like himself to work. The captain in charge of Karenko let it be known that he expected everyone to work nonetheless. The Japanese had mobilized their entire society for war, he had explained in his welcoming speech. "Everyone in the country is willing to endure all sorts of hardships and fighting for the final victory in the war. You must understand that it is nothing but natural that you are not allowed to lead an idle life." To keep up appearances, the Japanese presented Wainwright with what he deemed a "wily way" around the Geneva Conventions. His fellow officers would have the opportunity to work on a prison farm. If they took it, their food would improve. If they refused, well, they would see. The Japanese called the farm program "volunteer." Wainwright called it coercion and refused.

As it stood, the prisoners could not have accomplished much in the fields, anyway. They managed ten minutes of calisthenics in the morning but had energy for little else. Their swollen ankles presaged the return of beriberi, the vitamin deficiency they had come to know on Bataan. Wainwright developed the dry kind, which resulted in less swelling but a slapping sound every time he took a step. He had lost the muscle control needed to stop his toes from swinging down like a mouse trap the moment his heel touched the ground. The wooden clogs, which were many sizes too small, added to the discomfort. Nevertheless, camp rules required the Americans to stay on their feet. Except for a short siesta after lunch, the prisoners could not be in bed during the day. They would pass the time walking the gravel paths, reading what books they had, playing cards, and talking. Conversation often turned to what the men would eat once back in the United States. "As soon as I get to San Francisco, I am going to order a sirloin steak an inch thick with all the trimmings and wind up with apple pie a la mode," they would say to one another before turning back to the question never far from their thoughts: When would they go home?

The only clues came either from the guards or from the Japanese English-language newspapers that occasionally arrived at the camp. Skimming through the articles could give some idea of events in the Atlantic, where American and British troops under the command of MacArthur's old chief of staff, Eisenhower, would soon open a second front in North Africa, but almost no sense of events in the Pacific, where, the *Japan Times Advertiser* claimed, Japanese soldiers might soon achieve a "foothold" on the west coast of the United States from which they could march on Washington. Younger officers looked to Wainwright for their cues. When a conversation with him turned pessimistic or optimistic, their spirits would do the same.

On Sundays, the Japanese would let the prisoners hold church services. Catholics met inside, Protestants outside under the trees. As the great-grandson of an Episcopal bishop, Wainwright would go to the latter. The men had some Episcopal prayer books but no chaplain to lead them, only volunteers. In the midst of prayers for family members and loved ones, they would sometimes weep. Despite having sung in an Episcopal choir as a boy, Wainwright did not join the one that some of the men formed, but he did encourage those closest to him to do so. Music, he believed, served as a source of solace.

So did writing. "Karenko was beginning to be a place that prompted a man to look to the job of summing up, of trying to leave some record of how he felt and what he had done," Wainwright wrote. Not until mid-October did the Japanese allow him to write to his wife—and then only once with no prospect of doing so again. They urged the prisoners to focus instead on writing their wills. The Americans found other outlets for expression—diaries, imaginary dinner menus, cookbooks, and even novels—with the caution that the Japanese might seize these papers without any notice. The prisoners also drafted citations for awards they were in no position to present but hoped fellow soldiers would one day receive for acts of heroism on Bataan. Worried the real story of the campaign there would go untold if he did not survive, Wainwright made copies of his thoughts for a few fellow prisoners. "These were merely written to give expression to my thoughts and were meant as an accusation to no one, least of all General MacArthur," he wrote in his diary on September 24.

Three days later, Wainwright added several more pages to the dozens he had already written in his diary about the fall of Corregidor. "I will probably be asked why I surrendered Corregidor without a 'last ditch' stand," he began. What would the history books have written about him, he wondered, if he had fought to the last man as had happened at the Alamo or Little Bighorn? The eulogies, he reasoned, would have declared his troops "brave men" but him "a fool or perhaps a criminal for sacrificing all my troops without any possible chance of good coming from so doing." In the memoir he would write after the war, he would claim he resolved to write this entry after a conversation with a visiting Japanese news reporter who asked whether Wainwright expected to be court-martialed if he made it back home.

"Court-martialed?" Wainwright asked. "Why?"

"For surrendering," the reporter supposedly responded.

That possibility, Wainwright would claim, would haunt him in the months ahead, and no doubt it did. But there is reason to doubt the impetus for the diary entry being a conversation with a Japanese newsman because something far more poignant happened that night. It was the first time Wainwright saw some of the Americans who had surrendered on his orders in distant parts of the Philippines despite MacArthur's insistence they fight on as guerrillas. After a long journey, William Sharp, Bradford Chynoweth, and two other American generals, as well as twenty colonels and sixteen enlisted men, arrived at Karenko. Upon seeing them, Wainwright apologized with an expression that Chynoweth would remember as "utter abjection."

In addition to the Americans from the Visayas and Mindanao, Karenko began receiving high-ranking British prisoners, including Lieutenant General Arthur Percival, who had surrendered Singapore to the Japanese. Dutch and Australian officers came, too, in violation of an article of the 1929 Geneva Convention against mixing different nationalities in prison camps. The new arrivals made the barracks even tighter and the rations even slimmer.

At the end of September, Wainwright and Percival, as the two highest-ranking prisoners, asked to deliver a joint letter of complaint to the head of the prison. But the old captain refused to speak with them. Instead, they received a meeting with his second-in-command, a burly lieutenant the prisoners called "Boots" because of his odd choice in footwear. Boots, Wainwright recorded, "shouted that we would not see the camp commander and that if we ever wrote another such letter of protest, he would personally see to it that we were severely dealt with."

A change seemed to come over Wainwright afterward. He did not even protest when a guard stole something from his room. It would give the Japanese an excuse for another beating, someone heard him say. "What a leader to protect our interests!" wrote Paul Bunker, the old colonel who had sewn the scrap of red from the Corregidor flag into his shirt. In his diary, Bunker wrote that Wainwright had "folded up and quit," and even wondered if he had grown scared of being slapped. That, as the days ahead would show, was not true. But it was true that Wainwright was no longer the man he had been. The transformation that had begun on Bataan had reached its conclusion. At the war's start, he had presumed "that the Jap fighter was a human being much like the rest of us." But never again would he think so. There was no humanity he could see in the Japanese. There was no mercy he could expect from them. And if he did not accept their proposal to work on a farm, there would be no hope for more food.

Most of his fellow prisoners had come around on the idea long before, and so finally did he. "We decided that it was either work or death by starvation," Wainwright wrote. "But the Jap mind is a baffling nest, and going to work was not as easy as expressing the willingness. We had to appeal to them to permit us to work, to make it appear that we were breaking down their lofty resolve to uphold the Geneva Convention." On October 26, 1942, the Japanese allowed him and the other prisoners to go to work on a little land on the other side of the prison gate. "Slowly and painfully," he wrote, "we did clear our first patch of ground and prepared it for the planting of various seeds." It was exhausting work, and the extra calories the prisoners received in exchange did not seem to compensate for the ones expended. The older officers struggled just to walk across the field in their clogs, let alone wield the long and heavy dull blade provided for breaking the soil. "I came to depend more and more on the light walking stick which MacArthur had left for me on Corregidor when he departed," Wainwright remembered.

A few days after work began on the farm, the Japanese gave Wainwright a break—not because they thought he needed one but because they had somewhere else for him to be: a tea in town with the mayor of Karenko. The cameramen also in attendance took pictures they could share with the world for propaganda. "What lying evidence!" Bunker wrote in his diary. "All evidently to show how well American prisoners are treated and the great privileges accorded them!" As if on cue, the *Japan Times Advertiser* topped its front-page with a picture of a handwritten letter thanking a Japanese general for cigarettes and pork. The signature read, "J. M. Wainwright."

Only by seeing Wainwright and his fellow prisoners at bath time— only by smelling them, for they went with almost no soap and with never enough toilet paper—could their countrymen in the United States have known the reality. In his memoirs written years later, Wainwright would provide one of the most vivid descriptions.

> *Our weekly baths in the common bathing tank were shocking spectacles, for only the mass nakedness of our men brought home to each one of us our terrible state. Our labors had used up the inner muscles of our buttocks. The skin of our buttocks just hung down the backs of our skeletonized legs like deep pockets. But we were beyond all mortification over our appearance. There was nothing in our minds except food.*

The boniness made Wainwright's legs appear even more bowed. They looked, a fellow prisoner said, "like a pair of badly warped pieces of bamboo." Colonel Bunker would die of malnutrition within months, and Wainwright did not look far behind. By December 12, his weight had fallen to 125 pounds, his waist size to 27 inches. A fever kept him in bed that day and for days after. With no fat on his body and no heat in his room, he needed every blanket and every article of clothing he could muster as the temperature fell below fifty degrees.

In 1941, Wainwright had spent Christmas on the run. In 1942, he spent it unable to go anywhere. In the spirit of the holiday, the Japanese let the prisoners decorate their barracks with some foliage and added some pork and duck to their soup. "I had about four pieces of pork the size of my thumbnail," Beebe noted, and, for this, Wainwright's chief of staff was grateful. Wainwright received no less and no more; he and the other officers had appointed a fellow general they trusted to dole out the meat equally. For the sake of one another, they resolved to try to make the best of the holiday. Wainwright forced himself from his bed for some of the day, but he was back in it when the Japanese allowed the prisoners' choir to go caroling from cell to cell. When the members reached his, he could hear them singing one of his favorites, "Hark! The Herald Angels Sing." But he would not let them see him crying behind the door, with his head in his hands.

The year ended with some of the most depressing news yet. It came courtesy of several prisoners who arrived at Karenko from the Philippines in late December. A new camp in the town of Cabanatuan had replaced Camp O'Donnell as the chief prison on Luzon. According to the numbers shared with Wainwright, about 25 percent of Americans who had spent time at either place had not lived to see the end of 1942.

There was little reason to suppose 1943 would prove any better. Even seemingly good news had a way of turning bad. An order exempting older officers from farming in January should have saved Wainwright from the indignity of slave labor. But the arrival of some goats at the camp soon after created an opening for a new job, and the Japanese assigned the old cavalryman to herding. In response to a series of articles in the *Nippon Times*, as the *Japan Times Advertiser* now called itself, guards at Karenko had begun to talk more about prisoner rights. But the talk did not have the effect that the prisoners at Karenko might have hoped, because the newspaper coverage did not concern their treatment but rather the treatment of internees in the United States. Franklin Roosevelt had signed an order allowing the military to relocate and intern Japanese immigrants and their children living on the west coast. The evidence suggests their plight probably would not have concerned Wainwright had not their treatment, as he discovered, enraged his captors.

On February 26 came a summons for a meeting with Boots. After bowing, Wainwright listened with several other high-ranking prisoners as the Japanese lieutenant made a rare concession. There had been times when guards could have disciplined prisoners without striking them. But, Boots continued, if the treatment of prisoners in American and British camps did not improve, punishments would grow even harsher in Japanese camps. "It is but natural that sentries learn from the news of cruel treatment of our Nipponese internees and lose their kind hearts," Boots said. Then he gave the prisoners assembled before him a choice: either agree to draft letters calling on their governments to live up to their ideals or prepare to face, as he put it, "consequences."

What sort of consequences became obvious before bedtime when Wainwright went out back to the latrines. Knowing it was the place no prisoner could avoid going, the Japanese made it the place where they posted their most sadistic guards. It was sometimes hard to see them standing there in the dark. One night Wainwright had failed to bow to them as a result, and they had punished him by demanding he do what no bowlegged person could: click his feet and knees together at the same time. When his feet went in, his knees went out, and vice versa. The guards had made a game of it by putting their hands on his limbs and playing with them, a witness recorded, "as a child would play with a jack in the box."

On the night of February 26, Wainwright did see the Japanese private on duty and bowed, as the rules required. This time, it did no good. The private yelled something Wainwright could not understand and then slapped him on the cheek and yelled something he could understand, "Japanese in America." Wainwright's face stung. "In my throat," he remembered, "I felt a rising gorge of hate and despair." He wanted to hit back, as he believed any real American would, but knew doing so here at this moment would mean death. So he stood and did nothing. Four times the private slapped Wainwright. Four times the private repeated the phrase about Japanese in America. "The blows made my legs weaker but I was determined not to fall at the feet of a rat like that," Wainwright wrote. "He saw that I was not going down, so he took a lunge at me and hit me on the left jaw with his fist. And then I fell. I was only half conscious from the blow, but the part of my consciousness that was alive told me that this was the very pit of my life." He had risen from a plebe at West Point to a lieutenant general in command of all forces in the Philippines—and now he lay at the feet of a Japanese private. "A private should never strike a lieutenant general"—that was all he could think.

Wainwright shook in bed through the night and could not stop the next morning even as he turned to dusting the shelf where his bowls sat. Suddenly, a guard carrying a rifle with a bayonet barged into the room. "In my nervousness," Wainwright remembered, "I accidentally knocked one of the bowls off the shelf." He watched it shatter, as if in slow motion, and then felt a bayonet go into his left wrist and a fist pound his face over and over for what felt like an eternity. Only after the guard had tired himself out did he let Wainwright fall to his knees and gather the shards. Before allowing him to go to the hospital, the guard demanded Wainwright go to the guardhouse and report his offense. The blood dripping from his wrist left a trail through the barracks for other prisoners to see as proof that their general had shared in the beatings that they had so often experienced and never more so than over the past twenty-four hours, which all would remember as the worst period of their captivity. "The heat," as they called it, "was on." It would not go off unless Wainwright sent the letter the Japanese had demanded. After receiving a bandage, he decided to do so. People back home, he hoped, would recognize he had no choice.

The next day brought the most unexpected news: a short radio message from his wife. It was the first word Wainwright had received from Adele since his surrender. She said she had written letters. But he had received none from her. He had not seen her handwriting since the letter she had sent on November 17, 1941, weeks before Pearl Harbor. Before surrendering on Corregidor, he had received word via radio of her plan to move with her mother from Monterey, California, to the town of Skaneateles in upstate New York, where she had lived for a time as a child. He would often allow himself to dream of being there with her. His imagination would turn the early mornings into the evenings and the evenings into the early mornings so as to adjust for the time difference, and there he would find her walking their dog. He longed to know how she was. He longed to see her for real. "There are many forms of torture," he would write afterward, "but isolation of this kind is not the least of these varied cruelties."

*   *   *

As the wife of America's highest-ranking prisoner of war, Adele Wainwright found herself a prisoner of another kind. There were places she had to be. There was a ceremony in Hartford, Connecticut, where she had to accept the thanks of the state assembly on behalf of her husband in a voice that newspapers described as "choked with emotion." Manuel Quezon, the ailing president of the Philippines, had come, too, so he could remind the people of America that they owed his people and Adele's husband their day of liberation. There was an event in Baltimore, where she christened the cargo ship on which her son, Jack, would serve as master and sail into the war across the Atlantic. There was an award to accept in New York on behalf of her husband, who had won his second Distinguished Service Medal. At the request of the War Department, MacArthur relayed some words of his own for the occasion. "Please tell Mrs. Wainwright of my sincere hope that before too long elapses I may have her husband back on active service again under my command."

As far as is known, MacArthur never wrote to Adele directly. So George Marshall, while managing a war spanning two oceans and generals with personalities that seemed as large, made it his duty to do so. "You have been in my thoughts pretty constantly for a long time, and I have wanted to write to you," Marshall wrote. "There must be a great deal of consolation to you at this time in the knowledge that he [your husband] has made for himself a great place in history." Marshall sent Adele what information he could about her husband and made a point of keeping tabs on her son's travels at sea. Very few made it to a first-name basis with Marshall. Adele did. He called her "my dear Adele." She called him "my dear George" and confided her struggles. "Each day of my life seems worse than the last as I look into the future," she wrote.

When the news about Bataan falling in April 1942 had arrived, she had still been in Monterey. The newspapers described her as "exhausted" and "under heavy strain." She had her mother put out a statement saying, "There is a limit to human endurance." Adele was close to hers. When the news of Corregidor's fall followed the next month, reporters described her as being in "a highly nervous state." By then, she had moved with her mother to Skaneateles. "Difficult as your situation is, I am confident that you can keep your chin up for that is just what Wainwright would want you to do," Marshall wrote. She tried to occupy herself. She worked shifts as an airplane spotter. But rumors about her husband always found her. They popped up from time to time in newspapers picking up reports from the Japanese press. On the eve of the one-year anniversary of Pearl Harbor, Adele finally received the first direct word from her husband. The Japanese had allowed him to broadcast a short radio message. Marshall confirmed its authenticity. "Am well and cared for," Wainwright said. He said he had written to her and told her to try sending him a letter. She had. Evidently, none had made it through.

Adele had planned to take part in events commemorating the one-year anniversary of the fall of Bataan. But when the day came, she had a bad cold and could go nowhere. Instead, she called in for a radio interview for which she could barely speak. "The pauses between words were long, with the tedium of prodigious effort," a newspaper correspondent wrote. But she seemed insistent on trying, as if hoping her words might somehow make it to her husband.

Not until later that spring did Adele receive her husband's letter dated October 13, 1942. "Each day that goes by, darling, makes it one day nearer the time when I can get home to you and I am sure that I am going to get home some time," he wrote. "This can't last forever." There were, he wrote, "a lot of personal things" he wanted to share but dared not write, he explained, "as someone else must of course read this." By someone else, she knew what he meant. For the sake of the Japanese censors, no doubt, he described himself as "comfortably housed" and "quite well fed." For Adele's sake, however, he snuck in a detail that suggested otherwise. "About the size and weight I was when we were married," he wrote. The image of how thin he had been back then came to her immediately. And so did a sense of how much weight he had lost.

Adele could tell that her husband had changed in other ways. The Japanese believed society had no place for those who surrendered, and he seemed as if he expected his own countrymen to ostracize him the same way if he returned home. Apparently, he had no idea that Americans had named a shipyard and streets after him and hailed him as a hero. If he returned home, he said, he could not imagine living in Washington, where he believed himself reviled. "I don't think I will want much in the way of society," he wrote. "Perhaps the people at home don't understand my fatal decision in the Philippines." He could not mount a defense now but expected to have his opportunity to do so in the future. "I have no self-criminations as to my action and will explain all when the time comes, and I will be fully backed by all the senior officers who *were still there at the end*." He underscored those words, as if to suggest the senior officers *not* still there at the end might not stand with him. MacArthur had supposedly recommended Wainwright for the Distinguished Service Medal Adele had accepted. What higher medal her husband would have received without his commander's meddling, Adele did not know. Nor did she know that a member of MacArthur's staff had angered the secretary of war during a recent visit to the War Department by making more of the same insinuations about her husband. But she knew enough now to question the sincerity of Douglas MacArthur. He had abandoned her husband once and, if the letter from Formosa hinted at the truth, might do so again.

CHAPTER TEN

Bypass

There was another field commander beginning to feel forsaken by Douglas MacArthur. In late November 1942, the highly regarded fifty-six-year-old major general Robert L. Eichelberger received a summons to the forward headquarters MacArthur had finally opened at Port Moresby on the southeastern coast of New Guinea. The failure to seize Buna on the other side of the mountains in July still haunted the headquarters staff. "Bob" Eichelberger remembered MacArthur saying while pacing the screened veranda of the commodious house he had taken, "I want you to take Buna, or not come back alive." MacArthur promised to reward Eichelberger with newspaper coverage if he returned triumphant. But when he succeeded in doing so in early 1943 after a battle that proved far bloodier than the navy's better-known simultaneous struggle for Guadalcanal in the Solomon Islands, MacArthur seemed less than eager to share the headlines, even though he himself had once again stayed away from the front lines. The paperwork supporting a Medal of Honor bid for Eichelberger mysteriously went missing at MacArthur's headquarters. When copies inconveniently surfaced, MacArthur torpedoed the nomination, albeit without the insinuations he had made against Wainwright. For the next year, Eichelberger would find himself stuck on training duty in Australia.

There were other people whom MacArthur had better reason to keep out of the headlines—the army and navy cryptologists chosen to leave Corregidor for their ability to decipher Japanese code. It was thanks to them that MacArthur learned how the Japanese planned to ferry reinforcements to New Guinea from their stronghold at Rabaul. When the ships were spotted on March 1, 1943, MacArthur's air force commander, George Kenney, had his airplanes ready. Over the next few days, they annihilated the convoy. MacArthur put Japanese losses at fifteen thousand men and twenty-two ships, never mind that the best intelligence indicated that the convoy had included only sixteen ships to start. Some in Washington would quibble with the numbers, especially when MacArthur refused to revise them, but no one could doubt the importance of what had transpired in what would become known as the Battle of the Bismarck Sea. "Billy Mitchell, Billy Mitchell," was all MacArthur could say to his wife after the battle. If a skeptic of airpower before, MacArthur never would be again. "Control of such sea lanes no longer depends solely or even perhaps primarily upon naval power, but upon air power operating from land bases held by ground troops," read the communiqué MacArthur issued. It sounded, as he surely knew it would, like an insult to his real rival, the United States Navy.

At the same time, MacArthur knew that the next stage of operations against Rabaul would require cooperation between the army and navy. He had suffered the indignity of the joint chiefs adjusting his boundary lines before the Battle of Guadalcanal and would not allow a recurrence. With Guadalcanal won, the next step up the Solomons chain would bring the navy's South Pacific commander, Admiral William F. Halsey, under MacArthur's strategic direction.

In April 1943, Halsey requested a meeting in Brisbane with Mac-Arthur. If Halsey worried about serving under a general whose pronouncements had made enemies of so many admirals, seeing MacArthur in person immediately allayed his concerns. "I have seldom seen a man who makes a quicker, stronger, more favorable impression," Halsey wrote of MacArthur. "His hair was jet black; his eyes were clear; his carriage was erect. If he had been wearing civilian clothes, I still would have known at once that he was a soldier." Halsey made a similar impression on MacArthur, who described the sixty-year-old, square-jawed admiral as a naval officer in the mold of Admiral George Dewey, who had steamed into Manila Bay all those years ago without fear of losing a ship. No doubt MacArthur intended that compliment as a contrast with the admirals who had refused to do the same when he had called for carriers on Corregidor. Halsey offered a more unifying recollection. He remembered that his father, also a naval officer, had met MacArthur's father in the Philippines and that the two had formed a friendship. The sons would resolve to put aside their service rivalries and do the same.

The plan that would come out of this meeting would consume the rest of 1943 and early 1944 and take the name Operation Cartwheel, a series of landings by which Halsey would advance northwest through the Solomons and MacArthur northwest up the coast of New Guinea. Their lines of advance would eventually come together to put Rabaul in the crosshairs. But even as Cartwheel began in the summer of 1943, some already questioned the endgame. Instead of fighting a climactic battle against the hundred thousand troops the Japanese had in Rabaul, planners in Washington wondered if the base could be "neutralized" by destroying its airpower, chasing away its ships, cutting off its supply lines, and isolating it much as the Japanese had MacArthur's own forces in the Philippines. The strategy would become known as bypassing. Though initially resistant to it, MacArthur would make it his signature move in the year ahead. It would lead to his most brilliant triumphs but also threaten the one he sought most: returning to the Philippines.

*   *   *

As MacArthur would later tell the story, the idea of bypassing Rabaul had sprung from his own head. He had kept it locked there until a meeting one day in early 1943 when he heard staffers despairing as to how he would take the base that served as the linchpin of the Japanese position in the Southwest Pacific. "General," MacArthur recalled one staffer saying, "I know your peculiar genius for slaughtering large masses of the enemy at little cost in the lives of your own men, but I just don't see how we can take these strongpoints with our limited forces." MacArthur agreed, even though his ground forces now totaled eighteen divisions and his aircraft fourteen hundred planes, to say nothing of those on Halsey's five carriers. This force, MacArthur told his staffers, would not suffice. But what he said next, according to his account, stunned them. "[I] said I did not intend to take them [the Japanese strongpoints]—I intended to envelop them, incapacitate them, apply the 'hit 'em where they ain't—let 'em die on the vine' philosophy." Instead of charging up the ridge as his father had, MacArthur planned to move around it so as to strand the enemy on its summit. "New conditions and new weapons require new and imaginative methods," he told his staffers. "Wars are never won in the past."

If MacArthur did give this speech, it seems odd that he protested the same idea when George Marshall proposed it in the run-up to the conference President Roosevelt, Prime Minister Churchill, and their respective joint chiefs held in Quebec in August 1943. How to assign resources to competing offensives in Europe dominated the discussion. The Americans wanted to focus on building up forces in England for Operation Overlord by which the Allies would cross the English Channel for an invasion of Europe scheduled for the spring of 1944. The British, meanwhile, preferred to keep momentum in the Mediterranean, where Eisenhower's forces had defeated Axis ones in North Africa and landed on the underside of Europe in Sicily.

A similar dispute loomed in the Pacific. Unlike in Europe, however, this dispute pitted not the American strategists against the British ones but rather the Americans against the Americans, or more specifically, the United States Army against the United States Navy. All these months after the Japanese had attacked the Philippines—all these months after Wainwright had carried out the retreat to Bataan—the navy was finally set to carry out its part of War Plan Orange. In the fall, the fleet under the command of Admiral Nimitz would begin an advance across the central Pacific. And unlike Halsey, Nimitz would in no way be under MacArthur's command. The Americans at Quebec described their plans for Nimitz and MacArthur as "mutually supporting," but the British hearing them wondered if the two advances—Orange and Cartwheel— might not prove, as one historian puts it, "mutually competing." In a sense, they already had. Instead of receiving the reinforcements he would need to take Rabaul, MacArthur received orders informing him of the decision to bypass it.

Of greater concern to MacArthur was the fate of the Philippines. Shortly before the Quebec conference, MacArthur heard from three American officers who had escaped from prisons in the islands. They told him, for the first time, about the Bataan Death March and the survivors starving in prison. "The Japanese will pay for that humil- iation and suffering," he said. Thousands of Americans, he learned, had already died at Camp O'Donnell and Camp Cabanatuan, and that number would only grow if liberation did not come soon.

When MacArthur made it out of the Philippines and vowed to return, he had made his promise personal. He might have guessed that the American soldiers who called him Dugout Doug on Bataan would have mocked his egotism. But he believed his words had resonated with the Filipino people. "I spoke casually enough," he later explained, "but the phrase 'I shall return' seemed a promise of magic to the Filipinos. It lit a flame that became a symbol which focused the nation's indomitable will. . . . It was scraped in the sands of the beaches, it was daubed on the walls of the barrios, it was stamped on the mail, it was whispered in the cloisters of the church." MacArthur himself approved a plan for proliferating the phrase. To counter Japanese propaganda, his aides set about emblazoning the words "I shall return" with his signature on cigarettes packs and candy wrappers that submarines smuggled to the Philippines. In spite of the terms of Wainwright's surrender, some Filipino and American fighters had escaped into the jungles and mountains in the hope of fighting another day. After a period of radio silence, they had begun making contact with MacArthur's forces in Australia. One early message read, "Your victorious return is the nightly subject of prayer in every Filipino home."

It remained MacArthur's prayer, too. But anyone looking at a map of the Pacific could see that the joint chiefs had put the two advances on a collision course. If Nimitiz made his way through the Gilbert and Marshall Islands to the Carolines—and if MacArthur continued to make his way northwest up the coast of New Guinea after neutralizing Rabaul—their trajectories both pointed toward the Philippines.* As to who would have the honor of landing ashore first, the joint chiefs refused to give an opinion at this juncture.

MacArthur did not hold back his own. He had not liked War Plan Orange at the beginning of the war and liked it even less now. "From a broad strategic viewpoint, I am convinced that the best course of offensive action in the Pacific is a movement from Australia through New Guinea to Mindanao," he wrote Marshall. While Nimitz would have only his carriers for air support, MacArthur boasted he would have his new favorite weapon: land-based aircraft. As he explained, he would advance by striking places that lent themselves to the quick development of airfields, which, once constructed, could serve to provide the cover needed to carry out new landings farther up the coast in areas that would yield yet more airfields.

If the joint chiefs gathering in Quebec required a demonstration, Kenney gave them one on August 17. Having developed a secret new airfield in the interior of New Guinea from which both his bombers as well as shorter-range fighters could reach the main Japanese air base on the island at a place called Wewak, he launched a surprise raid. As his pilots approached, they found two hundred Japanese planes, many of them lined up in neat rows. Almost 90 percent of them would never fly again after the attack. MacArthur issued a communiqué celebrating

---

* Within months, the Marianas would join the list of islands for Nimitz to take.

the outcome. "Numerically the opposing forces were about equal in strength, but one was in the air and the other was not," he wrote. "Nothing is so helpless as an airplane on the ground. In war, surprise is decisive." Those who had witnessed the fiasco at Clark Field would have agreed. Like the Japanese invading the Philippines, the Americans climbing their way up the coast of New Guinea would now enjoy overwhelming air superiority.

With Cartwheel off and running, MacArthur would not have to worry about Japanese planes interrupting the attack he had planned on a strategic village called Lae, which sat up the coast from Buna at the base of a peninsula stretching toward New Britain, home of Rabaul.* The plan called for putting Lae in a pincer: by landing one force amphibiously farther up the peninsula to the east and by parachuting another force into a site inland to the west. Before the paratroopers boarded their planes at Port Moresby on September 5, 1943, Kenney announced he would observe the jump from the relative safety of a bomber flying overhead. Even that struck MacArthur as too dangerous. He ordered Kenney not to go. "They were my kids," Kenney remembered telling MacArthur, "and I was going to see them do their stuff."

Something about the argument impressed MacArthur. Perhaps it reminded him of the arguments he had made during World War I when asked why he risked his life for what seemed like showmanship. Perhaps it reminded him of the unflattering nickname the boys on Bataan had given him. "You're right, George," MacArthur said. "We'll both go. They're my kids, too." Now it was Kenney who protested. But MacArthur insisted. He could see, he said, anxiety on the faces of the paratroopers. None of them had conducted such an operation before. No one in the Pacific theater had. "I did not want them to go through their first baptism of fire without such comfort as my presence might bring to them," MacArthur wrote. Kenney remembered the sixty-three-year-old MacArthur watching "the show," as he called it, from his B-17

---

* For reference, see the map of eastern New Guinea on pages 214 and 215.

while "jumping up and down like a kid." MacArthur would admit the medal he received afterward for heroics in the sky did him "too much credit" but made a mention of it nonetheless in his memoirs. Within days, his forces had captured Lae and, within a short time afterward, executed another landing at the tip of the peninsula.

At this rate, MacArthur estimated he would reach the Philippines around February 1945. There was, however, growing doubt that he would return at all. "Garrison Post for MacArthur" was the way an Australian newspaper headlined a story predicting that his part of the fighting would take him no farther than the beaches of New Guinea and last no longer than six more months, at which time he would move to an administrative role. There was more to it than gossip, as Sutherland found when sent to represent MacArthur at a major Allied conference in the fall of 1943 in Cairo, Egypt. It was there that the joint chiefs decided that priority in the Pacific should go to Nimitz instead of MacArthur in the belief that "operations in the Central Pacific promise, at this time, a more rapid advance toward Japan," never mind the high casualties that marred the first of Nimitz's island chain landings that November in the Gilberts.

On the plane flying east out of Cairo toward New Guinea, Sutherland was not the only general who might have felt disappointed. George Marshall had learned that he would not have the honor of commanding the troops destined to make history by crossing the Channel from England to France in the spring of 1944. Command of Operation Overlord would go to MacArthur's old chief of staff, Eisenhower, because Roosevelt did not believe he could make do without Marshall as the army chief of staff. Informed of the decision, Marshall decided to take the long way back to Washington by accompanying Sutherland to the Southwest Pacific.

Marshall and MacArthur had not seen each other in years, and whether they would see each other even now remained uncertain. Reaching the far-flung Southwest Pacific theater was no guarantee of receiving a meeting with its often reclusive commander, as Eleanor Roosevelt had learned a few months earlier. "I am delighted that she will be able to see you," President Roosevelt had written to MacArthur in August in advance of the first lady's visit. But she never did see Mac-Arthur. Although MacArthur had limited his time away from Australia after the victory at Buna in early 1943, he arranged his schedule so that he would be in New Guinea when Eleanor arrived in Australia. He pawned the job of escorting the president's wife off on General Eichelberger, still paying penance for the press he had received post-Buna. Jean MacArthur also saw Eleanor a few times: once at a luncheon when an Australian governor asked the two women whether their husbands might run against each other in the 1944 United States presidential election, and another time at a dinner when Eleanor asked Jean to explain why her husband would refuse the first lady permission to come see him in New Guinea. Perhaps Eleanor suspected that the answer to her question was the same as the answer to the governor's. In the months ahead, MacArthur's behavior would give many the impression that he had his eye on the presidency.

When Marshall touched down in Brisbane on December 13, Mac-Arthur did not show up to greet him either but for seemingly a better reason. To an island called Goodenough off the northeastern coast of New Guinea, he had gone to oversee the next Cartwheel landings. Having seized one side of the narrow strait between New Guinea and New Britain, he would now dispatch marines to seize the other, which would put them on the same island as Rabaul, albeit at the opposite end. "There are some people in Washington who would rather see Mac-Arthur lose a battle than America win a war," officers heard MacArthur rage after discovering he did not have as many ships and planes as he wished for the operation. It has been said that MacArthur considered not seeing Marshall at all during his visit for fear of embarrassing the chief of staff responsible in some way for these alleged shortages. That claim is hard to reconcile with what happened when the two finally did meet on Goodenough Island on December 15.

By his own account, MacArthur showed no hesitancy about delivering his usual complaints about "the paucity of men and material I was receiving as compared with all other theaters of war." Although the United States had committed about the same number of men— more than 1.8 million—to battling Japan as to Germany, the lack of unity of command in the Pacific had required dividing the forces sent there among different theater commanders. Accounts of the meeting suggest that Marshall, with his blue eyes and graying hair, shared MacArthur's skepticism toward the Central Pacific route. In fact, according to MacArthur's own version, Marshall went so far as to confirm the existence of a conspiracy against the Southwest Pacific in Washington and to place Admiral King, the commander in chief of the United States fleet, at its head. King, MacArthur recalled Marshall saying, "resented the prominent part I had in the Pacific War." Incredibly, without intending any irony or showing any self-awareness, MacArthur remembered himself responding, "I felt it fantastic, to say the least, that interservice rivalry or personal ambitions should be allowed to interfere with the winning of the war." Operation Cartwheel's success so far, he insisted, owed to the unity of command he had exercised over army, navy, and air force units in the Southwest Pacific. The failure to extend the arrangement across the entire Pacific, he warned, would waste time and supplies, to say nothing of human lives.

The dueling paths across the Pacific had one upside that MacArthur never acknowledged. As a boy at the West Texas Military Academy, he had discovered that competition brought out the best in him. The same now happened in the Pacific. By early 1944, Cartwheel had almost reached its conclusion. MacArthur's progress up the coast of New Guinea and ultimately successful landing on New Britain had cut Rabaul off from the south and southwest. Meanwhile, Halsey's climb up the Solomons had cut the Japanese base off on the east and soon around its north, and Kenney's bombers had pummeled its airfields and harbors from above. To finish the encirclement of Rabaul—or to "put the cork in the bottle," as MacArthur liked to say—Cartwheel called for an April landing in the Admiralty Islands, which included Los Negros and Manus, northwest of Rabaul.

In February, however, pilots flying over the Admiralties reported the Japanese bases there stripped of planes and free of antiaircraft fire. Charles Willoughby, MacArthur's intelligence chief, worried that appearances could deceive. The Japanese probably had four thousand men there. Nonetheless, MacArthur bet he could take them by surprise. His own officers could not believe the audacity of the plan he announced on February 24 for what he called a "reconnaissance in force" in just five days' time. He would need troops ready to "piss in the fire" and "get going," and he had them: a division of American cavalrymen who had given up their horses but not their heritage. He remembered himself as a boy watching them ride out after Geronimo on the frontier, and now he would go with them: a thousand of them on transports, he on a naval cruiser leading the warships whose guns would bombard the beaches. Eight hours after the cavalrymen began landing on Los Negros, MacArthur joined them ashore. Officers had tried to talk him out of it—Kenney even tried to bribe him by offering to let him drop a bomb from a plane instead—but MacArthur insisted he needed to be on the ground so he could call for a retreat if necessary. The moment he stepped onto the beach, he made up his mind. "Hold what you have taken, against whatever odds," he told the cavalrymen. "You have your teeth in him now. Don't let up."

As MacArthur moved from the beach to an airfield, he ventured closer to the jungle beyond the perimeter the cavalrymen had established. Shown two Japanese bodies killed within the half hour, he stopped, stared at the corpses, and declared, "That's the way I like to see them." They would not surrender otherwise, he knew. His men would have to kill the rest of the Japanese on the island. At any moment, he felt they might come sprinting out of the trees, yelling "Banzai!" Warned that a Japanese sniper had been killed in the jungle just moments earlier, he responded, "Fine. That's the best thing to do with them," as if more concerned for the consciences of the cavalrymen than for his own safety. They could not understand how the Japanese had failed to shoot him already. He made such an easy target with his corncob pipe leaving

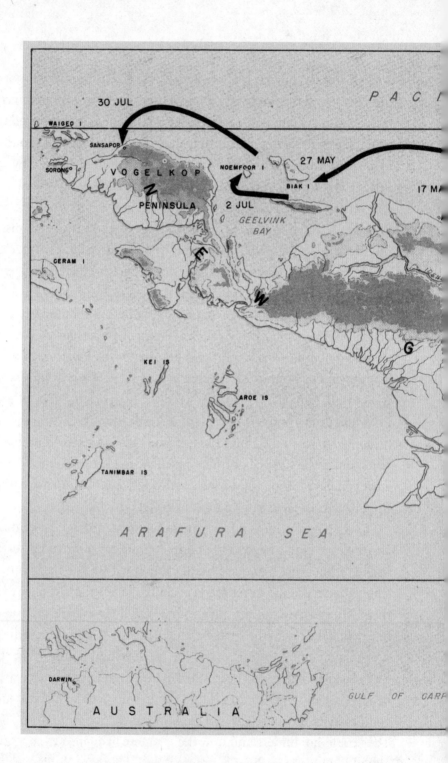

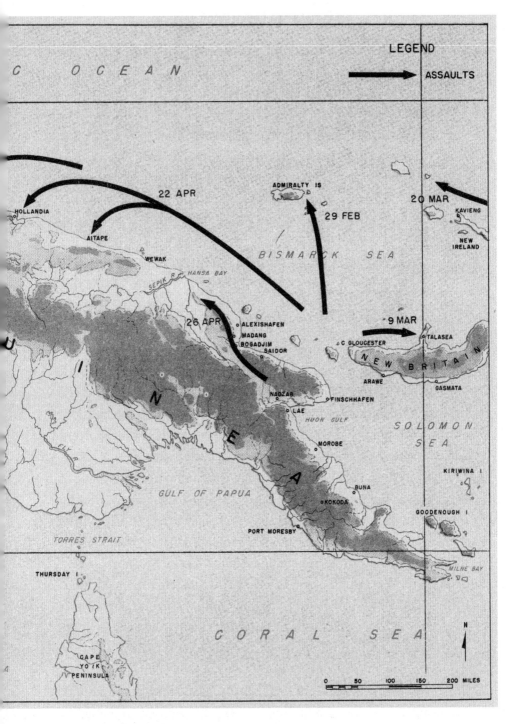

A map made for MacArthur's reports showing his major operations from February to July 1944, including his landing on the Admiralty Islands and the landings that brought his forces up the coast of New Guinea.

a trail of smoke. Rather than trying to blend in with the cavalrymen dressed in green fatigues, he donned khaki pants, a twill trench coat, and the world-famous gold-braided cap.

In truth, MacArthur did take one precaution for his health. He had a personal physician named Roger Egeberg come ashore, too. Seeing that MacArthur refused to wear a steel helmet, the terrified Egeberg felt no choice but to take his chances without one, too. Only later when they had returned to the cruiser did MacArthur tell the doctor he need not repeat the performance in the future. "Doc, I noticed you were wearing an officer's cap while we were ashore. You probably took a look at me and put it on," MacArthur said. "Well, I wear this cap with all the braid. I feel in a way that I have to. It's my trademark . . . a trademark that many of our soldiers know by now, so I'll keep on wearing it, but with the risk we take in a landing, I would suggest that you wear a helmet from now on." MacArthur knew the risk. He wanted his men to see him running it. He also wanted readers of newspapers and magazines back home to do the same. For that reason, he made sure reporters observed his first amphibious landing of the war. "Throughout the inspection, lasting a full hour, General MacArthur showed his usual magnificent lack of concern for possible danger," wrote a wire service reporter.

That sentence must have pleased MacArthur all the more because of his outrage at the very different conclusions contained in a mysteriously sourced but seemingly knowledgeable essay published in January in *The American Mercury* magazine. The essay contended that a growing chasm had formed between, as the headline put it, "General MacArthur: Fact and Legend," between the general celebrated for facing enemy fire and the one known to his troops as Dugout Doug, between the strategist likened to Napoleon and the one whose grand plan to meet the Japanese on the shores of the Philippines had collapsed within days, between the airpower genius advancing up the coast of New Guinea toward the Philippines under the cover of Kenney's planes and the one caught with his own planes on the ground hours after Pearl Harbor. In the weeks after that disaster, the essay conceded, Americans had needed a hero.

MacArthur had made a good one, and his friends in the press—to say nothing of his press censors—had made him appear an even better one. MacArthur had given orders ensuring his Filipino press aide, Carlos Romulo, made it off Corregidor, and Romulo had—to become the author of a bestselling book depicting MacArthur as an indomitable hero at the fall of the Philippines. In Washington, according to the essay, leaders aware of the messier truth had suppressed it in the interest of giving their countrymen a figure to rally around. But these good intentions had laid the foundation for a plan by the Republican Party to elevate MacArthur to the presidency in the 1944 election. "Although no general has ever left the field to become a candidate for the presidency—even the dashing George McClellan had been retired before he ran against Lincoln—the number of those who are determined to take a chance with MacArthur seems to be growing," stated the article, adding that he could end the distraction by taking a page from another Civil War general, William Tecumseh Sherman, and declaring, "I will not accept if nominated and will not serve if elected."

MacArthur wrote a letter calling the article "libelous." He did not, however, write a statement declaring himself unwilling to accept the Republican nomination. On the contrary, Republicans hoping to stop President Roosevelt from winning an unprecedented fourth term had found much to convince themselves that the commander of the Southwest Pacific theater might offer their best hope. During visits to Washington for meetings about the war, staffers including Sutherland and Willoughby had made time for meetings with Senator Arthur Vandenberg, a prominent Michigan Republican. "I want you to know the absolute confidence I would feel in your experienced and wise mentorship," read a message MacArthur had relayed to the senator.

Vandenberg took it as permission to form a movement to "draft" the general, a word purposely used not only because of its connotations of military necessity but also because of the consensus that a general could not openly seek the nomination. According to a poll in March 1944, voters believed MacArthur would do a better job "running the war" than his two main Republican rivals: Governor Thomas Dewey of New York and the party's 1940 nominee, Wendell Willkie. Both of these men, however, topped MacArthur when pollsters asked about other subjects such as the economy, where MacArthur had spoken out less, at least, publicly. He confided more in personal correspondence with a Nebraska congressman named A. L. Miller. When Miller predicted that four more years of "left wingers and New Dealism" would destroy democracy in the United States, MacArthur responded, "We must not inadvertently slip into the same condition internally as the one which we fight externally," by which he meant tyranny.

There were those especially on "the lunatic fringe of the left," as *Time* magazine put it, who believed MacArthur himself favored a more authoritarian model of government. They had not forgotten his role in putting down the Bonus March, and some on his staff spoke in ways that gave currency to such slanders. George Kenney remembered once hearing Dick Sutherland over dinner propose democracies do away with elections during wartime. To his credit, MacArthur shot down the idea. "No, Dick," MacArthur said, "you are wrong," and then explained that dissent and elections gave democracies an advantage that dictatorships did not enjoy: the freedom to change course in the midst of a conflict. "As long as a democracy can withstand the initial onslaught," MacArthur said, "it will find ways of striking back and eventually it will win." He trusted the voters to choose their own course. And in early April 1944, those participating in the Wisconsin primary did just that. As close to a political base as MacArthur had, given his family's history, the state handed him a defeat that crushed Vandenberg's hopes but not Congressman Miller's. On April 14, the congressman took it upon himself to reinvigorate the movement by publishing his correspondence with MacArthur.

By this time, MacArthur was days away from boarding a cruiser for his boldest move yet: a five-hundred-mile westward leap that would land his troops on either side of a port that the Dutch had christened Hollandia. Cartwheel had left the hundred thousand troops the Japanese had at Rabaul, as MacArthur put it, "to die on the vine" like unpicked grapes. In one swoop, this jump would do the same to the tens of thousands of Japanese troops spread around the Wewak area, where Kenney had continued his destruction of their air capabilities and where they expected MacArthur would carry out his next landing. On April 22, the landing at Hollandia delivered the shock MacArthur hoped. As at Los Negros, Doctor Egeberg accompanied MacArthur ashore but struggled to keep pace as the general bounded through the sand. "He seemed in better shape than many of the soldiers," wrote Egeberg. "He didn't sweat, while they and I were pretty well soaking wet." MacArthur declared victory: The bypassed Japanese around Wewak now had his troops to the west and east, his naval forces to the north, the impassable mountains of the jungle to the south, and his air force overhead. "This enemy army is now completely isolated," he wrote. "Their ultimate fate is now certain. Their situation reverses Bataan."

Much as MacArthur could relish those words, they were not the ones that the newspapers hounded him to hear. Before leaving for Hollandia, he had issued a statement acknowledging the authenticity of the letters published without his permission but rejecting any interpretation of them as "intended as criticism of any political philosophy or any personages in high office," by which he meant Roosevelt. MacArthur added that he did not seek the presidency, but the phrasing left open whether he would accept the office, which, of course, had been the game all along. No longer would the press let him play it. On his return from Hollandia, there was no choice but to issue another statement: "I have had brought to my attention a number of newspaper articles professing in strongest terms a widespread public opinion that it is detrimental to our war effort to have an officer in high position on active service at the front, considered for nomination for the office of president," he wrote. "In view of these circumstances, in order to make my position entirely unequivocal, I request that no action be taken that would link my name in any way with the nomination. I do not covet it nor would I accept it."

MacArthur would relish a dubious account he received of Roosevelt's glee upon hearing the news. "I'm sure," MacArthur quoted the witness as saying, "that every night when he turned in, the president had been looking under the bed to make sure you weren't there." In reality, a showdown with MacArthur did not scare the president at all. Roosevelt had plans for one soon.

*   *   *

On July 6 came orders from George Marshall: Be in Pearl Harbor in twenty days' time for a meeting. The message did not specify with whom, but MacArthur could figure it out from the tone before commencing the first of the three legs of the flight that would bring him to the place where the war had begun for Americans. The aircrew had set up a cot for him, but he went twenty-eight hours without any sleep. For much of the time in the air, he paced. Democrats convening in Chicago days earlier had nominated Roosevelt for a fourth term and ratified his tepid selection of a Missouri senator named Harry Truman for vice president. Already en route to Pearl Harbor, Roosevelt himself had not bothered to accept in person. MacArthur wondered if the president had made a calculation that voters would prefer to see their commander in chief managing the war than managing party politics. If true, Roosevelt might have proposed the meeting at Pearl Harbor for nothing more than a photograph. The thought enraged MacArthur.

Not since 1937 had MacArthur visited any American territory closer than the Philippines. Not since the war had begun had he set foot, as he put it, "on soil over which I am not the commander." He did not think he should be away from his theater now. He had followed up his success at Hollandia with new landings that had him days away from reaching the far northwestern corner of New Guinea, which would put him a mere six hundred miles from Mindanao. His troops, however, were not the only ones nearing the Philippines. Only days before MacArthur had begun his journey to Pearl Harbor, Nimitz's forces had staged a return of their own to the American territory of Guam as part of the battle for the Marianas. The campaign had already cost thousands of American lives but also set up a naval victory west of the islands in the Philippine Sea, which leads, as the name suggests, to the Philippine Islands.

MacArthur knew Roosevelt would have Nimitz at Pearl Harbor, too. For months, the joint chiefs had put off answering who would lead the leap into the Philippines. On board the plane, MacArthur confronted a possibility even more disturbing than Nimitz receiving the job. Roosevelt might assign it to no one. In a cruel irony, MacArthur's success bypassing Japanese strongpoints had given planners in Washington a new idea: bypassing most of the Philippines, the islands to which he had vowed to return, in favor of invading Formosa to the north and thereby putting American forces closer to Japan. Unsurprisingly, MacArthur's nemesis, Admiral King, was the most vocal proponent of the plan. But even Marshall seemed taken with it. MacArthur would still land on Mindanao, but Marshall feared that reconquering the rest of the Philippines, especially the main island of Luzon, would require difficult fighting that could bog down the war. Leaping over Luzon to Formosa could save time and lives. "With regard to the . . . reconquest of the Philippines," Marshall had written MacArthur, "we must be careful not to allow our personal feeling and Philippine political considerations to override our great objective." By this time, two and a half years into a war, the phrase "our great objective" should have had a clear meaning. Yet Marshall deemed it necessary to add a clause defining those words as "the early conclusion of the war with Japan" because he knew his correspondent had always had a different definition. "The Philippine Islands had constituted the main objective of my planning from the time of my departure from Corregidor," MacArthur would later admit. Only six hundred miles and a meeting with the president now stood in the way.

On the afternoon of July 26, a crowd formed around the two-acre space authorities had roped off in preparation for the arrival of the naval cruiser carrying Roosevelt to Pearl Harbor. When the ship arrived, the white-haired Nimitz went up the gangplank with a group of other officers eager to welcome the president. Roosevelt asked where Mac-Arthur was. An awkward silence ensued. MacArthur had landed an hour before. By any measure of decorum, he should have been there waiting on Roosevelt—not kept him waiting. Suddenly, as if to answer the president's question, the party heard a loud siren and then saw what one of the president's speechwriters later described as "a motorcycle escort and the longest open car I have ever seen." The car drove right up to the gangplank. Out the back hopped its sole passenger, wearing a leather flying jacket that looked out of place on a summer day in Hawaii. Sunglasses covered his eyes, a gold-braided cap his face. But the crowd recognized Douglas MacArthur not in spite of his accoutrements but because of them. Partway up the gangplank, he stopped to wave. A staff member accompanying MacArthur heard "a tremendous ovation."

So did the president. "Hello, Doug," Roosevelt said when MacArthur stepped aboard. "What are you doing with that leather jacket on? It's darn hot today."

"Well, I've just landed from Australia," MacArthur said. "It's pretty cold up there."

MacArthur would make his own comments about the way Roosevelt looked, but not to his face. "When he was animated," MacArthur later said of the president, "he looked familiar, but otherwise his jaw sagged down and he looked to be in very poor physical condition." Roosevelt, who had contracted polio twenty-three summers earlier, "was carried every place he went" or pushed in his wheelchair. No longer did he have the strength, MacArthur observed, "[to] stand up as he used to do with the use of leg braces." Roosevelt might live to see victory in Europe, where the success of the Eisenhower-led landings the previous month on the beaches of Normandy in France had fueled hopes for the quick collapse of Germany. But MacArthur doubted Roosevelt would live to see victory in the Pacific. The president would be dead in half a year, MacArthur predicted.

Despite his manifest health problems at Pearl Harbor, Roosevelt insisted on covering as much ground as he could the next day. Together, in the backseat of an open car, Roosevelt and the general he had once ranked among the "most dangerous men" in America shuttled between army and navy facilities. As he had the day before, MacArthur put on a good face for the cameramen. At one point out of earshot, he asked the president about his odds of beating Dewey, who had captured the Republican nomination for president. Roosevelt, according to MacArthur's memory, "answered that he had not had time to think of politics." MacArthur laughed. Roosevelt paused and then did, too.

Not until after a dinner at the house where the president and his party had made their quarters did the discussion turn serious. Roosevelt beckoned Nimitz and MacArthur to the living room. Could the army and navy officers leading the main charges across the Pacific reach an agreement on the next step? As MacArthur looked around, he felt ambushed. Nimitz's aides had hung huge maps of the Pacific and various charts around the room. Evidently, Nimitz had known the purpose of the meeting and come ready. MacArthur had brought no maps and no materials. He felt outnumbered. Of the four men present, three counted themselves navy men. There was Nimitz. There was the president's chief of staff, William Leahy, a navy admiral himself. And there was the president, who had served, as his older cousin Theodore had, as assistant secretary of the navy earlier in his career. "I began to realize I was to go it alone," MacArthur remembered. He had barely closed his eyes since leaving Australia. He should have spent his first night in Hawaii sleeping, given he had not at all on the plane, but instead had stayed up musing aloud about the disappointments he had experienced. The conference ahead, he worried, might put him—to say nothing of his country—on the path for another one.

Roosevelt began by pointing to Mindanao on one of the navy's maps and asking, "Douglas, where do we go from here?"

"Leyte, Mr. President," answered MacArthur referring to a large island east of Cebu in the Visayas, "and then Luzon!" So often during his career MacArthur had silenced listeners with his ability to marshal arguments into seemingly impromptu yet somehow polished monologues.

The one he launched into now, however, was by no means spontaneous. Though he had not known he would be delivering the speech there in the living room, he had developed it in correspondence, communiqués, and conversations throughout the war. The southern route over which he had led his army had begun cutting the Japanese off from the natural resources that had drawn them south at the start of the war. "If I could secure the Philippines," he said, "it would enable us to clamp an air and naval blockade on the flow of all supplies from the south to Japan, and thus, by paralyzing her industries, force her to early capitulation."

"How many Japs are there in the Philippine Islands?" Roosevelt interrupted.

"About one hundred thousand," MacArthur said.

To MacArthur's chagrin, Roosevelt said the estimates he had seen put the number far higher. He worried, he said, "to capture Luzon would be very bloody."

"Mr. President," MacArthur protested, "my losses would not be heavy, any more than they have been in the past. The days of the frontal attack should be over. Modern infantry weapons are too deadly, and frontal assault is only for mediocre commanders. Good commanders do not turn in heavy losses." MacArthur did not need to say who he meant by mediocre commanders. He had often used the term "frontal attacks" to denigrate the navy's headfirst charge across the Pacific, and the resulting casualty numbers strengthened the analogy. Over just a few weeks in June and July, Nimitz had suffered 3,400 combat deaths in the fight for an island called Saipan above Guam in the Marianas—twice as many as MacArthur would record in all his operations between April and September 1944, a period including the Hollandia landings. His men had advanced under the shield of land-based air support. Bypassing Luzon in favor of Formosa would mean going without it. The result, MacArthur warned, would be far bloodier.

The discussion went on until midnight and then began again the next morning around ten. Despite MacArthur's barbs about the casualties in Nimitz's theater, Roosevelt and Leahy found the debate between the two theater commanders more cordial than reading the correspondence from the Southwest Pacific theater would have led one to suppose. Nimitz delivered the navy's case for bypassing the Philippines but seemed less than convinced by it himself. MacArthur sensed Nimitz had never shared King's enthusiasm for the idea. At one point, Nimitz even conceded that conditions might require the occupation of Manila under any circumstances.

By the time the meeting ended, it seemed to MacArthur that he had won over the president or at least worn him down. Roosevelt joked he needed aspirin. In truth, he had found his time with MacArthur stimulating and asked him to stay a little longer than planned so they could have a private chat. When MacArthur finally boarded his plane, he seemed, as his pilot, Weldon "Dusty" Rhoades, put it, "in rare good humor." When asked if he had gotten what he hoped from the meeting, MacArthur answered, "Yes, everything. We are going on." On his own way home from the trip, Roosevelt would send MacArthur a letter. "As soon as I get back, I will push on that plan for I am convinced that it is logical and can be done," Roosevelt wrote. "Someday there will be a flag-raising in Manila—and without question I want you to do it." The correspondence leaves no doubt that Roosevelt promised to back Luzon over Formosa. Did MacArthur promise anything in return? Some historians have conjectured so. According to this theory, he offered what any wartime president weeks away from an election would want: good headlines from the front. If the two men reached such a deal, neither received much. MacArthur could have obtained more from Roosevelt, who gave only his personal support for Luzon in deliberations with the joint chiefs when he could have given them orders that ended the debate in Washington altogether. Instead, the debate would go on. Meanwhile, Roosevelt received from MacArthur only what he had always given freely: hyperbolic reports of success.

This is not to say the Hawaii meeting was without political intrigue. Very likely MacArthur made an ominous prediction, though probably not in words that sounded as overtly threatening as he later recalled them to one of his staffers. "Mr. President," MacArthur remembered saying, "if your decision be to bypass the Philippines . . . I dare to say that the American people would be so aroused that they would register most complete resentment against you at the polls this fall." The United States had what MacArthur called a "moral obligation" to the Philippines. Unlike Formosa, the Philippines were American territory. "We had been thrown out of Luzon at the point of a bayonet and we should regain our prestige by throwing the Japanese out at the point of a bayonet," MacArthur explained. Almost all the seventeen million people on the archipelago, in his opinion, had stayed loyal to the United States in part because they believed his vow to return. Roosevelt had failed to send help when the Filipinos needed it in 1942. If he abandoned them a second time—if he delayed the day of their liberation—if he forced MacArthur to break his word—no one in Asia would ever again trust America's. The Filipino people would never forgive Roosevelt. Nor would the American people.

After all, it was not just Filipinos waiting for MacArthur. It was Americans, too. The War Department had barred MacArthur from discussing the Bataan Death March and succeeded in keeping it secret until January 1944, when the story became front-page news. Roosevelt could not leave, MacArthur remembered saying, "thousands of American internees and prisoners of war to continue to languish in their agony and despair." In May 1944, *Time* had evoked their memories in an article commemorating the two-year anniversary of Corregidor's fall. On the cover appeared a painting of Wainwright behind barbed wire. "Sorely remembered now are more than thirteen thousand U.S. soldiers, including thirty-five U.S. generals, now in Japanese prison camps," read the article. "Jonathan Wainwright, the man left behind to preside at his country's worst military fiasco, waits for death or liberation." Of his agony and despair, MacArthur said not a word. He knew the highest-ranking American taken prisoner was no longer in the Philippines. Wainwright was on Formosa, where MacArthur had no interest in going.

CHAPTER ELEVEN

Solitaire

Wainwright was still on Formosa but no longer at Karenko. The Japanese had moved him around the island multiple times. Each time, the group of officers with him had grown smaller. The first of these moves came on April 2, 1943, when the Japanese ordered all American, British, and Dutch prisoners of the rank of brigadier general and higher to pack up their belongings and march to a nearby train station. The Japanese let Wainwright take his orderly, Sergeant Carroll, with him but not his two aides, Pugh and Dooley. Wainwright saw them waving farewell from the barracks as he stepped out of the gates. "It will be for the better," Dooley consoled himself as he considered how Wainwright had suffered at Karenko.

The train crawled southward at a pace that never seemed to exceed ten miles per hour. After seven hours and several stops, the generals arrived at a place called Tamazato, where they found their new camp just yards from the tracks. "The military establishment was set in a rather beautiful piece of land at the foot of a steep and verdant mountain," Wainwright wrote. "There was a stream running along the camp." More picturesque scenery was not what any of the generals cared about seeing. They wanted to see their share of the seventeen thousand pounds of Red Cross packages that had arrived at Karenko just days before their departure.

On April 12, about 20 percent of the total made it to Tamazato. There was corned beef and cheese, biscuits and bacon, and pudding and plum jam. There was also the sugar, soap, and shoes the soldiers had missed so much, as well as the chocolate that they discovered they had missed most of all. It was like Christmas morning but with generals doing the unwrapping. "No package was ever opened by any child with a greater interest than was displayed by all the prisoners here," Wainwright's chief of staff, Lew Beebe, recorded in his diary. On March 24, Wainwright had weighed 126.5 pounds. By April 23, he weighed 132 pounds with almost all of the five and half new pounds put on in one week. After days of gorging themselves with disregard for the diarrhea they knew would follow, the officers imposed a system of rationing. All recognized the supplies would have to last.

For propaganda purposes, the Japanese carried on with the pretense of operating their camps in accordance with the Geneva Conventions. Allowing delivery of the relief packages was one part of the charade. Another part was allowing the prisoners to speak with a representative of the International Red Cross. But when the doctor from Switzerland visited on June 1, the Japanese provided Wainwright and fourteen other prisoners with a script, as he put it, "[of] what we could say and . . . mostly of what we could not say."

Something similar happened two days later on June 3 when a correspondent for a Japanese news agency interviewed Wainwright for a broadcast that would make it to America. Wainwright took the opportunity to send greetings to his wife but worried that the interview had made it seem that he agreed that lasting peace required a balance of power between the United States and Japan with the former maintaining stability in the western hemisphere and the latter maintaining it in East Asia. According to the report that United States intelligence officials analyzing the broadcast provided to President Roosevelt, the Japanese succeeded in forcing Wainwright to say far worse: that the

American advance in the Southwest Pacific would meet fierce resistance and that the war could last for a hundred years if the politicians who had started it did not agree to negotiate. Asked if the American president would negotiate, Wainwright said that he did not know enough about conditions outside the prison to guess but that he did know Roosevelt "was a very shrewd statesman"—shrewd enough, as it turned out, to recognize Wainwright's remarks for what they were: coerced.

The Americans at Tamazato did not have a propaganda arm of their own, but they did have an unofficial poet: a brigadier general named William Brougher. It was around this time that Brougher started planning out what he hoped would become an epic in praise of Wainwright and in opposition to the "silly idea" that he should feel any shame for his actions on Corregidor. "An old cavalryman and horse-lover, accustomed to taking the field with a free rein and hurdling a thousand traps that death has laid for him with the rollicking laugh of a hunter and racing rider, on his first and final big assignment as a war-time commander, 'Skinny' Wainwright finds himself not only dismounted, but chained to the rock of a small island fortress," read the notes Brougher made. "[Wainwright] starves with his heroic troops and not only 'eats his own heart out' in a helpless situation of isolation and futility, but sees his own beautiful thoroughbred hunters slaughtered and eaten by members of his command—in their last extremity." At times, some officers had griped about Wainwright's decisions, but few could imagine enduring without his example. No other officer, Beebe wrote, could have held the prisoners together the way Wainwright had.

But no longer could he. On June 5, 1943, the Japanese further pared down the prisoners. Beebe and the other brigadier generals departed for an unknown destination. Only the twelve highest-ranking British and Dutch prisoners, as well as the top three Americans—Wainwright, Ned King, and George Moore—and their orderlies stayed at Tamazato, but not for long. On June 23, they set off, first via train, and then in the cramped cargo hold of a boat that would take them to a port near the capital of Formosa at the island's top, where the Japanese had built a new camp in a village called Muksaq. With their army and navy on the retreat, the Japanese looked to their highest-ranking prisoners in the hope of scoring a public relations victory. The beatings Wainwright had suffered would end. But so would the camaraderie that had sustained him through his bitterest days. He had felt lonely before. He would feel lonelier now.

*   *   *

At least, Wainwright had one new friend. Sergeant Carroll had raised a duck at Tamazato. The prisoners had named him Donald, plied him with any food they could spare, and managed to take him with them when they left. As they entered their new prison on June 24, Wainwright described the duck as "the only healthy living thing in the line of march." If not for the electric fence around the acre of land that became their new home at Muksaq, the prisoners might have mistaken it for a rustic retreat. Built on a hill with orange trees, the camp overlooked fields of rice. In the one-story barracks made of pinewood, each officer received his own private room. "They were tiny—eight and a half feet by ten, as I measured them," Wainwright wrote. "But each room had an easy chair, a bamboo cot, and a table for our meals and writing." The Japanese provided books they had seized from an old British consulate as well as portions of rice and vegetables that would have been impossible to imagine at Karenko. Within weeks of his arrival, Wainwright would bring his weight back up to 138 with another five pounds.

A Japanese colonel named Sasawa welcomed the prisoners with an almost sycophantic show of friendliness. "If there's anything on your minds, just let me know," he said. "I will fix it. You can trust me." No one said a word in response. "We just looked at him, unable to answer, knowing that there must be a method in what was patently madness," Wainwright remembered.

Shortly afterward, Sasawa sent one of his officers to visit Wainwright in his room and ask, "What do you most want in the world?" When

Wainwright replied that he wanted the war "successfully terminated" and the right to go home, the Japanese officer acted as if he could not have agreed more. "I know a way to do just that," he said. "If you will just write to your President Roosevelt and tell him that there is no use for America to carry on this war any further."

Wainwright ended the conversation there, but the Japanese would miss no opportunity to continue it. On August 12, they invited him to a tea party. On August 18, they let him walk around the mountain outside the prison. On September 9, they took him and the other generals on a fishing expedition and served them iced pop and candy. Wainwright had the largest catch, a four-and-a-half-inch fish, and the Japanese let him keep it. On October 20, they held a picnic for the prisoners at a shrine on a nearby mountain. To reach it, Wainwright had to climb hundreds of stairs—no easy feat for a malnourished man with a limp—but what awaited him there made the hike seem worth it: a lunch of roast duck. Only after licking the bones clean did he learn that they belonged to poor Donald. The Japanese had seized the bird from Sergeant Carroll shortly before. "All of us had grown attached to Donald," Wainwright wrote, "so none of the officers at the picnic were in a receptive mood when Colonel Sawsawa stood up at its end, belched appreciatively, and launched into an attack on the Allies." He talked about how it had taken twenty thousand Americans to overcome a Japanese force a mere tenth of that number in a recent battle. "Now, there are one hundred million people in the Japanese Empire," Sasawa said. "It will therefore take ten times one hundred million people to defeat Japan." Given the United States had nowhere near this number of people—to say nothing of soldiers—the war could end only through a diplomatic solution. If Wainwright and the other prisoners did not push their president to negotiate, they would never see their homes and families again.

So often had Wainwright heard these arguments that he had begun to believe them. Perhaps because of this, the Japanese encouraged him to write home more often. "I long for the day when I will see you and my beloved homeland again, but I fear that it will be a long time," he wrote to Adele. He had predicted at Tarlac that MacArthur would return to the Philippines at the end of 1943 but no longer expected him to do so. And even if he did, it would not mean liberation for prisoners on Formosa. The Japanese guards would sometimes talk about prisoner exchanges with the United States and even describe ships set to sail for that purpose. Early on, such rumors would have raised Wainwright's spirits, but no longer. The two countries had exchanged civilian prisoners. But no soldier had gone home from the Pacific this way, and none ever would. Wainwright expected his captivity to last as long as the war.

How to fill the hours haunted Wainwright. For the most part, the guards at Muksaq followed the Geneva Conventions and required only enlisted men to work. Many of the Allied officers, however, had become so accustomed to farming that they requested permission to set up small gardens. Wainwright grew radishes, peanuts, and corn and looked after some farm animals.

Wainwright also continued to write. Though his daily diary entries grew shorter, he began compiling lists. One offered advice for younger officers. Underscored on it was "never criticize your superiors." But holding out the tantalizing possibility of contradicting that advice was another list he titled "Undesirable Qualities Sometimes Found in a High Commander." It surely would have disappointed some of those who had fought with him in the Philippines to learn that none of the entries on the list took aim at the famous commander who had left them behind.

Nothing captured the mood at Muksaq better than the craze the prisoners developed in August 1943 for the one-player card game whose name reflected how they felt: solitaire. They began teaching one another different ways to play, and Wainwright must have settled on a hard set of rules because the meticulous records he kept reveal that he won only 6.8 percent of the time—and not for lack of practice. Between August 1943 and August 1945, Wainwright would play 8,632 games in total or an average of twelve games per day.

Occasionally a copy of the *Nippon Times* disrupted the tedium. One carrying an October date but not arriving in the camp until November brought news Wainwright could hardly believe. Like the promotions he had received during World War I, the promotions he had received in recent years to major general and lieutenant general had been only temporary. When the war ended, his rank would revert to brigadier general, or so he thought until seeing a story saying Roosevelt had promoted a group of officers to the permanent rank of major general. "My name leaped out of the page," Wainwright remembered. From time to time had come signs that people in the United States did not view him the way he had feared. At Karenko, his fellow prisoners had found a story in a Japanese newspaper about plans to build a statue in his honor somewhere in the United States. But he had continued to worry about the rebuke awaiting him in Washington. Now that concern began to subside. "I appear in good standing," he concluded.

If he lived to see the end of the war—if he ever made it back to the United States—he could suddenly imagine a future other than ostracism. He could imagine living with Adele, as they once had, around Washington, DC. The promotion to the permanent rank of major general would allow them to retire comfortably. Instead of the $375 a month owed to a retired brigadier general, he would receive $500 a month. Only one hurdle stood in the way. He would receive the additional money only if he found a way to formally accept the promotion before his sixty-fourth birthday on August 23, 1947, at which point he assumed the army would retire him on account of age. Such was his state of mind—such was his pessimism about the war in the Pacific—that he worried he would not have the opportunity to communicate with the War Department before then, that he would still be a prisoner. For all the times the Japanese had tried to convince him to write to his superiors in Washington, they would not let him do so now. They would permit him only to write to his wife. He would have to ask her to accept the promotion on his behalf.

He had received another radio message from Adele on September 28, 1943. Unlike the message he had received earlier in the year, this one gave some sense of life back home. She told him about the house she had rented in Skaneateles and referred to Jonathan Wainwright V as "Captain Jack," which Wainwright took as proof that his son had become, as he put it, "skipper of his own ship." She mentioned more letters she had sent him. He had received none of them. Throughout the winter of 1943–44, he wrote to her over and over again with growing concern about the promotion and the steps she needed to take to secure it for the sake of both their futures.

It was a winter of waiting. The temperatures remained warm in theory, but the low of forty-three degrees might as well have been freezing for malnourished men still wearing the same threadbare, light khaki uniforms from the Philippines. The cold aggravated the old lower back injury Wainwright had suffered. No longer could he tend to the animals. His orderly, Sergeant Carroll, had it worse. The enlisted prisoners at Muksaq had to labor no matter how they felt and sleep in a single uninsulated room with benches for beds. The only mercy came on Christmas 1943, when the Japanese let Wainwright have Carroll over to the officers' barracks for dinner and let him have his share of some hog or, at least, the cuts of it the guards had rejected for themselves. On February 18, Wainwright marked his thirty-third wedding anniversary. "While they have had their ups and downs," he wrote Adele, "they have been generally happy years." A few days later, for the first time, General King received letters from his wife. Wainwright received a few letters, too, but none from Adele. "I am becoming very much discouraged," he wrote.

With the warm weather that spring came the largest mosquitos Wainwright had ever set eyes on but also the largest batch of mail he had received since his surrender. The letters came on May 1, 1944. There were several from American mothers and fathers he did not know but whose sons he had known on Bataan. They had served under his command and had gone missing. These letters defied, as he put it, "adequate reply," but he endeavored to answer every one of them. There were also letters from his own family: four letters from his daughter-in-law, Elfrida; one from his son, Jack; and three, at long last, from his

MacArthur standing beside Chief of Staff George C. Marshall during their meeting on Good-enough Island in December 1943. MacArthur complained, per his recollections, "[about] the paucity of men and material I was receiving as compared with all other theaters of war." Also shown are Generals George Kenney (second from left) and Walter Krueger (third from right).

MacArthur (center) with Vice Admiral Thomas Kinkaid (left) aboard a navy cruiser before the rapidly planned landing on Los Negros in the Admiralty Islands on February 29, 1944. Despite being advised not to join the cavalrymen ashore, MacArthur insisted on doing so.

3

4

A Japanese photograph staged for propaganda purposes of Wainwright writing a letter from the Muksaq prison camp on Formosa. Not until May 1944, two years after his surrender, did the first letter from his wife reach him there.

Franklin Roosevelt sitting aboard the cruiser that carried him to Pearl Harbor in July 1944 for a meeting with Admiral Chester W. Nimitz (right) and MacArthur, who wore his signature cap and leather flying jacket. In the meeting, MacArthur called returning to the Philippines a "moral obligation."

5

Part of the armada that would accompany MacArthur back to the Philippines in October 1944. When fully assembled, the vessels would number more than seven hundred. "Ships to the front, to the rear, to the left, and to the right, as far as the eye could see," MacArthur would later write.

6

MacArthur walking beside Philippine president Sergio Osmeña (also in sunglasses) around the beachhead on Leyte on October 20, 1944. MacArthur's pants appear waterlogged from him having waded ashore, as shown in the famous photograph on the cover of this book. "People of the Philippines: I have returned," he said. "By the grace of Almighty God, our forces stand again on Philippine soil—soil consecrated in the blood of our two peoples."

7

Liberated prisoners crowding around MacArthur (identifiable by his cap) during his visit to Santo Tomas on February 7, 1945. "The welcome was hysterical as he was thoroughly surrounded by happy, shouting, talking, weeping people," an aide remembered. "He couldn't move."

8

Some of the emaciated Bataan and Corregidor survivors liberated from the Bilibid in Manila in February 1945. "I promised I would be back, but I am a long time overdue," MacArthur told the prisoners. "My boys, my men—it's been so long—so long."

9

An American tank wedged into the walls of Fort Santiago, where the Japanese made their last stand in Manila's Intramuros. When the Japanese refused to surrender, American forces charged into the walled city on February 23, 1945.

10

The ruins of the once-splendid Manila Hotel. The penthouse, which MacArthur had called home, burned in front of his eyes. "I watched, with indescribable feelings, the destruction of my fine military library, my souvenirs, my personal belongings of a lifetime," he wrote.

The blocks of devastation that remained after the battle for Manila in 1945. MacArthur would call the scene "a panorama of physical and spiritual disaster."

The flag-raising ceremony MacArthur attended on Corregidor after taking a PT boat back to the island on March 2, 1945. "I see that the old flagpole still stands," MacArthur said. "Hoist the colors to its peak and let no enemy ever haul them down."

13

The moment when MacArthur and Wainwright reunited in Yokohama, Japan, after the latter's liberation from a prison camp in Manchuria. "The emotion that registered on that gaunt face still haunts me," MacArthur wrote years later.

14

Wainwright watching MacArthur sign the surrender agreement aboard the USS *Missouri* on September 2, 1945. "When halfway through it," Wainwright remembered, "[MacArthur] stopped, turned to me, and asked me to step forward. He gave me the pen, a wholly unexpected and very great gift."

15

General Tomoyuki Yamashita being brought to a prison after the surrender ceremony that Wainwright attended in the Philippines on September 3, 1945. "This might seem a little strange coming from me," Wainwright said, "but I hope Yamashita is shown the courtesy due his rank, in the matter of personal accommodations, housing, and food."

General Masaharu Homma wearing a coat and tie and sitting at a table while on trial in Manila for war crimes. The court had earlier sentenced Yamashita to hang but gave Homma the privilege of a firing squad. "That is too good for him," Wainwright wrote upon hearing the news. "He should have been hanged like Yamashita."

17

Wainwright sitting next to his wife, Adele, and wearing the Medal of Honor after receiving it from President Harry Truman at the White House on September 10, 1945. Four years had passed since Wainwright had last seen Adele. Little could he know that he would not spend the last years of his life living with her.

The ticker-tape parade held for Wainwright in New York City three days after he received the Medal of Honor in Washington. Police estimates put the crowd at four million. Truman worried Americans would "kill" Wainwright "with kindness."

MacArthur standing with Emperor Hirohito at the United States embassy in Tokyo a few weeks after Japan's surrender. "I tried to make it as easy for him as I could," MacArthur wrote, "but I knew how deep and dreadful must be his agony of humiliation."

20

MacArthur speaking in Manila at the independence ceremony for the Philippines on July 4, 1946. "Let history record this event in the sweep of democracy through the earth as foretelling the end of mastery of peoples by the power of force alone—the end of empire as the political chain which binds the unwilling weak to the unyielding strong," MacArthur said.

wife. The most recent letter from Adele carried the date of July 15, 1943. The other two were months older. Over and over, he read the words. "You can imagine how happy I was to get them," he said. That these old letters could say nothing about his promotion ended up not mattering. There was nothing Adele needed to do. On June 15, 1944, he received a message saying the War Department had presumed he accepted.

The next day, Wainwright sent Adele another letter. "I am very well and getting along all right," he wrote. "Of course I am awfully fed up, and long to get home to you, but that seems a long time away." There was so much he could not tell her: that his weight had returned to 145 pounds; that the change in weather had soothed his back and allowed him to return to work on the farm; that rumors of a landing in Normandy had reached him. The end of the war in Europe seemed near. But it made little difference to the prisoners of the Japanese. Nippon seemed nowhere near surrender. He was willing to bet Carroll a double-barreled Winchester shotgun that the war in the Pacific would not end before the last day of 1946. Wainwright had set his mind to at least two more winters away from Adele. He asked her, if possible, to have warmer clothes sent. As it turned out, he would lose the bet with Carroll but very much need the clothes.

*   *   *

The Japanese would not tell Wainwright where they planned to take him next. They would say only that it would be somewhere farther north, somewhere he could not take many of the papers he had amassed during his captivity. Before leading him and the other prisoners out of Muksaq on October 5, 1944, the guards scoured their belongings. Only by slipping his diaries to Sergeant Carroll did Wainwright manage to keep them. The generals went by trucks and train and then by plane to Kyushu, Japan's southernmost main island, and then by rail once more to a coastal town holding a surprise. Inside what seemed like a run-down old resort hotel waited Beebe and the other lower-ranking generals with whom Wainwright had parted ways at Tamazato. The Japanese had moved them into the hotel a few days before.

It was to be a short stay. The worst of the journey lay ahead. On October 10, the Japanese brought the generals farther up the coast and loaded them onto a crowded ship where they spent the night. "Packed in like fish" was how Wainwright described it. The next day, the ship set off—zigzagging as it went so as to elude American submarines and planes with no way of differentiating Japanese ships carrying prisoners of war from other Japanese vessels. At one point, Wainwright heard a gun on the ship begin to fire. He expected to see an American plane coming in, only to discover the target was a mine. He had assumed the voyage would end on some nearby Japanese island. But the ship had gone a different way: north toward Korea. "The matter of our tropical clothing began to concern us," Wainwright remembered. "We had suffered enough from the cold the previous two winters in relatively mild Formosa."

On the afternoon of October 11, the ship docked at Pusan at the bottom of the Korean peninsula. The next morning, the Japanese loaded the prisoners into train cars. Wainwright had a seat but nothing to cushion the wood jolting his back, which now ached as much as ever. Across three days and two nights, they traveled hundreds of miles northward until the mountainous landscape out the windows leveled into a great plain full of fields with all kinds of grain but no rice. The appearance of bread on the train confirmed it: The prisoners had passed out of, as Wainwright put it, "the rice-eating and watery-soup world." They began to see frost on the ground. None of them had any wool clothes. Their bodies began to shake. Some said the train would stop at a city called Mukden, where Arthur MacArthur had observed part of the Russo-Japanese War and where an explosion on the tracks in 1931 had given the Japanese the pretext they needed to seize Manchuria, as this region was known. But the train went on past Mukden for several hours until reaching a village whose name Wainwright recorded as Sheng Tai Tun.

Enclosed by five-foot earthen walls that the Japanese had reinforced with an electrified fence, the camp looked like a fort, which it had been. The Russians had built it long ago, and the coat of accumulated filth in the barracks showed their age. Each room had an antiquated Russian stove, which burned coal faster than the prisoners could feed it. They struggled to stay warm as the temperature dropped below freezing and then below zero. Sometimes, it snowed. For the most part, conditions remained dry, almost arid. To the west lay the Gobi Desert, and, when the wind picked up, as it often did, the dust became so heavy that Wainwright could barely see Ned King on the other side of the room they shared. Almost immediately, Wainwright took ill. Within days, he had lost most of the weight he had put on since leaving Karenko.

On November 14, an additional 259 prisoners arrived from Formosa. Wainwright hoped to see Pugh and Dooley in the group but did not. Only officers ranked colonel and higher had made the trip. The new arrivals had not seen Wainwright since he had left Karenko and, if anything, he looked worse, as if he would collapse without the walking stick he had carried since Corregidor. Of the stick's previous owner, there were tidings. En route to Sheng Tai Tun, the new arrivals had met a newspaperman who told them MacArthur had fulfilled his vow. He had returned to the Philippines. He had landed on the island of Leyte in the Visayas, where he had hoped soldiers fighting on after the surrender of Corregidor would pave the way for his speedy return from Australia. But it had taken far more time. "Two and a half years after Corregidor," Wainwright wrote in his diary. And according to the details he heard, it had taken far more than some scattered guerrillas. It had taken a naval armada the likes of which the Pacific had never seen and several army divisions equipped with supplies and provisions the likes of which the men who had started the war in the Philippines could not have imagined. Wainwright often cursed but rarely in his diary. This was such a time. "Guerrilla warfare," he wrote. "Hell!"

CHAPTER TWELVE

The Return

It happened this way. The debate between Luzon and Formosa had carried on in Washington until September 1944, when Admiral Halsey ended it. Having switched from MacArthur's theater to Nimitz's, Halsey had taken command of the carriers charging across the Central Pacific and had sent some of their planes flying over the Philippines. What the pilots saw convinced him that the Japanese had left the islands, as he put it, "a hollow shell," vulnerable in the middle. Here, he believed, lay an opportunity for his friend MacArthur to jump-start his return to the Philippines. Instead of beginning as always assumed with a landing at the bottom of the chain in Mindanao, he could leap ahead to the island of Leyte in the Visayas.

What would MacArthur say about the idea? "We shall execute Leyte operation on 20 October . . . MacArthur," read the response the joint chiefs received without delay. The message made it seem as if he had approved Halsey's idea. In truth, MacArthur had not even seen it. The criticism he had endured for staying away from Bataan and Buna never adequately accounted for the reverse risk a commander runs by being away from his headquarters. At sea headed to another landing—this one on an island between New Guinea and Mindanao—MacArthur could not receive radio messages from his staff members at the forward headquarters they had established at Hollandia in New Guinea. In his absence, his chief of staff, Richard Sutherland, had made the decision. Fortunately for Sutherland, MacArthur agreed with it. Unfortunately for Sutherland, it seemed to some that MacArthur was embittered that he had lost the chance to make the decision himself. Upon returning to Hollandia, MacArthur confronted Sutherland for having brought his Australian mistress to Hollandia. In fairness, Sutherland had received a warning about her before. Now he received so harsh a reprimand that he offered to resign. MacArthur did not accept but banished the woman.

Only one general could have his woman so close to the front lines, and that was MacArthur. But even his wife now seemed far away. He decided to make a final visit to Brisbane so he could spend a few afternoons driving around the city with her and little Arthur. "I won't be back," MacArthur told Jean privately. Once he made it to Leyte, he would not return to Australia. She would come to him in the Philippines. As soon as he retook Manila, he would summon her and little Arthur. "I want to get back there and see my friends," she said. He promised he would not make her wait a day longer than needed. She began packing immediately. If he landed on Leyte on October 20, he could land in Luzon as early as December 20, he said.

Faced with the speed of that timetable, even Admiral King had to abandon his cherished Formosa plan. For the return to the Philippines, the navy would give MacArthur what it called "the most powerful naval force ever assembled." George Dewey had entered Manila Bay with nine vessels. Douglas MacArthur would enter Leyte Gulf with 738. Dwight Eisenhower could say he had more at Normandy, but MacArthur's naval force boasted, as one historian writes, "much stronger . . . firepower." It had been American forces that had lost the Philippines in 1942, and MacArthur felt that American forces—and not the Australian ones he had used in so many other places—should take back the archipelago. On board the ships, he had 174,000 American ground troops provisioned with hundreds of thousands of tons of medical supplies, weeks of rations, and enough cigarettes to fill 120 cubic feet.

There was also tobacco for the corncob pipes MacArthur had begun to make famous. As he boarded the cruiser *Nashville* with his aides at Hollandia on October 16, a wave jolted the ship and caused him to lose his balance and fall. The sailors watching him held their breath. As if nothing had happened, he picked himself up and saluted. And out to sea they went. On October 18, they converged with the rest of the convoy. "On the waters around me lay one of the greatest armadas of history," MacArthur wrote. "It is difficult even for one who was there to adequately describe the scene of the next two days. Ships to the front, to the rear, to the left, and to the right, as far as the eye could see." But as he drew near the entrance of Leyte Gulf late the next night under a cloudy moonless sky, all the ships beside him vanished into what he described as "the stygian waters below and the black sky above." On the deck of his ship, he felt as alone as he had the night of his escape from the Philippines aboard PT-41. When he tired of staring into the darkness, he returned to his cabin, wrote a letter to his wife, and fell asleep over his Bible.

Soon it was October 20, 1944. In the past, MacArthur had referred to landings by the usual term of D-Day. But everyone around him would call this one A-Day so no one would confuse it with Eisenhower's Normandy landing. By dawn, MacArthur had returned to the bridge with his pants pocket now holding a gun he had inherited from his father. "The ominous clouds of night," he wrote, "still hung over the sea, fighting the sun for possession of the sky, but the blackness had given way to somber gray, and even as we saw the black outline of the shore on the horizon, the cloak of drabness began to roll back." The sun was behind him. But there were flashes of fire all around as ships bombarded the beaches. With his pipe lit, MacArthur stared through his sunglasses. He knew the coastline well. He had surveyed it, he told news correspondents summoned to his side, as a young lieutenant fresh from West Point. He could see the familiar sandy beaches and the jungle rising on the hills behind. Before long, the scene gave way to the smoke that the explosions had come together to form and then to the first wave of landing craft heading into it. Around ten in the morning, they reached the beaches. The correspondents then watched him down a chocolate soda with his lunch, as if unconcerned about the prospect of losing it on the journey that lay ahead of him.

Around one in the afternoon, MacArthur boarded a landing barge and took a seat near the stern. With him were four correspondents and a group of officers including Sutherland, George Kenney, the pilot Dusty Rhoades, and Doctor Egeberg, who by this time had become the general's aide-de-camp and confidant. MacArthur had hoped to have seated beside him his old friend Manuel Quezon, but the president of the commonwealth had died in the United States in August. Instead, it would be Quezon's old rival, Sergio Osmeña, whom the landing barge picked up from a nearby ship. The old "Voice of Freedom" from Corregidor, Carlos Romulo, boarded, too. "Carlos, my boy," MacArthur exclaimed, "here we are—home." For the rest of the voyage, the other passengers kept repeating the phrase. "Well, here we are," as if they themselves could not believe it. "Son," MacArthur yelled to a sailor aboard a boat returning from the beaches, "where is the hardest fighting going on?" The sailor pointed ahead. "Head for that beach," MacArthur said. But the barge could not make it all the way. Less than fifty yards from the beach, it bottomed out. After the image of MacArthur wading the rest of the way ashore had become famous, rumors would spread that he had staged the entire scene. To the contrary, an aide had tried to avoid it by calling for a special boat to carry MacArthur and his party to dry land. The harried officer receiving the request had hundreds of vessels to worry about unloading. "Let 'em walk," he responded. Some of those around MacArthur perceived displeasure in his face as he sank his khakis into the knee-deep water filled with debris. But the cameramen fast enough to capture him striding ashore in fewer than forty footsteps produced pictures that made him look as persevering and prophetic as his promise to return had made him sound.

The smell of burning palm trees greeted him. So did the sound of Japanese gunfire. The American soldiers who had landed on the beach hours earlier had not cleared the last of the pillboxes the Japanese had conscripted Filipinos into constructing. "Hey, there's General Mac-Arthur," Kenney heard one soldier crouching behind a palm tree tell another.

"Oh yeah? And I suppose he's got Eleanor Roosevelt along with him," said the other soldier in disbelief. But the whole world would soon hear the news. With some help from the CBS News correspondent William Dunn, army technicians readied a radio transmitter. By the time they had the microphone ready for MacArthur, it had begun to rain.

For weeks, MacArthur had labored over what to say. As late as the evening before, he remained open to edits. Now the words would reverberate around the globe. "People of the Philippines: I have returned. By the grace of Almighty God, our forces stand again on Philippine soil—soil consecrated in the blood of our two peoples," he said. "Rally to me. Let the indomitable spirit of Bataan and Corregidor lead on. As the lines of battle roll forward to bring you within the zone of operations, rise and strike." The words would open him to the criticism that he had made the moment about himself. It was true he could not have returned to the Philippines alone, but it was also true that he alone had committed America to the course. He had fulfilled part of the vow he had made two and a half years earlier from the train station in Australia, but he had promised more than just a return to a place. He had promised to return to people: the soldiers who remained prisoners on the islands; the Filipino people who had put their faith in his word; Jean and little Arthur, who wanted to return to their old home atop the Manila Hotel. Keeping his promise to all of them would prove more painful than anyone imagined.

*   *   *

"I know well what this means to you," read the message from President Roosevelt. "I know what it cost you to obey my order that you leave Corregidor in February 1942, and proceed to Australia. Ever since then you have planned and worked and fought with whole-souled devotion for the day when you would return with powerful forces to the Philippine Islands. That day has come." As more congratulations made their way to MacArthur in the days after his landing, a more urgent message made its way to Admiral Halsey on the morning of October 25: "Where is Task Force 34?" The ships in the task force should have been guarding the San Bernardino Strait, which offered a backdoor route to Leyte Gulf from the north. But Vice Admiral Thomas Kinkaid, the commander of the armada escorting MacArthur, discovered that a Japanese naval force, including the colossal battleship known as the *Yamato*, had somehow made it clear through the strait. Without informing Kinkaid, Halsey had taken the ships in Task Force 34 with his fleet in pursuit of some carriers the Japanese had dangled as bait as part of a plan to descend on MacArthur's forces in Leyte Gulf from two directions. Luckily, Kinkaid had foiled one part of the plan by obliterating the Japanese ships attempting to pass around the south of Leyte through the Surigao Strait but had only a hodgepodge of vessels to meet the *Yamato* and other Japanese ships coming from the north. Just when it looked as if the tides had turned against MacArthur's return, the Japanese commander became confused and ordered a retreat.

In a desperate bid to thwart MacArthur's return to the Philippines and salvage their empire, the Japanese had brought about a naval engagement that would go into the history books as the largest ever fought. A decisive American victory, the Battle of Leyte Gulf could easily have turned out otherwise as a result of the miscommunication between Kinkaid, who fell under MacArthur's command, and Halsey, who no longer did. The near debacle validated, as MacArthur saw it, the years of warnings he had sent to Washington about the dangers of divided command. During the battle, he had been able to do little but await the result.

For all MacArthur's talk at the Pearl Harbor conference about the superiority of advancing under the cover of land-based aviation, the jump to Leyte had taken him out of the range of his fighter planes. As

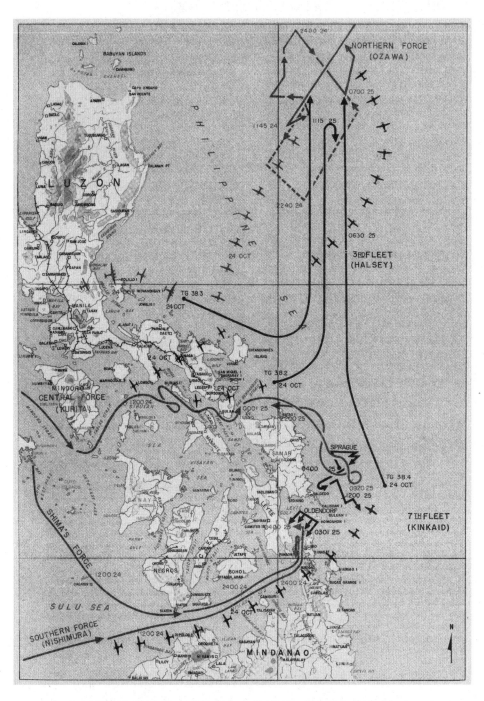

A map made for MacArthur's reports showing the Battle of Leyte Gulf. Had the Japanese emerged victorious from what has become known as the largest naval battle in history, they would have endangered the forces MacArthur had landed on the beaches of Leyte.

a result, he found himself back under enemy aerial bombardment. For weeks after the invasion, bombs fell around the provincial capital of Tacloban, which his men had secured after the landing and where he and Osmeña had held a ceremony marking the revival of civil government on Leyte. MacArthur established his headquarters in a stucco mansion that stood out as the town's largest and, thus, its easiest target. As he had on Corregidor, MacArthur made a habit of either coming outside to watch the air raids or carrying on with meetings inside as if unconcerned about explosions only yards away. While he slept one night, a plane strafing the house planted bullets in a beam over his bed. "Papa is sending you two big bullets that were fired at him and missed," he wrote to his son afterward. MacArthur sometimes seemed not to sleep at all. By the light of his pipe, people would see him walking back and forth along the house's porch late into the night even during the storms that dropped thirty-five inches of rain in about as many days on the island. So much precipitation fell that engineers struggled to build the runways Kenney needed to get his fighter planes into the skies. The lack of progress in the air allowed the enemy to bring more troops to the island by sea. Although the position of the Japanese remained hopeless, their reinforcements dragged out the fighting.

By the end of November, MacArthur had to acknowledge the obvious: He would not land in Luzon by Christmas, as he had hoped. Pushing back his invasion of the island meant pushing back the landings the navy had scheduled afterward for Iwo Jima and Okinawa—to say nothing of his reunion with his wife and son. He had been counting the days since he had last seen them. He would not, he now knew, have them home at the Manila Hotel for Christmas. The only holiday cheer came from Washington, where Congress had passed a new law allowing generals to receive a fifth star. MacArthur became the second general to do so after George Marshall but, importantly, before Eisenhower. Guests at the Tacloban headquarters heard MacArthur bash his old chief of staff, whose drive toward Germany suffered a setback at the Battle of the Bulge.

It was MacArthur's current chief of staff who bore most of his boss's frustration. Shortly before Christmas, MacArthur learned that Sutherland had once again brought his Australian mistress to the front and, even worse, ordered the already overtaxed engineers to build a house for her in Tacloban. MacArthur summoned his chief of staff, dressed him down, and relieved him of his duties (some of which he would soon resume and others of which he never would).

By Christmas, MacArthur's forces on Leyte had suffered 3,000 deaths compared with an astonishing 56,000 for the Japanese. Pacifying the island would require slaying another 27,000 Japanese in the months ahead, but MacArthur did not wait for that bloody milestone to release a communiqué declaring the battle over the day after the holiday. The Japanese on Leyte might fight on, but he was ready to move on. "The Almighty has given me a job to do," officers heard him say, "and I expect to be able to finish it."

On January 4, 1945, he set off for Luzon aboard the cruiser *Boise*. He described it in a letter to Jean as "the most comfortable cruiser on which I have traveled," but the bigger cabin and superior cooking did not explain his change of ships. A few weeks earlier, the *Nashville* had taken a hit from the terrifying weapon the Japanese had debuted in defense of the Philippines: pilots trained to turn their planes into ship-seeking missiles. MacArthur would call them "suiciders." The history books would call them "kamikazes." On the deck of the *Boise*, MacArthur watched as his ship and others in the armada fired into the sky against the new foe taking aim at them over and over again. At one point, he saw a plane swooping downward and then smoke billowing from some less fortunate ship in the distance.

Aides described him as increasingly "restless" as he paced the deck. He kept returning to the rail as if waiting for something on January 8. Then, as he told the story years later, "there they were, gleaming in the sun far off on the horizon—Manila, Corregidor, [Mount] Mariveles, Bataan. I could not leave the rail. One by one, the staff drifted away, and I was alone with my memories. At the sight of those never-to-be forgotten scenes of my family's past, I felt an indescribable sense of loss, of sorrow, of loneliness, and of solemn consecration."

Past the outstretched claws of Bataan—around the head of the dragon-shaped island—and into the gulf between the nape of its neck and its outstretched wings—went the *Boise*. By the same logic that had led American forces in 1899 and Japanese ones in 1941 to Lingayen Gulf, MacArthur brought close to a thousand ships and more than two hundred thousand men into the shimmering violet-colored water there on the morning of January 9.

MacArthur expected little resistance on the beaches and found none. The Japanese would not repeat the mistake he had made three years earlier. Across twelve miles of beaches, four divisions of the United States Sixth Army under the field command of Lieutenant General Walter Krueger came ashore. By the time MacArthur joined them in the afternoon, his engineers had a pier ready so he would not have to soak his pants again. Either because he wanted to see more of the dramatic newspaper descriptions that he had read of himself striding ashore at Leyte or because he did not want soldiers to see him receiving special treatment, he ordered the boat away from the pier. He would later write about it as if he had no choice. "As was getting to be a habit with me," he wrote, "I had to wade in." He returned to the ship later in the day in an ecstatic state. "Mac sat down slick in his room and ate a quart of ice cream—just like a kid at a circus," recorded a brigadier general on staff named Bonner Fellers. "He is very happy tonight for he was playing high stakes and again he was right."

When the Americans had come to the Philippines a half century before, they had built schools. In one of them, MacArthur established his headquarters in the coastal town of Dagupan. Gone was the rain of Leyte. He found Luzon, as he had left it, in its dry season. "Don't you like the feel?" he said to his aides as if eager to share the brightly flowering bushes and palm trees. "Everywhere I went, jubilant Filipinos lined the roads and rent the air with cheers and applause," he wrote. "They would crowd around me, try to kiss my hand, press native wreaths around my neck, touch my clothes, hail me with tears and sobs. It embarrassed me no end."

MacArthur had made it to Luzon but not yet to Manila. As long as that remained the case, the restlessness inside him would not settle. He wanted Krueger to move there as fast as possible. MacArthur had set up a trap. With the Sixth Army coming from the north down the central plain, the Eighth Army under General Robert Eichelberger would land to the south, block the Japanese from retreating into Bataan, and, as MacArthur put it, "close like a vise on the enemy."

It would not be so simple. Roosevelt had been right at Pearl Harbor. The Japanese had more troops on Luzon than MacArthur believed. Rather than the 152,000 that his intelligence chief, Charles Willoughby, supposed, the Japanese had 287,000—about 80,000 more men than MacArthur had brought with him. But MacArthur had what counted more: control of the seas, as well as the skies thanks to the airfields Kenney had brought into operation and the planes the Japanese had squandered on suicide missions. The Japanese position in the Philippines resembled the American one at the start of the war: more men but no chance of victory unless one defined victory, as MacArthur had begun to do for the battle his men had waged on Bataan and Corregidor in 1942, as delaying the enemy. Their courage, he would argue, had made possible all of America's subsequent successes in the Pacific. Skeptics would point out that the Japanese had not let the stand around Manila Bay delay them from conquering other places—in effect, temporarily "bypassing" the starving garrisons there until ready to finish them. But leaders in Japan must have agreed, at least, in part with MacArthur's analysis, for they had changed commanders in the Philippines. Dissatisfied with the performance of General Homma, the Japanese had recalled him and ended his career not long after Wainwright's surrender.

To spoil General MacArthur's return to the islands, the Japanese turned to General Tomoyuki Yamashita, who had become known as the "Tiger of Malaya" for his conquest of Singapore in 1942. Rather than reprise the American withdrawal into Bataan, Yamashita split his army into three pieces. One went with him into the mountains of the dragon's wing rising off the eastern shore of Lingayen. Another dug into the hills west of Clark Field. The third had charge of southern Luzon, including Manila, but had instructions to vacate the city.

Only 110 miles now separated MacArthur from the Philippine capital. There had been no real battle for Manila when the Spanish had surrendered it to the Americans in 1898 or when MacArthur had declared it an open city for the Japanese in 1941. From the start, he assumed the Japanese would observe the precedent themselves. He assumed they would let history guide them as he felt it guided him now. He knew, he wrote, "every wrinkle of the terrain, every foot of the topography" because of the nearly half century of history that bound his family to the land. Aides, who rarely heard him talk about his father, now heard him do so, as Doctor Egeberg put it, "[with] a certain wistfulness, as though he wished that famous general could see what his son was doing now." At one point, Egeberg accompanied MacArthur on a car ride to the Sixth Army's left, or eastern, flank, which lay exposed to Yamashita's force on the dragon's wing. Before long, the car had come into range of Japanese guns shelling the road. Where the fire seemed heaviest, MacArthur ordered the car to stop. He then turned to Egeberg and jabbed a finger into his chest. "On that spot, Doc, about forty-five years ago, my father's aide-de-camp was killed standing right at his side." With the finger still stuck in his chest, Egeberg suddenly had an uncomfortable feeling. He was the aide-de-camp now.

In truth, the threat to the left flank did not concern MacArthur. He thought General Krueger should have already advanced his Sixth Army to Clark Field, where the Japanese had caught the American air force on the ground in 1941. Kenney would have American planes back there by now, MacArthur believed, if not for Krueger's cautiousness. MacArthur's headquarters, as the clerk Paul Rogers remembered, "bubbled and boiled with exasperation with Krueger." Sutherland, desperate to leave MacArthur's staff, even spoke of replacing Krueger. MacArthur would not hear of it. He did not want to reward Sutherland, and Krueger himself represented a tie to Luzon's past. Long before rising to a general officer, he had served under the first General MacArthur as an enlisted man in the Philippines. All the same, Krueger proved immune to the second General MacArthur's exhortations. "Walter's pretty stubborn," MacArthur said after a long meeting with Krueger produced no progress. "Maybe I'll have to try something else." If words could not coax the Sixth Army forward, perhaps embarrassing its field commander would.

On January 25, MacArthur moved his own headquarters far in front of Krueger's—about fifty miles south, not far from where the Japanese had held Wainwright and the other high-ranking prisoners in Tarlac during the summer of 1942. But where the Japanese had shut off the plumbing to the prison toilets, engineers had the swimming pool filled at Hacienda Luisita, the wealthy sugar plantation aides made ready for MacArthur. "We should have Clark Field by now," he said after his first dinner at the hacienda. "We should be announcing the capture . . . but I can't corroborate it." When he tried to drive there the next day to do so, Japanese shells forced him away but did not stop him from issuing a statement announcing the capture of Clark and, for good measure, Wainwright's old home Fort Stotsenburg, too. It was January 26, MacArthur's sixty-fifth birthday. Newspapers hailed Clark and Stotsenburg as the perfect presents, but the Japanese force burrowing into the foothills to the west of Stotsenburg had yet to give either. Not until January 28 did MacArthur's forces win Clark. And not until the last day of January could they raise an old 26th Cavalry flag back where it had formerly flown over Stotsenburg. "Five bitter days' fight after General MacArthur had announced its capture," complained an officer overseeing the operation. "Why does he do this?"

MacArthur had always done this with his communiqués. In this case, however, he had reason to hope he could rush reality into conforming to his rhetoric. A few days before the Luzon landing, army intelligence officers had interviewed American prisoners reporting to be the only survivors of a 150-man Japanese-run camp on the island of

Palawan, west of the Visayas. After seeing an American convoy sail by the island and American planes overhead, the guards had ordered the prisoners into the primitive air-raid shelters they had made by covering narrow trenches in the ground. With all the prisoners jammed inside, the Japanese had doused the trenches with gasoline and lit them on fire. MacArthur knew that the Japanese had thousands more prisoners on Luzon and worried they would meet a similar fate. "As soon as we have a foothold on those shores," he told a photographer for *Life*, "my aim is to push south before they know what's hitting them. I want to save as many of those prisoners as we can." On January 30, army rangers operating with guerrilla forces behind enemy lines carried out a raid east of Tarlac on the prison the Japanese operated at Cabanatuan. Of the eight thousand Americans once held there, only five hundred remained. The others had died or boarded boats bound for slave camps in other parts of the Japanese empire. The Japanese had left behind only the sickest of the sick. Surprising the guards, the rangers carted and, in some cases, carried these starving survivors of the Bataan Death March and Corregidor on one final march to freedom.

For the nearly four thousand American and other Allied civilians held prisoner at a university called Santo Tomas in Manila, freedom remained as far away as the army advancing down the central plain under Krueger. MacArthur had lost patience. With a far less motorized army, the Japanese had made far better time from Lingayen in December 1941. Determined to have no more delays, MacArthur harnessed a force that had always brought out the best in him: competition. His new plan pitted three divisions against one another in a race for the right to pin the phrase "First in Manila" to their battle flags. From the south would come an airborne division that had landed with Eichelberger's army. From the north along the highway on the western side of the central plain would come an infantry division. And along a parallel route to the east would come the cavalry. Three years after members of the 26th Cavalry had made the final cavalry charge in American history—three years after they had seen their horses slaughtered for sustenance—a new kind of cavalry had arrived on Luzon. Unlike the cavalry of old, this new cavalry traded horses for tanks and jeeps and even surveillance aircraft. But like their predecessors, these new cavalrymen would travel fast and light. MacArthur considered them his best fighters. "Go to Manila!" he told them. "Go around the Nips, bounce off the Nips, but go to Manila! Free the internees at Santo Tomas! Take Malacañan Palace [the president's house]!"

Right after midnight on February 1, 1945, two thousand cavalrymen set off with their vehicles arranged in three so-called flying columns. Past the cheering Filipinos who lined the road in every town to welcome their liberators—past checkpoints manned by Japanese soldiers too stunned to elude the bullets coming their way—the flying columns reached speeds of more than forty miles per hour. At 6:35 p.m. on February 3, the first cavalrymen reached Manila. Not long afterward, one of their tanks burst through the gates of Santo Tomas. With the cavalry rode Wainwright's favorite news reporter, Frank Hewlett, who had coined the words "battling bastards of Bataan." Hewlett had not set eyes on his wife since she had fallen prisoner with the city of Manila to the Japanese. Now, at Santo Tomas, he found all eighty pounds that remained of her. Despite suffering a nervous breakdown, she had survived thanks to a group of emaciated women the cavalrymen had not expected to find: the nurses whose fate had so worried Wainwright on Corregidor. In prison as on the Rock, they had stayed by the side of the sick till the end.

MacArthur wanted to join the cavalrymen in Manila immediately. He would have if they had not forgotten to leave behind a guard around a critical bridge they had crossed and the Japanese had subsequently blown up. Not until February 7 could he make it into the city but, even then, only at speeds of no more than five miles per hour through roads clogged with Filipino families walking the opposite way. "They're frightened, scared—look at their faces," MacArthur told the aides riding with him. "They're running away from something horrible." Whatever it was lay hidden behind the smoke he could see rising over the city's skyline.

U. S. TROOPS HIT LINGAYEN BEACHES 9 JANUARY IN FIRST DIRECT MOVE TOWARD MANILA.

DINGALAN BAY

San Jose

Victoria

Tarlac

Cabanatuan

Sangitan

Gapan

CLARK FIELD

San Fernando

Pampanga R.

Caloc

MANILA

MANILA BAY

Pa

Cavi

Abucay

Orion

San Antonio

Olongapo

Dinalupihan

Orani

BATAAN

Mariveles

SUBIC BAY

CORREGI

N

ELEMENTS OF U. S. EIGHTH ARMY LAND ON WESTERN LUZON ABOVE SUBIC BAY 30 JANUARY.

MANILA LIBERATED

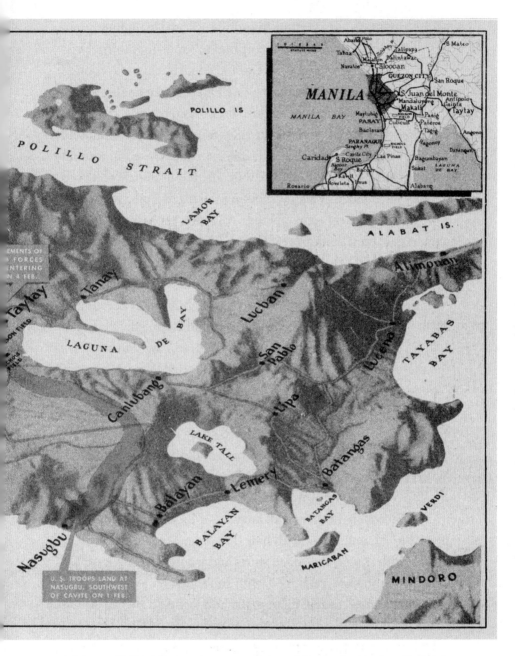

A February 1945 army news map giving a sense of the race for Manila with the infantry coming down the west side of the central plain, the cavalry coming down the east side, and the airborne troops coming up from around Nasugbu, where they had landed to the south. The cavalry won the race not on February 4, 1945, as shown, but on February 3.

At the city limits, MacArthur found his officers, including proud cavalry commanders, waiting to escort him to Santo Tomas. The prisoners there had not known when he would come but knew as soon as he did by the sight of his glimmering cap. Evidently, Japanese soldiers nearby had expected him, too, because they began lobbing shells into the university. As usual, MacArthur showed no concern for himself. But he showed some unease as skeletal internees closed in around him and reached to touch him. "The welcome was hysterical as he was thoroughly surrounded by happy, shouting, talking, weeping people. He couldn't move," Egeberg remembered. "And after ten minutes or so, I thought he gave me a signal to get him out." One woman shouted for his autograph. "I would have to sign hundreds," he protested and instructed the woman to make private arrangements with his staff. After touring the shanties the prisoners had built for themselves out of boards and seeing the children being treated by the nurses of Corregidor, he began to look, his doctor noted, "restless and uneasy." He needed to move on.

But there was something else MacArthur needed to see. His troops had found another prison nearby at a decrepit structure known as the Bilibid, which the Spanish had built as a jail and the Japanese had turned into a hospital, if that word could apply to a place of torture and starvation. Of the more than a thousand prisoners held there, many were soldiers from Bataan and Corregidor. Before he entered, MacArthur wanted it known that the prisoners should not rise from their cots. But many of them did, anyway. "I looked down the lines of men bearded and soiled, with hair that often reached below their shoulders, with ripped and soiled shirts and trousers, with toes sticking out of such shoes as remained, with suffering and torture written on their gaunt faces." Seeing them made him feel sick. He had always hated hospitals. But he could not look away now. Years later, he would remember the odd silence as the eyes staring out of the hollowed faces followed him across the room. He knew some of these men had cursed his name. But he heard no curses now, only whispers: "You're back" or "You made it." He quipped about being "a little late," but they knew the truth as well as he did. They could see it in his eyes. Having taken off his sunglasses, he could not conceal the tears. "I owe you men a lot. I promised I would be back, but I am a long time overdue," he said. "My boys, my men—it's been so long—so long."

The poignancy was more than MacArthur could bear. "I want to get out," he told his aides, "and I want to go forward until I am stopped by fire." The place he had in mind to go might expose him to a great deal of fire. Officers tried to talk him out of it. But he insisted he wanted to head deeper into the city, to Malacañan Palace. The cavalrymen had seized the president's house shortly after Santo Tomas but had not yet cleared the streets of snipers. Nonetheless, MacArthur arrived without incident at the mansion where his father had lived as military governor and where his late friend Quezon had reigned as the commonwealth's first president. Inside Quezon's old office, MacArthur removed his hat and asked the rest of his party to leave so he could be alone with his thoughts.

When MacArthur reemerged, he joined some of his field officers out on a porch. His communiqué the day before had described victory in the city as "imminent." In a statement to reporters, he had gone further. "Our motto becomes: On to Tokyo," he said. "The fall of Manila was the end of one great phase of the Pacific struggle and set the stage for another." He spoke as if the battle already belonged to the history books. Indeed, his staff members had begun drawing up a victory parade that would take him by the Manila Hotel as well as the legislature and other neoclassical government buildings. But between those buildings and the porch off which he stared into the distance lay the Pasig, the river dividing the north side of Manila from the south.

For all the talk of victory, his men had just begun to cross into the south side. The Japanese had blown up the bridges but not until after blowing up the city's commercial center on the north side. Major General Oscar Griswold, the corps commander who would take charge of the three divisions that had raced into the city, watched MacArthur gazing across the river and realized he had deluded himself into

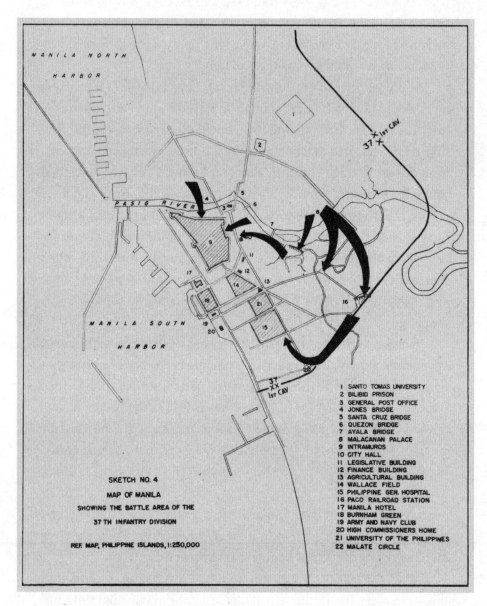

Map text labels:

MANILA NORTH HARBOR

PASIG RIVER

MANILA SOUTH HARBOR

37 X IST CAV

37 XX IST CAV

SKETCH NO. 4

MAP OF MANILA

SHOWING THE BATTLE AREA OF THE

37 TH INFANTRY DIVISION

REF. MAP, PHILIPPINE ISLANDS, 1:250,000

1 SANTO TOMAS UNIVERSITY
2 BILIBID PRISON
3 GENERAL POST OFFICE
4 JONES BRIDGE
5 SANTA CRUZ BRIDGE
6 QUEZON BRIDGE
7 AYALA BRIDGE
8 MALACANAN PALACE
9 INTRAMUROS
10 CITY HALL
11 LEGISLATIVE BUILDING
12 FINANCE BUILDING
13 AGRICULTURAL BUILDING
14 WALLACE FIELD
15 PHILIPPINE GEN. HOSPITAL
16 PACO RAILROAD STATION
17 MANILA HOTEL
18 BURNHAM GREEN
19 ARMY AND NAVY CLUB
20 HIGH COMMISSIONERS HOME
21 UNIVERSITY OF THE PHILIPPINES
22 MALATE CIRCLE

A map made for an infantry battle report showing select positions in Manila, including Santo Tomas, the Bilibid, and Malacañan Palace on the north side of the Pasig River and the legislative building, the Manila Hotel, and Intramuros on the south side. Only when the American infantry and cavalry crossed the river did the real fight for the city begin.

believing he could save the south side of the city. "He does not realize, as I do, that the skies burn red every night as they [the Japanese] systematically sack the city. Nor does he know that enemy rifle, machine gun, mortar fire, and artillery are steadily increasing in intensity," Griswold wrote in his diary. "My private opinion is that the Japs will hold that part of Manila south of the Pasig River until all are killed." By contrast, MacArthur said the Japanese would vacate the city as soon as the first American platoon crossed.

Events might have proved MacArthur correct had his counterpart, Yamashita, been present to enforce his own orders. Instead, Yamashita remained in the mountains east of Lingayen with the bulk of his troops. Rear Admiral Sanji Iwabuchi of the Japanese navy had command of the force of seventeen thousand men in the city and proved no more inclined than American admirals to take orders from a remote army general. As MacArthur toured the prisons and palace, his troops elsewhere in the city stumbled upon a copy of Iwabuchi's plans. There was something strange about them: With Manila Bay lying to the west and with three American divisions closing in from three other directions— the infantry crossing from the north, the cavalry crossing to the east before circling back toward the waterfront, and the airborne coming up from the south—the Japanese had a shrinking window to escape. If they were to do so, as Yamashita had wanted, Iwabuchi would have to move them soon. Yet Iwabuchi's orders, the Americans discovered, made no mention of escape. His men would fall back only when forced to do so and leave nothing behind that could aid the American advance. Because the population of Manila had always seemed sympathetic to MacArthur—because his words had encouraged guerrilla movements and spurred their attacks on Japanese forces—no Filipino man, woman, or child would be spared. In the eyes of the Japanese, everyone in Manila was a military target.

The realization dawned on MacArthur slowly. After visiting the city on February 7, he seemed in no rush to do so again. A curious twelve days would elapse before he did. William Dunn, the CBS correspondent, accused the headquarters staff back at the hacienda of shielding Mac-Arthur from the truth. "The general is going to look ridiculous!" Dunn said. "There is *no* possibility, physically, of a parade." Nevertheless, planning for one went on until February 13, when word finally went out that it would be "put off indefinitely." Manila was burning.

During the months of fighting in the jungles of New Guinea, the soldiers crossing the Pasig had dreamed of Manila's nightlife and neon lights but now found an urban hell where every room of every house became its own fight to the death. General Griswold requested air support from bombers. But MacArthur refused. "The use of air [attacks] on a part of a city occupied by a friendly and allied population is unthinkable," he said. "The inaccuracy of this type of bombardment would result beyond question in the death of thousands of innocent civilians." Innocent civilians were dying anyway, General Griswold griped. As his divisions converged on the southern part of the city, his men found the dead everywhere: heaped in piles behind gas stations, strewn across burned-out churches, hacked to death in houses, and bound with their hands behind their backs behind fences. The troops also encountered rape victims and other survivors who looked little better than the dead, with necks partly severed, breasts cut open, and arms clutching bayoneted babies no one had the heart to declare dead. "We know, too, that the Japs are burning large numbers to death, shooting them, and bayoneting them," Griswold wrote in his diary. "Horrid as it seems, probably death from bombing would be more merciful."

In one regard, MacArthur bowed to the wishes of his field officers. Orders went out relaxing rules that had restricted the use of artillery in the city. As the men MacArthur had left behind on Corregidor could have told him, wrecking a place did not require airpower. Artillery could more than handle the job. Little of what the Japanese did not purposely destroy would survive the artillery duel between the armies. "Block after ruined block marks the progress of the battle for Manila," a correspondent for *The New York Times* wrote. "Any building with intact walls stands defiantly alone in the midst of ashes and concrete rubble."

Among the walls still standing south of the Pasig on the morning of February 23 were the thick ancient Spanish-made ones forming Intramuros and the reinforced-concrete American-made ones forming the neoclassical government buildings. Behind these walls, the Japanese had planned what any child of Fort Custer would have recognized as a last stand. Out of the city's fourteen and a half square miles, the Americans had penned the Japanese into this last square mile. Griswold sent a message begging the Japanese in Intramuros to surrender if not for their own sake, then for the sake of the residents they had rounded up inside the walled city. "Your situation is hopeless—your defeat inevitable. I offer you an honorable surrender," read the statement. "In the event you do not accept my offer, I exhort you that, true to the spirit of the Bushido and the Code of the Samurai, you permit all civilians to evacuate the Intramuros." The message received no response. The Japanese had already given their answer in the destruction and carnage all around. The corollary to their law of no surrender was no mercy.

So at 7:30 in the morning, American guns fired the first of nearly eight thousand rounds that would make rubble of the old Spanish walls. Into the openings billowing with smoke at 8:30 went soldiers armed with flamethrowers and bazookas. Till the end, MacArthur refused to let planes participate in the operation. "I'm not going to let you bomb the Intramuros," he told Kenney. "The world would never forgive us." As it turned out, the Japanese had already burned most of the buildings inside the walls. They had blown up Manila Cathedral's dome and a convent beside the centuries-old San Agustin Church after having herded the residents inside the two. Some starving women and children who had survived made a dash for the American lines. The answer to what had happened to their husbands and fathers awaited at Fort Santiago, where the American flag had first gone up over Manila in 1898. Now the smell of death beckoned the American troops down beneath the fort. The Japanese had stuffed so many bodies inside the underground dungeons that no one would ever know the number.

Around the same time that American soldiers made this sickening discovery, MacArthur made his own a block outside the walls to the south. Amid the destruction, he had prepared himself to accept the total loss of his old penthouse atop the Manila Hotel. "Do not—repeat not—be too distressed over the house," he had written to Jean after hearing of a fire in the hotel. "It was a fitting end for our soldier home." But upon receiving surprising reports that the hotel had survived with the penthouse undamaged, he rushed to the city on the morning of the Intramuros battle only to find himself, as he put it, "temporarily pinned down on Burnham Green [part of the Luneta] by machine-gun fire from the hotel itself." He had endured so many delays on his long journey back to his home, but this final one would prove the most painful. "Suddenly, the penthouse blazed into flame," he remembered. "They had fired it. I watched, with indescribable feelings, the destruction of my fine military library, my souvenirs, my personal belongings of a lifetime." Up the stairs of the burned-out building he went to see the results for himself. At the entrance of the penthouse lay a dead Japanese colonel amid smashed fragments of the vases Emperor Hirohito's grandfather had given MacArthur's father. Jean had hoped the Japanese would recognize the vases and spare their belongings. It seemed for a moment as if some of Arthur MacArthur's books had survived. But the pages crumbled when touched.

Iwabuchi had barricaded himself nearby inside the columned Agriculture Building. American troops would give him one final chance to surrender. He chose to disembowel himself instead. The fight to clear his marines from the last of the neoclassical government buildings east of the Luneta would drag into the beginning of March, but MacArthur would not wait to restore the system of government the architecture represented. To mark the occasion, he returned to Malacañan Palace for a ceremony with President Osmeña on February 27.

There was a terrible silence as MacArthur stepped through the red drapes and began addressing the audience gathered in the ornate room on the other side. He said he had done all he could to spare the city's "churches, monuments, and cultural centers" from the ravages of war, but "the enemy would not have it so." Ninety percent of the buildings in many of the city's most famous areas no longer stood. As he thought about the 613 blocks of absolute wreckage—the hundreds of years of culture lying beneath—his face turned pale. "Cruelly punished though it be," he continued, "[your capital city] has regained its rightful place—citadel of democracy in the East. Your indomitable . . . " Words had always served as his armor. But they deserted him now. "My voice broke," he wrote afterward. "I could not go on."

Perhaps MacArthur remembered that his father had died while giving a speech to his old Civil War regiment after stopping amid a sentence that had begun with those same words: "your indomitable." It felt as if his father were in the room now. Theodore Roosevelt and William Howard Taft, too. They and so many other Americans had filled a half century with promises of democracy and freedom to the Philippines. By keeping his promise, MacArthur had redeemed theirs but at an incalculable cost to the city he loved and the people who called it home. Of the million or so people living in Manila at the time of his arrival, an estimated one hundred thousand had died. "To others it might have seemed my moment of victory and monumental personal acclaim," he wrote of the ceremony afterward, "but to me it seemed only the culmination of a panorama of physical and spiritual disaster."

There would be those who would ponder the perverse irony: Had he not returned—had he bypassed Luzon as many in Washington had wanted him to do—would Manila have burned? But he would not countenance that counterfactual, and not just because bypassing Luzon would have required blockading it and hastening the famine toward which Japanese rule had inched the island. For him, the cruelty with which he had seen the Japanese deal with prisoners and the people of the Philippines made him regret only that he had not returned sooner. The proof lies in what he did immediately after. His motto might have changed to "On to Tokyo," but his orders to Eichelberger could be paraphrased otherwise: "Back to the rest of the Philippines." Without waiting for authorization from Washington—without clear strategic rationale—MacArthur ordered his men to turn their backs on Tokyo to the north and carry out landings to the south in Cebu, Mindanao, and other Philippine islands his forces had bypassed. He could have left the Japanese on those islands, as he had done in other places, "to die on the vine." But to do so in the Philippines would have left people who had put their faith in him to hang as well. He would not leave them waiting till the war's end for freedom. He would keep his promise.

*   *   *

Amid the fighting for Manila, newspapers across the United States ran headlines about a poignant trip MacArthur had taken to Bataan. On February 16, several jeeps full of correspondents had tailed his own to the peninsula and down the road up which the Japanese had led the Death March. Having seen what had happened to the Americans and Filipinos who had made their stand on Bataan, the Japanese had chosen not to make the peninsula central to their defensive plans but had not abandoned it either. As MacArthur made his way south, he reached an active front, a fact made obvious by the American soldiers who had just fought off a "Banzai" charge and had the freshly killed Japanese bodies to prove it. Told that if he continued down the road he would enter a no-man's-land, he looked around and said, "You can't stop me here. We'll go on."

So he did with the correspondents following. At one point, they heard him ask rhetorically if Bataan had changed since 1942. "No," he said. "This could almost be January '42. I feel more at home now than I have for years," never mind that at no point during the war had Bataan served as his home. So far beyond his own lines went his convoy that his aides worried an American fighter pilot circling overhead would mistake the jeeps for Japanese vehicles. The more dangerous the expedition became, the more delighted MacArthur seemed. "This visit is easing an ache that has been in my heart for three years," he said. He hoped to make it all the way to the tip of Bataan, where he would find a view of Corregidor once again under siege but this time by American guns. The paratroopers he had seen make their debut in the skies over New Guinea had scheduled another jump onto the heights of Topside, and he wanted to see some of the show. To his chagrin but very much to the relief of his aides, a demolished bridge kept him from going that far. A return to the Rock had to wait.

When the day came on March 2, 1945, he returned to Corregidor as only he could have: in a convoy of four PT boats with as many members of the so-called Bataan Gang as he could round up. Among them were not only Sutherland but also Richard Marshall, Charles Willoughby, Hugh Casey, and Sid Huff, who had become a full colonel just as MacArthur had promised that dark night aboard PT-41. All the men returning to Corregidor with MacArthur did so with loftier titles and ranks than they had held at the hour of their departure. Press officer LeGrande Diller had earned his own general's star. Even the stenographer Paul Rogers had become a commissioned officer. All of them stepped ashore with MacArthur that morning and joined him in the debris collected around the entrance of the Malinta Tunnel. Rather than surrender as Wainwright had, the Japanese inside the tunnel had blown themselves up. Altogether, about five thousand Japanese soldiers on Corregidor had chosen to sacrifice their lives rather than risk their honor. With his foot, MacArthur rotated one of their skulls so the eyes faced him. "They made it tough for us," he said, "but it was a lot tougher for them." A little east of the tunnel entrance, he saw the foundation of the gray cottage where he had lived with Jean. "I am home again," reporters heard him say. Then it was on to the Topside parade ground. "I see that the old flagpole still stands," MacArthur said, staring at the mangled hundred-foot mast that Wainwright had ordered denuded before raising the white flag. "Hoist the colors to its peak and let no enemy ever haul them down."

There was one more promise to keep. On March 6, he boarded a boat to meet a freighter stuck out in Manila Bay. It could not make it into the harbor because of all the damage, and he could not wait any longer to see its precious cargo: Jean, Arthur, and Ah Cheu. Ever since they had boarded the vessel in Brisbane on February 21, he had ticked off the days till their arrival. Ironically, it was Sutherland who took it upon himself to warn MacArthur that "unfriendly columnists" might publish newspaper articles accusing him of putting his own needs above Manila's. The space Jean, Arthur, and Ah Cheu had taken on the ship could have gone to food and other supplies that the city's population needed. MacArthur showed Sutherland to the door. A press relations officer simply issued a statement saying Mrs. MacArthur had come "to aid and assist in such way as she can in the care of internees and the rehabilitation of the city and its inhabitants." And she wasted no time in doing so. The day of her arrival, she made a visit to Santo Tomas. But those closest to MacArthur knew the real reason he had rushed her to Manila. He needed her for himself. His health remained enviable for a sixty-five-year-old fighting beside much younger men, most of whom could not remember a time when he was not America's most famous soldier. Yet aides heard him say he might not have many years left with his wife. Especially now that Sutherland had forfeited his place as a confidant, MacArthur needed Jean.

It was not easy to find a place to live amid the ruins. Before Jean's arrival, MacArthur heard George Kenney mention a white house he had found for himself north of the Pasig. Fittingly called Casa Blanca, the mansion had a swimming pool and a garden. By the next morning, Kenney discovered the house no longer belonged to him. "George," MacArthur said, "I did a kind of dirty trick on you today. I stole your house." MacArthur tried to make it feel like home. He hired a house-boy named Castro who had served the family before the war. Another loyal Filipino had managed to conceal the family silver from the Japanese, and MacArthur brought it to the house. He and Jean would sleep upstairs, Arthur and Ah Cheu downstairs. Unlike their residence at the Manila Hotel, their new one had no air-conditioning. They would need mosquito nets. The first night there, Jean could hear gunfire coming from outside the city, where Yamashita's forces still fought on. "I think I'd better go down and check on Arthur," she told her husband. She found Ah Cheu asleep but the boy upright. "Do you hear those guns?" she asked.

"Yes, Mommy," Arthur said. "I hear those guns."

"I just want you to know that they're our guns," she said.

"Oh, that's all right," he said, and lay back down as if eager to convince his mother that the sounds had not scared him.

The performance did not persuade her. When she went back upstairs, she told her husband what had happened. "He remembers," she said of the boy, "when we were shelled on Corregidor." She worried the experience had scarred him. The years living in the Brisbane hotel had left their own mark. Instead of dressing up like one of the sergeants he had seen on Corregidor, he sometimes would dress up like the brides at the many weddings he had witnessed at the hotel. Other times he would ask to dress like one of the dancers he had seen in the ballets he liked. Everyone agreed he had a gift for music. He could hear a song one time and, without ever seeing sheet music, play it back on the piano. The bugles MacArthur had fallen in love with as a boy growing up in America's southwest had put him on the path to a soldier's life. The music his son fell in love with in the Southwest Pacific showed signs of leading elsewhere.

MacArthur tried his best to instill the values he cherished in the boy and wrote a prayer that they would read in unison when together. "Build me a son, O Lord," it began, "who will be strong enough to know when he is weak, and brave enough to face himself when he is afraid; one who will be proud and unbending in honest defeat, and humble and gentle in victory." There was more. "Lead him, I pray, not in the path of ease and comfort, but under the stress and spur of difficulties and challenge. Here let him learn to stand up in the storm; here let him learn compassion for those who fail." MacArthur had come through such a storm, but his compassion for those who had not remained difficult to see.

Shortly after welcoming his family back to Manila, MacArthur received a visit from General Eichelberger, who reported how "valuable" guerrillas had proven to operations to retake the island of Mindanao. MacArthur responded that there would have been more guerrillas had the soldiers there taken to the mountains as he wanted in 1942. "I ordered them to keep on fighting, and Skinny [Wainwright] ordered them to surrender while he was a prisoner. It was not a very creditable thing." Eichelberger did not know how to respond. He could see Wainwright's side. But MacArthur, it seemed, could not. "It is all a very peculiar thing," Eichelberger wrote afterward. "I do not know how history will deal with it." An answer to that would have to wait.

CHAPTER THIRTEEN

The Other Return

No longer did Wainwright worry as much about history. If he made it back to the United States, he expected a committee would call him to Washington as part of an investigation into the surrender, but his anxiety as to the outcome had waned. The promotion he had received and the belated discovery that Adele had accepted a Distinguished Service Medal on his behalf in 1943 seemed, he told his diary, "to indicate that the president and the American people have accepted my action with a generous understanding, and that I was left to lead a forlorn hope—the outpost that was bound to be sacrificed." The army, he thought, might let him retire in peace.

There were other matters to concern a man in Manchuria in the middle of the winter. In December 1944, the Japanese once again separated out the three highest-ranking American generals and their orderlies, as well as their British and Dutch counterparts, and transported them on yet another uncomfortable train to yet another penned-in prison yard—this one outside a town called Sian, east of Sheng Tai Tun. "Christmas! Hell!" Wainwright declared in his diary after finding a holiday dinner of five chickens for the thirty-four members of his group to split. "This is a rotten, cold barracks, entirely unfit for persons of our ranks and station. It is the worst of the camps I have been in," he wrote before crossing out the words, almost surely because he remembered the beatings at Karenko. At least here, he had his own room, if one could call it that given the partitions between the cells did not even rise to the ceiling. A heating system piped steam through the barracks, and the prisoners would need all they could get that winter.

At four in the morning on February 2, 1945, Wainwright recorded the mercury on the thermometer hanging outside the barracks at minus forty-nine degrees. "Groundhog Day," Wainwright wrote in his diary. "He sees his shadow. Six weeks more of winter." For such a cold climate, remarkably little snow fell. The winds brought only more and more dust from the desert over the mountains to the west. By March, the worst days began to remind Wainwright of the so-called Dust Bowl in Kansas. When the sun showed at all, it did so with a silvery hue. It was hard to see any evidence of spring, but it made no difference to the Japanese. As if bound by the calendar, the guards began reducing the heat—first in mid-March to only an hour and a half in the mornings and evenings, and then in early April to almost none at all. On April 3, the mercury stood at sixteen degrees outside and forty-four degrees inside. Wainwright wore all the clothes he had, and even those were not enough because the Japanese had taken back the only heavyweight ones provided. Wainwright guessed that at least three more weeks would have to pass before the weather really warmed. "Well, I guess I can take it," he wrote.

The watch he had used to keep time throughout his captivity, however, could not take it. He had devoted entire pages of his diary to measuring how many seconds the timepiece gained or lost during the course of days. But now it could not keep time at all. "That is a real calamity," he wrote. "Now I will have no way of knowing what time it is *for the duration.*" He tried to pass the hours the best he could. Two enlisted men to whom he would feel indebted ever after had managed to transform an old cot into an easy chair where he could rest, as he put it, "my old bones" and read. There were no newspapers to read anymore. The Japanese would not share them. So Wainwright read the few books he found over and over. He kept playing solitaire and smoked eight cigarettes a day—four from the ration the Japanese provided and four from Red Cross packages. The Japanese offered to let him keep a vegetable garden or tend to chickens. "I do NOT," Wainwright wrote in his diary. "I had enough grief with animals at Muksaq." Besides, he had found a new vocation: sharpening razor blades for fellow prisoners. He even gave the service a name: Wainwright Razor Blade Sharpening Establishment.

There were still more hours to fill. Although no letters ever reached Wainwright in Sian, the Japanese let him send some with the caveat, of course, that he not share his real thoughts. Those could go only in his diary. At Sian, he fell into the habit of writing a lengthy recap of the week every Sunday and ending it with a phrase he remembered American Indians using: "I have spoken." But the more he wrote, the more, it seemed, he withdrew into himself.

Part of the problem was Wainwright's own hearing. He had always struggled to understand what the Japanese were saying. Now he could not even make out the British and Dutch. That was the explanation he offered, anyway, for resigning from the central governing committee the prisoners from the three countries had set up among themselves. In his diary, he offered another reason. "I cannot stomach the British arrogance and bullheadedness, and the suave, slick, and insincere Dutch diplomatic talk," he wrote. Fellow prisoners had previously credited Wainwright with helping hold the different nationalities together. Now he swore to have no future dealings with them. The British especially had begun to infuriate him. They should have received the same diet as all the other prisoners—cornmeal mush to start the day, soup in the midday, and soybeans to end the day—but without consulting their fellow prisoners, five Britons had asked the cook to set aside an extra helping of cornmeal mush for dinner because they suffered flatulence from eating beans. Everyone, Wainwright roared in his diary, suffered flatulence because of beans. And because of this selfishness, he had more of them and less cornmeal mush, which everyone agreed was "the only palatable thing we have to eat." If that was not bad enough, there was another British officer who kept his window open no matter the temperature. Who could blame the Japanese for shutting the heat off if the British were going to waste it? "There certainly is no sense in burning up good coal to try and heat the whole of outdoors Manchuria," Wainwright wrote. The British and Dutch begged him to join them in writing a letter of protest. But he refused. "I want nothing to do with them as a whole," he wrote. "I have spoken."

For the first time, Wainwright even had bad words for Sergeant Carroll, whom the Japanese forced to work seven days a week with the other enlisted men. Carroll made the mistake of removing a paper liner he had put over the windows a few weeks prematurely and letting a draft and dust into the barracks. "As usual, he will not listen to anyone else," Wainwright wrote. "I have spoken." But in this case, he had spoken too soon. He would need Carroll more than ever.

On May 12, Wainwright "slipped," as he put it, his sacroiliac between his spine and pelvis. He had injured the joint, which accounted for his lower back pain, many times before, but now it set off the sciatic nerve. The pain traveled through his buttocks and thigh and sent him to bed. A few times he thought himself improving. At least once he forced himself up for roll call. But bowing to the emperor, as the Japanese still made the prisoners do, worsened his pain. By June 12, which Wainwright noted to be the "39th anniversary of my graduation from West Point," he had begun to fear he would never recover. "I am afraid it is now chronic," he wrote. "If so, that is the end of my soldiering." No longer could he rise from bed. Carroll moved his cot into the room. "Carroll," Wainwright wrote, "cares for me, day and night. He is at his best under these conditions." The agony grew so severe over the next week that sleep itself became a dream. A shot of morphine gave Wainwright only a few hours relief. "If this keeps up, I know I can't survive," he wrote. "Thin and weak as I am and no proper food, I doubt if I can endure this pain for any long period of time." His weight fell to 131 pounds.

What saved Wainwright was a memory. His body could go nowhere, but his mind went back to his lowest point in the Philippines. He had held on as long as humanly possible. That was what he wanted the world to say of his stand on Bataan and Corregidor, and that was what he wanted said again of his struggle for life now. "I will make a fight for life, as I fought against overwhelming odds in the Philippine Islands," he wrote in his diary on June 19. The Japanese had taken his freedom but not his pride. "No one called me yellow then, and, by God, I won't be now. . . . I have spoken." On the struggle went. "There seems to be no end to it," he wrote on June 24, "but I *will* fight on." And he did for weeks more until, by mid-July, he could go for short walks again with help from the walking stick he had picked up on Corregidor.

There was another force pushing Wainwright. Four years had passed since he had seen Adele board the ship out of Manila. The years apart had made him realize the sacrifices she had made for him, the hardships she had endured. "I realize more and more how much she has done for me. Without her, I never would have risen to my present rank and station in life," he wrote. She had built her life around his career. If he returned alive, he wanted to build the rest of his life around her wishes. "How I do long to see her," he had written on their most recent anniversary in February. "But that will have to wait for at least two, or possibly three years."

In August 1945, Wainwright decided to revisit that estimate. Hard as he looked, he still could see no way around two more Manchurian winters. Unusual events around the camp, however, began to make other prisoners think otherwise. At four in the morning on August 9, the prisoners awoke to the sound of an explosion. Wainwright passed it off as insignificant, just another one of the air-raid drills the Japanese liked to conduct. But they began doing the drills twice a day afterward and blackouts at night, too. On August 12, the Japanese ordered the prisoners to begin packing for another move but, a few days later, called it off. "There is a decided feeling of unrest," Wainwright wrote in his diary on August 18. "Something seems to be going on that causes a lot of uncertainty." As to what, he had to wait to find out until that night when he received a visit from a fellow prisoner. "I congratulate you, General."

"Really?" Wainwright remembered responding with all sincerity. "Upon what?"

"The war is over."

*   *   *

The news seemed impossible. Wainwright could not believe it. More than a half year had passed since he had seen a newspaper or received mail. From time to time, guards had admitted that "the war was going well for the Americans." He could not have imagined how well.

Wainwright had assumed that victory in the Pacific could not come before victory in Europe. He had not known that, with American and British forces in Germany and with Soviet ones actually in Berlin, the Nazis had surrendered in May 1945. He had believed the Japanese would never follow suit unless his countrymen found some way to take the fight to the Japanese homeland. He had not known all the ways his countrymen had found. He had heard that American forces had taken the Marianas. He had not known that the United States now had a bomber, the B-29 Superfortress, with a range far greater than that of the old B-17 Flying Fortress and able to fly missions covering the fifteen hundred miles between the Marianas and targets in Japan. He had learned that the Japanese way of building with paper and wood made their houses fire-prone. He had not known that American bombers armed with a new incendiary called napalm had burned entire cities, including Tokyo. He had heard that an American submarine had sunk a Japanese ship carrying Red Cross supplies in recent months. He had not known that the better part of the Japanese navy had also gone to the bottom. He had believed that airpower and sea power alone would not suffice to defeat Japan and that the United States would need, as he put it, "possession of an island near enough to Japan to permit of a landing on the mainland." He had not known that his countrymen had already acquired such an island in Okinawa, 350 miles below Japan, and that the joint chiefs had begun planning for his old chief, Douglas Mac-Arthur, to lead the invasion of the home islands: Kyushu in November 1945 and Honshu in early 1946. Wainwright had expected American forces on the islands would face terrible resistance—the Japanese, he knew, did not believe in surrender. He had not known about the new weapon developed in Los Alamos, New Mexico. Not even MacArthur had known about the atomic bomb until days before a B-29 dropped one on Hiroshima on August 6, 1945.

Another bomb had leveled Nagasaki on August 9, but that had not been the noise that had woken Wainwright and his fellow prisoners at Sian early that morning. He had known that MacArthur had hoped to bring the Soviets into the fight against Japan as part of a fanciful plan to save the Philippines at the start of the war. Wainwright had not known that the Soviets had finally notified the Japanese on August 8 that a state of war would exist between their countries as of the next day and, sure enough, sent troops into Manchuria at midnight. That explained why the Japanese had almost moved Wainwright afterward. An unprecedented radio broadcast by the Japanese emperor on August 15 announcing the decision to surrender—"[to] bear the unbearable," as Hirohito privately put it—explained why the guards had called off the move.

On the morning of August 19, Wainwright and his fellow prisoners assembled for *tenko*, the word they had learned to use for roll call. The camp commander who everyone called Lieutenant Marui delivered a short speech, which the prisoners could not understand until an interpreter began translating. "By order of the Emperor, the war has now been amicably terminated. . . ." The interpreter did not make it a word more. None of the prisoners had discussed how to react. But almost every one of them, as Wainwright remembered it, reacted the same way. "We roared suddenly with laughter . . . roared until the rest of his words were blotted out. There was no stopping the laughter. It came in me, and in the others, with an irresistible force: something born of a combination of our relief, the look on the Jap's face, the blind preposterousness of his beginning, the release from years of tension, the utter, utter joy over having survived to see this blessed day." Their war had ended. And yet, as the interpreter took the opportunity to remind them, they remained prisoners of war. Whether any friend beyond the prison walls even knew their whereabouts, no one could say.

The answer to that question came with shocking speed. After roll call, a guard told Wainwright that two Americans had arrived at the camp and wanted to see him. He should report immediately to the commander's office. Wainwright walked over but dared not breach the doorway without permission. Inside, he saw Lieutenant Marui speaking with two strangers. More than three years had passed since Wainwright had seen Americans the way he remembered them back home: healthy and well-fed. He could not contain himself. "Are you really Americans?"

One of the men nodded. He introduced himself as Major Robert Lamar and his comrade as Sergeant Harold Leith. They belonged to an intelligence agency called the OSS, or Office of Strategic Services. Wainwright had never heard of it, not because it had been kept secret from him but because it had not existed at the time of his surrender. If the appearance of these two men confused him, his appearance appalled them. Leith thought Wainwright "looked like a tattered scarecrow." Worse was watching how he behaved when Marui finally motioned him into the room. As had become customary, Wainwright bowed. Lamar asked Wainwright to take a seat. "He must remain standing," Marui yelled, as if offended his visitor did not know the protocol for meetings with prisoners. Lamar insisted Wainwright sit. Finally, Marui conceded.

"General, you are no longer a prisoner. You're going back to the States," Lamar said.

These were the words for which Wainwright had waited. And yet they did not bring the relief he had imagined. They brought back instead the fear he had fought against for so long. All the evidence he had stockpiled to the contrary, as it turned out, had not put his mind at ease. The question still haunted him: "What do the people in the States think of me?"

"You're considered a hero there," Lamar said. "Your picture is even in *Time* magazine." Wainwright looked skeptical, yet the very story of how Lamar and Leith had come to the prison should have removed any doubt. The mission had its origins with George Marshall, who had worried about what the defeated Japanese would do to their prisoners, especially to those now caught in the chaos of the Soviet invasion of Manchuria. He had assigned responsibility for bringing these men home to the American commander in China, Lieutenant General Albert C. Wedemeyer, who in turn had assigned teams of OSS operatives to parachute into places suspected of housing prison camps. Lamar and Leith belonged to a six-man team code-named Cardinal, which had jumped on August 16 into Mukden, where intelligence indicated the Japanese operated their largest prison camp in Manchuria. Indeed, not far from the landing spot, the members of Cardinal had found seventeen hundred prisoners of war, including many officers, but not the highest-ranking of the generals and not the one whose fate had most concerned Wedemeyer and Marshall. They wanted Wainwright. So Lamar and Leith had broken off from the rest of their team and set off for Sian, about 150 miles to the northeast. Now that they had located Wainwright, they faced the harder half of their mission: getting him out.

With the Soviets having severed communication between Sian and Mukden, Lamar and Leith had no way of notifying their team that they had found the highest-ranking generals. So Lamar set off alone for Mukden on August 20 with the promise he would return with transportation for the prisoners. But days passed, and he did not return. Having finished packing in mere hours, Wainwright and the other prisoners had nothing to do but interrogate Leith about how the world had changed during their captivity. "The general," Leith noted in his diary, "had not yet heard about jet planes." Perhaps to discourage Wainwright, the Japanese had shared one piece of news that he had refused to believe until Leith confirmed it. Franklin Roosevelt, whose final message to Corregidor had given Wainwright some consolation when nothing else could, had died in April. Harry Truman had taken office.

On August 23, Wainwright celebrated his sixty-second birthday. "The prospect of getting home soon makes this the happiest birthday in many years," he wrote in his diary. He took the opportunity to send his fellow prisoners a "notice" declaring, "The Wainwright Razor Blade Sharpening Establishment is hereby closed." At the bottom, he left room for his "customers" to endorse a statement reading, "I am delighted with the cause which enables the proposition to retire from business at the great age of sixty-two." Wainwright had not lost his humor, but he also found himself increasingly impatient. There was a bottle of scotch said to be waiting in Mukden with his name on it. "We were in a mood to hitch up our belts and walk," he wrote.

Then on August 24, Wainwright heard the sound of jeeps. A Soviet column had arrived, and at its head was, as he put it, "about the toughest-looking fighting man I have ever seen." With Leith translating, the Soviet commander said his men were on their way to Mukden. If the prisoners could procure transportation, they could come, too. The Japanese, Wainwright knew, had a few old trucks and buses. Wainwright asked for them. "Yes, sir," Lieutenant Marui responded. By the time the vehicles appeared, the Soviets had stripped the Japanese commander of his sword. "I will no longer allow myself or the other Americans here to be considered prisoners of war," Wainwright said. "We will take no further orders from you or your men, and we will leave with the Russians." And so at around six o'clock in the evening, Wainwright and the other prisoners drove out of the prison gate. "Officially released from captivity as P.O.W. and now under Russian military escort to Mukden," he wrote in his diary.

The road to freedom was not smooth. The engines of the old buses and trucks kept breaking down. Mud kept swallowing the wheels. When the prisoners gratefully switched to a train, it derailed after just a few hundred yards. When a new train came, it broke down, too. Finally, at one in the morning on August 27, Wainwright reached Mukden, where so many of his old friends awaited: not only his old chief of staff, Lew Beebe, and the other generals and colonels Wainwright had last seen in December 1944 at Sheng Tai Tun but also the lower-ranking officers he had left behind at Karenko in April 1943—most important, his two aides, Johnny Pugh and Tom Dooley. There was no time to see any of them that night. Major Lamar, who had feared the worst had happened to Wainwright on the road from Sian, escorted him to a hotel. "A real bed," Wainwright wrote in his diary, "first one in over three years." He could sleep for only a few hours. He had a flight to catch after sunrise. He had learned he was not going home yet. He had somewhere else to be on September 2, the place where any fighting man would want to be, aboard the USS *Missouri* in Tokyo Bay for the official surrender ceremony. MacArthur himself would be presiding.

Wainwright believed his invitation had come from MacArthur. In a sense, it had, but only after George Marshall had forced the issue. The American people, the army chief of staff told MacArthur, would expect to see Wainwright at the ceremony, and the old cavalryman deserved no less. MacArthur could hardly say no. He would be "delighted," he responded, to have his old lieutenant there. Wainwright accepted the invitation on one condition. He knew room aboard the *Missouri* on September 2 would be hard to find. But he wanted some space set aside for Beebe, Pugh, and Dooley, as well as the faithful Sergeant Carroll. "All this group were with me on the tragic day when I had to surrender," Wainwright wrote MacArthur, "and I'm especially anxious that they be present when we accept the Japanese surrender." They would be among the thirty-eight passengers—a mix of American, British, and Dutch officers—flying out of Mukden with Wainwright at ten o'clock in the morning on two army planes sent specially for him. Tears streamed down his face as he saw Beebe, Pugh, and Dooley for the first time at the airport.

The next few days would be a blur of takeoffs and landings. At the first American base at which the prisoners landed in China, they had their fill of ice cream. "You should have heard Skinny say, 'Aah!' after his first bite of ice cream in three years," wrote a witness. At a second American base in China, the prisoners found as much alcohol as they could drink, per unofficial orders Wedemyer had received. "Chocolate, cigarettes, food, liquor have been rained on us in profusion, and I find that I cannot keep up," Pugh wrote. "My insides so shrunken cannot get used to such plenty." As the freed prisoners ate and drank, they compared the fare to the rice they had consumed in prison and cursed their former captors. "The utterances were as polite as polite conversation will permit but I couldn't help but feel the vehemence of their stored up hate," said an officer on Wedemeyer's staff. "Hate is a part of their lives, their manners, their speech, and—I'm sure—a part of their soul." The staff member worried about Wainwright in particular. "He's not doing too well. The effects are quite apparent and he's gotten quite deaf not to mention detached." When he spoke, he spoke too loudly, as if unable to modulate his voice.

Nonetheless, Wainwright could hear a bugle play reveille in the morning as soldiers raised the Stars and Stripes over the base. "It was a blood-tingling sight for all of us, for it was the first American flag we had seen since the last one came down on Corregidor," he wrote. He also received his first look in four years at his wife. Through a service called radiophoto, she sent him a picture with a handwritten message. He sent her one back of himself. A press conference gave reporters their own look at Wainwright. They described him as "gaunt, stooped, and looking his nickname, Skinny." For now, he would tell reporters only this: "I have had little contact with the outside world, but what little I have had has caused me to believe that the administration, the War Department, and the American people have accepted my dire disaster with a forbearance and generosity greater than any in the experience of any other defeated commander."

On August 30, Wainwright left China aboard a B-17 with Beebe, Pugh, Dooley, and Carroll, along with the highest-ranking British prisoner of war, General Percival, and his orderly, both of whom had their own invitation to the USS *Missouri*. Before heading there, the seven of them had a stop to make in Manila, where MacArthur had ordered his aide Sid Huff to have a team of barbers and tailors ready to go to work. "Give them the best we have," Huff recalled MacArthur saying. As the plane neared Luzon, Wainwright requested to fly over Bataan so he could see the place he had hoped to be—the place he had promised to be if still alive—when MacArthur returned. Across the bay in Manila, President Osmeña waited to welcome Wainwright as he limped off the plane with his cane. He hardly recognized the city as he drove into it. "Manila was shockingly destroyed," Wainwright wrote. "The very contour of the city seemed changed. We entered Dewey Boulevard by a route which was totally unfamiliar to me, and, as we proceeded down that avenue, I saw that the spacious mansions which once lined it had been burned or broken to the ground. In their places stood barracks and supply dumps." The war had ended, but the task of rebuilding had barely begun. There was no time for sightseeing. At six o'clock the next morning, Wainwright and his party set off for Okinawa, where they had a short layover before flying to Atsugi Airfield, outside the city of Yokohama on Tokyo Bay.

MacArthur had arrived the day before aboard a new plane he had named like his old one, *Bataan*. Winston Churchill supposedly declared MacArthur's landing at Atsugi the bravest "of all the amazing deeds of bravery of the war," and, no doubt, it had required bravery. Fellow officers worried they did not have enough American troops on the ground to protect MacArthur. The Japanese themselves worried they would be unable to subdue the committed kamikaze pilots the airfield housed. They did not worry MacArthur, however. As he stepped off the *Bataan* with his corncob pipe, he told the members of his party not to carry any guns. "If the Japs didn't really mean what they had said about surrendering, those pistols wouldn't do us much good," he joked. In seriousness, he wanted the Japanese to see him unarmed in their native land. "It told them more than anything else that they had lost the war," George Kenney wrote afterward. "MacArthur's instinct for figuring out the workings of the Oriental mind was still paying off."

The Japanese soldiers lining both sides of the road to Yokohama faced away from MacArthur's motorcade as it made its way to the bombed-out city. The formation baffled the Americans until someone explained the Japanese usually reserved it for the emperor, who they deemed a god but who, according to the surrender terms, "[would] be subject to the Supreme Commander of the Allied Powers." Truman had given MacArthur the job. Wanting to wait to enter Tokyo until after the official surrender, the new supreme commander set up quarters at the New Grand Hotel in Yokohama.

That was where Wainwright headed after landing at Atsugi on the afternoon of August 31. Memories of his arrival have faded in a haze of controversy, and most of it owes to President Truman, who told the story two decades afterward that MacArthur refused to see Wainwright when he entered the hotel dining room during lunch. "General Wainwright walked in on him and started to salute and talk to him," Truman said. "MacArthur—instead of asking him to sit down and have lunch—he said, "General, I told you I'd see you at 3 o'clock! I'll see you at that time." Being on the other side of the world on the day of the reunion, Truman did not witness it, and none of those who did would corroborate his version of events.

For starters, Wainwright had eaten lunch during his layover in Okinawa. By the time he arrived at the hotel, it was past eight o'clock in the evening. MacArthur had started supper in the dining room. Some members of the Wainwright family would later blame MacArthur for not immediately coming out to the lobby. But MacArthur would claim he tried. "I was just sitting down to dinner when my aide brought me the word that they had arrived," he remembered. "I rose and started for the lobby, but before I could reach it, the door swung open and there was Wainwright." Wainwright himself seemed not to care one way or the other. According to his memory, MacArthur had left instructions to meet him at the table. "I washed up and went in," Wainwright wrote. "And there he was, looking fine and fit and every inch the leader he is. He got up when he saw me coming toward him on the cane he had left me years before. He reached his arms out, took hold of me, cocked his head, and looked me over."

A photographer captured the moment the two men embraced. MacArthur pulled his head back not to escape but as if to bring a face from the past back into focus. Wainwright, MacArthur wrote, "was haggard and aged. His uniform hung in folds on his fleshless form. He walked with difficulty and with the help of a cane. His eyes were sunken and there were pits in his cheeks. His hair was snow white and his skin looked like old shoe leather." At first, neither man opened his mouth. Neither man knew what to say. In the three and a half years since MacArthur and Wainwright had last seen each other, an age had gone by. A war that had begun with American soldiers sampling monkey and iguana on Bataan had ended with American generals ordering steaks in a Japanese hotel. A war that had begun with men on horseback had ended with men manufacturing an atomic bomb. It was hard to reconcile, and it was perhaps unfair to expect even a man as eloquent as MacArthur to find the words to do so.

"Well, I'm glad to see you," MacArthur said.

The words still did not come to Wainwright. Reporters saw him swallow. "I'm glad to see you, too," he finally said. Both men had tears in their eyes.

The staff members sitting with MacArthur at the table reshuffled their seats so the two generals could sit beside each other and continue talking. Wainwright spoke of the years he had spent worrying that Americans would never forgive him—never give him a new command—because he had surrendered his last one. "Shocked" was how MacArthur described his own reaction to hearing this, never mind the words he himself had used to characterize Wainwright's surrender not only at the time ("unbalanced") but also much more recently ("not . . . very creditable").

Accounts of what happened next diverge. According to one version, MacArthur said Wainwright could have any command he wished. Wainwright supposedly replied, "I want command of a corps—any one of your corps." If true, the request represented a major departure from Wainwright's usual way of thinking. Why would a professional soldier who had always taken promotions so seriously have asked for what would have amounted to a demotion? As a lieutenant general, Wainwright's rank put him in line to command far more than one corps. When he had surrendered in the Philippines, he had commanded all forces on the islands. By a seemingly more plausible account, it was MacArthur who offered Wainwright a corps. "Why, Jim," this version has MacArthur saying, using his old nickname for Wainwright, "you can have command of a corps with me any time you want it!" Notably, this was essentially the account that MacArthur himself endorsed. He had not wanted to leave Wainwright in charge of the full Philippines and, as others knew, still blamed him for what had happened.

That is not to say MacArthur made his offer disingenuously. In the ruins of Manila, his soldiers had recently discovered communications between Wainwright and the generals in the Visayas and Mindanao during those fateful days in May 1942 when he had believed the Japanese would murder all the men and women on Corregidor if American forces elsewhere in the archipelago did not surrender. The documents did not contain any information that MacArthur could not have known before, but perhaps reading them made him slightly more sympathetic to the dilemma Wainwright had faced. Whatever the truth, MacArthur believed what he said at the dinner table touched Wainwright. Probably it did. "The emotion that registered on that gaunt face still haunts me," MacArthur later wrote. When Wainwright stepped out of the dining room, he told reporters he had never felt more elated. He had a gun back in his holster and soon would have revenge against the people he hated most: the Japanese.

On the morning of September 2, 1945, Wainwright and his aides boarded the destroyer that took them to where the USS *Missouri* waited in Tokyo Bay. Christened only the previous year, the *Missouri* reminded Wainwright of a "gigantic hedgehog" with guns for bristles. "I simply could not believe that anything could be so huge, so studded with guns," he thought as he stepped aboard. Here, he was in Tokyo Bay on a battleship of the sort that the men on Bataan and Corregidor could only have dreamed of sailing to their rescue in Manila Bay in 1942, per the old War Plan Orange. Over the *Missouri* flew two five-star pennants for the two five-star officers on board: Admiral Nimitz and General MacArthur. The latter could not have failed to see the irony: On board the ship, he had finally achieved unity of command. He would run the show, but, first, he needed to run to the bathroom. As always before a major moment, MacArthur felt sick.

The surrender documents lay ready on a table draped in green and flanked on three sides by American army and navy officers, representatives of the other Allied powers, and members of the media. "The fourth side of the square," Wainwright noted, "was left open for the Jap delegates." He watched as the eleven men representing Japan—some wearing frockcoats and top hats and others wearing military garb—took their places with an expression he described knowingly as "glum." Wainwright remembered how the Japanese had subjected him to their cameras as he waited for General Homma on Bataan. Now cameras from around the world turned their lenses on the Japanese as they waited for MacArthur. He did not make them wait nearly as long. In a few minutes, he appeared in a plain khaki uniform notable only for the five stars on the collar and the braid on the worn-out cap. Up to a microphone standing across the table from the Japanese, he stepped. "We are gathered here, representatives of the major warring powers, to conclude a solemn agreement whereby peace may be restored," he said. He had written out what he wanted to say. And rather than rely on his famous memory, he read from a sheet that shook in his fingers. Unlike the Homma-Wainwright meeting where neither party had known what the other would do, the ceremony MacArthur had scripted left only the trembles of his hands to chance.

When MacArthur finished, Sutherland showed the Japanese where to sign. A representative from every Allied power would need to sign, too. Nimitz would sign for the United States but not before MacArthur signed as supreme commander. He had brought six pens for the job—three for the Allied copy, three for the Japanese one. As he sat at the table, he signaled for Wainwright and Percival to stand behind the chair. Marshall had said Americans would expect to see the former prisoners. MacArthur would make sure his fellow citizens did. He wanted to teach them a lesson, an aide remembered, "[about] the unpreparedness of two great democracies" at the start of the war. No one represented the cost of that failure better than Percival and Wainwright. MacArthur started to sign his name with the first pen. "When halfway through it, he stopped, turned to me, and asked me to step forward," Wainwright remembered. "He gave me the pen, a wholly unexpected and very great gift." Percival received one, too. So eventually would Jean.

Once the Allies had finished signing, MacArthur said, "These proceedings are closed," even though he had one more speech to make. While fighting on faraway fronts, he had never forgotten the home front. Over the radio now, he spoke directly to his countrymen. "As I look back on the long, torturous trail from those grim days of Bataan and Corregidor, when an entire world lived in fear, when democracy was on the defensive everywhere, when modern civilization trembled in the balance, I thank a merciful God that He has given us the faith, the courage and the power from which to mold victory." Then, alluding to the new age of nuclear weapons, he said, "We have had our last chance. If we do not now devise some greater and more equitable system, Armageddon will be at our door." The only hope, as he saw it, lay in the Pacific islands on which his father had planted the American flag. "In the Philippines, America has demonstrated that peoples of the East and peoples of the West may walk side by side in mutual respect and with mutual benefit. The history of our sovereignty there has now the full confidence of the East. And so, my fellow countrymen, today I report to you that your sons and daughters have served you well and faithfully." He could have said the same about himself to his father.

Wainwright was thinking about his own son. The army had made plans to fly Wainwright back to San Francisco and then to Washington. Word had it that he might miss seeing Jack, who was in San Francisco but about to cross the Pacific the other way. Before bidding farewell to MacArthur at the pier in Yokohama, Wainwright mentioned the concern. MacArthur promised to help. On that subject, there was another area where MacArthur said he would be happy to give assistance: Wainwright's as-of-yet unwritten memoirs. There was talk of a bidding war for the rights to publish them. "I hear that you've been offered a lot of money," MacArthur said. Wainwright did not deny it. Some of the unsolicited offers had gotten so large—six figures—that he had no clue what to make of them. "Bully," said MacArthur. "You write them [the memoirs], then send them to me, and I'll check them and send them on to the War Department." Wainwright had spent years worried what MacArthur would say. Now, to borrow the expression Wainwright used to explain his glee at the Japanese surrender, "the shoe was on the other foot."

It was farewell to MacArthur and then right back to Luzon, where Wainwright had another ceremony to attend the next day. Disappointed that the Japanese had not selected Homma to represent them aboard the *Missouri*, Wainwright would have the pleasure of witnessing the surrender of another Japanese general reviled in the Philippines: Yamashita. More than fifty thousand of the troops under the command of the Tiger of Malaya had managed to hold out on the wing of the dragon-shaped island until the end of the war. They had made it months longer than the men under Wainwright had made it on Bataan and Corregidor. Only after the emperor had announced Japan's surrender did Yamashita present himself to the American forces, who now placed him on the other side of a long table with documents to sign. In a mere eleven minutes, it was all over. As on the *Missouri*, one of the pens went to Wainwright, and another to Percival, who had met Yamashita in Singapore under very different circumstances in the early days of the war. Yamashita concealed his emotions until military police led him out of the room and off to prison. Only then did Wainwright see tears. Something compelled Wainwright to walk over to the officer charged with handling Yamashita's detention. "This might seem a little strange coming from me," Wainwright said, "but I hope Yamashita is shown the courtesy due his rank, in the matter of personal accommodations, housing, and food."

"He'll be given everything he's entitled to, under the Geneva Conventions," the officer replied. "We don't want to be guilty of treating anyone as the Japs treated you and your men."

Reporters wanted another statement. "The war in the Philippines is now over," Wainwright told them. The next day, he had a pleasant lunch with Mrs. MacArthur, who always referred to him as General Wainwright because he always refused to call her by her first name despite her pleas for him to do so. It was finally time to go home. On September 5, he boarded the first of several flights that would take him, Beebe, Pugh, Dooley, and Carroll across the Pacific. As the plane flew over Luzon and out over the Philippine Sea, Wainwright took a last look at the coastline of the land he was leaving behind. "I will come back," he scribbled in his diary and then, perhaps remembering the pledges he and MacArthur had made to each other three and a half years earlier, wisely added the word "perhaps."

*   *   *

By the time Wainwright reached Washington, he had already had a homecoming the likes of which he could not have imagined in prison. At the airport in San Francisco on September 8, 1945, he had stepped out of the plane onto the continental United States for the first time in five years with a cane clutched in his hand and four stars strapped to his slender shoulders. He had learned that the Senate had unanimously confirmed him to the wartime rank of full general. His sister Jennie hurried to embrace him. Then another body came rushing in from the side and almost knocked him over. It was Jack. The next day, a half million people flooded the streets to watch Wainwright lead a twenty-thousand-person victory parade. The cheers for him drowned out the sound of the bombers flying overhead.

Only two of Wainwright wishes had gone unfulfilled. One was relief from the pain in his mouth. A molar of his had broken during his captivity in Manchuria, and a Japanese dentist had filled it rather than extract the roots, which had become infected. Emergency dental visits in San Francisco early in the morning before the parade and then in Omaha, Nebraska, at 2:30 the next morning during a layover en route to Washington, had dulled the pain but not fixed the root cause because his schedule had not given the doctors time to do so.

The other wish—the one he had pined for during his years in prison—was the opportunity to hold Adele, his dear Kitty. When he emerged from the plane at National Airport across the Potomac from Washington on September 10 at 12:31 p.m., George Marshall had her positioned at the bottom of the stairs. As she rushed for her husband, the wind nearly swept off the oversized black straw hat covering her face. "Hello, darling," she said. He tried to reply but, as when seeing MacArthur for the first time, no words came out. The crowd closing in around the couple blocked photographers hoping to capture the moment when the world's most famous prisoner of war drew his long-suffering wife into his arms. They begged the Wainwrights to re-create their kiss for the cameras, but the couple would not oblige. Adele was on no sleep and no food. The hat made it hard to see her eyes, but reporters could hear her sobbing.

It was Marshall who escorted the Wainwrights through the crowd to the car that whisked them away to the massive new five-sided structure where the chief of staff had moved his headquarters on the Virginia side of the Potomac in 1942. The size of the Pentagon astonished Wainwright. Inside waited a few dozen veterans of Corregidor and Bataan, including Carlos Romulo, whom Wainwright had ordered out of the Philippines. "You, my friends of Bataan and Corregidor," Wainwright said, "I am glad to see you here. It is too bad that all of you are not here but more are coming. They are on the way," by which he meant more freed prisoners of war—men not so fortunate as to have flights waiting to take them home, to say nothing of motorcades to take them across the Arlington Memorial Bridge.

At the Washington end of the bridge, motorcycles traveling in a V formation led the way under the American flag and welcome sign hanging from two large ladders covered in red, white, and blue and angled to form an inverted V over the road. Next came Wainwright and Adele in a large roofless car that even MacArthur might have envied. Behind them in similar cars came Beebe and his wife, Pugh and his wife, Dooley and his mother, and Sergeant Carroll and his sister. Past the Lincoln Memorial, through the crowds lining either side of Constitution Avenue, past the American flags waving from lampposts adorned with pictures of Wainwright's face, the motorcade made its way to the Washington Monument, where a crowd of hundreds of thousands had formed around a stage. Government agencies had let employees out so they could see Wainwright accept his membership in the Disabled American Veterans, as well as the keys to the city for having "made a triumph of defeat." Adele looked uncomfortable throughout. "During the half-hour ceremony at the Monument Grounds, Kitty Wainwright sat nervously off the edge of her chair, twisting her handkerchief and dabbing at her face," a reporter wrote. Oddly, the organizers had placed five seats between her and her husband.

When the time came for Wainwright to stand before the microphone, he thanked his fellow citizens for the honors they had heaped upon him, and said he hoped they would draw the same lessons he had from the unlikely journey he had made from humiliation to triumph.

As I stood on the deck of the Missouri, *at the right hand of General MacArthur, watching the signing of the surrender document, I fervently wished that every American could feel the full significance of that moment. Nearly four years had elapsed since the Japs launched their attacks on Pearl Harbor and the Philippines. That moment of surrender in Tokyo Bay had been bought with the blood of more than a million Americans who died or were wounded in the struggle. Billions of dollars and countless hours of work by Americans at home had been required to bring that little party of beaten Japs to the* Missouri's *deck.*

All because for a while we were careless of the nation's safety. We let
down our guard.

    It is over now, and we are at peace. But in the name of all my com-
rades, who suffered with me, I pray that this nation will never again
neglect the strength of its defenses. . . .

    This is truly such a welcome as a man dreams of, locked away behind
barbed wire and the bayonets of cruel jailers. It is the surest evidence
I could have that you still keep before you the words which I know
fired you to great effort after our sorrowful defeat: Remember Bataan!
Remember Corregidor!

Preparedness was a theme he would preach for the rest of his life, most immediately in short speeches to the House and Senate, where members greeted him with what newspapers described as "a deafening din of cheers [and] applause" and even "a scattering of rebel yells," surely from the southern members whose fathers had undergone their own surrender.

One more stop awaited: a visit to the White House. Wainwright had expected a perfunctory meeting in the Oval Office and nothing more. He remembered meeting Truman twice during the 1930s but could not have imagined that the new president had reached the startling conclusion that his predecessor had rescued the wrong general from the Philippines. "I don't see why in Hell Roosevelt didn't order Wainwright home and let MacArthur be a martyr," Truman had privately written in 1945. "We'd have had a real general and a fighting man if we had Wainwright and not a play actor and a bunko man such as we have now." Had the politics not dictated the selection of MacArthur, Truman would have appointed someone else to be supreme commander in Japan. From the start, the decision to rescue MacArthur from the Philippines had disgusted Truman. "If he'd been a real hero, he'd have gone down with the ship," Truman had written in June 1942. But what precisely caused the man from Missouri to go from those understandable sentiments to referring to MacArthur in terms as personally insulting as "prima donna," "brass hat," and "stuffed shirt" a mere three years later has eluded biographers.*

The point of no return for Truman might have come upon learning about a folder labeled "super secret" on George Marshall's orders. Inside lay the only copy the chief of staff had retained of MacArthur's letter blackballing Wainwright's nomination for the Medal of Honor. With the war ending and Wainwright returning, Marshall had decided the time had come to reopen the file. The fear he had felt upon reading MacArthur's objections in 1942 had not gone away. Marshall had navigated disputes between MacArthur and his rivals whether they be in the navy or elsewhere throughout the war but could see no solution to this one. On September 5, he handed the file to Secretary of War Stimson. "The possibility of a row coming up between MacArthur and Wainwright," Marshall warned Stimson, "would strain the memories of the present war." Unable to make the decision himself, Marshall asked Stimson to do so. The secretary of war wasted no time. In less than twenty-four hours, he made up his mind. He had advocated ignoring MacArthur's objections in 1942 and now found them to be "untrue" and "untenable." Marshall, Stimson remembered, seemed "much relieved" upon hearing the news.

The citation from 1942 required revision. While the new one would still credit Wainwright with having set an example for his soldiers by joining them on the "firing line," it would also credit him with having set an example for defenders of democracy everywhere. "The final stand on beleaguered Corregidor, for which he was in an important measure personally responsible, commanded the admiration of the nation's allies. It reflected the high morale of American arms in the face of overwhelming odds. His courage and resolution were a vitally needed inspiration to the then sorely pressed freedom-loving peoples of the world."

---

* The famous conflict between Truman and MacArthur over Korea still lay years in the future.

Theodore Roosevelt, who as assistant secretary of the navy had begun America's journey into the Philippines, had subsequently set the precedent as president that the commander in chief should personally present the Medal of Honor if possible. Almost nothing in his life, Truman said, would give him "more pleasure" than presenting the award to the war's most famous prisoner. When the Wainwrights entered the Oval Office, Truman bounded out from behind his desk with flowers for Adele. Wainwright's legs had begun to look less sturdy as the day had dragged on, so he was grateful when Truman motioned for everyone to sit. But soon the president was back on his feet. "Come on, General, let's take a walk in the garden. Some photographers out there want to get a picture of us together." Reluctantly, Wainwright rose and followed. Arm in arm, they walked outside to a group of microphones set up in the Rose Garden. For a moment, Wainwright worried he would have to give another speech. Then Truman began to read from a piece of paper he had concealed in the pocket of his seersucker suit.

General Jonathan M. Wainwright, commanding United States Army forces in the Philippines from 12 March to 7 May 1942, distinguished himself by intrepid and determined leadership against greatly superior enemy forces. At the repeated risk of life above and beyond the call of duty . . .

Wainwright did not know how close he had come to receiving the medal in 1942. But he knew those words—those "magic words," as he called them—"above and beyond the call of duty." He had not viewed the decision he had made on Corregidor in those terms at the time. He had viewed it as the least he could do. "No other course of action would be honorable," he had written in his diary. So he had stayed with his men and shared their fate, and he could see some of them—Beebe, Pugh, Dooley, and Carroll—smiling now. The president had a grin, too, as he finished reading the citation and draped the blue ribbon around the long, thin neck. Wainwright had not needed a medal to find honor. He had found it for himself on that tadpole-like island in the clutches of the dragon's claws. The only course he could see consistent with his definition of honor had demanded all the mettle he could muster and had led him here, he now knew, to the highest honor his country could bestow: the Medal of Honor.

When Men Have to Die

By all rights, MacArthur had earned his own parade. Even Truman thought so. Eight years had passed since MacArthur had seen the continental United States. Little Arthur had never seen it, and he would not do so anytime soon. MacArthur deemed himself unable to leave Japan because, as he put it, "[of] the extraordinarily dangerous and inherently inflammable situation which exists here." Actually, on the road into Tokyo from Yokohama, the landscape looked remarkably nonflammable. Almost every structure that could burn already had. About two million Japanese had died in the war. More than seven times as many had nowhere to live.

To build a new Japan, MacArthur would need to be more than a soldier. He would have to be, in his words, "an economist, a political scientist, an engineer, a manufacturing executive, a teacher, even a theologian of sorts." He would have to be, in sum, his father's son. But where William Howard Taft and his commission had clipped Arthur MacArthur's wings before he could fully spread them as military governor of the Philippines, Douglas MacArthur refused to allow history to repeat itself, even when his government gave in to Soviet demands for a joint Allied commission in Japan. An

American diplomat serving under MacArthur summed up the situation this way: "Never before in the history of the United States had such enormous and absolute power been placed in the hands of a single individual."

Letters from Japanese men and women to MacArthur would often address him as their "new shogun," a reference to the military leader who had served as the power behind the throne in centuries past. The role required MacArthur to keep a distance from the people, and, as the men on Bataan could attest, that remoteness came easily to him. He let the masses see his famous cap and sunglasses only when he climbed into and out of the Cadillac shuttling him between the home Jean set up in the old American embassy and the headquarters his staff established, as in Brisbane and Melbourne, at an insurance headquarters—this time, the Dai-Ichi Building. He made almost no social calls, not even to the emperor. Hirohito would have to come to MacArthur, and did so on his own accord in late September 1945. With Jean and Arthur watching behind a curtain, MacArthur offered the emperor a cigarette and saw his hand trembling as he accepted. "I tried to make it as easy for him as I could," MacArthur wrote, "but I knew how deep and dreadful must be his agony of humiliation." When Hirohito asked to "bear sole responsibility" for what his country had done, MacArthur was, as he put it, "moved to the very marrow of my bones." Some wanted to send the emperor to the gallows as a war criminal. MacArthur wanted to harness Hirohito's ancient power over the people as an engine for remaking Japan into a modern democracy.

If that sounded like a contradiction, it was the sort MacArthur relished. He believed the Japanese needed to make their own reforms but ordered his own staff to prepare a constitution when the Japanese draft disappointed him. He had mocked American pacifists who believed they could avoid war through disarmament but insisted the Japanese include an article in their constitution renouncing "war as a sovereign right of the nation" and declaring "land, sea, and air forces . . . will never be maintained."* As Sutherland had learned the hard way, MacArthur did not relish having women (Jean aside) around when he worked but took pride in the dozens of women who won election to the Japanese legislature, even after hearing that one was a former prostitute. Informed that she had won a few hundred thousand votes, he quipped, "Then I should say there must have been more than her dubious occupation involved." He wanted a future of free enterprise for Japan but believed the country could achieve it only through redistributing land and weakening the Japanese family conglomerates known as *zaibatsu*. He encouraged participation in labor unions but took action to prevent a general strike. He opposed taking vengeance against the Japanese but sought it himself against the two principal antagonists he had faced in the Philippines: Masaharu Homma and Tomoyuki Yamashita.

On October 29, 1945, inside a ballroom rigged with stage lights, the Pacific theater's first war crime trials debuted in Manila. General Yamashita went first. MacArthur had established the rules for the trial, and everyone involved, including the five judges responsible for rendering a verdict, knew they would have to answer to him. Yamashita argued that he had wanted to abandon Manila, not destroy it. But that made no difference. Prosecutors had not charged him with ordering the murders, mutilations, and rapes but with abdicating his responsibility as a commander to have stopped them. In December 1945, after hearing weeks of testimony recalling the mayhem that the Japanese had inflicted on Manila, the judges sentenced Yamashita to hang.

Next up was General Homma. After being recalled in the wake of Wainwright's surrender, Homma had faded into obscurity in Japan only to learn that the Americans sought his arrest. They transported him back to Manila so he could stand trial under the stage lights. To testify against him, Johnny Pugh returned, too. Wainwright did

---

* In his memoirs, MacArthur explained that the constitution did not deprive Japan of the right to self-defense. "If attacked," he wrote, "she will defend herself."

not but submitted a deposition. In Japan, MacArthur teared up as he read details he had not known. "Indefensible" was how he described Homma's behavior toward Wainwright. Interestingly, the judges found otherwise and acquitted Homma on the charge of refusing to "grant quarter" on the day the white flag had gone up over Corregidor. Nonetheless, Homma received a death sentence. He might not have planned the Bataan Death March but, like Yamashita, had failed to prevent atrocities.

By this time, the United States Supreme Court had rejected a challenge to the way MacArthur had set up the trials, though not without two dissents, including one arguing that the commissions violated the Geneva Conventions by denying the accused the same legal protections American soldiers on trial for their lives would have received. If true, it was not the sort of violation that troubled Wainwright. "That double bastard Homma," Wainwright thought, had gotten off easy with a firing squad. "That is too good for him," Wainwright wrote. "He should have been hanged like Yamashita." Homma had one last appeal, and his wife made it for him face-to-face at the Dai-Ichi Building. She asked MacArthur to consider the case one more time. He did and issued a statement upholding the verdict. "There are few parallels in infamy and tragedy with the brutalization of troops who in good faith had laid down their arms," he said. When he had first learned of the Bataan Death March during the war, he had sworn that "the Japanese will pay." On April 3, 1946, the general who had forced MacArthur from the Philippines did.

There was another promise MacArthur would keep. His father had believed that Filipinos hungered for independence. The United States had promised it to them. On July 4, 1946, Douglas MacArthur was in Manila for the ceremony where the American flag came down and the Philippine flag went up. "For forty-eight years since my father first led our army down the long road to liberate this great city of Manila, close identification with you has been my personal privilege," he said. "Let history record this event in the sweep of democracy through the earth as foretelling the end of mastery of peoples by the power of force alone—the end of empire as the political chain which binds the unwilling weak to the unyielding strong."

That is not to say there would be no political chain. MacArthur himself had twisted it a few months earlier during the election that determined the first president of the independent Philippines. The contest pitted the incumbent Osmeña against Quezon's protégé, Manuel Roxas, who served as president of the Philippine senate and had recently shepherded through resolutions giving MacArthur honorary citizenship in the islands and placing his name in "perpetuity" on the rolls of the Philippine Army. "At parade roll calls, when his name is called," the resolutions said, "the senior non-commissioned officer shall answer, 'Present in spirit.'" MacArthur said he wept when he read the words. It was the least Roxas could do. Accusations that he had collaborated with the Japanese during their occupation of the Philippines might have hurt his election campaign had MacArthur not made it known that he considered Roxas a patriot. That was the reassurance Filipino voters needed to elect him president.

MacArthur still had his own interest in being president. Americans surveyed by Gallup at the end of the war had ranked MacArthur the "greatest person, living or dead, in world history" behind only Franklin Roosevelt, Abraham Lincoln, Jesus, and George Washington. But World War II veterans surveyed by *Fortune* said MacArthur was not the general they thought should run for president. By significant margins, not only European theater veterans but also Pacific theater ones preferred Dwight Eisenhower. Having replaced George Marshall as chief of staff in late 1945, Eisenhower had already made plans by early 1948 to become president of another institution, Columbia University, and issued a statement saying that "the necessary and wise subordination of the military to civic power will be best sustained . . . when lifelong professional soldiers, in the absence of some obvious and overriding reasons, abstain from seeking high political office." In response, MacArthur issued his own statement from Japan: He did not seek the presidency, he said, but it "would be recreant to all my concepts of good citizenship were I to shrink . . . from accepting any public duty to which I might be called by the American people." In other words, he would accept the Republican nomination. He would not get it.

At the June 1948 party convention, which MacArthur did not attend in Philadelphia, his forces numbered only eight pledged delegates. Not until the wee hours of the morning did one of his backers have the opportunity to nominate him. Newspapers reported that he received the "shortest of the ovations" of any candidate. By the time the man chosen to second the nomination spoke, only a quarter of the seats at the convention had bodies. "MacArthur is probably the world's greatest authority on national preparedness," said the speaker. "I know Douglas MacArthur intimately; in fact, I have known him since we were cadets together at West Point, forty-six years ago. I have fought side by side with him in two great wars, and my respect and admiration for him are unbounded." There was another ovation at the end but this time not for MacArthur but for the speaker himself. It was Wainwright. "When I went to the Republican Convention in your behalf, I felt that it would be a forlorn hope but you and I, side by side, have fought a forlorn hope before now," Wainwright wrote to MacArthur afterward. "The professional politicians had us beaten from the start with the big machine they had set up and the vast amount of money." For the second time in four years, Thomas Dewey won the nomination but not the election. Truman did.

From the start, the president had worried that Americans eager to celebrate Wainwright would "kill him with kindness." Three days after receiving the Medal of Honor, Wainwright arrived in New York City for a ticker-tape parade. The police commissioner put the crowd at four million, and the sanitation department put the amount of paper thrown from buildings at 490 tons. On September 19, 1945, Wainwright and his wife headed to White Sulphur Springs, West Virginia, where the army had converted the famous Greenbrier resort into a hospital. He and Adele moved into a cottage where doctors hoped he would begin a period of rest. Instead, he began work the next day on his memoirs. For the right to serialize the story into articles that would appear daily in newspapers later that fall, a syndicate gave him $155,000. For the book rights, Doubleday would kick in $25,000. The book would become a *New York Times* bestseller and might have become an MGM movie if studio executives had not worried that Americans would not sit for a film about surrender.

A newspaperman named Robert Considine, who had capitalized on America's MacArthur mania in 1942 with a book called *MacArthur the Magnificent*, assisted Wainwright with the writing. Every morning, the two would meet on the porch of the Greenbrier cottage to talk, or yell in the case of Considine, who found the general unable to hear otherwise. Over a few hours, Wainwright would narrate one part of the story. Considine would ask questions and then have the installment ready to review the next morning. "I would bring with me a first draft of what he had related the day before," Considine wrote. "He'd put on his glasses, take a stubby pencil out of his breast pocket, and carefully read the material." To the ghostwriter's relief, the copy usually pleased Wainwright. Only self-effacingly would Wainwright later refer to it as "my very bad book." One of the few lines he added came after a description of how his men on Corregidor had "stood at attention and saluted" him after he had surrendered them to the Japanese. "I am a student of the Civil War," Wainwright wrote, "but not until then did I know how General R. E. Lee felt after Appomattox." Sometimes Adele would listen in on the sessions. She saw her husband tear up as he recalled the slaps that he had received from the Japanese private at Karenko. "Mrs. Wainwright cupped her sad face in her right hand," Considine remembered.

At no point did Wainwright take MacArthur up on his offer to review material in advance. "For all his admiration, Wainwright could poke fun at MacArthur," Considine recalled. But when Wainwright went back to praising his old commander, Adele would walk away. Considine could sense her revulsion for the man who had left her husband behind. "She always does that," Wainwright said the first time Adele excused herself in front of Considine. When she did it again over a meal, Wainwright yelled, "Damnit, cut that out and come back to dinner."

But Adele could not cut it out. After the stay at the Greenbrier, she kept humiliating her husband at the dinners and banquets thrown in his honor. She could not stop drinking. A combination of alcohol and sedatives had sustained her through the long nights of his captivity. Her son, Jack, had begged her to seek medical assistance. She blamed Jack's wife, Elfrida, for monopolizing his attention. When a reporter had called with the news that the war had ended, Adele could not speak. A friend had picked up the phone for her and explained that she had become so excited that she had become "hysterical." Upon returning to America, Wainwright "had hoped," his son wrote, "to control her drinking, etc., himself but found to his dismay that it was beyond him . . . after a number of embarrassing experiences." That fall, Wainwright made the decision to take Adele to a neuropsychiatric institute in Hartford, Connecticut. His mother-in-law, who had lived with Adele throughout the war, was furious. Adele herself could not see the need. She was no worse than she had been during the war. Probably that was true.

Wainwright celebrated his first Thanksgiving back in America not with his wife but with his sister's family in Seattle. Though he had regained some of the weight he had lost during the war, looking at the turkey heaped on his plate made him think of the emaciated faces he had seen during the war. "Try to forget those terrible times," a niece said. "You're home now."

"Home!" Wainwright said. "I don't have any home without Adele."

The army had planned to give Wainwright a command that would have given him a home on Governors Island in New York, but he said he worried that the "social obligations in New York would have proven very strenuous for me," by which he meant Adele. With almost no public explanation, in January 1946, the army changed his assignment and sent him to San Antonio, Texas, where he took command of the

Fourth Army. When newspaper reporters asked why they had not seen his wife recently, he explained, "She worried so much about this worthless carcass of mine while I was gone that now she is sick." He wrote to Adele less than his son thought a husband should, but perhaps being unable to communicate with her during the years in prison had made it feel almost natural now. He was not alone in Texas. During those early days, he had the family he had made in the Philippines: Hubert Carroll, Tom Dooley, Johnny Pugh, and Lew Beebe. In addition, a busy speaking schedule forced the "hero of Bataan and Corregidor," as people called Wainwright, to spend much of his time on the road—"hero stuff," as his son called the work. With Americans wanting to move on with the lives they had set aside for the war, Wainwright begged them not to let down their guard.

In March 1946, Wainwright flew to Connecticut and checked Adele out of the institute. A few days later, newspapers printed a photograph of them together with some of his fellow former prisoners making toasts over drinks. The doctors worried she would relapse. Not surprisingly, she did. She had gone to the institute in Connecticut voluntarily. In April, Wainwright obtained a court order to have her committed to a sanitarium in Dallas, where she began electroshock therapy. "Lonesome" and "low" were how he described himself afterward. In September, he moved her to a hospital in Colorado Springs. She told doctors she would never drink again. She wondered why her husband would not take her back. A few times, he tried. The experiments always ended the same way. His own lifestyle could not have helped. "Get out your best drinking shoes and be ready for a party," he wrote to a niece before visiting her.

It has been suggested that Wainwright's own drinking problems prompted his retirement from the army in August 1947. That is not true. Sad as he was to leave the army, he had always planned to do so upon his sixty-fourth birthday, which he celebrated that month. He claimed doctors had a "hell of a time finding enough to retire me on for physical disability," a status he sought only for the advantage it carried for his taxes. Choosing to stay in San Antonio, he purchased a two-story house he named Fiddlers' Green after an old cavalry poem he loved.

> Halfway down the trail to Hell,
> In a shady meadow green,
> Are the souls of all dead troopers camped
> Near a good old-time canteen,
> And this eternal resting place
> Is known as Fiddlers' Green.
>
> Marching past, straight through to Hell,
> The Infantry are seen,
> Accompanied by the Engineers,
> Artillery and Marine,
> For none but the shades of Cavalrymen
> Dismount at Fiddlers' Green.
>
> Though some go curving down the trail
> To seek a warmer scene,
> No trooper ever gets to Hell
> Ere he's emptied his canteen,
> And so rides back to drink again
> With friends at Fiddlers' Green.

Whatever the truth about the mythical Fiddlers' Green, canteens never ran dry at Wainwright's. The house had its own official beer. Wainwright had negotiated an endorsement deal with Pabst Blue Ribbon, which ran advertisements showing him serving the brew in his den. He had stronger stuff, too. He liked the scotch whisky in Texas but the bourbon even better. "We will have no drought," he promised friends coming to visit him.

Wainwright could not ride much anymore but could shoot and fish and received invitations to do so all across the country. He also organized annual reunions of the so-called Travelers Club, which he and twenty-five fellow prisoners had formed at Karenko. He judged the success of their annual reunions by how much liquor they consumed. Men brought their wives but knew not to ask too much about Wainwright's. He did not like to talk about Adele anymore. For a time starting in 1947, he had brought her to live with him at Fiddlers' Green but, in May 1948, sent her back to Colorado Springs. "I don't think it advisable at this time to bring her home for fear that she would go back to her old ways—and I'm quite certain she would," he wrote. They would never live together again. Although there were always people eager to see him, he felt alone. The sycophants coming over to his table at restaurants agitated him. When possible, he preferred to eat whatever his live-in African-American cook, Sarah, made. In some ways, she gave him the only sense of home he was to know.

There was discussion of drafting Wainwright to run for the United States Senate from Texas in 1948. The idea intrigued him enough that he decided to come out as a Democrat because, as he explained to reporters, "Now I'm a Texan. There's only one Republican in Texas I know of, and it isn't me." When pressed, he admitted to having "never cast a vote in my life." A congressman named Lyndon Johnson ended up winning the seat, and Wainwright went back to the rule that had guided him before: "keep out of politics." Only "friendship" and "admiration" for MacArthur, Wainwright said, made him go to the opposing party's convention that same year. MacArthur repaid the favor a few months later by supporting Wainwright's nomination for national commander of the Disabled American Veterans. "I know of no person better qualified vigorously to lead this distinguished organization than he," read the message sent from Japan. "He has won the respect and admiration of all men with whom he has served."

Everyone, it seemed, had ideas for how to make money off the respect Wainwright had earned. For a time, a grocery company in San Antonio named him chairman. A stock farm raising cattle made him its manager. He had little to offer these ventures, and they did not care.

Surely, they just wanted his name. "Cockroach" was the word he used for strangers wanting something from him. "Everyone wants to know why the cockroach," he joked. "Because I am the Boss Cockroach." The secretary he employed in his business pursuits made him put a nickel in a "swear box" every time he cursed. By 1948, he had moved on to the presidency of a company selling insurance to members of the armed forces. One of the first pitches he made was to MacArthur.

More and more, Wainwright began to turn down speaking engagements, which he said had left him "near ragged" but continued to speak out when forced to do so. Relatives and random correspondents alike never stopped asking what he "really" thought about MacArthur. It was as if they could not believe the answer Wainwright always gave. "Among the great captains of all time." Only Robert E. Lee and Ulysses S. Grant belonged in the same sentence as Douglas MacArthur, Wainwright would say. Even his son, Jack, was not sure whether to believe it. "No one's ever going to know what Dad thinks about either MacArthur or Roosevelt," Jack said. "They're his commanding officers." As for the greatest fighting unit in American history, Wainwright left no doubt: None exceeded the Philippine Scouts of the 26th Cavalry. So long as much of the world did not have roads suitable for vehicles, he warned that the army had made a grave mistake by not maintaining at least one division of horse cavalry "as a modest nucleus for expansion and to retain our precious traditional 'know-how.'" As a reminder of what had been lost, he kept a photograph on his desk of Little Boy, his horse that had died with the 26th Cavalry covering his retreat to Bataan. He would never have made it without the cavalry, and he would believe horse soldiers could have played a similar role for American forces fighting on another Asian peninsula—the one known as Korea.

The Soviet invasion of Manchuria in the final days of World War II had resulted in an unhappy division of neighboring Korea, with a Communist regime coming to power above the 38th Parallel and an American ally coming to power below. When North Korea threw its forces across the border in June 1950, Harry Truman and the United

Nations looked to seventy-year-old Douglas MacArthur to save South Korea. Once again, aggression had found the United States unprepared. Once again, American forces found themselves retreating toward the bottom of a peninsula only to be penned in. Once again, MacArthur himself was not with them most of the time; he still had an occupation to oversee in Tokyo. This time, however, he really did have help on the way. The brilliant landing he staged in September higher up the peninsula at Inchon put enemy forces on the run and his own on the path not only to liberate South Korea's capital of Seoul but also, with the approval of the United Nations, to capture the North's capital of Pyongyang.

In late October, the first of MacArthur's forces made it as far north as the Yalu River. On the other side lay Manchuria and, in it, the forces belonging to the Communist Chinese who had chased their Nationalist rivals off the mainland to the island of Formosa (Taiwan). Charles Willoughby, whose intelligence had convinced MacArthur that Manila lay open for the taking in the winter of 1945, now convinced him that the Communist Chinese forces would not cross the Yalu as winter neared. At a conference, MacArthur assured Truman of the same. But the Chinese did cross, in enormous numbers that engulfed entire units of MacArthur's army and sent the rest into retreat. MacArthur would blame Washington for not having let him bomb the bridges over the Yalu for fear of provoking what had resulted anyway: a larger war.

By spring 1951, the lines had reset around where the fighting had begun. MacArthur had ideas for taking the fight back into North Korea. Some may have been more realistic than his idea of sealing Korea off from Manchuria by "laying a field of radioactive wastes" between the two. But to his disgust, members of the Truman administration seemed content with reaching a draw in Korea, as if convinced the contest against Communism in Europe mattered more. MacArthur had been here before with the Europe-firsters during World War II. When they had stood in his way then, he had not hesitated to bypass them just as he had bypassed so many Japanese on the way back to the Philippines. So often the paths he had found brought him onto the front pages as well as into political back channels where other military men dared not go.

It was fitting, then, that MacArthur's military career ended the same way as his 1944 presidential campaign: with an ill-advised letter agreeing with a Republican congressman, in this case one who had written in favor of widening the war by having Chinese Nationalists on Taiwan open a "second Asiatic front" against Communism. "It seems strangely difficult for some to realize that here in Asia is where the Communist conspirators have elected to make their play for global conquest," MacArthur responded. "We must win. There is no substitute for victory." When the letter became public in April, Truman called it "rank insubordination." The joint chiefs did not go that far but backed the president's decision to relieve MacArthur of his commands. Jean heard the news before her husband. "Jeannie," he said after she shared it, "we're going home at last." Alongside the road to Atsugi airport, the Japanese stood as they had in 1945 but no longer did they have their backs to MacArthur. He could see the tears in their eyes.

Fifty years had passed since his father had returned home after his own feud with civilian authority as military governor of the Philippines. When Arthur MacArthur had arrived in San Francisco, no crowds had greeted him. Not even his family had come. Douglas had his family, including Ah Cheu, but worried any crowds on the ground would cheer only, as he put it, "because they feel sorry for me." He need not have worried. Massive crowds greeted him in San Francisco and then in Washington, where he had an invitation to address a joint session of Congress on April 19, 1951. Predictions that the speech would lead to the Republican presidential nomination the next year overlooked the change of heart of one Dwight Eisenhower, who would win the nomination and the election, surely to his former commander's chagrin. The closing lines of MacArthur's address to Congress more accurately, albeit unintentionally, portended his own future. "Old soldiers never die, they just fade away," said MacArthur, quoting an old army ballad. In the chamber to hear those words was Wainwright. He had waited at National Airport so he could welcome MacArthur to Washington as soon as he landed. "Hello, Skinny," MacArthur had said, using the nickname he usually disdained. Wainwright smiled and reached his hand out before being pushed back into the crowd and disappearing.

One day in July 1953, Wainwright showed up at Brooke Army Medical Center in San Antonio for an appointment and never left. Doctors admitted him for problems with his arteries and liver. Whatever role alcohol played, his family blamed the Japanese. So did newspapers reporting on his condition. From across the country came letters wishing Wainwright a speedy recovery. By his family's account, he kept asking whether MacArthur had written. He never did. Days before turning seventy on August 23, Wainwright began suffering a series of strokes. Adele wanted to see him one more time. Jack decided it would be best if she stayed in Colorado Springs. When conscious, Wainwright made Jack promise that Adele would "never want." Early on the morning of September 2—the eighth anniversary of the Japanese surrender aboard the *Missouri*—doctors rushed Jack into his father's room. "I believe he's gone," they said several times only for Wainwright to surprise them with another breath. Twenty-seven minutes past noon, he took his final one. The hero of Bataan and Corregidor had fought to the end. They would bury him near his mother and father at Arlington National Cemetery, straight behind the mansion where Lee had lived. The riderless horse trailing Wainwright's body carried the sword his mother had given him. He had left it at Fort Stotsenburg at the start of the war. A Filipino had found it on the corpse of a Japanese officer and returned it. Beside Jack throughout the funeral stood George Marshall. A spokesperson explained MacArthur had business elsewhere.

MacArthur had become chairman of Remington Rand, famous for its typewriters. He and Jean had never owned a house and did not buy one now. They moved into a suite in New York's Waldorf Towers. Herbert Hoover was their neighbor. MacArthur had hoped his son would go to West Point but realized it was not to be. When the boy did not graduate at the top of his high school class, MacArthur said,

"I am glad that he is not number one in his class standing, as I believe that brings little reward." Still passionate about the performing arts, Arthur would go on to Columbia University and eventually to a life of anonymity in the city.

In 1961, on the orders of President John F. Kennedy, the air force flew MacArthur and his wife to the Philippines for the fifteenth anniversary of its independence. Now the ambassador to the United States, Carlos Romulo accompanied the MacArthurs on their journey. Not since the Revolutionary War hero Lafayette's return in 1824 to the United States from France had an old soldier from a foreign land received such a welcome in a young republic. Asked by a reporter for *Life* what Filipinos thought of MacArthur, one said, "What do you think of God?" The neon lights illuminated the city again, but it had lost the luster that made it the Pearl of the Orient. The neoclassical legislative building stood once again, but Intramuros still lay in ruins. Where MacArthur had once had his headquarters on the walls had become the realm of squatters. But where he would speak nearby on July 4, 1961, assembled a crowd that Manila police described as the "biggest ever gathered on the Luneta." He wore, as a newspaper put it, "the familiar sweat-stained" cap he had worn through the war, but the face underneath now belonged to an eighty-one-year-old. Many struggling to hear his remarks made out "I shall return" and cheered, but the context went unheard. He had said those three words only to explain he could not make the same pledge again. He would not return. He hated hospitals to the end and waited too long to go to Walter Reed in Washington to have his gall bladder removed. On April 5, 1964, weeks after the surgery, he died at the hospital. In both the United States and the Philippines, flags fell to half-mast.

Harry Truman observed no mourning period. Almost without pause, he went public with his account of MacArthur snubbing Wainwright at their reunion in Yokohama. To the end, the former president remained convinced that his predecessor in office should have ordered Wainwright out of the Philippines and left MacArthur behind. Roosevelt, however, had his reasons. In those desperate days, the United States had needed two very different generals: one for the headlines and one for the front lines. No general as committed to the chain of command and as uncomfortable with celebrity as Wainwright could have forced 130 million of his fellow Americans to live up to their responsibilities to a distant island chain—and bent the path of a war across the world's widest ocean—on the strength of his own word the way MacArthur did. No general as self-centered and certain of his place in history as MacArthur could have made the sacrifice Wainwright did: not to die a glorious death but to live as a prisoner for the sake of his fellow soldiers. Neither vow was easy. Both had to be kept. America's honor demanded no less.

Jean, who insisted on staying near her husband during the war, had to wait thirty-six years after his death to join him in the crypt of the MacArthur Memorial in his mother's hometown of Norfolk, Virginia. Adele did not have to wait as long to reunite with her husband. She died in 1970 and now shares his gravestone, just as she shared his sacrifice during the war. Several rows away lies Wainwright's most trusted aide, John Ramsey Pugh, who went on to become a general himself. His stone reads, "He was loyal," and he was. Given the chance to escape Corregidor and save himself, he refused to leave his general. If Wainwright deserved a Medal of Honor—if MacArthur deserved a Medal of Honor—Pugh did, too. And so did many others—Americans and Filipinos—left to fight without hope on Bataan and Corregidor. "There are times," it was said during those dark days, "when men have to die." But when there is time to prepare, may no man have to fall with the flag because his country wavered and left him waiting. May that be the fate of no soldier. May it always be above and beyond the call of duty.

Acknowledgments

The idea for this book came from the discovery of Wainwright diaries, letters, and other primary sources not available four decades ago when a biographer last attempted a full account of the general's life. These documents are split between two repositories. At the United States Army Heritage and Education Center in Carlisle, Pennsylvania, Thomas E. Buffenbarger and his colleagues shared with me their Wainwright papers and several other indispensable collections. No less important are the Wainwright papers in the Archives and Special Collections of the United States Military Academy at West Point, where Susan Lintelmann, Corey Flatt, and Kirsten L. Cooper handed me a treasure trove of documents, many of which, as far as I know, had never been examined by anyone outside the Wainwright family.

For letters and other papers related to MacArthur and, by extension, Wainwright's service in the Philippines, there is no substitute for a visit to the Library and Archives of the MacArthur Memorial in Norfolk, Virginia, and no substitute for the knowledge and generosity of James Zobel. He not only showed me the documents I requested but also steered me toward many I would have otherwise missed.

For the third book in a row, I have felt fortunate to live near the Library of Congress in Washington, DC, where the staff of the

Manuscript Reading Room has always opened its collections to me. Unable to travel to other repositories as easily, I am grateful to the archivists and librarians who sent me copies of letters and other primary sources. Special thanks to Melissa Davis at the George C. Marshall Foundation Library in Lexington, Virginia; David Clark and Lindsay Closterman at the Harry S. Truman Library and Museum in Independence, Missouri; Katelyn M. Miller and Max Wagh at the Special Collections Research Center at Syracuse University Libraries; Jennifer McGillan at Mississippi State University Libraries; Liz Phillips at the Hoover Institution Library and Archives at Stanford University; Amanda Nelson at the Special Collections and Archives at Wesleyan University; Jimmy DeButts at *Shipmate*; and Mark Fritch in the Archives and Special Collections of the Mansfield Library at the University of Montana. At the National Archives and Records Administration, I thank Sarah Bseirani, George Fuller, Lori Norris, Christine Rheem, Katherine Stinson, Phillip Wong, Brian Quann, and many others who assisted with my requests for documents, maps, audio recordings, and pictures (both still and motion) from the era.

Especially valuable to my research were diaries kept by men who shared Wainwright's fate in the Philippines. I am indebted to David Pugh, who shared the incredible diary his father, General John R. Pugh, kept while serving as Wainwright's most trusted aide. My gratitude also goes to General Pugh's granddaughter Nancy Later Lavoie for her willingness to help me. I also thank Whitney Galbraith for speaking with me and sharing a great wealth of information including the diaries of his father, Colonel Nicoll F. Galbraith, who served under Wainwright.

Important as letters and diaries are to this book, it would not have been possible to write without seeing the places where the history happened. Within days of the Philippines lifting its Covid travel restrictions in 2022, I was on a plane to Manila. The success of this trip owes to the hospitality and deep historical knowledge of the people I met. Most important was Desiree Ann C. Benipayo, who helps lead the Philippine World War II Memorial Foundation and wrote a moving book called *Honor* about the courageous Philippine chief justice Jose Abad Santos, a relative of her husband, Mario. Desiree and Mario not only accompanied me on much of my travels around Luzon but also introduced me wherever we went to people who knew the history of the war in the Philippines in a way impossible to learn in the United States.

On Bataan, Bong Mamuad and Bob Hudson were generous with their time. For a trip across the channel in a banca to Corregidor, Tony Feredo was the perfect guide. He knew every inch of the island's history and wrote a trip summary for me afterward. At Clark Museum, near the site of Fort Stotsenburg and Clark Field, Jada San Andres arranged a visit. A little to the north, Rhonie Dela Cruz shared his Bamban World War II Museum (a marvel not to be missed) and then helped me find the site of Wainwright's prison in Tarlac. At the site of Camp O'Donnell, where the prisoners on the Bataan Death March ended their journey, Darwin Campo provided a tour of the Capas National Shrine. On the shores of Lingayen, Captain Angelito Gumarang invited me to pass through his property for a special view of the landing area. At the site of the old Fort McKinley, Vicente Lim IV showed me around the Manila American Cemetery and Memorial, dug up some old photographs, and discussed his great-grandfather General Vicente Lim, a Filipino West Point graduate who fought with Wainwright on Bataan and later died at the hands of the Japanese. At the Manila Hotel, Annie Alejo and Tyne Dignadice Jr. gave me a sense of MacArthur's old home and showed me a reconstruction of his penthouse. At Intramuros in Manila, Guiller Asido and John "Rancho" Arcilla arranged a tour. In Quezon City, Desiree and Mario introduced me to Professor Ricardo Jose. Everyone I met in the Philippines referred to him as the most eminent scholar of World War II, and it took only one meal with him for me to see why. I am thankful for the research suggestions he gave me.

As I planned this trip, I benefited from the assistance of the United States embassy in Manila, especially Pong Aureus, Nina Lewis, and Pauline Anderson. I also thank Fred Ayala, Carol and Nando Roa,

Soleil Tropicales of the Philippine Department of Tourism, and Cecilia I. Gaerlan, who shared much advice as the head of the Bataan Legacy Historical Society.

The prologue required a visit to relatively not-so-far-away Chattanooga, Tennessee, where I had the good fortune of seeing Lookout Mountain with Ali Williams, a Forest Service hydrologist who knew the lay of the land. She introduced me to Michael F. Shillinger, a retired army officer, who proved the ideal person with whom to see Missionary Ridge.

Long before I considered writing a book that would require any travel, I made a different sort of journey with my editor, Colin Harrison, at Scribner. Having written books for him about figures from the eighteenth and nineteenth centuries, he suggested I move to the twentieth century. As I went off in search of an idea—and even when I could not seem to find my way—Colin stuck with me and believed I would find a book worth writing. I am lucky to have him as my editor, and I am thankful for the revisions and suggestions he gave me. The book also benefited from the wisdom and patience of associate editor Emily Polson and so many others at Scribner, including Jason Chappell, John McGhee, Nan Graham (who came up with the perfect title), Brian Belfiglio, Mark Galarrita, Kyle Kabel, and the design team that gave these pages such a cover as I can only hope they prove worthy of. This is my third book with Glen Hartley as my agent, and I could not ask for a finer one. He has always been a strong advocate for me and become a friend, too. I am thankful for all he did to make this book a reality.

When my fellow Maryland-based author David O. Stewart heard the topic of this book, he recommended I reach out to Christopher L. Kolakowski. I immediately recognized Christopher as the former director of the MacArthur Memorial and the author of *Last Stand on Bataan*, an outstanding book I had already read and cited. Christopher kindly read an early version of this book and offered suggestions for improving it. So fortunately for me did David Martin, the legendary

CBS News national security correspondent. Historians researching America's more recent wars will be wise to start with David's reporting because no one did it better than he did during his decades at the Pentagon. I am grateful for the advice he gave me on this manuscript.

In nothing have I been so fortunate as in my family, both immediate and extended. My uncle Eric, who passed away in 2020, knew more World War II history than anyone I knew growing up, and I wish I could have shared this book with him. My wife's parents helped her take care of our children during my time in the Philippines. My brothers, Michael and Steven, gave me their advice and encouragement. In too many ways to say, my mom and dad have helped me with this book and beyond. Much of this story is about sons following in the footsteps of their fathers: Wainwright into the cavalry, MacArthur to the Philippines. As for me, I learned to write from my dad and so much more from both him and my mom, who set a standard of selflessness that I can only try to live up to as a parent myself.

Nothing has made me prouder—"infinitely prouder," as MacArthur would have me put it—than being a father to Laura and Emma. As this book grew, they did, too, but far faster. They amazed me with their own stories and with the way they welcomed the historical figures and places from this book into our lives. It is usually for parents to remind children about deadlines, but Laura and Emma have done so much to help me meet mine that it seems only fitting that this book should be dedicated to them and to my wife, Caroline. When Caroline told me to "just go write" some years ago, neither of us knew where those words would lead or how much else we would both have to do and how often we would wonder how it would all get done. Often there is no easy answer, but I do know this book would not have gotten done—would not have even gotten started—without her. She is my best friend and most trusted reader. And though she could not join me in the Philippines, she always helps me find the way.

For all the names acknowledged and the thanks given at the end of a book, writing remains a pursuit best done alone unless an author is lucky enough to have a dog as good as the one we had in our girl Berkeley for eight years, much of them with her at my feet under my desk. She did not live to see the end of this book, but she left my family with a gift: memories that inspired us to bring home a new dog, Marley. He has found his way into our hearts and, with his own nose for history, under my desk, where I am lucky to have him now.

Notes

ABBREVIATIONS

GCMFL: George C. Marshall Foundation Library, Lexington, Virginia
HILA: Hoover Institution Library and Archives, Stanford University, California
HSTLM: Harry S. Truman Library and Museum, Independence, Missouri
JMWP: Jonathan M. Wainwright Papers
LC: Library of Congress, Washington, DC
MMLA: MacArthur Memorial Library and Archives, Norfolk, Virginia
MSSUL: Mississippi State University Libraries, Mississippi State, Mississippi
NARA: National Archives and Records Administration, Various Locations
PC: Private Collection
RG: Record Group
SU: Syracuse University, Special Collections Research Center, Syracuse, New York
USAHEC: United States Army Heritage and Education Center, Carlisle, Pennsylvania
USMA: United States Military Academy Library, West Point, New York
WHS: Wisconsin Historical Society, Madison, Wisconsin
WP: Wainwright Papers
YU: Yale University Library, Manuscripts and Archives, New Haven, Connecticut

AW: Adele Wainwright
DM: Douglas MacArthur
GCM: George C. Marshall
JM: Jean MacArthur
JMW: Jonathan Mayhew Wainwright
JRP: John R. Pugh
LCB: Lewis C. Beebe

DMREM: Douglas MacArthur, *Reminiscences: General of the Army* (Annapolis: Naval Institute Press, 1964)

FOP: Louis Morton, *The Fall of the Philippines* (Washington, DC: Center of Military History, 1953)

GWS: Jonathan M. Wainwright, *General Wainwright's Story*, ed. Robert Considine (Garden City, NY: Doubleday, 1946)

POTRS: John M. Beebe, ed., *Prisoner of the Rising Sun: The Lost Diary of Brig. Gen. Lewis Beebe* (College Station: Texas A&M University Press, 2006)

TBAB: Jerry C. Cooper, ed., *To Bataan and Back: The World War II Diary of Major Thomas Dooley* (College Station: Texas A&M University Press, 2016)

YOM: D. Clayton James, *The Years of MacArthur*, 3 vols. (Boston: Houghton Mifflin, 1970–85)

In lieu of a bibliography, full publication information appears for sources on their first reference. Citations for letters containing incomplete dateline information reflect omissions in the originals.

PROLOGUE **Paths to Honor**

3 "Who ordered": Peter Cozzens, *The Shipwreck of Their Hopes: The Battles for Chattanooga* (Urbana: University of Illinois Press, 1996), 7–9, 15, 192, 199–204, 245–49, 257–88, and 307–8; Shelby Foote, *The Civil War: A Narrative* (New York: Vintage Books, 1986), vol. 2, 842–56; Ron Chernow, *Grant* (New York: Penguin, 2017), 322–24; Kenneth Ray Young, *The General's General: The Life and Times of Arthur MacArthur* (Boulder: Westview Press, 1994), 5, 13, 18–21, 42, 62–67, and 72–75. For other details, see DMREM, 8–9; Eunoia [pseud.], "The Recent Victory of Gen. Grant at Chattanooga," November 26, 1863, in Quiner Scrapbooks, vol. 10, 291–92, WHS, online; James Heth, "The 24th Wis. at the Storming of Missionary Ridge," in Quiner Scrapbooks, vol. 10, 293, WHS, online; Arthur MacArthur Jr. to Arthur MacArthur Sr., Camp near Chattanooga, November 26, 1863, in Quiner Scrapbooks, vol. 10, 297–98, WHS, online; William J. K. Beaudot, *The 24th Wisconsin Infantry in the Civil War: The Biography of a Regiment* (Mechanicsburg, PA: Stackpole, 2003), 264; J. A. Watrous, "How the Boy Won: General MacArthur's First Victory," *Saturday Evening Post*, February 24, 1900, 770–71; *New York Sun*, February 26, 1899. **4** "On, Wisconsin": DMREM, 8–9. For other details including various accounts of what Arthur MacArthur said, see Watrous, "How the Boy Won," 770–71; United States War Department, *The War of the Rebellion: A Compilation of the Official Records of the Union and Confederate Armies* (Washington, DC: Government Printing Office, 1880–1901), series I, vol. 31, part 2, 194–95 and 207–8; Eunoia [pseud.], "The Recent Victory of Gen. Grant at Chattanooga," November 26, 1863, in Quiner Scrapbooks, vol. 10, 291–92, WHS, online; Heth, "The 24th Wis. at the Storming of Missionary Ridge," in Quiner Scrapbooks, vol. 10, 293, WHS, online; Arthur MacArthur Jr. to

Arthur MacArthur Sr., Camp near Chattanooga, November 26, 1863, in Quiner Scrapbooks, vol. 10, 297–98, WHS, online; Cozzens, *The Shipwreck of Their Hopes*, 242, 286, and 307–8. **4** "Chickamauga": Thomas J. Ford, *With the Rank and File: Incidents and Anecdotes During the War of the Rebellion, as Remembered by One of the Non-Commissioned Officers* (Milwaukee: Press of the Evening Wisconsin, 1898), 29. For MacArthur's condition and the flag, see Arthur MacArthur Jr. to Arthur MacArthur Sr., Camp near Chattanooga, November 26, 1863, in Quiner Scrapbooks, vol. 10, 297–98, WHS, online; Heth, "The 24th Wis. at the Storming of Missionary Ridge," in Quiner Scrapbooks, vol. 10, 293, WHS, online. **5** "no more": Cozzens, *The Shipwreck of Their Hopes*, 308–11. For the credit MacArthur received and other feats of similar courage, see Eunoia [pseud.], "The Recent Victory of Gen. Grant at Chattanooga," November 26, 1863, in Quiner Scrapbooks, vol. 10, 291–92, WHS, online; Beaudot, *The 24th Wisconsin Infantry in the Civil War*, 264; DMREM, 9; United States War Department, *The War of the Rebellion*, series I, vol. 31, part 2, 188–93 and 207–8; Indiana Battle Flag Commission, *Indiana Battle Flags and a Record of Indiana Organizations in the Mexican, Civil, and Spanish-American Wars* (Indianapolis, 1929), 122–23; James Gindlesperger, "First Flag to be Planted on the Parapet: George Banks and the Battle at Missionary Ridge," in Congressional Medal of Honor Society, November 25, 2021, online. **5** "racked with": DMREM, 8–9. For the regiment's commanding officer not knowing MacArthur was eligible, see Carl von Baumbach to Redfield Proctor, Milwaukee, June 7, 1890, RG 94, NARA. **5** "such non-commissioned": Edwin Stanton, *Annual Report of the Secretary of War* (Washington, DC: Government Printing Office, 1865), 18–19. For other details, see Young, *The General's General*, 155–62; Dwight S. Mears, *The Medal of Honor: The Evolution of America's Highest Military Decoration* (Lawrence: University Press of Kansas, 2018), 27–37. **6** "I feel very": Arthur MacArthur to the Adjutant General, Fort Wingate, New Mexico, October 13, 1883, RG 94, NARA. **6** "very recently": Carl von Baumbach to Redfield Proctor, Milwaukee, June 7, 1890, RG 94, NARA. For receipt of the medal, see War Department to Arthur MacArthur, Washington, DC, June 30, 1890, RG 94, NARA. **7** "silhouetted": DMREM, 5, 8–9, and 16–17. For other details, see Young, *The General's General*, 161–63; *Washington Evening Star*, August 27, 1896; Affidavits of George Allanson (April 1890), Edwin B. Parsons (May 1890), J. E. Armitage (May 1890), RG 94, NARA.

CHAPTER ONE **Fatherland**

11 "Anything else": Carol Morris Petillo, *Douglas MacArthur: The Philippine Years* (Bloomington: Indiana University Press, 1981), 47 and 257. For other details, see Young, *The General's General*, 130–31, 136–37, 175, and 178–84; Stanley Karnow, *In Our Image: America's Empire in the Philippines* (New York: Random House, 1989), 104–5; Henry C. Corbin to Mary Hardy MacArthur, Washington, DC, June 2, 1898, RG 94, NARA; Arthur MacArthur to Henry C. Corbin, Tampa Bay, May 2 and 3,

1898, RG 94, NARA; Arthur MacArthur to Henry C. Corbin, Chickamauga Park, Georgia, June 2, 1898, RG 94, NARA; DMREM, 14; *Report of the Commission Appointed by the President to Investigate the Conduct of the War Department in the War with Spain*, 56th Cong., 1st session, Senate Doc. 221, vol. 1, 443–46. **12** "took the form": Young, *The General's General*, 186. For other details, see Jesse George, *Our Army and Navy in the Orient, Giving a Full Account of the Operations of the Army and Navy in the Philippines* (Manila, 1899), 54; F. D. Millett, *The Expedition to the Philippines* (New York: Harper & Brothers, 1899), 33–35; FOP, 7–8 and 296; Karnow, *In Our Image*, 106 and 125; John Barrett, "Manila and the Philippines," *Harper's Weekly*, August 6, 1898; "A Trooper's Diary: From Honolulu to Manila," *The Outlook*, October 29, 1898. **17** "In the event": Gregg Jones, *Honor in the Dust: Theodore Roosevelt, War in the Philippines, and the Rise and Fall of America's Imperial Dream* (New York: New American Library, 2012), 5–7, 10–11, 41–44, and 86–94. For the prehistory of the islands, Magellan, the revolutionary tide, and deliberations in Washington, DC, see Luis H. Francia, *A History of the Philippines: From Indios Bravos to Filipinos* (New York: Overlook, 2014), 5–31; Karnow, *In Our Image*, 33–47, 51–77, and 79–91; Laurence Bergreen, *Over the Edge of the World: Magellan's Terrifying Circumnavigation of the Globe* (New York: Perennial, 2003), 231–82; Antonio Pigafetta, *Magellan's Voyage: A Narrative Account of the First Circumnavigation*, trans. R. A. Skelton (New York: Dover Publications, 1994), 99–158; David J. Silbey, *A War of Frontier and Empire: The Philippine-American War, 1899–1902* (New York: Hill and Wang, 2007), 8–15, 22–25, 34, 41, and 52–53. **18** "The heated": Petillo, *Douglas MacArthur*, 44–46. For other details, see Arthur Herman, *Douglas MacArthur: American Warrior* (New York: Random House, 2016), 62; William Manchester, *American Caesar: Douglas MacArthur, 1880–1964* (New York: Back Bay Books, 1978), 23; Young, *The General's General*, 127–51 and 175; Edmund Morris, *The Rise of Theodore Roosevelt* (New York: Modern Library, 2001), 478–80; Silbey, *A War of Frontier and Empire*, 23–24. **18** "Self-interest": Herman, *Douglas MacArthur*, 21. **19** "simple feint": *Affairs in the Philippine Islands*, 57th Cong., 1st session, 1902, Senate Doc. 331, part 2, 1402–9. For the details of the battle and description of Intramuros, see Young, *The General's General*, 193–200; Silbey, *A War of Frontier and Empire*, 47–49; Arthur MacArthur, "General MacArthur's Account," in *Harper's Pictorial History of the War with Spain* (New York: Harper & Brothers, 1899), 418–21; George, *Our Army and Navy in the Orient*, 105–6; Joseph L. Stickney, *Life and Glorious Deeds of Admiral Dewey* (Chicago: Chas B. Ayer, 1898), 113–14 and 202; Jones, *Honor in the Dust*, 88; Robert Ross Smith, *Triumph in the Philippines* (Washington, DC: Center of Military History, 1993), 240. **20** "to carry": *Affairs in the Philippine Islands*, 862. For other details, see Karnow, *In Our Image*, 59–60, 124–26, and 130–31; "Manila and the Philippines," *Harper's Weekly*, August 6, 1898; J. B. Babcock, General Orders, No. 4, Manila, August 15, 1898, in *Annual Reports of the War Department: Miscellaneous Reports* (Washington, DC: Government Printing Office, 1898), 50; Brian McAllister Linn, *The Philippine War, 1899–1902* (Lawrence: University Press of Kansas, 2000),

13 and 26; George, *Our Army and Navy in the Orient*, 123–24; Young, *The General's General*, 203–5; Jones, *Honor in the Dust*, 98 and 137. **20** "neatness": Young, *The General's General*, 207. **20** "year of observation": *Affairs in the Philippine Islands*, 862. For the bookdealer, see Silbey, *A War of Frontier and Empire*, 143. **21** "I became": *Affairs in the Philippine Islands*, 867–77. For the value of being provost marshal and for the bigotry Americans brought, see Petillo, *Douglas MacArthur*, 49; Jones, *Honor in the Dust*, 97–98. **22** "gulp": John F. Bass, "The Philippine Revolt: The Malolos Campaign," *Harper's Weekly*, June 17, 1899. For other details, see Young, *The General's General*, 218–34; Karnow, *In Our Image*, 128–30; *Affairs in the Philippine Islands*, 894–900; Silbey, *A War of Frontier and Empire*, 70–86 and 116–43; Linn, *The Philippine War*, 52; *Military Notes on the Philippines* (Washington, DC: Government Printing Office, 1898), 23; Petillo, *Douglas MacArthur*, 257; Jones, *Honor in the Dust*, 120–22; Rowland T. Berthoff, "Taft and MacArthur, 1900–1901: A Study in Civil-Military Relations," *World Politics* 5, no. 2 (January 1953), 198. **24** "The more": Berthoff, "Taft and MacArthur," 196–208. For more on the commission, the feud, the constabulary, and the creation of the Scouts, see Petillo, *Douglas MacArthur*, 52; Karnow, *In Our Image*, 167–69; Young, *The General's General*, xv, 254–60, 273, and 277; Christopher Capozzola, *Bound by War: How the United States and the Philippines Built America's First Pacific Century* (New York: Basic Books, 2020), 14–15. **24** "a profound": Young, *The General's General*, 272–76. **24** "academical": *Affairs in the Philippine Islands*, 861–69. For more about MacArthur's vocabulary, see Young, *The General's General*, 276. **25** "psychological conditions": Berthoff, "Taft and MacArthur," 199–200. **25** "great majority": Linn, *The Philippine War*, 185–217. For the election and education, see also Silbey, *A War of Frontier and Empire*, 158–66; Young, *The General's General*, 266. **26** "the humiliation": Berthoff, "Taft and MacArthur," 208–10. For the capture and other details, see Young, *The General's General*, 285–90; Karnow, *In Our Image*, 182–84 and 235. For Quezon's memory, see Manuel Luis Quezon y Molina, "The MacArthurs in Philippine History" (speech, Malacañan Palace, Manila, August 24, 1936), *Official Gazette of the Republic of the Philippines*, online; Silbey, *A War of Frontier and Empire*, 172–86. **26** "MacArthur Is": *Milwaukee Journal*, August 24, 1901. For other details of the return, see Young, *The General's General*, 274 and 293–95; *Milwaukee Journal*, August 19, 1901; Karnow, *In Our Image*, 170; Helen Herron Taft, *Recollections of Full Years* (New York: Dodd, Mead, 1914), 211. **27** "gallantry": Theodore Roosevelt to Elihu Root, Buffalo, September 7, 1901, Theodore Roosevelt Digital Library, Dickinson State University. For background on Robert Powell Page Wainwright and other details, see William T. Wood, Alexander D. Schenk, and Frederick C. Johnson, "Robert Powell Page Wainwright," Military Order of the Loyal Legion of the United States, January 20, 1903, JMWP, USAHEC; Betty Mears Wainwright, "Skinny," unpublished manuscript, WP, USMA, 5, 27–28, and 36–38; United States Naval War Records Office, *Official Records of the Union and Confederate Navies in the War of the Rebellion* (Washington, DC: Government Printing Office, 1894–1922), series 1, vol. 19, 443 and 456; "How Wainwright Died,"

JMWP, USAHEC; W. H. Miller, "Robert Powell Page Wainwright," in *Thirty-Fifth Annual Reunion of the Association Graduates of the United States Military Academy at West Point* (Saginaw, MI: Seemann and Peters, 1904), 27–32; Silbey, *A War of Frontier and Empire*, 113, 171, 181, 197–201, and 205–6; Jones, *Honor in the Dust*, 195. **28** "Cardiac": William T. Wood, Alexander D. Schenk, and Frederick C. Johnson, "Robert Powell Page Wainwright," JMWP, USAHEC. For the theory that the older Wainwright might have died of a tropical disease, see Duane Schultz, *Hero of Bataan: The Story of General Jonathan M. Wainwright* (New York: St. Martin's Press, 1981), 16. **28** "strategical": *Affairs in the Philippine Islands*, 867 and 1918–19. For Wainwright starting at West Point, see George W. Cullum, *Biographical Register of the Officers and Graduates of the U.S. Military Academy at West Point, New York, 1900–1910*, ed. Charles Braden (Saginaw, MI: Seemann & Peters, 1910), 781; Betty Mears Wainwright, "Skinny," unpublished manuscript, WP, USMA, 101–5.

CHAPTER TWO **The Call of History**

29 "the most thoroughly": Karnow, *In Our Image*, 14, 196–203, 211–12, and 226. For additional details, see Tom Nicoll, "Some Golf Courses in the Philippines," *Golfer's Magazine* 34, no. 3 (March 1919), 11; Thomas S. Hines, "The Imperial Façade: Daniel H. Burnham and American Architectural Planning in the Philippines," *Pacific Historical Review* 41, no. 1 (February 1972), 45; Joseph P. McCallus, *The MacArthur Highway & Other Relics of American Empire in the Philippines* (Washington, DC: Potomac Books, 2010), 275 and 278; *Report of the Philippine Commission to the Secretary of War, 1908* (Washington, DC: Government Printing Office, 1909), part 2, 627; FOP, 79. **30** "TOJO DECLARES": Clark Lee, *They Call It Pacific: An Eye-Witness Story of Our War Against Japan from Bataan to the Solomons* (New York: Viking, 1943), 23–42. For other details about the hotel and social life, see *The Building Age*, January 1913, 17–18; Clare Boothe, "Destiny Crosses the Dateline," *Life*, November 3, 1941, 107–9; *New York Times*, September 19, 1941; James Bollich, *Bataan Death March: A Soldier's Story* (Gretna, LA: Pelican, 1993), 34–35. **31** "attractive": Richard M. Gordon, *Horyo: Memoirs of an American POW* (St. Paul: Paragon House, 1999), 40. For the order sending wives and children home, see *New York Times*, April 23, 1941. **31** "very best": James McAfee, ed., *The 27th Reports*, online. For background on Brereton and other details, see Roger G. Miller, "A 'Pretty Damn Able Commander'—Lewis Hyde Brereton, Part I," *Air Power History* 47, no. 4 (Winter 2000), 16 and 21; Karl H. Lowe, "World War II," in *The 31st Infantry Regiment: A History of "America's Foreign Legion" in Peace and War* (Jefferson, NC: McFarland, 2018), 87; Lewis H. Brereton, *The Brereton Diaries: The War in the Air in the Pacific, Middle East and Europe* (New York: Da Capo, 1976), 38; Paul P. Rogers, *The Good Years: MacArthur and Sutherland* (New York: Praeger, 1990), 93. **32** "The more": Brereton, *The Brereton Diaries*, 17–25. For other accounts of MacArthur's penthouse, pacing, and predictions, see Clare Booth, "MacArthur of the Far East," *Life*, December 8, 1941, 139; Janet Flanner, "General and

Mrs. Douglas MacArthur," *Ladies' Home Journal*, June 1942, 59; Sid Huff, *My Fifteen Years with General MacArthur: A First-Hand Account of America's Greatest Soldier* (New York: Paperback Library, 1964), 27; GWS, 13; Geoffrey Perret, *Old Soldiers Never Die: The Life of Douglas MacArthur* (New York: Random House, 1996), 193 and 245–46; John Hersey, *Men on Bataan* (New York: Alfred A. Knopf, 1942), 279–81; Lee, *They Call It Pacific*, 32; Rogers, *The Good Years*, 15–16; Manchester, *American Caesar*, 320; Frazier Hunt, *The Untold Story of Douglas MacArthur* (New York: Devin-Adair, 1954), 223; John Dos Passos, *Tour of Duty* (Boston: Houghton Mifflin, 1946), 170; *New York Times*, January 26, 1945; Special Personal Report and Statement, December 18, 1919, Official Military Personnel File for Douglas MacArthur, RG 319, NARA. **32** "at the head": DMREM, 14–15. For "lonely" and other details, see Young, *The General's General*, 145–47. **33** "a great man": Hunt, *The Untold Story of Douglas MacArthur*, 11. For the skirts, see Petillo, *Douglas MacArthur*, 20 and 254n; Jean Edward Smith, *FDR* (New York: Random House, 2007), 21. **33** "We were": DMREM, 15 and 16. For the reality of Selden, see Young, *The General's General*, 125–26, 143, and 149–51. **34** "Washington was": DMREM, 16 and 17. For "competitive speaking" and other details, see YOM, vol. 1, 58–61; Clark Lee and Richard Henschel, *Douglas MacArthur* (New York: Henry Holt, 1952), 96. **35** "I never": DMREM, 17–19. For the attempts at admission and the final score, see YOM, vol. 1, 63–66; *Milwaukee Journal*, June 7, 1898. **35** "flashing dark": Robert E. Wood, "An Upperclassman's View," *Assembly* 23, no. 1 (Spring 1964), 4. For the move to West Point, see YOM, vol. 1, 67–69; Hunt, *The Untold Story of Douglas MacArthur*, 18–19. **35** "Is it": *Milwaukee Journal*, December 29, 1900. For MacArthur's convulsions, which he himself denied having, see *Hazing at the Military Academy*, 56th Cong., 2nd session, 1901, H. R. Rep. 2768, part 3, 916–17 and 1200–13. **36** "Like mother": DMREM, 25–26. For the poem's earlier publication and the reality of the testimony, see L. A. Goodman, *Thirtieth Annual Report of the State Horticultural Society of the State of Missouri* (Jefferson City: Tribune, 1888), 463; *Milwaukee Journal*, December 29, 1900; *Hazing at the Military Academy*, 917. **36** "This rating": DMREM, 27. For other details, see YOM, vol. 1, 77–78; William A. Ganoe, "An Appreciation of Douglas MacArthur—The Man," *Assembly* 23, no. 1 (Spring 1964), 20–21; Herman, *Douglas MacArthur*, 50; "Graduation Week at West Point," *Army and Navy Journal* 40, no. 41 (June 13, 1903), 1033; Hunt, *The Untold Story of Douglas MacArthur*, 33. **36** "The Philippines charmed": DMREM, 29–30. For the change in loyalties and malaria, see Karnow, *In Our Image*, 187 and 231–37; YOM, vol. 1, 89–90. **38** "the most important": DMREM, 30–32 and 287–88. For other details, see Young, *The General's General*, 308–21 and 323–27; Petillo, *Douglas MacArthur*, 72–85; *Washington Evening Star*, December 11, 1903; John Toland, *The Rising Sun: The Decline and Fall of the Japanese Empire, 1936–1945* (New York: Modern Library, 2003), 7 and 54; YOM, vol. 1, 91–94. **38** "I was": Summary of Efficiency Reports, 1908, Official Military Personnel File for Douglas MacArthur, RG 319, NARA; YOM, vol. 1, 95–101. For other details, see Manchester, *American Caesar*, 69. **39** "My whole": DMREM, 35–36. For Arthur's final disappointment and his widow, see Young,

The General's General, 328–40; Petillo, *Douglas MacArthur*, 110–11. **39** "victim": Petillo, *Douglas MacArthur*, 113–15. For additional details of the incident and the dispute over the medal, see DMREM, 40–43; YOM, vol. 1, 123–26. **40** "stretch over": DMREM, 43–52 and 61; YOM, 130–45. **40** "a roaring": DMREM, 56, 58, and 70. For additional details about MacArthur's appearance, see YOM, vol. 1, 156, 158–60, 216–17, and 253; Manchester, *American Caesar*, 87 and 107; Petillo, *Douglas MacArthur*, 120–22. **40** "the bloodiest": YOM, vol. 1, 165 and 181. **41** "I cannot fight": DMREM, 54. **41** "all of Germany": YOM, vol. 1, 211–12. **41** "There are times": Hunt, *The Untold Story of Douglas MacArthur*, 87–88. **41** "a list": DMREM, 66. **41** "d'Art- agnan": Manchester, *American Caesar*, 89 and 98. **41** "considered the most": YOM, vol. 1, 169–72. **41** "the show-off": Manchester, *American Caesar*, 91. For other details, see Herman, *Douglas MacArthur*, 143; YOM, vol. 1, 238–39. **42** "Careless": Herman, *Douglas MacArthur*, 173–74. For Louise and the other girls, also see DMREM, 27; Petillo, *Douglas MacArthur*, 102–6 and 140–41; Walter R. Borneman, *MacArthur at War: World War II in the Pacific* (New York: Little, Brown, 2016), 29; *New York Times*, June 1, 1965. **42** "flapper": Petillo, *Douglas MacArthur*, 123–25 and 140–41; Man- chester, *American Caesar*, 127–29. For the newspaper controversy, see *New York Times*, February 10, 1922. **42** "new roads": DMREM, 84. For the baggage and ponies, see Perret, *Old Soldiers Never Die*, 129–30; Petillo, *Douglas MacArthur*, 126. **43** "as soon as": Karnow, *In Our Image*, 231–52. For other details, see YOM, vol. 1, 297–303; Rich- ard Meixsel, "The Philippine Scout Mutiny of 1924," *South East Asia Research* 10, no. 3 (November 2002), 353; Theodore Friend, *Between Two Empires: The Ordeal of the Philippines, 1929–1946* (New Haven: Yale University Press, 1965), 47–53. **43** "[as] our heel": Capozzola, *Bound by War*, 71–73. For the development of War Plan Orange, see Ronald H. *Spector, Eagle Against the Sun: The American War with Japan* (New York: Free Press, 1985), 54–59; Edward S. Miller, *War Plan Orange: The U.S. Strategy to Defeat Japan, 1897–1945* (Annapolis: Naval Institute Press, 1991), 53–65; Louis Mor- ton, "War Plan Orange: Evolution of a Strategy," *World Politics* 11, no. 2 (January 1959), 221–50; YOM, vol. 1, 298, 334–36, and 473. **44** "I covered": DMREM, 84. **45** "he may": Bob Considine, *It's All News to Me: A Reporter's Deposition* (New York: Mere- dith, 1967), 342. For other details, see "First Mrs. Mac Speaks Up," *Washington Sunday Star*, April 19, 1964; YOM, vol. 1, 303–5 and 319–21; *New York Times*, September 28, 1924; Perret, *Old Soldiers Never Die*, 168; Herman, *Douglas MacArthur*, 240. **45** "If only": Manchester, *American Caesar*, 141–44. For the Olympics, divorce, and Cooper, see Herman, *Douglas MacArthur*, 192–95 and 237–38; Manchester, *American Caesar*, 141; Petillo, *Douglas MacArthur*, 152–56 and 164; Vernadette Vicuña Gonzalez, *Empire's Mistress: Starring Isabel Rosario Cooper* (Durham: Duke University Press, 2021), 33. **46** "No one": Herman, *Douglas MacArthur*, 191–92 and 217–25. For details about the world situation and Bonus March, see David M. Kennedy, *Freedom from Fear: The American People in Depression and War, 1929–1945* (New York: Oxford University Press, 1999), 1–9, 79, 92, and 385–89; Toland, *The Rising Sun*, 7–8; DMREM, 92–97. **46** "most dangerous": YOM, vol. 1, 411. For the libel suit, see Petillo,

Douglas MacArthur, 165. **46** "When we": DMREM 100–101. For MacArthur's relationship with Hoover and Roosevelt's decision, see YOM, vol. 1, 352–54 and 427–29; Herman, *Douglas MacArthur*, 224–28. **47** "An army": YOM, vol. 1, 354–62, 378–81, and 426–27. For Billy Mitchell, see DMREM, 85–86; "Billy Mitchell's Prophecy," *American Heritage* 13, no. 2 (1962), online; Spector, *Eagle Against the Sun*, 12–15; Douglas Waller, *A Question of Loyalty: Gen. Billy Mitchell and the Court-Martial That Gripped the Nation* (New York: Harper Collins, 2004), 56. **47** "Daddy": Manchester, *American Caesar*, 144–45 and 156. **48** "Do you think": Manuel Luis Quezon, *The Good Fight* (New York: D. Appleton, 1946), 153–54. For the legislation, see Karnow, *In Our Image*, 252–56. **48** "I don't": Friend, *Between Two Empires*, 160–64. For MacArthur's plan and pay, see DMREM, 103–4; Quezon, *The Good Fight*, 153–55; Petillo, *Douglas MacArthur*, 179; YOM, vol. 1, 501–4; FOP, 10; Perret, *Old Soldiers Never Die*, 188 and 192. **49** "my general": Huff, *My Fifteen Years*, 13–25 and 125. For other details, see Hunt, *The Untold Story of Douglas MacArthur*, 170 and 179–80; DMREM, 103; Interview with JM, New York City, June 19–24, 1984, RG 13, MMLA; Clare Booth, "MacArthur of the Far East," 132 and 139; Flanner, "General and Mrs. Douglas MacArthur," 59; Lee and Henschel, *Douglas MacArthur*, 9 and 64–68; Herman, *Douglas MacArthur*, 254–56; Petillo, *Douglas MacArthur*, 186–87. **51** "On any": Jean Edward Smith, *Eisenhower in War and Peace* (New York: Random House, 2013), 101–5 and 126–30. For the daily routine and enrollment problems, see Interview with JM, New York City, June 19–22, 1984, RG 13, MMLA; YOM, vol. 1, 505–6, 521–38, and 557; Manchester, *American Caesar*, 164 and 179; Dwight D. Eisenhower, *The Eisenhower Diaries*, ed. Robert H. Ferrell (New York: Norton, 1981), 22; Huff, *My Fifteen Years*, 9; Dwight D. Eisenhower, *At Ease: Stories I Tell to Friends* (New York: Doubleday, 1967), 214; Excerpt from Oral Reminiscences of Dwight D. Eisenhower, August 29, 1967, D. Clayton James Papers, MMLA. **52** "Some day": Friend, *Between Two Empires*, 192–94; Herman, *Douglas MacArthur*, 278. **52** "new order in": Toland, *The Rising Sun*, 1 and 43–86. For more details of the march to war, see YOM, vol. 1, 516; Spector, *Eagle Against the Sun*, 43 and 62–69; Kennedy, *Freedom from Fear*, 418–52 and 502–12; FOP, 14–15 and 46. **53** "This action": YOM, vol. 1, 502–3, 546–47, 579–80, 584, and 590–95. For Quezon's reaction and the Rainbow details, see Kennedy, *Freedom from Fear*, 479–82; FOP, 63–65, Friend, *Between Two Empires*, 201. **54** "contagious optimism": Henry L. Stimson and McGeorge Bundy, *On Active Service in Peace and War* (New York: Harper Brothers, 1947), 388. For the numbers and the B-17, see YOM, vol. 1, 594–95; Mark Skinner Watson, *Chief of Staff: Prewar Plans and Preparations* (Washington, DC: Historical Division Department of the Army, 1950), 433; Spector, *Eagle Against the Sun*, 16 and 74–75; FOP, 39–42; Perret, *Old Soldiers Never Die*, 244–45. **54** "acted like": Brereton, *The Brereton Diaries*, 17–19. For the content of the secret letter and the shipping of equipment, see GCM to DM, November 27, 1941, in *Hearings Before the Joint Committee on the Investigation of the Pearl Harbor Attack*, 79th Cong., 1st session, 1946, part 14, 1329; FOP, 37 and 48; GCM to Frederick Gilbreath, Washington, DC, November 29, 1941, in George C. Marshall,

The Papers of George Catlett Marshall, ed. Larry I. Bland (Baltimore: The Johns Hopkins University Press, 1986), vol. 2, 687. **55** "Japanese future": GCM to DM, November 27, 1941, in *Hearings Before the Joint Committee on the Investigation of the Pearl Harbor Attack*, part 14, 1329. For other details, see Walter D. Edmonds, *They Fought with What They Had: The Story of the Army Air Forces in the Southwest Pacific, 1941–1942* (Boston: Little, Brown, 1951), 14 and 62–63; Brereton, *The Brereton Diaries*, 34–35; Wesley Frank Craven and James Lea Cate, eds., *The Army Air Forces in World War II* (Washington, DC: Office of Air Force History, 1983), 191; John Toland, *But Not in Shame: The Six Months After Pearl Harbor* (New York: Random House, 1961), 11–13; Lee, *They Call It Pacific*, 32; GWS, 13; Perret, *Old Soldiers Never Die*, 245–47; Lee and Henschel, *Douglas MacArthur*, 136–37; YOM, vol. 2, 11. **56** "a large number": Toland, *But Not in Shame*, 22–23. **56** "Pearl Harbor?": Hunt, *The Untold Story of Douglas MacArthur*, 223. For MacArthur's continuing disbelief, see DMREM, 117. **56** "sound": Lee and Henschel, *Douglas MacArthur*, 166. For the first conference between Brereton and Sutherland and other details, see George C. Kenney, *General Kenney Reports: A Personal History of the Pacific War* (Washington, DC: Office of Air Force History, 1987), 33; Brereton, *The Brereton Diaries*, 36–44; Rogers, *The Good Years*, 94; Edmonds, *They Fought with What They Had*, 63, 68, and 86–93; Toland, *The Rising Sun*, 212; Craven and Cate, eds., *The Army Air Forces in World War II*, 204–7; FOP, 81–84. **57** "The general says": Toland, *But Not in Shame*, 41. **57** "If hostilities": FOP, 71. For other details, see Brereton, *The Brereton Diaries*, 39; Toland, *But Not in Shame*, 41–42; Edmonds, *They Fought with What They Had*, 81. **57** "more like a": Hersey, *Men on Bataan*, 287–88. For the bedroom and flags, also see Huff, *My Fifteen Years*, 27. **58** "turned away": Perret, *Old Soldiers Never Die*, 209–10; "The Cradle of Philippine Democracy," RG2, MMLA. **58** "Personally": Booth, "MacArthur of the Far East," 127. **58** "The Philippines, while": Charles A. Willoughby, *MacArthur, 1941–1945* (New York: McGraw-Hill, 1954), 24–25; YOM, vol. 2, 10–11. For MacArthur's belief that the Japanese had not yet attacked the Philippines, also see John Jacob Beck, *MacArthur and Wainwright: Sacrifice of the Philippines* (Albuquerque: University of New Mexico Press, 1974), 13–14. **59** "glorious": Perrett, *Old Soldiers Never Die*, 235 and 240–47. For "a people's contest," see Abraham Lincoln, Message to Congress in Special Session, July 4, 1861, in Don E. Fehrenbacher, ed., *Abraham Lincoln: Speeches and Writings, 1859–1865* (New York: Library of America, 1989), 259.

CHAPTER THREE **First Steps to a Last Stand**

62 "lean, tough": Amea Willoughby, *I Was on Corregidor: Experiences of an American Official's Wife in the War-Torn Philippines* (New York: Harper & Brothers, 1943), 142–43. For other details, see Edmonds, *They Fought with What They Had*, 46, 79–86, and 98–100; H. Jordan Theis, "Fort Stotsenburg Today," *The Cavalry Journal* 41, no. 169 (January–February 1932), 27–28; Interview with David J. Duran, undated, John Toland Papers, LC; Mary Henry Howze, "Diary of Mary Henry Howze," October

24, 1938, Philippine Diary Project, online; Edwin Price Ramsey and Stephen J. Rivele, *Lieutenant Ramsey's War: From Horse Soldier to Guerrilla Commander* (Washington, DC: Brassey's, 1990), 34–35; John K. Herr and Edward S. Wallace, *The Story of the U.S. Cavalry, 1775–1942* (Boston: Little, Brown, 1953), 250–54; Andrew Roberts, *The Storm of War: A New History of the Second World War* (New York: Harper, 2011), 24; Alexander M. Bielakowski, "The Role of the Horse in Modern Warfare as Viewed in the Interwar U.S. Army's 'Cavalry Journal,'" *Army History*, no. 50 (Summer–Fall 2000), 23–24; JMW, "Mobility," *The Cavalry Journal* 44, no. 191 (September–October 1935), 20; JRP, Diary, November 28, 1941, PC; Interview with Virgil McCollum, undated, John Toland Papers, LC; Interview with Don Adams, undated, John Toland Papers, LC; Interview with John Connor, undated, John Toland Papers, LC; Interview with Charles Frances, undated, John Toland Papers, LC; *Detroit Times*, December 30, 1941. **63** "Mother of": GWS, 20–22 and 234. **63** "imperturbable": Ramsey and Rivele, *Lieutenant Ramsey's War*, 43–44. For Wainwright's activities the day before, see also JMW, Diary, December 7, 1941, JMWP, USAHEC; GWS, 17–18; Jeffrey W. Woodhall, "The 26th Cavalry in the Philippines," *Armor* 92, no. 1 (January–February 1983), 9. **63** "The cat": GWS, 18–21. For the field equipment, see JMW, Diary, Memoranda, 1941, JMWP, USAHEC; Lucian K. Truscott Jr., *The Twilight of the U.S. Cavalry: Life in the Old Army, 1917–1942*, ed. Lucian K. Truscott III (Lawrence: University Press of Kansas, 1989), 20–22; Herr and Wallace, *The Story of the U.S. Cavalry*, 78; *Washington Evening Star*, March 24, 1942; J. K. Mizner, "Some Changes in Equipment," *Journal of the United States Cavalry Association* 2, no. 4 (March 1889), 35–36; Schultz, *Hero of Bataan*, 21 and 270. **64** "jerky": *St. Paul Daily Globe*, July 4, 1886. **64** "Home is where": Betty Mears Wainwright, "Skinny," WP, USMA, 1–4, 36–46, and 92. For Wainwright's reflection later in life and the timing of these moves, see JMW to Percy McElwaine, March 26, 1951, WP, USMA; Robert Powell Page Wainwright, *Cullum's Register*, University of Chicago, online. **65** "first distinct": *Billings Gazette*, June 26, 1952. For tending the grounds and the story of the rifle, see Jerome A. Greene, *Stricken Field: The Little Bighorn Since 1876* (Norman: University of Oklahoma Press, 2008), 15–16 and 31–35; *Winnemucca Silver State*, February 8, 1886; *Charleston News and Courier*, June 28, 1952; JMW to Robert M. Utley, September 19, 1950, WP, USMA; JMW, Statement, January 14, 1949, JMWP, USAHEC; JMW to Walter Siegmund, October 5, 1949, JMWP, USAHEC; Walter Siegmund to E. S. Luce, December 14, 1949, JMWP, USAHEC; JMW to Walter Siegmund, December 30, 1949, JMWP, USAHEC. **65** "fillies": Betty Mears Wainwright, "Skinny," WP, USMA, 40–49, 89–96, 170, and 182. **66** "He was": *Chicago Sun*, April 12, 1942. For the Roosevelt letter, see Theodore Roosevelt to Elihu Root, Buffalo, September 7, 1901, Theodore Roosevelt Digital Library, Dickinson State University. **66** "he came": Charles G. Mettler, "Jonathan M. Wainwright, 1906," West Point Association of Graduates, online. **66** "rare": Perret, *Old Soldiers Never Die*, 45. For MacArthur's place, see "West Point," *Army and Navy Journal* 39, no. 42 (June 21, 1902), 1074. **66** "The only person": GWS, 3 and 189–90. For Jim and the rankings, see

Schultz, *Hero of Bataan*, 1 and 20; DMREM, 142; United States Military Academy, *The Howitzer of 1906* (Springfield, MA: F. A. Bassette, 1906), 67; *Watertown Daily Times*, August 29, 1945; *Charleston Evening Post*, March 27, 1942; *Official Register of the Officers and Cadets of the U.S. Military Academy* (West Point: USMA Press, 1903), 18; *New York Times*, November 21, 1902; Betty Mears Wainwright, "Skinny," WP, USMA, 97–106; *Official Register of the Officers and Cadets of the U.S. Military Academy* (West Point: USMA Press, 1906), 14; JMW, Demerit Book, USMA. **67** "Who would": United States Military Academy, *The Howitzer of 1906*, 67, 72, 155, 179, 185, 269, 272, and 275. For his classmates' respect, the sword, and early career, see Charles G. Mettler, "Jonathan M. Wainwright, 1906," West Point Association of Graduates, online; JMW to Wilhem D. Styer, Fort Sam Houston, Texas, October 21, 1946, John Toland Papers, LC; JMW to Gordon L. Harris, Fort Sam Houston, Texas, January 28, 1947, USAHEC, online; JMW to Francis J. Martin, September 11, 1952, JMWP, USAHEC; J. Mayhew Wainwright, *Those Who Came Before Us: Wainwrights, Mayhews, Stuyvesants, and Others* (Salem, 1953), 33; Jerome J. Comello, *Jonathan M. Wainwright: Planning and Executing the Defense of the Philippines* (Temple University, Dissertation, 1999), 10–28; Schultz, *Hero of Bataan*, 23–24; Caroline S. Shunk, *An Army Woman in the Philippines* (Kansas City: Franklin Hudson, 1914), 28–51; Jonathan M. Wainwright, *Cullum's Register*, University of Chicago, online; "Biography of Jonathan Mayhew Wainwright," JMWP, USAHEC. **69** "brown": Betty Mears Wainwright, "Skinny," WP, USMA, 121–42, 161, and 174. For the details of the engagement, wedding, and life together, see *Milwaukee Sentinel*, August 26, 1945; *Salt Lake Tribune*, February 19, 1911; JMW to Elfrida Wainwright and Jack Wainwright, Fort William McKinley, August 17, 1941, JMWP, USAHEC; *Watertown Daily Times*, August 29, 1945. **69** "remarkably energetic": Frederick S. Folts to R. E. L. Michie, Presidio of Monterey, July 11, 1915, JMWP, USAHEC. For the injury and Jack's birth, see Detached Service of JMW, JMWP, USAHEC; Schultz, *Hero of Bataan*, 25; Wainwright, *Those Who Came Before Us*, 36; Betty Mears Wainwright, "Skinny," WP, USMA, 133–34. **70** "good judgment": Frederick S. Folt to JMW, Douglas, Arizona, July 12, 1916, JMWP, USAHEC. For the fair and the cavalry, see *San Francisco Chronicle*, October 12, 1915; JMW to Commanding Officer, Presidio of San Francisco, October 13, 1915, JMWP, USAHEC; Herr and Wallace, *The Story of the U.S. Cavalry*, 241–48. **70** "snoot full": Betty Mears Wainwright, "Skinny," WP, USMA, 144. For other World War I details, see Colonel Beebe to Major General Burnham, September 24, 1918, JMWP, USAHEC; Director General Staff College to JMW, Army General Staff College, May 29, 1918, JMWP, USAHEC; Edward M. Coffman, *The War to End All Wars: The American Military Experience in World War I* (Lexington: University of Kentucky Press, 1998), 323–25; Schultz, *Hero of Bataan*, 28–29; *Charleston Evening Post*, March 27, 1942. **71** "exceptional ability": Colonel Beebe to Major General Burnham, September 24, 1918, JMWP, USAHEC. For the medal, see Henry T. Allen to the Adjutant General, October 18, 1920, JMWP, USAHEC. **71** "first boat": *Milwaukee Sentinel*, August 26, 1945. For the horse shows, see J. C. Montgomery to

JMW, August 15, 1920, JMWP, USAHEC. **71** "the bravest": Betty Mears Wainwright, "Skinny," WP, USMA, 151–65. For the German class, see Schultz, *Hero of Bataan*, 30. **72** "entirely up": Malin Craig to Hamilton S. Hawkins, December 6, 1924, JMWP, USAHEC. For the relationship with Craig and other biographical details, see Comello, *Jonathan M. Wainwright*, 10–12, 41, 44–45, 48, 51–52, and 98; JMW to John R. Pugh, November 29, 1948, WP, USMA; *Expenses of Burial in Arlington Cemetery of Unknown Member of American Expeditionary Forces*, 67th Cong., 1st session, 1921, 1–16; Morris S. Daniels Jr. to JMW, War Department, August 29, 1923, JMWP, USAHEC; "Biography of Jonathan Mayhew Wainwright," JMWP, USA-HEC. **72** "I could do": Schultz, *Hero of Bataan*, 32–34. For details of Wainwright's interactions with War Plan Orange, see Comello, *Jonathan M. Wainwright*, 24–114. **72** "Mastership of": JMW, "History of Cavalry School Hunt, 1895–1935," *The Cavalry Journal* 44, no. 192 (November–December 1935), 69–71. For other details, see Frederick Gilbreath, "The Fort Leavenworth Museum: During Its First Four Years of Struggle," Frontier Army Museum (May 1968), online; Betty Mears Wainwright, "Skinny," WP, USMA, 170; "Biography of Jonathan Mayhew Wainwright," JMWP, USAHEC. **72** "Cavalry leaders": JMW, "Farewell Speech by the Commanding Officer," *Fort Myer Haltershank* 9, no. 24 (August 25, 1936), 1–2. For the reverence for Wainwright and the years at Riley, see Schultz, *Hero of Bataan*, 35; J. C. Montgomery, Special Report, Jonathan M. Wainwright, Fort Riley, May 16, 1916, JMWP, USAHEC; Truscott Jr., *The Twilight of the U.S. Cavalry*, 75–104. **72** "Modern firearms": Bielakowski, "The Role of the Horse in Modern Warfare as Viewed in the Interwar U.S. Army's 'Cavalry Journal,'" 22–24. For the 1st Cavalry, see Herr and Wallace, *The Story of the U.S. Cavalry*, 248–50. **73** "broke his": *Washington Evening Star*, March 28, 1942. **73** "the fastest": JMW, "Mobility," 20. **73** "When you": Schultz, *Hero of Bataan*, 35. **73** "quick footed": JMW to the Quartermaster General, Fort Myer, Virginia, November 14, 1938, JMWP, USAHEC. For the move and Craig's role, see JMW to JRP, November 29, 1948, WP, USMA; Schultz, *Hero of Bataan*, 34–35; YOM, vol. 1, 492–93 and 502–3. **73** "an omnivorous": United States Military Academy, *The Howitzer of 1932* (West Point, 1932), 67. For Pugh's appointment and the books, see *Washington Sunday Star*, November 6, 1938; R. L. Cave to J. M. Wainwright, Finance Office, July 5, 1936, JMWP, USAHEC; Schultz, *Hero of Bataan*, 35. **74** "They have been": *Washington Evening Star*, December 10, 1938. For the Society Circus, see *New York Times*, April 2, 1937; Truscott Jr., *The Twilight of the U.S. Cavalry*, 113–17. **74** "there has never": *Washington Times*, November 19, 1938. **74** "Gentlemen": Schultz, *Hero of Bataan*, 23. For the culture, bourbon, and an example of the gossip, see Truscott Jr., *The Twilight of the U.S. Cavalry*, 116–17; JMW to Ben Keith, February 28, 1950, WP, USMA; Oral Reminiscences of Colonel James V. Collier, August 30, 1971, D. Clayton James Papers, MMLA. **74** "I guess": William Edward Brougher, *Baggy Pants and Other Stories* (New York: Vantage, 1956), 74–75; Schultz, *Hero of Bataan*, 23. **75** "like an officer": Betty Mears Wainwright, "Skinny," WP, USMA, 229. **75** "a completely": TBAB, 61–62. For Pugh's view, see

JRP, "J's Story about Wainwright," circa 1981, PC. **75** "outmoded": Thomas E. Ricks, *The Generals: American Military Command from World War II to Today* (New York: Penguin, 2012), 32–34. **75** "a sideburned": *Dallas Morning News*, May 16, 1940. **75** "Natural leader": *Washington Evening Star*, March 28, 1942. For the choice of commands, see AW to Jack Wainwright, Thursday Morning, WP, USMA. **76** "dodged": *Dallas Morning News*, May 16, 1940. For background on the maneuvers, see Mary Kathryn Barbier, "George C. Marshall and the 1940 Louisiana Maneuvers," *Louisiana History: The Journal of the Louisiana Historical Association* 44, no. 4 (Autumn 2003), 389–410. **76** "Our family": JMW to Jack and Elfrida Wainwright, San Francisco, October 7, 1940, WP, USMA. For the marital advice and other family details, see JMW to Jack Wainwright, Fort Clark, Texas, January 1, 1940, WP, USMA; Jack Wainwright to Elfrida Wainwright, At Sea, April 25, 1940, WP, USMA; Betty Mears Wainwright, "Skinny," WP, USMA, 173–76; AW to Jack Wainwright, Fort Bliss, Texas, early 1940, WP, USMA; JRP, Diary, November 1940, PC. **76** "miss the war": *Dallas Morning News*, April 9, 1942. **76** "out to pasture": Gordon, *Horyo*, 20–26. For other details, see AW to Jack Wainwright, October 10–24, 1940, WP, USMA; GWS, 6–7; FOP, 21–24; AW and JMW to Jack Wainwright, November 19, 1940, Fort McKinley, WP, USMA; JRP, Diary, December 1940, PC. **77** "Orange": JMW, Diary, January 1941, JMWP, USAHEC. For the assumption about the timing, see FOP, 61. **77** "A defense must": GWS, 9–10. **77** "Sometimes I": JRP, Diary, January 1941, PC. **78** "namby-pamby": *Providence Sunday Journal*, March 29, 1942. **78** "I ride": JMW to Elfrida Wainwright, Fort William McKinley, May 28, 1941, JMWP, USAHEC. For other details, see JMW, Diary, various 1941, JMWP, USAHEC; Ramsey and Rivele, *Lieutenant Ramsey's War*, 35 and 43; JMW to Jack Wainwright, Fort McKinley, December 5, 1940, WP, USMA. **78** "the sparkle": GWS, 9–10. For notice of the evacuation, see JMW, Diary, February 12, 1941, JMWP, USAHEC. **78** "Oh!": JMW, Diary, May 14, 1941, JMWP, USAHEC. For the teeth, see JMW to Elfrida and Jack Wainwright, Fort William McKinley, August 17, 1941, JMWP, USAHEC. **78** "ache": JRP, Diary, May and June 1941, PC. For other details, see Interview with JM, New York City, June 22, 1984, RG 13, MMLA; YOM, vol. 1, 583; DM, "They Died Hard—Those Savage Men," *Life*, July 10, 1964, 74; GWS, 4 and 8–9; JMW to Ruth B. Milliken, October 11, 1950, WP, USMA; YOM, vol. 1, 560–61; JMW, Diary, various 1941, JMWP, USAHEC; Oral Reminiscences of Colonel James V. Collier, August 30, 1971, D. Clayton James Collection, MMLA. Although Collier said he never heard Wainwright call MacArthur by his first name, Wainwright claimed to do so sometimes. The correspondence he sent to MacArthur supports the claim. **79** "Which do": GWS, 11–15. For other details, see YOM, vol. 1, 510 and 593–96; FOP, 25–26 and 69–71; JMW, Diary, September 1, 1941, JMWP, USAHEC. **80** "A paper": Malcolm M. Champlin, "Bataan, February 1942," *Shipmate* (February 1972), 3–6. **80** "The Philippine Army troops": JMW to Elfrida and Jack Wainwright, Fort William McKinley, August 17, 1941, JMWP, USAHEC. For the challenge of preparing the army, see Celedonia A. Ancheta, ed., *The Wainwright*

Papers (Quezon City: New Day, 1980), vol. 1, 69; FOP, 6, 27–30, and 86; John C. McManus, *Fire and Fortitude: The US Army in the Pacific War, 1941–1943* (New York: Caliber, 2019), 56 and 61; YOM, vol. 1, 514; DM to GCM, Manila, October 28, 1941, RG2, MMLA. **81** "You'll probably": GWS, 12–18. For Wainwright taking command and his aides, see Richard K. Sutherland, Special Orders, no. 77, Manila, November 21, 1941, RG 2, MMLA; JRP, Diary, September–November 1941, PC. **81** "filthy": JMW, Diary, December 1941, JMWP, USAHEC. **81** "at all costs": FOP, 69. For Wainwright's reflections, see GWS, 13–19. **81** "ready for": YOM, vol. 1, 609. For the travel plans, see GWS, 19. **82** "damned fool": GWS, 22–24. For the aides and aftermath, see TBAB, 2, 6–16, and 21; Edmonds, *They Fought with What They Had*, 101–4; FOP, 90–97. **83** "It was like": FOP, 107. For other details, see Toland, *But Not in Shame*, 84. **83** "mopping up": Press Releases of the C in C's Daily Communiques, December 11, 1941, RG 2, MMLA. **83** "JAPANESE FORCES": *New York Times*, December 14, 1941. **84** "It is hard": GWS, 27–35. For other details of the landings and the horse, see FOP, 98–114 and 123–38; Toland, *But Not in Shame*, 93–95; JMW, Diary, December 1941, JMWP, USAHEC; E. B. Miller, *Bataan Uncensored* (Long Prairie, MN: Hart, 1949), 8–9 and 94; JMW to AW, October 13, 1942, WP, USMA. **84** "Give me": GWS, 35–36. For the headquarters, see Schultz, *Hero of Bataan*, 92–93; TBAB, 16 and 25. **85** "MacArthur and Sutherland": Oral Reminiscences of Brigadier General Clifford Bluemel, July 8, 1971, D. Clayton James Collection, MMLA. For the view being widespread, see Toland, *But Not in Shame*, 114. **85** "major": Champlin, "Bataan, February 1942," 6. **85** "scrap": Betty Mears Wainwright, "Skinny," WP, USMA, 184–85. For the memoirs, see GWS, 9–10. **86** "It was unlike": GWS, 37 and 41–42. For more about the challenge, see Alvin P. Stauffer, *The Quartermaster Corps: Operations in the War Against Japan* (Washington, DC: Office of the Chief of Military History, 1956), 6–7; FOP, 163–68, 203, 210, and 254; GWS, 37 and 41–42; JMW, Diary, January 1941, JMWP, USAHEC; YOM, vol. 2, 29–37. **88** "Banzai": Peter F. Stevens, *The Twilight Riders: The Last Charge of the 26th Cavalry* (Guilford, CT: Lyons, 2011), 109–13; GWS, 35 and 38–39. **88** "I'm going": Oral Reminiscences of Brigadier General Clifford Bluemel, July, 8 1971, D. Clayton James Collection, MMLA. **88** "characteristic": Stevens, *The Twilight Riders*, 118–21; William E. Chandler, "26th Cavalry (PS): Battles to Glory, Part II," *Armored Cavalry Journal* 56, no. 3 (May–June 1947), 10–11. For other Binalonan details, see GWS, 39–41; TBAB, 21–22. **88** "A bleak": JMW, Diary, December 25, 1941, JMWP, USAHEC. **88** "[the] Christmas tree": GWS, 25 and 40–46. For the pattern, see also FOP, 168; Ancheta, ed., *The Wainwright Papers*, vol. 1, 24–25. **89** "Our troops": JRP, Diary, December 26, 1941, PC. For the loss of men and food, see YOM, vol. 2, 38 and 45; FOP, 179–80 and 256. **89** "I'm giving": Toland, *But Not in Shame*, 138–43; Interview with Albert Jones, undated, John Toland Papers, LC. For details about the race to Calumpit, see FOP, 180–81 and 199–210; TBAB, 23; GWS, 42–44; JMW, Diary, December 29, 1941–January 1, 1942, JMWP, USAHEC. **91** "deafening": GWS, 43–44. **91** "The general's": TBAB, 28–29. For the final stage of the retreat, see JMW, Diary, January 1942, JMWP, USAHEC; FOP, 181–82, 210–11, 223–25, 254, and 262–63; JRP, Diary, January 3, 1942, PC; GWS, 43–46.

CHAPTER FOUR **Tunnel View**

93 "spooky": Interview with JM, New York City, June 24, 1984, RG 13, MMLA. For other details, see Huff, *My Fifteen Years*, 24–25; FOP, 115–19; McManus, *Fire and Fortitude*, 73; Jose Avelino to DM, Manila, November 7, 1939, RG 10, MacArthur Memorial Archive, Philippine Archives Collection, online. **94** "Sir Boss": Huff, *My Fifteen Years*, 37–38. For other details, see Interview with JM, New York City, June 24, 1984, RG 13, MMLA; Manchester, *American Caesar*, 179; Flanner, "General and Mrs. Douglas MacArthur," 59; YOM, vol. 2, 27. **95** "Mummy": Interview with JM, New York City, June 24, 1984, RG 13, MMLA. For other details, see Huff, *My Fifteen Years*, 38–39; Rogers, *The Good Years*, 120; Beck, *MacArthur and Wainwright*, 36; Elizabeth E. Sayre, "Submarine from Corregidor," *Atlantic*, August 1942, 24. **95** "I hope": Brereton, *The Brereton Diaries*, 61–62. **95** "Take every": Hersey, *Men on Bataan*, 40; Press Releases of the C in C's Daily Communiques, December 15, 1942, RG 2, MMLA. For manning the parapets and pacing, see Huff, *My Fifteen Years*, 34; Carlos P. Romulo, *I Saw the Fall of the Philippines* (Garden City, NY: Doubleday, 1942), 61. **96** "Rogers": Rogers, *The Good Years*, 119. **96** "I'll be": Romulo, *I Saw the Fall of the Philippines*, 61–62. For other details about the departure, see Diary of General Douglas MacArthur, December 24, 1941, RG 2, MMLA; Rogers, *The Good Years*, 119–20; Steve Mellnik, *Philippine Diary, 1939–1945* (New York: Van Nostrand Reinhold, 1969), 50; Donald Knox, *Death March: The Survivors of Bataan* (New York: Harcourt Brace Jovanovich, 1981), 34; Interview with JM, New York City, June 24, 1984, RG 13, MMLA; Manchester, *American Caesar*, 217; Beck, *MacArthur and Wainwright*, 20–21 and 39; Huff, *My Fifteen Years*, 39, Herman, *Douglas MacArthur*, 334; FOP, 91–97 and 146–52; LCB, "Personal Experience Sketches," 1945, Beebe Papers, USAHEC. **98** "We have never": Huff, *My Fifteen Years*, 39–43. For other details, see FOP, 471–78; Barrett, "Manila and the Philippines," *Harper's Weekly*, August 6, 1898; James H. Belote and William M. Belote, *Corregidor: The Saga of a Fortress* (New York: Harper & Row, 1967), 10–23 and 70; Miller, *War Plan Orange*, 54–55; Romulo, *I Saw the Fall of the Philippines*, 60–61 and 91–100; Diary of General Douglas MacArthur, December 24, 1941, RG 2, MMLA; Quezon, *The Good Fight*, 214–16; Manchester, *American Caesar*, 224; *Washington Evening Star*, June 12, 1942; GWS, 95–96. **100** "You better": Interview with JM, New York City, June 24, 1984, RG 13, MMLA. For details about life on the Rock and the raid, see Lee, *They Call It Pacific*, 162–66; Belote and Belote, *Corregidor*, 6–9; Rogers, *The Good Years*, 127–30; Huff, *My Fifteen Years*, 43. **101** "One half": Lee and Henschel, *Douglas MacArthur*, 70–71. **101** "MacArthur did not": Rogers, *The Good Years*, 127–30. **101** "The Japs": Quezon, *The Good Fight*, 244–45. **101** "General MacArthur narrowly": Press Releases of the C in C's Daily Communiques, January 1, 1942, RG 2, MMLA. **102** "insult":

Herman, *Douglas MacArthur*, 256–59. For other details, see Quezon, *The Good Fight*, 228–29; Diary of General Douglas MacArthur, December 30, 1941, RG 2, MMLA; *New York Times*, November 12, 1941. **102** "At the present": Quezon, *The Good Fight*, 228–31 and 301. **102** "Never before": DM, Remarks, December 30, 1941, RG 2, MMLA. For Lincoln and the tears, see DMREM, 6; Huff, *My Fifteen Years*, 47–48. **103** "like a tired": Romulo, *I Saw the Fall of the Philippines*, 61, 95, and 100. For the daily routine, see Hersey, *Men on Bataan*, 123–24; Huff, *My Fifteen Years*, 49; Rogers, *The Good Years*, 131–34 and 138; Interview with JM, New York City, June 24, 1984, RG 13, MMLA; GWS, 3. **103** "Good morning, Dick": Rogers, *The Good Years*, 138–39. For the tunnel and Sutherland as the successor, also see Lee, *They Call It Pacific*, 165 and 168; Romulo, *I Saw the Fall of the Philippines*, 172; DM to Adjutant General, January 23, 1942, RG 4, MMLA. **104** "Somebody": YOM, vol. 2, 76–78. **104** "keeping a baseball": Romulo, *I Saw the Fall of the Philippines*, 120–23. For watching the raids, also see Huff, *My Fifteen Years*, 41 and 44–45; Mellnik, *Philippine Diary*, 61. **105** "No bombers": Interview with JM, New York City, June 24, 1984, RG 13, MMLA. For other details including MacArthur's estimate that a "greater concentration of bombs dropped on Corregidor than on any other area on earth," see Lee, *They Call It Pacific*, 170; Diary of General Douglas MacArthur, December 30, 1941, RG 2, MMLA. **105** "Air raid": Manchester, *American Caesar*, 229. **105** "Good morning, General": Huff, *My Fifteen Years*, 45–46. **105** "cafeteria fashion": Romulo, *I Saw the Fall of the Philippines*, 96, 127–30, and 166. For other details, see YOM, vol. 2, 100; Lee, *They Call It Pacific*, 161–62 and 173–74; Hersey, *Men on Bataan*, 124; Interview with JM, New York City, June 24, 1984, RG 13, MMLA; Willoughby, *MacArthur*, 42; Rogers, *The Good Years*, 132; FOP, 534; POTRS, 35. **106** "As things": Beck, *MacArthur and Wainwright*, 64. For supplying Bataan, see Stauffer, *The Quartermaster Corps*, 9–14 and 28; Belote and Belote, 43; FOP, 232–36 and 256–57; Romulo, *I Saw the Fall of the Philippines*, 134. **107** "How are": Romulo, *I Saw the Fall of the Philippines*, 137. **107** "Sagging": Beck, *MacArthur and Wainwright*, 66–67. For other details of the visit, see Diary of General Douglas MacArthur, January 10, 1942, RG 2, MMLA; Romulo, *I Saw the Fall of the Philippines*, 136; GWS, 48–49; DM, General Orders No. 56, January 6, 1942, RG 2, MMLA; FOP, 245; Eisenhower, *At Ease*, 214. **107** "fit": GWS, 49–50 and 274. For MacArthur's appearance, see *Washington Evening Star*, June 12, 1942; Schultz, *Hero of Bataan*, 137; Romulo, *I Saw the Fall of the Philippines*, 139. **108** "Our 155s": Diary of General Douglas MacArthur, January 10, 1942, RG 2, MMLA. **108** "enemy's temporary": JRP, Diary, January 10, 1942, PC. For sharing the notes, see TBAB, 31. **109** "always with": McManus, *Fire and Fortitude*, 108; Interview with Richard K. Sutherland, November 12, 1946, Morton Papers, USAHEC. For the global situation and press team, see Spector, *Eagle Against the Sun*, 100–106 and 128–32; FOP, 145; Roberts, *The Storm of War*, 193–95; Smith, *FDR*, 541–42; Kennedy, *Freedom from Fear*, 565–69; Romulo, *I Saw the Fall of the Philippines*, 43; Lee, *They Call It Pacific*, 65; Christopher L. Kolakowski, *Last Stand on Bataan: The Defense of the Philippines, December*

1941–May 1942 (Jefferson, NC: McFarland, 2016), 81. **109** "greatly outnumbered": Office of Government Reports, *Information Digest*, Washington, DC, December 22, 1941, and January 10, January 15, and March 9, 1942. For Japan moving troops away, see FOP, 261–63; YOM, vol. 2, 24 and 49; McManus, *Fire and Fortitude*, 82–83 and 95. **110** "Of 142": YOM, vol. 2, 89–90. **110** "M'ARTHUR FIGHTS": *New York Times*, January 1, 2, 12, 15, 22, and 26, 1942. **110** "MACARTHUR OF THE PHILIPPINES": *Time*, December 29, 1941. For the anecdotes and summaries, see *New York Times*, December 16, 1941; Press Releases of the C in C's Daily Communiques, January 1, 1942, RG 2, MMLA; Carlos Romulo, Excerpts from Radiograms, January–March 1942, RG 2, MMLA. **111** "The Philippine theater": Beck, *MacArthur and Wainwright*, 20–21, 59–61, and 65. For other details, see YOM, vol. 1, 85–90; Dwight D. Eisenhower, Diaries, January 13, 1942, Dwight D. Eisenhower Library, online; David L. Roll, *George Marshall: Defender of the Republic* (New York: Caliber, 2020), 195–206; Romulo, *I Saw the Fall of the Philippines*, 172; FOP, 150–51; Borneman, *MacArthur at War*, 96–97 and 110–11; Kennedy, *Freedom from Fear*, 522. For MacArthur's quotation about fighting the War Department, see Interview with Richard K. Sutherland, November 12, 1946, Morton Papers, USAHEC. **111** "damn nonsense": Roll, *George Marshall*, 173 and 299; Larry I. Bland, ed., *George C. Marshall Interviews and Reminiscences for Forrest C. Pogue* (Lexington, VA: George C. Marshall Research Foundation, 1991), 244. For an explanation of the Illinois National Guard incident, see YOM, vol. 1, 436–47. **112** "It will be": Smith, *Eisenhower in War and Peace*, 174–85. For the failure of blockade runners, see FOP, 152–55 and 391–401. **112** "every day": GCM to DM, January 4, 1942, RG 2, MMLA. **112** "an epic of": DMREM, 133n–34n. **112** "MacArthur is": Dwight D. Eisenhower, Diaries, January 19, 1942, Dwight D. Eisenhower Library, online. **112** "Unquestionably": DM to GCM, Fort Mills, January 17, 1942, RG 2, MMLA. For the reminder about the troop composition, see Beck, *MacArthur and Wainwright*, 60. **113** "Help is": Beck, *MacArthur and Wainwright*, 60 and 69. For MacArthur's claim and his actions, see Lee and Henschel, *Douglas MacArthur*, 151; YOM, vol. 2, 56–58; POTRS, 46. **114** "Listen to what": Willoughby, *MacArthur*, 55–56. For the dust and enemy propaganda, see Belote and Belote, *Corregidor*, 66 and 84–85; Romulo, *I Saw the Fall of the Philippines*, 120 and 178; Press Releases of the C in C's Daily Communiques, February 5, 1942, RG 2, MMLA; Beck, *MacArthur and Wainwright*, 92; DMREM, 134–38; YOM, vol. 2, 53. **114** "My people": DM to GCM, Fort Mills, February 8, 1942, RG 4, MMLA. **114** "bombshell": Dwight D. Eisenhower, *Crusade in Europe: A Personal Account of World War II* (Baltimore: The Johns Hopkins University Press, 1948), 26. **114** "We can't": Forrest C. Pogue, *George C. Marshall: Ordeal and Hope, 1939–1942* (New York: Viking, 1963), 247–48. **115** "worse": Henry Lewis Stimson, Diary, February 9, 1942, Stimson Papers, YU; Beck, *MacArthur and Wainwright*, 91–109. For MacArthur's recollection as well as the excuses he made for Quezon, see DMREM, 138–39. **115** "The temper": DM to GCM, Fort Mills, February 8, 1942, RG 4, MMLA. **115** "It is mandatory": Franklin D. Roosevelt to DM, February 10, 1942,

RG 4, MMLA. For the drafting of the letter, see Dwight D. Eisenhower, Diaries, February 8-9, 1942, Dwight D. Eisenhower Library, online; Beck, *MacArthur and Wainwright*, 100. **115** "There are times": Beck, *MacArthur and Wainwright*, 100. **115** "This type": DM to GCM, Fort Mills, February 8, 1942, RG 4, MMLA. **115** "Thanks": Huff, *My Fifteen Years*, 8. For MacArthur's normal custom of carrying no arms, see Romulo, *I Saw the Fall of the Philippines*, 100. **116** "I'm just": Interview with JM, New York City, June 24, 1984, RG 13, MMLA. For the submarines, see FOP, 398-400. **116** "My son": Romulo, *I Saw the Fall of the Philippines*, 166. **116** "will share": DM to Franklin D. Roosevelt, Fort Mills, February 11, 1942, RG 2, MMLA. **116** "Manuel": DM, "They Died Hard—Those Savage Men," *Life*, July 10, 1964, 73. For other details of the departure, see GCM to DM, February 10, 1942, RG 2, MMLA; Beck, *MacArthur and Wainwright*, 60; Romulo, *I Saw the Fall of the Philippines*, 183-87. **116** "military logic": Dwight D. Eisenhower, Diaries, February 23, 1942, Dwight D. Eisenhower Library, online. For the discussions, see Beck, *MacArthur and Wainwright*, 90-91. **116** "bring Douglas": Beck, *MacArthur and Wainwright*, 111. **116** "one of the outstanding": *Washington Post*, January 27, 1942. For the naming honors, see Carlos Romulo, Excerpts from Radiograms, January-March 1942, RG 2, MMLA; *Charleston News and Courier*, March 31, 1942. **117** "Dugout Doug": Miller, *Bataan Uncensored*, 193-94. For not returning to Bataan, see GWS, 50; YOM, vol. 2, 54-55, 67-68, and 90; Manchester, *American Caesar*, 235-36; Huff, *My Fifteen Years*, 16. **118** "fighting general": Carlos Romulo, Excerpts from Radiograms, January-March 1942, RG 2, MMLA.

CHAPTER FIVE **Battling Bastards**

119 "[of] the powers": Clark Lee, "The Fighting 26th," *The Cavalry Journal* 52, no. 2 (March-April 1943), 4. For the censorship, see Lee, *They Call It Pacific*, 178-89; Steven Casey, *The War Beat, Pacific: The American Media at War Against Japan* (New York: Oxford University Press, 2021), 22-38; *New York Times*, April 23, 1942; Melville Jacoby, "The Press: Press on Bataan," *Time*, February 9, 1942. **120** "Ramsey": Ramsey and Rivele, *Lieutenant Ramsey's War*, 59-69. For other details about the 26th, see Stevens, *The Twilight Riders*, 197-224; Chandler, "26th Cavalry (PS): Battles to Glory, Part II," 14-15; John Wheeler, "Rearguard in Luzon," *The Cavalry Journal* 52, no. 2 (March-April 1943), 6. **121** "The jungle": William E. Chandler, "26th Cavalry (PS): Battles to Glory, Part III," *Armored Cavalry Journal* 56, no. 4 (July-August 1947), 15-16; TBAB, 31; *Washington Evening Star*, June 12, 1942. **124** "personally selected": DM to Adjutant General, January 23, 1942, RG 4, MMLA. For other details, see FOP, 245-54, 290-315, 325-26, and 337-39; Interview with Richard K. Sutherland, November 12, 1946, Morton Papers, USAHEC; Interview with R. J. Marshall, April 7, 1948, Morton Papers, USAHEC; Rogers, *The Good Years*, 175; Toland, *But Not in Shame*, 153-54 and 180; GWS, 48-55; JMW, Diary, January 23, 1942, JMWP, USAHEC; JMW, Memorandum, January 27, 1942, RG 2, MMLA; JRP, Diary, January 27, 1942,

PC; Richard K. Sutherland to JMW, January 28, 1942, RG 2, MMLA. **124** "It will not": JMW, Diary, January 26, 1942, JMWP, USAHEC. **125** "What do I": Champlin, "Bataan, February 1942," 3–7. For the road and the headquarters, see *New York Times*, February 9 and 10, 1942; Lee, *They Call It Pacific*, 190; *New York Times*, April 22, 1942; *Washington Evening Star*, June 12, 1942; FOP, 296–98; Michael Norman and Elizabeth M. Norman, *Tears in the Darkness: The Story of the Bataan Death March and Its Aftermath* (New York: Farrar, Straus and Giroux, 2009), 71–72 and 94–95; Ramsey and Rivele, *Lieutenant Ramsey's War*, 65; Toland, *But Not in Shame*, 176; TBAB, 43–46; *Washington Evening Star*, June 13, 1942. **126** "Imagine": TBAB, 21, 22, 29, 31, 34, and 40. For the food situation, see also Stauffer, *The Quartermaster Corps*, 14 and 26–28; FOP, 257 and 367–77; McManus, *Fire and Fortitude*, 120; *Washington Evening Star*, June 12 and 14, 1942; Schultz, *Hero of Bataan*, 158. **127** "veterans": GWS, 49. **127** "nice time": TBAB, 33–58. For the poetry, see *Washington Evening Star*, June 12, 1942. **127** "dry humor": *Charleston Evening Post*, March 27, 1942. For an early Bataan dinner with Hewlett, see *Washington Evening Star*, June 12, 1942. **127** "If the United States": Lee, *They Call It Pacific*, 189–90 and 224–25. For other details of Lee's dinner, see *New York Times*, February 9 and 10, 1942. **127** "You can't": *Washington Evening Star*, June 12, 1942. For other details, see TBAB, 27, 33, 35, 37–38, 54, 55, and 58; JRP, Diary, January 22 and February 17, 1942, PC; GWS, 53; Romulo, *I Saw the Fall of the Philippines*, 102 and 106–7; JMW, Diary, February 2, 1942, JMWP, USAHEC; FOP, 398–400. **128** "I live": JRP, Diary, January 23, 1942, PC. **128** "practically dumps": TBAB, 49–50. For the blankets, see Lee, *They Call It Pacific*, 225. **128** "native": *Washington Evening Star*, June 12, 1942. **128** "Hard to": TBAB, 33, 53, 55, and 57. For the temperature and soap, see FOP, 325; JRP, Diary, February 17, 1942, PC; Romulo, *I Saw the Fall of the Philippines*, 234. **129** "carrying his": *Charleston Evening Post*, March 27, 1942. For the distance to the front and snipers, see Lee, *They Call It Pacific*, 224–25; Toland, *But Not in Shame*, 172; TBAB, 40; Champlin, "Bataan, February 1942," 6. **130** "General Wainwright": Champlin, "Bataan, February 1942," 6–7. For other details, see TBAB, 42; *Charleston Evening Post*, March 27, 1942; GWS, 59–60. **130** "God damn": GWS, 59. For what Dooley and Pugh saw, see TBAB, 35, 39, and 42; JRP, Diary, January 19, 1942, PC; JMW, Diary, January 18, 1942, JMWP, USAHEC. **130** "Dead generals": *Washington Evening Star*, June 13, 1942. For morale, see *Washington Evening Star*, June 14, 1942. **131** "We had to": GWS, 61–62. For other details about the Battle of the Pockets, see FOP, 339–46; TBAB, 48. **131** "All right": Toland, *But Not in Shame*, 182–83. **131** "When this was": GWS, 55–57, 62, 187, 286, and 299. For other details about the Battle of the Points and prisoners, see FOP, 303–6, 308–22, and 372–73; TBAB, 48–50; JRP, Diary, February 9, 1942, PC; JMW, Diary, February 5, 1942, JMWP, USAHEC; Betty Mears Wainwright, "Skinny," WP, USMA, 160; McManus, *Fire and Fortitude*, 136. **132** "quiet": JMW, Diary, February 21, 1942, JMWP, USAHEC. For the Japanese falling back, see FOP, 347–52; JMW, Diary, February 22, 1942, JMWP, USAHEC. **133** "food stories": TBAB, 60 and 64. For the food crisis, see FOP, 367, 369, 370, 376, 377, and 383; Stauffer, *The*

Quartermaster Corps, 29; GWS, 48–49 and 205; Norman and Norman, *Tears in the Darkness*, 118–19. **133** "Rotten": JMW, Diary, February 27, 1942, JMWP, USAHEC. For the smell, see McManus, *Fire and Fortitude*, 122; FOP, 377–79; JMW, Diary, February 14, 1942, JMWP, USAHEC; JRP, Diary, February 17, 1942, PC. **133** "Quinine Point": Kolakowski, *Last Stand on Bataan*, 111. For other details, see FOP, 314 and 378; JMW, Diary, March 3, 1942, JMWP, USAHEC; McManus, *Fire and Fortitude*, 122–23; Elizabeth M. Norman, *We Band of Angels: The Untold Story of the American Women Trapped on Bataan* (New York: Random House, 1999), 33–82. **134** "the finest damn": Schultz, *Hero of Bataan*, 162. For the meeting at the command post, see JMW, Diary, February 14, 1942, JMWP, USAHEC. **134** "Bataan was": GWS, 60. **134** "Hope of": JRP, Diary, February 17 and March 7 and 8, 1942, PC. For the anger over the disparity, see FOP, 375–76. **135** "We're the battling": Kolakowski, *Last Stand on Bataan*, 142. For the reaction of the aides, see TBAB, 61. **135** "Out of a": Herr and Wallace, *The Story of the U.S. Cavalry*, 252. For the executive order, see Pogue, *George C. Marshall: Ordeal and Hope*, 293–96. **135** "The horses had": GWS, 53. **136** "They are": JRP, Diary, March 14, 1942, PC. For the origin of the much-repeated account and Wainwright's own account, see Champlin, "Bataan, February 1942," 7; JMW to AW, October 13, 1942, WP, USMA; Perry B. Griffith, "The Mystery of Melhap," *Horse and Horseman* 9, no. 2 (April 1981), 54–56 and 65. **136** "Get the hell out": Champlin, "Bataan, February 1942," 7. For the summons, see GWS, 1; TBAB, 65–66. **136** "scared stiff": TBAB, 64–65. **136** "strafed by": JMW, Diary, March 9, 1942, JMWP, USAHEC. **136** "Wish to": GWS, 1–5, 64, and 187. For other details, see TBAB, 65; *Charleston Evening Post*, March 27, 1942; Champlin, "Bataan, February 1942," 6. **138** "not only relief": *Charleston Evening Post*, March 27, 1942. **138** "major military": Champlin, "Bataan, February 1942," 6. **139** "Good-bye": GWS, 5. For remembering the names of the aides, see TBAB, 65.

CHAPTER SIX **The Trough**

141 "Where's Jean": Huff, *My Fifteen Years*, 50. For the orders and memories of the conversation, see GCM to DM, Washington, DC, February 23, 1942, RG 4, MMLA; DM to GCM, Fort Mills, February 24, 1942, RG 4, MMLA; Lee and Henschel, *Douglas MacArthur*, 156; Interview with JM, New York City, June 24, 1984, RG 13, MMLA. **141** "entire staff": DMREM, 140. **141** "Where in the": Beck, *MacArthur and Wainwright*, 263n. **142** "men, arms": DMREM, 140. **142** "a great deal": DM to GCM, Fort Mills, February 24, 1942, RG 4, MMLA. For MacArthur's skepticism about Australia, see DM to GCM, Fort Mills, January 17, 1942, RG 2, MMLA. **142** "many observers": *New York Times*, February 14, 1942. For court-martial and political considerations, see Lee and Henschel, *Douglas MacArthur*, 156; Dwight D. Eisenhower, Diaries, February 23, 1942, Dwight D. Eisenhower Library, online. **142** "It would mean": Perrett, *Old Soldiers Never Die*, 272. **143** "humanity and": Hugh S. Johnson, "MacArthur's Gallant Battle," *Richmond Times-Dispatch*,

February 26, 1942. For a short summary of Donelson, see James M. McPherson, *Battle Cry of Freedom: The Civil War Era* (New York: Ballantine, 1988), 397–402 and 405n. **143** "needless triumph": Winston S. Churchill, *Their Finest Hour* (New York: Houghton Mifflin, 1949), 94–96. **144** "the captain": Manchester, *American Caesar*, 251–53. For MacArthur's view, see DMREM, 140. **144** "A sudden collapse": DM to GCM, Fort Mills, February 24, 1942, RG 4, MMLA. For Marshall's letter and his response to MacArthur, see GCM to DM, Washington, DC, February 23, 1942, RG 4, MMLA; GCM to DM, Washington, DC, February 25, 1942, RG 4, MMLA. **144** "nucleus": Huff, *My Fifteen Years*, 50–51. For Sutherland's and Ah Cheu's inclusion, see GCM to DM, Washington, DC, February 23, 1942, RG 4, MMLA; DMREM, 141. **144** "anticipated contribution": DMREM, 141. For the lack of consideration for the inverse question, see GWS, 70; Beck, *MacArthur and Wainwright*, 178. **145** "It was almost": Huff, *My Fifteen Years*, 51–52. **145** "never in my": Huff, *My Fifteen Years*, 26–30. For the development of PT boats, see Robert J. Bulkeley, *At Close Quarters: PT Boats in the United States Navy* (Washington, DC: Naval History Division, 1962), 29–59; FOP, 13, 47, and 155. **146** "mighty midgets": Curtis L. Nelson, "They Were Commendable," *Naval History* 16, no. 2 (April 2002), online; *Washington Sunday Star*, February 1, 1942. For other details, see Beck, *MacArthur and Wainwright*, 151–52; Cineworld Interview with John D. Bulkeley, October 5, 1982, RG 32, MMLA; Bulkeley, *At Close Quarters*, 8–9 and 29. **146** "When you ride": "With the Mosquito Fleet," *Popular Mechanics*, April 1941, 487–90. For other details, see Bulkeley, *At Close Quarters*, 29; Huff, *My Fifteen Years*, 52–53. **146** "get a feel": Cineworld Interview with John D. Bulkeley, October 5, 1982, RG 32, MMLA. For Bulkeley's authority, also see Oral Reminiscences of John D. Bulkeley, July 2, 1971, D. Clayton James Papers, MMLA. **147** "one of the most": Champlin, "Bataan, February 1942," 4. **147** "tobogganing": "With the Mosquito Fleet," 487–90. For Jean's test, see Huff, *My Fifteen Years*, 52–53. **147** "No": Oral Reminiscences of John D. Bulkeley, July 2, 1971, D. Clayton James Papers, MMLA. For other details, see Cineworld Interview with John D. Bulkeley, October 5, 1982, RG 32, MMLA; Interview with JM, New York City, June 24, 1984, RG 13, MMLA. **147** "a sheer": Cineworld Interview with John D. Bulkeley, October 5, 1982, RG 32, MMLA. For the plan, see Francis Rockwell to John D. Bulkeley, Fort Mills, March 10, 1942, RG 4, MMLA; Huff, *My Fifteen Years*, 52–53; Manchester, *American Caesar*, 254; JMW, Diary, 1942, moon phases. **147** "It is time": DMREM, 141–42. For the packing, also see Interview with JM, New York City, June 24, 1984, RG 13, MMLA; Lee and Henschel, *Douglas MacArthur*, 72 and 83; Oral Reminiscences of John D. Bulkeley, July 2, 1971, D. Clayton James Papers, MMLA; Huff, *My Fifteen Years*, 50 and 55; Courtney Whitney, *MacArthur: His Rendezvous with History* (New York: Alfred A. Knopf, 1956), 44; Manchester, *American Caesar*, 257. **148** "The amounts": Paul P. Rogers, "MacArthur, Quezon, and Executive Order Number One: Another View," *Pacific Historical Review* 52, no. 1 (February 1983), 93–100. For other details, see Carol Morris Petillo, "Douglas MacArthur and Manuel Quezon: A Note on an Imperial Bond," *Pacific Historical Review* 48, no. 1 (February 1979), 107–17; Petillo, *Douglas MacArthur*, 204–13; Perret, *Old Soldiers Never Die*, 271–72; Inflation Calculator, Federal Reserve Bank of Minneapolis, online; Manuel Quezon, Executive Order No. 1, January 3, 1942, RG 2, MMLA; DM to Chase National Bank, Fort Mills, February 15, 1942, RG 2, MMLA. **149** "My eyes": DMREM, 142–43. **150** "George": Beck, *MacArthur and Wainwright*, 144. For the flag flying, see FOP, 538. **150** "I shall return": Huff, *My Fifteen Years*, 56. **150** "What's his": DMREM, 142–43. **150** "He was just": Interview with JM, New York City, June 24, 1984, RG 13, MMLA. **150** "You may": DMREM, 143. **150** "I was": Cineworld Interview with John D. Bulkeley, October 5, 1982, RG 32, MMLA. **150** "Sinister outlines": DMREM, 143. **150** "we cranked": Cineworld Interview with John D. Bulkeley, October 5, 1982, RG 32, MMLA. **151** "We would": DMREM, 143–44. For other details, see Interview with JM, New York City, June 24, 1984, RG 13, MMLA; Huff, *My Fifteen Years*, 56. **151** "That's not": Beck, *MacArthur and Wainwright*, 145–48. For other details, see Huff, *My Fifteen Years*, 59–61. **152** "I warned": Cineworld Interview with John D. Bulkeley, October 5, 1982, RG 32, MMLA. **152** "Dick": Toland, *But Not in Shame*, 272. **152** "It was rougher": Cineworld Interview with John D. Bulkeley, October 5, 1982, RG 32, MMLA. For other details, see Lee and Henschel, *Douglas MacArthur*, 72–73; Interview with JM, New York City, June 24, 1984, RG 13, MMLA. **153** "That's going": Huff, *My Fifteen Years*, 9 and 61–65. For other details, see Interview with JM, New York City, June 24, 1984, RG 13, MMLA; DMREM, 144; Toland, *But Not in Shame*, 273–74; Manchester, *American Caesar*, 262–63; Francis Rockwell to John D. Bulkeley, Fort Mills, March 10, 1942, RG 4, MMLA. **154** "You have taken": Cineworld Interview with John D. Bulkeley, October 5, 1982, RG 32, MMLA. For the Medal of Honor, see Borneman, *MacArthur at War*, 528n. **154** "not fit": Beck, *MacArthur and Wainwright*, 152–55. For the woman looking for Jean, see Huff, *My Fifteen Years*, 19–20 and 65–66; Interview with JM, New York City, June 24, 1984, RG 13, MMLA; Interview with JM, New York City, August 17, 1984, RG 13, MMLA; Manchester, *American Caesar*, 265–66. **155** "with chewing gum": DMREM, 145. For other details, see Interview with JM, New York City, June 24, 1984, RG 13, MMLA; Interview with JM, New York City, August 17, 1984, RG 13, MMLA; Huff, *My Fifteen Years*, 66–67. **155** "Never, never": Huff, *My Fifteen Years*, 67–68. For other details, see Beck, *MacArthur and Wainwright*, 157. **155** "Don't ask": Interview with JM, New York City, June 24, 1984, RG 13, MMLA. **156** "Get that": Huff, *My Fifteen Years*, 68–72. For other details, see Interview with JM, New York City, June 24, 1984, RG 13, MMLA; Interview with JM, New York City, August 17, 1984, RG 13, MMLA; Beck, *MacArthur and Wainwright*, 158; Borneman, *MacArthur at War*, 158–59. **156** "Welcome": *Adelaide Advertiser*, March 21, 1942. For other details, see Borneman, *MacArthur at War*, 158–59; Whitney, *MacArthur*, 52. Accounts of MacArthur's exact words differ. The text here reflects the words reported closest to the time and place of delivery. **157** "The horrible": Huff, *My Fifteen Years*, 73–74. For the evidence that the Marshall meeting took place after the statement, see Interview with JM, New York City, August 17, 1984, RG 13, MMLA;

Melbourne Age, March 21, 1942; *Adelaide Advertiser*, March 21, 1942. **157** "the greatest": Lee and Henschel, *Douglas MacArthur*, 160. **157** "I understand": Manchester, *American Caesar*, 264. **158** "God have": Lee and Henschel, *Douglas MacArthur*, 161. **158** "We shall return": Manchester, *American Caesar*, 271–72. For the distorted memories of where MacArthur said his famous line and memories of his anguish after, see DMREM, 145; Willoughby, *MacArthur*, 64–65; Interview with JM, New York City, August 17, 1984, RG 13, MMLA; Huff, *My Fifteen Years*, 74–75. **159** "I know": Franklin D. Roosevelt, Press Conference, March 17, 1942, FDR Library, Digital Collections, online. **159** "deserter": Manchester, *American Caesar*, 275. **159** "Secretary of War": GCM to Richard Sutherland, Washington, DC, January 31, 1942, RG 2, MMLA. **159** "utter contempt": Richard Sutherland to GCM, March 16, 1942, The President's Secretary's Files, Box 83, FDR Library, Digital Collections. **160** "incontestable proof": Mears, *The Medal of Honor*, 101–2. **160** "There is no": Editorial Note, George C. Marshall, Memorandum for the President, March 25, 1942, in George C. Marshall, *The Papers of George Catlett Marshall*, ed. Larry I. Bland and Sharon Ritenour Stevens (Baltimore: The Johns Hopkins University Press, 1991), vol. 3, 147–48. **160** "for sitting": McManus, *Fire and Fortitude*, 562n. For Eisenhower's opposition, see YOM, vol. 2, 129. **160** "gallantry and": Editorial Note, George C. Marshall, Memorandum for the President, March 25, 1942, in Marshall, *The Papers of George Catlett Marshall*, vol. 3, 147–48. **160** "to offset": GCM to Franklin D. Roosevelt, Washington, DC, August 22, 1944, President's Secretary's Files, Box 83, FDR Library, Digital Collections. For the congressional process, see YOM, vol. 2, 130–32. **160** "We shall win": *Sydney Daily Telegraph*, March 27, 1942. For the awards being the same day, see *New York Times*, June 30, 1942; Young, *The General's General*, 162. **161** "I feel": DM to GCM, Melbourne, March 29, 1942, RG 2, MMLA. For a draft of this letter dated the previous day, see DM to GCM, Melbourne, March 28, 1942, RG 2, MMLA. **161** "Just announced": JMW to DM, March 28, 1942, Fort Mills, RG 30, MMLA.

CHAPTER SEVEN   **A Dreadful Step**

163 "They were all": GWS, 2 and 67. For the meeting being on March 11 and not March 12 as Wainwright later remembered in his memoirs, see JMW, Diary, March 11, 1942, JMWP, USAHEC. For the staff and food, see TBAB, 67–69; JRP, Diary, March 14–16, 1942, PC. **164** "barely sufficient": JMW to DM, Fort Mills, March 27, 1942, Morton Papers, USAHEC. For the calculations, see JMW, Diary, March 17 and 18, 1942, JMWP, USAHEC; JRP, Diary, March 18, 1942, PC. **164** "irked": GWS, 2–3 and 67–68. For MacArthur's instructions, see POTRS, 46 and 57–62; Perret, *Old Soldiers Never Die*, 276; JRP, Diary, March 18, 1942, PC; FOP, 535. **165** "of the confidence": FOP, 362–63. For more about the confusion and timeline of these events, see George C. Marshall, Memorandum for the President, Washington, DC, March 19 and 22, 1942, in Marshall, *The Papers of George Catlett Marshall*, vol. 3, 139–40 and 143–45; Beck, *MacArthur and Wainwright*, 176; POTRS, 61; General Headquarters, Southwest Pacific Area, Chronological Index and Summary of Communications, March 1942, NARA, ProQuest History Vault. **165** "Thank goodness": POTRS, 62. **165** "native gin": TBAB, 71. For evidence that Wainwright's memoir conflated news of his promotion to lieutenant general with news of his new command, see also POTRS, 62; JMW, Diary, March 20, 1942, JMWP, USAHEC. **165** "Yes, yes": GWS, 68–69. For packing and other details, also see JRP, Diary, March 21, 1942, PC; Beck, *MacArthur and Wainwright*, 177–78. **166** "Special problems": FOP, 364; DM to GCM, March 21, 1942, in General Headquarters, Southwest Pacific Area, Chronological Index and Summary of Communications, March 1942, NARA, ProQuest History Vault. For other details, see Toland, *But Not in Shame*, 279; GWS, 70; Interview with Richard K. Sutherland, November 12, 1946, Morton Papers, USAHEC. **166** "impracticable": George C. Marshall, Memorandum for the President, Washington, DC, March 22, 1942, in Marshall, *The Papers of George Catlett Marshall*, vol. 3, 143–45. For MacArthur's thinking, see Rogers, *The Good Years*, 213; Kolakowski, *Last Stand on Bataan*, 144. **167** "At the least": Schultz, *Hero of Bataan*, 209. For the funny reaction, also see *Charleston Evening Post*, March 27, 1942. **167** "Your Excellency": Commander in Chief of the Imperial Japanese Army and Navy to JMW, March 19, 1942, Morton Papers, USAHEC. **167** "No answer": *Washington Post*, March 29, 1942. **167** "Lee marched": JRP, Diary, March 16, 1942, PC. For the numbers, see FOP, 401; GWS, 72. **168** "He was the": *Providence Sunday Journal*, March 29, 1942. **168** "I am glad": JRP, Diary, March 20, 1942, PC. **168** "old-time": *Providence Sunday Journal*, March 29, 1942. **168** "master strategist": *Washington Post*, March 29, 1942. For "most front going," see *Washington Evening Star*, March 27, 1942; *Charleston Evening Post*, March 27, 1942. **168** "the spiritual": *Providence Sunday Journal*, March 29, 1942. **168** "Looks like": *Washington Post*, April 4, 1942. **168** "We still": *Charleston Evening Post*, March 27, 1942. **168** "I am going": YOM, vol. 2, 126–27; Toland, *But Not in Shame*, 280. **169** "Here's where": GWS, 73. For the food and health, see TBAB, 71; Schultz, *Hero of Bataan*, 228; McManus, *Fire and Fortitude*, 144; Romulo, *I Saw the Fall of the Philippines*, 234. **169** "nothing has": JMW, Diary, March 22, 1942, JMWP, USAHEC. For the house, see JRP, Diary, March 26, 1942, PC. **169** "a royal": POTRS, 65. **169** "We field": Mellnik, *Philippine Diary*, 95. For the close escape, see TBAB, 72–74; Beck, *MacArthur and Wainwright*, 178. **169** "After taking": JRP, Diary, March 26, 1942, PC. For the bombing and the move, also see POTRS, 64; GWS, 74–75; TBAB, 72–74. **170** "you can": Beck, *MacArthur and Wainwright*, 178. **171** "utterly frank": Beck, *MacArthur and Wainwright*, 181–83 and 189–90. For Wainwright's thoughts being with Bataan and other details, see Schutz, *Hero of Bataan*, 228; GWS, 71–73; JMW, Diary, March 5, 22, and 28, 1942, JMWP, USAHEC; JMW to DM, Fort Mills, March 28, 1942, RG 30, MMLA; JMW to DM, Fort Mills, April 3, 1942, RG 30, MMLA; DM to JMW, April 4, 1942, RG 4, MMLA; TBAB, 74–75; FOP, 401, 411–14, 440, and 535. **171** "On this": JMW, Diary, April 2, 1942, JMWP, USAHEC. **172** "disintegrated": TBAB, 78. For other details, see FOP,

326 and 421; Toland, *But Not in Shame*, 282–83; POTRS, 67–68. **172** "Under no": DM to JMW, April 4, 1942, RG 4, MMLA. For holdovers remembering MacArthur thinking Bataan doomed and for his knowledge of Wainwright's letter to Marshall, see JRP, Diary, April 9, 1942, PC; JMW, Diary, July 26, 1942, JMWP, USAHEC; DM to GCM, Australia, March 31, 1942, Morton Papers, USAHEC. **173** "hollow-eyed": GWS, 77–78. For other details, see TBAB, 78; Toland, *But Not in Shame*, 285; Romulo, *I Saw the Fall of the Philippines*, 270–71. **173** "The troops have": JMW to DM, April 6, 1942, RG 30, MMLA. **173** "Very bad": JMW, Diary, April 4 and 5, 1942 JMWP, USAHEC. **173** "I would travel": *Richmond Times-Dispatch*, April 9, 1942. For the location, see *San Francisco Chronicle*, February 8, 1942; Elfrida Wainwright to Jack Wainwright, November 19, 1941, WP, USMA. **174** "Fellow Americans": Schultz, *Hero of Bataan*, 233. For the broadcast, also see POTRS, 69. **174** "like a brush": Willoughby, *I Was on Corregidor*, 142–43; Romulo, *I Saw the Fall of the Philippines*, 250 and 271. For other details, see Toland, *But Not in Shame*, 285–86; FOP, 440. **175** "asinine": Oral Reminiscences of Colonel James V. Collier, August 30, 1971, D. Clayton James Papers, MMLA. For other details, see Interview with Richard K. Sutherland, November 12, 1946, Morton Papers, USAHEC; Thaddeus Holt, "King of Bataan," USAHEC, online, 2–10 and 41; JRP, Diary, April 12, 1942, PC; JMW to DM, April 7, 1942, RG 4, MMLA; Toland, *But Not in Shame*, 291; FOP, 447. **175** "his face": GWS, 79. For General King never saying exactly what he had in mind, see JMW to DM, Fort Mills, May 4, 1942, RG 4, MMLA. For Roosevelt's "keep our flag" order still being in effect, see Franklin D. Roosevelt to DM, February 10, 1942, RG 4, MMLA; FOP, 456; JMW to Louis Morton, January 14, 1949, WP, USMA. **176** "I have had": JRP, Diary, April 7 and 9, 1942, PC. For Wainwright weeping and alcohol, see Romulo, *I Saw the Fall of the Philippines*, 272; Oral Reminiscences of Colonel James V. Collier, August 30, 1971, D. Clayton James Papers, MMLA. **176** "He was sitting": Romulo, *I Saw the Fall of the Philippines*, 272–73. **176** "If any": JMW to DM, Fort Mills, May 4, 1942, RG 4, MMLA. For the escape attempts, see Toland, *But Not in Shame*, 296–98; GWS, 76–79, 80–81, and 86–87. **177** "The troops on": FOP, 453 and 459–60. For the earthquake being felt in the tunnel, see JRP, Diary, April 10, 1942, PC. **177** "regardless": Toland, *But Not in Shame*, 301; Holt, "King of Bataan," 37–38. For other details, see POTRS, 70; JMW to DM, Fort Mills, May 4, 1942, RG 4, MMLA; JMW to Louis Morton, January 14, 1949, WP, USMA. **177** "Go back": GWS, 82–83. For King's thinking, see Holt, "King of Bataan," 24–38. **177** "He has taken": JRP, Diary, April 9, 1942, PC. For the Appomattox comparison, see FOP, 461; Elizabeth R. Varon, *Appomattox: Victory, Defeat, and Freedom at the End of the Civil War* (New York: Oxford University Press, 2014), 73–74. **177** "The decision": JMW to DM, Fort Mills, May 4, 1942, RG 4, MMLA. **177** "Physical exhaustion": DM to GCM, Australia, April 9, 1942, Morton Papers, USAHEC. **178** "I had": GWS, 83. **178** "[by] conveying": TBAB, 83. **178** "King had": JRP, Diary, April 9, 1942, PC. **178** "[I] am keenly": Beck, *MacArthur and Wainwright*, 193–94. **179** "simultaneously": DM to GCM, Australia, April 9, 1942, Morton Papers,

USAHEC. **179** "not concur": JMW to DM, Fort Mills, April 13, 1942, RG 30, MMLA. For other details, see GWS, 83–84 and 88–89; Beck, *MacArthur and Wainwright*, 199; FOP, 563; YOM, vol. 2, 147. **179** "complete authority": DM to JMW, April 14, 1942, RG 4, MMLA. **179** "You can't": Mellnik, *Philippine Diary*, 111–12. For other details, see Paul D. Bunker, *Bunker's War: The World War II Diary of Col. Paul D. Bunker*, ed. Keith A. Barlow (Novato, CA: Presidio 1996), 126; POTRS, 71; GWS, 87–88. **180** "Bataan has": JRP, Diary, April 12, 1942, PC. For the new arrivals and overall numbers, see *New York Times*, April 11, 1942; POTRS, 71 and 73; GWS, 86–87; Raymond G. Woolfe Jr., *The Doomed Horse Soldiers of Bataan: The Incredible Stand of the 26th Cavalry* (Lanham, MD: Rowman & Littlefield, 2016), 365; FOP, 529. **180** "Morale": TBAB, 85. For the older officers, see GWS, 99. **180** "prepare": DM to JMW, Headquarters USAFFE, April 12, 1942, RG 4, MMLA. **181** "only experienced": JMW to DM, April 16, 1942, RG 4, MMLA. For Cebu and the bomber raid, see FOP, 404 and 503–6; JMW to DM, April 10, 1942; *New York Times*, April 16, 1942; POTRS, 72; GWS, 72–73, 88, 98, and 107; DM to JMW, Melbourne, April 13, 1942, RG 4, MMLA; Ancheta, ed. *The Wainwright Papers*, vol. 1, 44–45. **181** "The Bataan peninsula": GWS, 91; Belote and Belote, *Corregidor*, 110–11; Bunker, *Bunker's War*, 130; Mellnik, *Philippine Diary*, 112. **181** "It is": POTRS, 73–74. For the searchlights, see FOP, 537–38 **181** "the most": GWS, 72 and 96. For other details, see Bunker, *Bunker's War*, 128–30; POTRS, 77; FOP, 491, 521, 533–34, and 546; "Swimming at the 2024 Paris Olympic Games," June 1, 2022, NBC Olympics, online. **182** "I don't": POTRS, 76–77 and 79. For the hospital and air blowers, see Charles S. Drake, "So Goes Corregidor: An Eyewitness Account of the Surrender of the Gibraltar of the Pacific," Morton Papers, USAHEC. **182** "living room": GWS, 96 and 102–4. For the rooms, also see POTRS, 64–65 and 87. **182** "I liked": LCB, "Personal Experience Sketches," 1945, Beebe Papers, USAHEC. **184** "with anybody": GWS, 96, 101, 104–5, and 138. For other details, see FOP, 534 and 542; POTRS, 78 and 79; JRP, Diary, April 25, 1942, PC. **184** "The Japs": POTRS, 76 and 79–80. **184** "Wish you": Toland, *But Not in Shame*, 338. For other details, see GWS, 81, 96–98, and 101–2. **184** "I have been": *New York Times*, May 7, 1942. For other details, see GWS, 107–8; JMW to DM, April 12, 1942, RG 4, MMLA. **185** "blackmail": Beck, *MacArthur and Wainwright*, 210–11. For the quotation about "General MacArthur's headquarters," also see JRP, "Story about Wainwright," undated, PC. **185** "I am making": LCB to Richard K. Sutherland, Fort Mills, May 2, 1942, RG 4, MMLA. For Wainwright not approving and the situation on Mindanao, see JMW to DM, Fort Mills, May 3, 1942, RG 4, MMLA; Toland, *But Not in Shame*, 357. **186** "it was the hope": Richard K. Sutherland to LCB, May 3, 1942, RG 4, MMLA. For MacArthur's demands, see DM to GCM, April 22, 1942, RG 4, MMLA; DM to JMW, May 3, 1942, RG 4, MMLA. **186** "That was just": JMW to JRP, January 17, 1951, WP, USMA. For Wainwright's worries and guns, see Beck, *MacArthur and Wainwright*, 212 and 278–79n; GWS, 108–9; Schultz, *Hero of Bataan*, 269–70; JMW to AW, October 13, 1942, WP, USMA; JRP, Diary, December 30, 1942, PC. **187** "It will": AW to GCM, Skaneateles,

July 1942, GCMFL. **187** "It took": GWS, 110–14. **187** "[had] literally": JMW, Diary, May 12, 1942, JMWP, USAHEC. For other details, see JMW to DM, Fort Mills, May 3, 1942, RG 4, MMLA; *United States of America vs. Masaharu Homma*, ICC Legal Tools Database, online, vol. 18, 2392; JMW to GCM, May 5, 1942, RG 4, MMLA; FOP, 550; LCB, "Personal Experience Sketches," 1945, Beebe Papers, USAHEC; GWS, 113–14 and 119–20; W. L. Marshall, "Japanese Treasure Hunt in Manila Bay," *United States Naval Institute Proceedings* 84, no. 3 (March 1958), online. **188** "I don't": LCB, "Personal Experience Sketches," 1945, Beebe Papers, USAHEC. For the moon, which rose a little before 11 that night, and other details, see GWS, 115; FOP, 551 and 555; U.S. Department of Commerce, *Tide Tables: Pacific Ocean and Indian Ocean* (Washington, DC: Government Printing Office, 1941), 278 and 280. **188** "The Nips": GWS, 90, 98, and 115–18. For the reaction to the landing and the battle overnight, see Charles S. Drake, "So Goes Corregidor: An Eyewitness Account of the Surrender of the Gibraltar of the Pacific," Morton Papers, USAHEC; LCB, "Personal Experience Sketches," 1945, Beebe Papers, USAHEC; FOP, 557; JMW to DM, Fort Mills, May 5, 1942, Morton Papers, USAHEC; Toland, *But Not in Shame*, 343; *New York Times*, April 27, 1942; JMW to AW, October 13, 1942, WP, USMA. **189** "All done": JMW to Franklin Roosevelt, May 6, 1942, RG 4, MMLA. **190** "This thing": LCB, "Personal Experience Sketches," 1945, Beebe Papers, USAHEC. For other details, see Charles S. Drake, "So Goes Corregidor: An Eyewitness Account of the Surrender of the Gibraltar of the Pacific," Morton Papers, USAHEC; GWS, 118; FOP, 558–601; JMW, Diary, May 12, 1942, JMWP, USAHEC; Norman, *We Band of Angels*, 111. **190** "a limit": GWS, 90–91, 109–10, and 120–23. For other details, see FOP, 506 and 538; LCB, "Personal Experience Sketches," 1945, Beebe Papers, USAHEC; *New York Times*, November 15, 1945; Belote and Belote, *Corregidor*, 172; *Official Register of the Officers and Cadets of the U.S. Military Academy* (1903), 10. **192** "It was": *Nippon Times*, April 28, 1943; Kazumaro Uno, *Corregidor: Isle of Delusion* (Shanghai, 1942), Corregidor Historic Society, online. For other details, see LCB, "Personal Experience Sketches," 1945, Beebe Papers, USAHEC, 27–30; GWS, 128–29; POTRS, 84–85; FOP, 568; JMW, Diary, May 12, 1942, JMWP, USAHEC. For Japanese film of the surrender, see American Surrender at Manila, 1942, Motion Picture Films from G-2 Army Military Intelligence Division, NARA. **192** "I think": GWS, 129–30. For the sashes, see LCB, "Personal Experience Sketches," 1945, Beebe Papers, USAHEC, 30. **192** "thin as": FOP, 567–68. For Wainwright's and Homma's appearance, also see GWS, 124 and 129–30; Uno, *Corregidor*, online; LCB, "Personal Experience Sketches," 1945, Beebe Papers, USAHEC, 29–30. **192** "How they": GWS, 130. For the seating, also see LCB, "Personal Experience Sketches," 1945, Beebe Papers, USAHEC, 29; POTRS, 84–86. **193** "Welcome": *Nippon Times*, April 28, 1943; Uno, *Corregidor*, online. For Uno saying Wainwright used the word "unconditionally" in his response and the decision to exclude that word from the end of his quotation here, see *United States of America vs. Masaharu Homma*, vol. 28, 3182. There are many accounts of the surrender, both from the American and Japanese perspective.

Drawing upon them, the author has tried to reconcile differences where possible. **193** "We will": GWS, 123–26. For the earlier attempts at surrender, also see FOP, 566; *United States of America vs. Masaharu Homma*, vol. 18, 2371–74. **194** "Tell him": GWS, 130–31. For Wainwright's document and the initial reaction to the claim he made, also see *United States of America vs. Masaharu Homma*, vol. 18, 2377–79, and vol. 28, 3181; Uno, *Corregidor*, online. **194** "Since when": *United States of America vs. Masaharu Homma*, vol. 19, 2470–71. For Wainwright's evident embarrassment and Homma's smile, see GWS, 131; POTRS, 84. **194** "Hostilities": *United States of America vs. Masaharu Homma*, vol. 16, 2282. **195** "At the time": *Nippon Times*, April 28, 1943; Uno, *Corregidor*, online. For the offer of the plane and the back-and-forth, see GWS, 131; *United States of America vs. Masaharu Homma*, vol. 18, 2379, and vol. 26, 3085. **195** "strongly recommend": POTRS, 84. While Morton and others have concluded that Wainwright agreed to surrender the entire archipelago at this point in the negotiations, the account Beebe wrote in his diary at the time leaves little doubt that Wainwright offered this compromise instead. **195** "It is useless": *United States of America vs. Masaharu Homma*, vol. 26, 3085. For the departure and aftermath, see GWS, 120 and 131–32; POTRS, 84–85; Uno, *Corregidor*, online. **196** "General": GWS, 132. **196** "[to] compensate": JMW, Diary, May 12, 1942, JMWP, USAHEC. For the decision, also see GWS, 132–33; JMW, Diary, September 27, 1942, JMWP, USAHEC. **197** "It was": GWS, 133–38. For coming ashore, also see POTRS, 87.

CHAPTER EIGHT **Down Under**

201 "You are listening": "General Wainwright's Surrender," May 7, 1942, Motion Picture, Sound, and Video Branch, NARA. For this account, the author has drawn on a few different versions of the recording, including one in the records of the Office of Strategic Services and another transcribed by NBC in San Francisco, as well as a typed transcript in the John Toland Papers, LC. **202** "Corregidor needs": Romulo, *I Saw the Fall of the Philippines*, 313. For evidence of Romulo being wrong about the timing of the statement and a day passing, see Whitney, *MacArthur*, 59; *Melbourne Herald*, May 6, 1942; *Sydney Mirror*, May 7, 1942; Norman and Norman, *Tears in the Darkness*, 234; Rogers, *The Good Years*, 202–3. **203** "I place": DM to GCM, May 8, 1942, RG 4, MMLA. For Sharp and the analysis, see FOP, 575; "General Jonathan M. Wainwright Surrender Speech," May 7, 1942, Records of the U.S. Information Agency, Motion Picture, Sound, and Video Branch, NARA; George C. Marshall, Memorandum for Mr. Forster, May 8, 1942, in Marshall, *The Papers of George Catlett Marshall*, vol. 3, 192–93. **203** "I believe": DM to GCM, May 9, 1942, RG 4, MMLA. For the evidence of authenticity, see *Manila Tribune*, May 8, 1942; William F. Sharp to DM, Headquarters North Western Area, May 10, 1942, RG 4, MMLA. **203** "Orders emanating": DM to William F. Sharp, May 9, 1942, RG 4, MMLA. **204** "a few": DM to GCM, May 4, 1942, RG 4, MMLA. **204** "I now": DM to GCM, May 12, 1942, RG 4, MMLA. For Sharp's order to surrender, see William F. Sharp to DM, Headquarters North Western Area, May 10, 1942, RG 4, MMLA. **206** "a New Deal": Lee and Henschel, *Douglas MacArthur*, 160–65. For other details, see Willoughby, *Douglas MacArthur*, 3 and 81–83; *Reports of General MacArthur*, vol. 1 (Washington, DC: Government Printing Office, 1966), 20–23 and 40–42; Toland, *The Rising Sun*, 277–84; Samuel Milner, *Victory in Papua* (Washington, DC: Center of Military History, 1957), 1–25; DMREM, 152; Borneman, *MacArthur at War*, 158, 186–89, and 207–10. **206** "I cannot": DM to GCM, May 8, 1942, RG 4, MMLA. **207** "having left": Lee and Henschel, *Douglas MacArthur*, 159–66. For the rationalization, see Willoughby, *MacArthur*, 2–3 and 43–45; Spector; *Eagle Against the Sun*, 137–39. **207** "the Atlantic": DM to GCM, May 23, 1942, RG 4, MMLA. **208** "I fully": FDR to DM, Washington, DC, May 6, 1942, RG 4, MMLA. For MacArthur's indirect suggestion to Churchill and the broader picture, see DM to GCM, May 3, 1942, RG 4, MMLA; Kennedy, *Freedom from Fear*, 568–69 and 577; Roberts, *The Storm of War*, 133–34 and 315–20. **208** "much more": DM to GCM, May 23, 1942, RG 4, MMLA. For MacArthur's ideas with the Soviets and the buildup, see DM to GCM, May 8, 1942, RG 4, MMLA; Herman, *Douglas MacArthur*, 330; McManus, *Fire and Fortitude*, 199. **209** "has brought": DM to GCM, June 8, 1942, RG 4, MMLA. For early warnings, the battle, and strategic considerations, see GCM to DM, May 23, 1942, RG 4, MMLA; Kennedy, *Freedom from Fear*, 532–42; DM to GCM, June 9, 1942, RG 4, MMLA; Louis Morton, *Strategy and Command: The First Two Years* (Washington, DC: Center of Military History, 1962), 294–95; Rogers, *The Good Years*, 293. **209** "Extreme delicacy": DM to GCM, June 11, 1942, RG 4, MMLA. **210** "psychological reasons": Morton, *Strategy and Command*, 240–49; Borneman, *MacArthur at War*, 172–77. For more details, see Directive, March 30, 1942, RG 4, MMLA. **210** "[would be] relegated": DM to GCM, June 28, 1942, RG 4, MMLA. For the dispute, see Morton, *Strategy and Command*, 294–301. **210** "I am engaged": GCM to DM, Washington, DC, June 28, 1942, RG 4, MMLA. For the compromise and the move, see GCM to DM, Washington, DC, July 4, 1942, RG 4, MMLA; Morton, *Strategy and Command*, 302–4; Spector, *Eagle Against the Sun*, 156–63 and 186; YOM, vol. 2, 191–93; Borneman, *MacArthur at War*, 208–13; *Reports of General MacArthur*, vol. 1, 40–41; DM to GCM, July 16, 1942, RG 4, MMLA. **212** "Arthur has": "The General's Son," *Life*, August 3, 1942, 67. For other family details, see Interview with JM, New York City, August 17, 1984, RG 13, MMLA; Huff, *My Fifteen Years*, 78–85 and 101. **212** "Boom": Huff, *My Fifteen Years*, 83–84. **213** "America's number": Alvin Austin to DM, New York, June 16, 1942, RG 10, MacArthur Memorial Archive, Philippine Archives Collection, online. **213** "By profession": DM to Alvin Austin, June 18, 1942, RG 10, MacArthur Memorial Archive, Philippine Archives Collection, online. For MacArthur Day and other details, see Interview with JM, New York City, August 17, 1984, RG 13, MMLA; Manchester, *American Caesar*, 289–90; *New York Times*, June 6, 1942. **213** "Hostesses": YOM, vol. 2, 195. For the cap, see Huff, *My Fifteen Years*, 9–10. **213** "Dick": Rogers, *The Good Years*, 287–88. **213** "Hello":

George H. Johnston, *Pacific Partner* (London: Victor Gollancz, 1945), 82. For the office, see Rogers, *The Good Years*, 203 and 287–88. **216** "the old man": Kenney, *General Kenney Reports*, 28–31. **216** "shell shocked": YOM, vol. 2, 191–93, 202–3, and 211. For the dye, see George C. Kenney, *The MacArthur I Know* (New York: Duell, Sloan and Pearce, 1951), 243. **217** "George": Kenney, *The MacArthur I Know*, 19–28 and 39–42. For other details, see Kenney, *General Kenney Reports*, xi–xiv; GCM to DM, Washington, DC, July 7, 1942, RG 4, MMLA. **217** "Kenney rushed": YOM, vol. 2, 193, 200–201, and 232. **217** "distinguished himself": GCM to DM, Washington, DC, July 31, 1942, RG 4, MMLA. **218** "utterly disregarded": Thomas W. Doyle, Statement, Washington, DC, July 15, 1942, 201 Wainwright, RG 165, NARA. **218** "remarks": GCM to DM, Washington, DC, July 31, 1942, RG 4, MMLA. **218** "fell far short": DM to GCM, August 1, 1942, RG 4, MMLA. For not objecting more vehemently to Wainwright's command being expanded at the time, see FOP, 365. **219** "strategically": Interview with Richard K. Sutherland, November 12, 1946, Morton Papers, USAHEC. For more criticism of the gap, see also Interview with R. J. Marshall, April 7, 1948, Morton Papers, USAHEC. **219** "rigor": DM to GCM, Australia, March 31, 1942, Morton Papers, USAHEC. For the anger over the guerrillas, see Jay Luvaas, ed., *Dear Miss Em: General Eichelberger's War in the Pacific, 1942–1945* (Westport, CT: Greenwood, 1972), 238. **219** "General MacArthur's": Joseph McNarney to GCM, War Department, August 3, 1942, 201 Wainwright, RG 165, NARA. For details, see Pogue, *George C. Marshall: Ordeal and Hope*, 258–59; Schultz, *Hero of Bataan*, 335. **219** "If the papers": Henry Lewis Stimson, Diary, September 8, 1942, Stimson Papers, YU. **220** "public airing": Joseph McNarney to GCM, War Department, August 3, 1942, 201 Wainwright, RG 165, NARA.

CHAPTER NINE **Honor of Another Kind**

221 "If anyone": William C. Braly, *The Hard Way Home* (Washington, DC: Infantry Journal, 1947), 35. For other details, see JRP, Diary, June–July 1942, PC; POTRS 98; GWS, 158 and 161–62; JMW, Diary, August 17, JMWP, USAHEC. **222** "He was": Charles S. Drake, "So Goes Corregidor: An Eyewitness Account of the Surrender of the Gibraltar of the Pacific," Morton Papers, USAHEC. **222** "We drove": GWS, 140–54 and 174–75. **224** "filthy": JMW, Diary, December 1941, JMWP, USAHEC. For details of the Bataan Death March, see Hampton Sides, *Ghost Soldiers: The Epic Account of World War II's Greatest Rescue Mission* (New York: Vintage Books, 2001); McManus, *Fire and Fortitude*; Norman and Norman, *Tears in the Darkness*; Toland, *But Not in Shame*. **224** "Your high": POTRS, 92–95. For other details, see GWS, 155–59; *Chicago Sun*, September 24, 1945; LCB, "Personal Experience Sketches," 1945, Beebe Papers, USAHEC; JRP, Diary, June 18, 1942, PC. **225** "while all facts": JMW, Diary, May 12, 1942, JMWP, USAHEC. For other details, see GWS, 165–67; TBAB, 99; JRP, Diary, August 1, 1942, PC. **225** "The Philippine Army was": JMW, Diary, August 1, 1942, JMWP, USAHEC. **225** "doomed": JMW, Diary, July 26, 1942, JMWP,

USAHEC. **225** "A foul": D. Clayton James, ed., *South to Bataan, North to Mukden: The Prison Diary of Brigadier General W. E. Brougher* (Athens: University of Georgia Press, 1971), 32. For the lack of confidence, see Bunker, *Bunker's War*, 179. **226** "a very": GWS, 170–71. **226** "way of": Norman and Norman, *Tears in the Darkness*, 81–82 and 100–101; Sarah Kovner, *Prisoners of the Empire: Inside Japanese POW Camps* (Cambridge: Harvard University Press, 2020), 13–41 and 222n. For other details, see Gavan Daws, *Prisoners of the Japanese: POWs of World II in the Pacific* (New York: William Morrow, 1994), 96–98; James, ed., *South to Bataan, North to Mukden*, 69 and 75; Young, *The General's General*, 316. **227** "centered": GWS, 170–76. For other details, see Braly, *The Hard Way Home*, 43–47 and 54–55; POTRS, 101, Bunker, *Bunker's War*, 220 and 239. **228** "Old Sourpuss": Braly, *The Hard Way Home*, 47–56. For other details, see GWS, 176; LCB, "Personal Experience Sketches," 1945, Beebe Papers, USAHEC. **229** "We stood": GWS, 178–79. For other details, see LCB, "Personal Experience Sketches," 1945, Beebe Papers, USAHEC; POTRS, 101. **230** *"kiotsuke"*: JMW, "Japanese Orders," Diary, JMWP, USAHEC. For other details, see POTRS, 103; Braly, *The Hard Way Home*, 50–52 and 58–59; GWS, 178–82; Daws, *Prisoners of the Japanese*, 101–2; Bunker, *Bunker's War*, 225. **230** "watery": GWS, 178–81, 187, and 201–3. For other details, see POTRS, 103; Braly, *The Hard Way Home*, 51–52; JMW, Diary, August 29 and September 15 and 26, 1942, JMWP, USA-HEC; LCB, "Personal Experience Sketches," 1945, Beebe Papers, USAHEC. **231** "turn the other": Braly, *The Hard Way Home*, 49, 54, and 63–65. For other details and evidence the work proposal came earlier than Wainwright recalled, see Kovner, *Prisoners of the Empire*, 60 and 129; JRP, Diary, September 22 and 23, 1942, PC; GWS, 187 and 203–4; Bunker, *Bunker's War*, 227 and 231. **232** "wily": GWS, 187. **232** "As soon as": POTRS, 102–6, 119, and 123. For other details including the "foothold," see *Japan Times Advertiser*, November 5, 1942; Braly, *The Hard Way Home*, 62–63, 73, and 76–80; LCB, "Personal Experience Sketches," 1945, Beebe Papers, USAHEC; GWS, 183, 190, and 199; Bunker, *Bunker's War*, 221; TBAB, 108–12; Betty Mears Wainwright, "Skinny," WP, USMA, 49. **233** "Karenko was": GWS, 186–87 and 211. For other details, see Bunker, *Bunker's War*, 239; POTRS, 109; Braly, *The Hard Way Home*, 84–85. **233** "These were": JMW, Diary, September 24, 1942, JMWP, USA-HEC. **233** "I will probably": JMW, Diary, September 27, 1942, JMWP, USA-HEC. **234** "Court-martialed": GWS, 184–85. **234** "utter abjection": Beck, *MacArthur and Wainwright*, 239–40. For other details including Chynoweth's belief that his men on Cebu could have held out, see TBAB, 111; JMW, Diary, September 28, 1942, JMWP, USAHEC; Bunker, *Bunker's War*, 244; Oral Reminiscences of Bradford G. Chynoweth, August 22, 1971, D. Clayton James Papers, MMLA. **234** "Boots": GWS, 184 and 188. For other details, see Daws, *Prisoners of the Japanese*, 135; Braly, *The Hard Way Home*, 53; Bunker, *Bunker's War*, 242–44. **235** "What a leader": Bunker, *Bunker's War*, 259–60. For the shirt, see *New York Times*, November 15, 1945. **235** "that the Jap": GWS, 58 and 190–91. For the men coming around on the farm and the timing of it beginning, see Bunker, *Bunker's War*, 234–35 and

259. **236** "What lying": Bunker, *Bunker's War*, 262. For the tea and the newspaper, see A. E. Percival, *The War in Malaya* (London: Eyre & Spottiswoode, 1949), 314; *Japan Times Advertiser*, November 4, 1942. **236** "Our weekly": GWS, 200. For the lack of soap and toilet paper, see JMW, Diary, December 15, 1942, JMWP, USAHEC; Daws, *Prisoners of the Japanese*, 118–20; Braly, *The Hard Way Home*, 86. **236** "like a pair": Richard C. Mallonée II, ed., *The Naked Flagpole: From the Diary of Richard C. Mallonée* (San Rafael, CA: Presidio, 1980), 183. For weight and sickness, see JMW, Diary, December 12, 1942, JMWP, USAHEC; JRP, Diary, December 12 and 20, PC; GWS, 190 and 195–96; LCB, "Personal Experience Sketches," 1945, Beebe Papers, USAHEC. **237** "I had": POTRS, 125. For the equal portions, Christmas details, and worsening news, see GWS, 187–88 and 198–99; JMW, Diary, July 28 and December 12, 1942, JMWP, USAHEC; TBAB, 124, 128, and 132; Edward King, Diary, December 23, 1942, National American Defenders of Bataan & Corregidor Museum, online. **238** "It is but": Braly, *The Hard Way Home*, 76–80, 104–5, and 113–15. There are discrepancies in Wainwright's and Braly's accounts of the conferences in terms of timing and personnel involved, but other accounts leave no doubt that the meeting took place in late February, as Braly recalled, and with Wainwright present, as Wainwright recalled. For other details including Wainwright's eventual animosity toward even Japanese-Americans, see GWS, 191–92 and 196; TBAB, 141; *Japan Times Advertiser*, November 7, 1942; *Nippon Times*, February 19, 1943; Bunker, *Bunker's War*, 267; Betty Mears Wainwright, "Skinny," WP, USMA, 226; Kennedy, *Freedom from Fear*, 748–60; Nicoll F. Galbraith, Diary, February 1943, PC; Edward King, Diary, February 26, 1943, National American Defenders of Bataan & Corregidor Museum, online. **238** "as a child": Mallonée II, ed., *The Naked Flagpole*, 182–84. **238** "Japanese in America": GWS, 192–93 and 196. For accounts confirming the February timing, see Nicoll F. Galbraith, Diary, February 1943, PC; TBAB, 141; Edward King, Diary, February 1943, National American Defenders of Bataan & Corregidor Museum, online. **239** "A private should": Considine, *It's All News to Me*, 275. **239** "In my": GWS, 192–94. For a slightly different account of the timing on February 27, see *Chicago Sun Times*, September 25, 1945; Edward King, Diary, February 1943, National American Defenders of Bataan & Corregidor Museum, online. For "the heat," see Braly, *The Hard Way Home*, 115. **240** "There are many": GWS, 211–12. Wainwright's diaries and letters leave no doubt he received a radio message this day from Adele, but evidently it said so little that he did not even count it as a communication from her when he wrote his memoirs after the war. For confirmation of its existence, his dreams of seeing her, and Skaneateles, see JMW to AW, October 13, 1942, WP, USMA; JMW to AW, August 2, 1943, WP, USMA; JMW to AW, February 15, 1944, WP, USMA; JMW, Diary, April 10, 1945, JMWP, USAHEC; Betty Mears Wainwright, "Skinny," unpublished manuscript, WP, USMA, 122; *Army and Navy Journal* 31, no. 23 (February 10, 1894), 409. **240** "choked": *Washington Evening Star*, April 20, 1943. For the ship, see *Washington Post*, April 12, 1943; Citation for Jonathan M. Wainwright V, Merchant Marine Distinguished Service Medal, December 23, 1943, JMWP,

USAHEC. **240** "Please tell": DM to B. M. Fitch, January 29, 1943, RG 3, MMLA; *New Orleans Times-Picayune*, February 11, 1943. For the award, also see J. A. Ulio to AW, War Department, November 9, 1942, JMWP, USAHEC; Alexander Surles to DM, January 29, 1943, RG 3, MMLA. **240** "You have been": GCM to AW, May 7, 1942, GCMFL. For checking on her son, see GCM to AW, July 15, 1942, GCMFL. **241** "My dear": AW to GCM, Skaneateles, [July 1942], GCMFL. **241** "exhausted": *Washington Post*, April 10, 1942. **241** "a highly": *Richmond Times-Dispatch*, May 6, 1942. For the move, see *Buffalo Evening News*, April 20, 1942. **241** "Difficult": GCM to AW, July 15, 1942, GCMFL. **241** "Am well": GCM to AW, December 12, 1942, GCMFL. For rumors and Adele writing and staying busy, see *Washington Evening Star*, November 20, 1942; *Washington Evening Star*, September 25, 1942; JMW to AW, August 31, 1943, WP, USMA; Schultz, *Hero of Bataan*, 369. **241** "The pauses": *Greensboro Record*, April 9, 1943. **241** "Each day that goes": JMW to AW, October 13, 1942, WP, USMA. For receipt of the letter and other details, see Memorandum for General Watson, June 29, 1943, RG 135, MMLA; *Washington Evening Star*, June 18, 1943; GWS, 189–90; *Richmond Times-Dispatch*, August 12, 1942; *Philippine Postscripts*, March 1, 1944, Ike Skelton Combined Arms Research Library Digital Library, online; Schultz, *Hero of Bataan*, 370; DM to GCM, August 1, 1942, RG 4, MMLA; JMW to AW [undated prisoner-of-war letter], WP, USMA; Considine, *It's All News to Me*, 275–76; Henry Lewis Stimson, Diary, February 25, 1943, Stimson Papers, YU.

CHAPTER TEN **Bypass**

243 "Bob": Robert L. Eichelberger, *Our Jungle Road to Tokyo* (New York: Viking, 1950), 21–22. For the house, not visiting the front, and the Medal of Honor, see Borneman, *MacArthur at War*, 247 and 370; Kenney, *General Kenney Reports*, 136; YOM, vol. 2, 270, 274–77, and 445; Luvaas, ed., *Dear Miss Em*, 53–54. **244** "Control of such": YOM, vol. 2, 292–303. For the intelligence, see Edward J. Drea, *MacArthur's Ultra: Codebreaking and the War Against Japan, 1942–1945* (Lawrence: University Press of Kansas, 1992), 15–16 and 68–72; Borneman, *MacArthur at War*, 276–77. For "Billy Mitchell," see Interview with JM, New York City, August 17, 1984, RG 13, MMLA. **244** "I have": William F. Halsey and J. Bryan III, *Admiral Halsey's Story* (New York: McGraw-Hill, 1947), 138 and 154–55. For MacArthur's comments, see DMREM, 173–74. For a short background on Halsey, see Ian W. Toll, *Pacific Crucible: War at Sea in the Pacific, 1941–1942* (New York: Norton, 2012), 201–2. **245** "neutralized": YOM, vol. 2, 316–35. For the number of troops in Rabaul and MacArthur's explanation, see Spector, *Eagle Against the Sun*, 276; DMREM, 176–77. **246** "General": DMREM, 168–69. For the strength of his forces, see YOM, vol. 2, 311. **247** "mutually supporting": Spector, *Eagle Against the Sun*, 252–56 and 276–78. For other details, see Roll, *George Marshall*, 266–67; YOM, vol. 2, 318 and 330–35. **247** "The Japanese": Mellnik, *Philippine Diary*, 276–80. For background, see

Norman and Norman, *Tears in the Darkness*, 344–45; *New York Times*, January 26, 1944. **247** "I spoke": DMREM, 145. For evidence he knew of the nickname, see Manchester, *American Caesar*, 236. **248** "Your victorious": Whitney, *MacArthur*, 128–34. For background on the guerrillas, see YOM, vol. 2, 506–10. **248** "From a broad": YOM, vol. 2, 318–19 and 333–34. For the competing paths and MacArthur's strategy, see Spector, *Eagle Against the Sun*, 277–79; DMREM, 165–66. **249** "Numerically": *Reports of General MacArthur*, 121–22. For details of the strike and the plan for Lae, see YOM, vol. 2, 324–25; Kenney, *General Kenney Reports*, 276–77; DMREM, 179. **249** "They were": Kenney, *The MacArthur I Know*, 104–6. **249** "I did not": DMREM, 179. **250** "jumping": Kenney, *General Kenney Reports*, 292–93. **250** "too much": DMREM, 179–80. **250** "Garrison Post": *Brisbane-Courier Mail*, September 27, 1943; YOM, vol. 2, 333 and 363–69. **250** "operations in the Central": Spector, *Eagle Against the Sun*, 279–80. For other details, see YOM, vol. 2, 365–69; Roll, *George Marshall*, 293–98; Smith, *FDR*, 592–98; Forrest C. Pogue, *George C. Marshall: Organizer of Victory, 1943–1945* (New York: Penguin, 1973), 323. **250** "I am delighted": Franklin D. Roosevelt to DM, August 15, 1943, Franklin D. Roosevelt Presidential Library & Museum, online. For the days away and details of Eleanor's visit, see YOM, vol. 2, 361 and 369; Interview with JM, New York City, August 17, 1984, RG 13, MMLA. **251** "There are": YOM, vol. 2, 341 and 369. For not being there when Marshall arrived, see Roll, *George Marshall*, 298–99; Weldon E. Rhoades, *Flying MacArthur to Victory* (College Station: Texas A&M University Press, 1987), 165; Hunt, *The Untold Story of Douglas MacArthur*, 313–14; *Reports of General MacArthur*, 128–32. **251** "the paucity": DMREM, 173 and 183–87. For the troop numbers and other details, see YOM, vol. 2, 350; Kenney, *General Kenney Reports*, 333–34; Pogue, *George C. Marshall: Organizer of Victory*, 506. **252** "put the cork": Kenney, *General Kenney Reports*, 359–60. For "reconnaissance in force," the strategic picture, and Kenney's bribe, see YOM, vol. 2, 377–84; *Reports of General MacArthur*, 132–38; DMREM, 188; John C. McManus, *Island Infernos: The US Army's Pacific War Odyssey, 1944* (New York: Penguin 2021), 74. **253** "Hold what": Charles A. Rawlings, "They Paved Their Way with Japs," *Saturday Evening Post*, October 7, 1944, 44. **253** "That's the way": *New York Times*, March 1, 1944. For the perimeter, see Noel F. Busch, "MacArthur and His Theater," *Life*, May 8, 1944, 102. **253** "Banzai": *Reports of General MacArthur*, 140–41. For MacArthur's expectation of an assault, see Roger Olaf Egeberg, *The General: MacArthur and the Man He Called 'Doc'* (Washington, DC: Oak Mountain, 1993), 30. **253** "Fine": Busch, "MacArthur and His Theater," 102. For being an easy target, also see Rawlings, "They Paved Their Way with Japs," 44; *New York Times*, March 1, 1944; William C. Chase, *Front Line General: The Commands of William C. Chase* (Houston: Pacesetter, 1975), 51–52. **256** "Doc": Egeberg, *The General*, 6–7 and 28–33. **256** "Throughout": *New York Times*, March 1, 1944. For his awareness of the press, see Casey, *The War Beat, Pacific*, 154; McManus, *Island Infernos*, 78. **257** "Although no": John McCarten, "General MacArthur: Fact and Legend," *The American Mercury*, January 1944, 7–18. For the argument that the article inspired MacArthur to land on the Admiralties, the Sherman quotation, and Romulo's bestseller, see YOM, vol. 2, 413 and 429–30; Robert L. O'Connell, *Fierce Patriot: The Tangled Lives of William Tecumseh Sherman* (New York: Random House, 2015), 323; Alexander G. Lovelace, *The Media Offensive: How the Press and Public Opinion Shaped Allied Strategy During World War II* (Lawrence: University Press of Kansas, 2022), 67–68. **257** "libelous": YOM, vol. 2, 414. **257** "I want": Philip J. Briggs, "General MacArthur and the Presidential Election of 1944," *Presidential Studies Quarterly* 22, no. 1 (Winter 1992), 33–37. **257** "running the war": YOM, vol. 2, 409. **258** "left wingers": A. L. Miller to DM, Washington, DC, January 27, 1944, RG 10, MacArthur Memorial Archive, Philippine Archives Collection, online. **258** "We must not": DM to A. L. Miller, February 11, 1944, RG 10, MacArthur Memorial Archive, Philippine Archives Collection, online. **258** "the lunatic": "The MacArthur Candidacy," *Time*, April 24, 1944. For not forgetting the Bonus March, see McCarten, "General MacArthur: Fact and Legend," 18. **258** "No, Dick": Kenney, *The MacArthur I Know*, 112–13. For the primary results, see YOM, vol. 2, 431–37. **259** "To die": DMREM, 169 and 189–90. For other details, see *Reports of General MacArthur*, 142–46; YOM, vol. 2, 443–50; Borneman, *MacArthur at War*, 368. **259** "He seemed": Egeberg, *The General*, 48–53. **259** "This enemy": *Reports of General MacArthur*, 146–48. **259** "intended as": YOM, vol. 2, 436–38. **260** "I'm sure": DMREM, 185. For Roosevelt's lack of fear, see Briggs, "General MacArthur and the Presidential Election of 1944," 40. **260** "on soil": Rhoades, *Flying MacArthur to Victory*, 256–58. For other details, see Borneman, *MacArthur at War*, 394; Ian W. Toll, *Twilight of the Gods: War in the Western Pacific, 1944–1945* (New York: Norton, 2020), 47–49; *Reports of General MacArthur*, 160–65; Spector, *Eagle Against the Sun*, 301–19. **261** "With regard": GCM to DM, Washington, DC, June 24, 1944, in George C. Marshall, *The Papers of George Catlett Marshall*, ed. Larry I. Bland and Sharon Ritenour Stevens (Baltimore: The Johns Hopkins University Press, 1996), vol. 4, 492–94. For more about whether to bypass the Philippines, see Spector, *Eagle Against the Sun*, 417–19; Robert Ross Smith, "Luzon Versus Formosa," in Kent Roberts Greenfield, ed., *Command Decisions* (Washington, DC: Center of Military History, 1987), 461–68; YOM, vol. 2, 521–24. **261** "The Philippine Islands had": DMREM, 209. **262** "a motorcycle escort": Samuel I. Rosenman, *Working with Roosevelt* (New York: Harper & Brothers, 1952), 456. For MacArthur's appearance and other details, also see Toll, *Twilight of the Gods*, 62–64; William D. Leahy, *I Was There: The Personal Story of the Chief of Staff to Presidents Roosevelt and Truman Based on His Notes and Diaries Made at the Time* (London: Victor Gollancz, 1950), 293–94; Samuel Eliot Morison, *History of United States Naval Operations in World War II*, vol. 12 (Boston: Little, Brown 1958), 9. For "a tremendous ovation," see Bonner Fellers to Dorothy Fellers, General Headquarters, Southwest Pacific Area, August 12, 1944, Bonner Frank Fellers Papers, HILA. **262** "When he was animated": Luvaas, ed., *Dear Miss Em*, 155–56. For predictions of victory in Europe, predictions of Roosevelt's death, and accounts of the tours, see Kennedy, *Freedom from Fear*, 732; Manchester, *American*

Caesar, 368; Smith, *FDR*, 187–91; Toll, *Twilight of the Gods*, 65–69; Leahy, *I Was There*, 294. **263** "I began": DMREM, 197. For other details, see Leahy, *I Was There*, 294–95. **263** "Douglas, where": Toll, *Twilight of the Gods*, 65; Morison, *History of United States Naval Operations in World War II*, vol. 12, 9. For other details, see Hunt, *The Untold Story of Douglas MacArthur*, 333. **264** "If I could": DMREM, 197. For examples of making arguments earlier, see YOM, vol. 2, 522–23; *Reports of General MacArthur*, 134–36. **264** "How many": Toll, *Twilight of the Gods*, 73. **264** "my losses would": DMREM, 198. **264** "frontal attacks": YOM, vol. 2, 319, 490, and 522–23. For Saipan numbers, see Kennedy, *Freedom from Fear*, 816–18. **265** "in rare": Rhoades, *Flying MacArthur to Victory*, 260. For other details of the meeting, see Leahy, *I Was There*, 294–95; DMREM, 197–99; Toll, *Twilight of the Gods*, 77. **265** "As soon": DMREM, 199. For the alleged deal, see YOM, vol. 2, 534–36. **266** "if your decision": Whitney, *MacArthur*, 125. **266** "moral obligation": DMREM, 198. **266** "We had been": Luvaas, ed., *Dear Miss Em*, 155. For Filipinos staying loyal and America's word, see DMREM, 198; YOM, vol. 2, 523–24. **266** "thousands of American": Whitney, *MacArthur*, 125. For the public's knowledge of the Bataan Death March, see *New York Times*, January 28, 1944; YOM, vol. 2, 512–13; Whitney, *MacArthur*, 147–48. **266** "Sorely remembered": *Time*, May 8, 1944.

CHAPTER ELEVEN **Solitaire**

267 "It will": TBAB, 142–43. For the move and waving, see POTRS, 146–48; JMW, Diary, April 2, 1943, JMWP, USAHEC. **267** "The military": GWS, 206–8. For the shipment, see JMW, Diary, March 24, 1943, JMWP, USAHEC. **268** "No package": POTRS, 150–52. For other details, see JMW, Diary, March 26 and April 12 and 23, 1943, JMWP, USAHEC; Edward King, Diary, April 14 and May 20, 1943, National American Defenders of Bataan & Corregidor Museum, online; James, ed., *South to Bataan, North to Mukden*, 67; GWS, 209. **268** "[of] what we": GWS, 210. For the Geneva Conventions and the interview, see Edward King, Diary, June 1, 1943, National American Defenders of Bataan & Corregidor Museum, online; Kovner, *Prisoners of the Empire*, 96–97. **269** "was a very": JMW, Diary, June 3, 1943, JMWP, USAHEC. For the American reaction to the broadcast and other details, see Text of Japanese Radio Broadcast, June 22, 1943, RG 135, MMLA; Franklin D. Roosevelt to AW, June 29, 1943, RG 135, MMLA. **269** "An old cavalryman": James, ed., *South to Bataan, North to Mukden*, 74–75. For Beebe's comment and departures, see POTRS, 157; JMW, Diary, June 5 and 23, 1943, JMWP, USAHEC; GWS, 209–15. **270** "the only healthy": GWS, 214–21. For other details, see *Chicago Sun*, September 27, 1945; Edward King, Diary, June 24, September 9, and October 20, 1943, National American Defenders of Bataan & Corregidor Museum, online; JMW, Diary, August 12, September 15, and October 20, 1943, JMWP, USAHEC. For evidence that Wainwright confused the dates of the picnic, see his and King's diaries. **271** "I long": JMW to AW, August 31, 1943, WP, USMA. For other details, see Edward King, Diary, February 22 and July 19,

1944, National American Defenders of Bataan & Corregidor Museum, online; TBAB, 109–10; Daws, *Prisoners of the Japanese*, 133; GWS, 217–21. **272** "never criticize": JMW, Diary, "Five Maxims for Young Officers," December 31, 1944, JMWP, USA- HEC. **272** "Undesirable": JMW, Diary, "Undesirable Qualities Sometimes Found in a High Commander," JMWP, USAHEC. For solitaire, see Edward King, Diary, August 3, 1943, National American Defenders of Bataan & Corregidor Museum, online; JMW, Diary, Solitaire, August 9, 1943–August 23, 1945, JMWP, USAHEC. **273** "My name": GWS, 219–20. For the promotion, also see JMW, Diary, November 30, 1943, JMWP, USAHEC; JMW to AW, January 8, 1944, WP, USMA. **273** "I appear": JMW to AW, undated, WP, USMA. For the statue and retirement, see JRP, Diary, February 16, 1943, PC; JMW to AW, February 15, 1944, WP, USMA; JMW to AW, Taiwan, June 16, 1944, WP, USMA; JMW, Diary, December 9, 1943, JMWP, USA- HEC. **274** "Captain Jack": JMW to AW, February 15, 1944, WP, USMA. For the date of the radio and his knowledge of her writing, see JMW, Diary, September 28, 1943, JMWP, USAHEC; JMW to AW, March 23, 1944, WP, USMA. **274** "While they": JMW to AW, February 15, 1944, WP, USMA. For the winter, see Edward King, Diary, March 11, 1944, National American Defenders of Bataan & Corregidor Museum, online; GWS, 221–24; JMW to AW, Taiwan, June 16, 1944, WP, USMA. **274** "I am becoming": JMW to AW, March 23, 1944, WP, USMA. For King's letters, see Edward King, Diary, February 21, 1944, National American Defenders of Bataan & Corregidor Museum, online. **274** "adequate reply": GWS, 226. For the letters, see JMW, Diary, May 1944, JMW Papers. **275** "You can imagine": JMW to AW, Taiwan, June 16, 1944, WP, USMA. For the dates of Adele's letters, the promotion being confirmed, and what else he could not tell her, see JMW, Diary, June 15 [two entries], June 29 and July 13, 1944, and May 6, 1945, JMWP, USAHEC; GWS, 224; Edward King, Diary, June 7, 1944, National American Defenders of Bataan & Corregidor Museum, online. **276** "Packed in": GWS, 233–41. For other details of the trip and the prison, see JMW, Diary, October 1944, JMWP, USAHEC; James, ed., *South to Bataan, North to Mukden*, 141–49; Edward King, Diary, October 1944, National American Defenders of Bataan & Corregidor Museum, online; Daws, *Prisoners of the Japanese*, 283–97; Braly, *The Hard Way Home*, 199–203; LCB, "Personal Experience Sketches," 1945, Beebe Papers, USAHEC; Young, *The General's General*, 314–18; Toland, *The Rising Sun*, 8. **277** "Two and a half": JMW, Diary, November 16 and 21, 1944, JMWP, USAHEC. For other details, see GWS, 234, 237, and 241; LCB, "Personal Experience Sketches," 1945, Beebe Papers, USAHEC; Braly, *The Hard Way Home*, 199.

CHAPTER TWELVE **The Return**

279 "a hollow": Halsey and Bryan III, *Admiral Halsey's Story*, 198–200. **279** "We shall": YOM, vol. 2, 536–41. For other details about the decision and the affair, see Pogue, *George C. Marshall: Organizer of Victory*, 453–54; Kenney, *General Kenney Reports*, 431–34; Rhoades, *Flying MacArthur to Victory*, 283–85; Egeberg, *The General*,

59–61; Paul P. Rogers, *The Bitter Years: MacArthur and Sutherland* (New York: Praeger, 1991), 145–66. **280** "I won't": Huff, *My Fifteen Years*, 95. For the drives, see Rhoades, *Flying MacArthur to Victory*, 288–89. **280** "I want to": Interview with JM, New York City, August 17, 1984, RG 13, MMLA. For the timeline, see YOM, vol. 2, 539; Toll, *Twilight of the Gods*, 93–94. **280** "the most powerful": YOM, vol. 2, 545. For Dewey and other details, see Jones, *Honor in the Dust*, 47–48; Borneman, *MacArthur at War*, 427; DMREM, 214; McManus, *Island Infernos*, 468–69. **281** "On the waters": DMREM, 199 and 214–15. For other details, see William J. Dunn, *Pacific Microphone* (College Station: Texas A&M University Press, 1988), 3–5 and 243; Rhoades, *Flying MacArthur to Victory*, 296–97; Whitney, *MacArthur*, 154–56; Kenney, *General Kenney Reports*, 446; McManus, *Island Infernos*, 476–78; Daniel E. Barbey, *MacArthur's Amphibious Navy: Seventh Amphibious Operations, 1943–1945* (Annapolis: United States Naval Institute, 1969), 168 and 244–45; *Chicago Daily News*, October 20, 1944; Egeberg, *The General*, 38. **282** "Carlos": Carlos P. Romulo, *I See the Philippines Rise* (Garden City: Doubleday, 1946), 90. **282** "Son": Dunn, *Pacific Microphone*, 6. **282** "Let 'em": YOM, vol. 2, 554–55. For other details including reports of MacArthur's displeasure, which some have disputed, see Manchester, *American Caesar*, 386–87; DMREM, 216; Rhoades, *Flying MacArthur to Victory*, 297; Perret, *Old Soldiers Never Die*, 421; William J. Dunn, "MacArthur's Mansion and Other Myths," *Army* 23, no. 3 (March 1973), 40–43. **283** "Hey, there's": Kenney, *General Kenney Reports*, 448. **283** "People of": DMREM, 216–17. For the edits and criticism, see YOM, vol. 2, 558–59; Egeberg, *The General*, 62–66. **283** "I know": DMREM, 218. **284** "Where is Task": Spector, *Eagle Against the Sun*, 429–41. For MacArthur's role and thoughts, see DMREM, 228–30; Egeberg, *The General*, 73–74. **286** "Papa is": DM to Arthur MacArthur IV, October 1942, RG 10, MacArthur Memorial Archive, Philippine Archives Collection, online. For the details about the days on Leyte, see Turner Catledge, *My Life and the Times* (New York: Harper & Row, 1971), 155–57; Kenney, *General Kenney Reports*, 463–90; Egeberg, *The General*, 82–83 and 90–93; DMREM, 228; YOM, vol. 2, 560–70, 583–91, and 602–3; McManus, *Island Infernos*, 498–502; Borneman, *MacArthur at War*, 448; Rhoades, *Flying MacArthur to Victory*, 333 and 337–38; Rogers, *The Bitter Years*, 181–217. **287** "The Almighty": Rhoades, *Flying MacArthur to Victory*, 298. **287** "the most comfortable": Borneman, *MacArthur at War*, 449 and 458. For the name "kamikaze," see Spector, *Eagle Against the Sun*, 440. **287** "restless": Egeberg, *The General*, 99–105. **287** "there they were": DMREM, 239–41. For other details, see YOM, vol. 2, 614 and 620–21; Barbey, *MacArthur's Amphibious Navy*, 299–300; Dunn, *Pacific Microphone*, 274–76; Egeberg, *The General*, 100; Manchester, *American Caesar*, 396. **288** "Mac sat": Bonner Fellers to Dorothy Fellers, General Headquarters Southwest Pacific Area, January 9, 1945, Bonner Frank Fellers Papers, HILA. **288** "Don't you": Egeberg, *The General*, 107–12. **288** "Everywhere": DMREM, 238, 241–42, 246, and 250. For "bypassing" and other details, see Dunn, *Pacific Microphone*, 279; John C. McManus, *To the End of the Earth: The US Army* *and the Downfall of Japan* (New York: Caliber, 2023), 4–11 and 19–25; Toll, *Twilight of the Gods*, 73; James M. Scott, *Rampage: MacArthur, Yamashita, and the Battle of Manila* (New York: Norton, 2018), 43 and 51–54; Willoughby, *MacArthur*, 43–45; FOP, 582; Norman and Norman, *Tears in the Darkness*, 348; YOM, vol. 2, 151–52, 335, and 625–29; Chase, *Front Line General*, 95.   **290**   "[with] a certain": Egeberg, *The General*, 112–16. For other details, see DMREM, 244; YOM, vol. 2, 626–27.   **290**   "bubbled": McManus, *To the End of the Earth*, 21 and 29–32; Rogers, *The Bitter Years*, 233–59. For other details, see Egeberg, *The General*, 118; Dunn, *Pacific Microphone*, 279; Kevin C. Holzimmer, *General Walter Krueger: Unsung Hero of the Pacific War* (Lawrence: University Press of Kanas, 2007), 12.   **291**   "Walter's pretty": Egeberg, *The General*, 114–19. For other details, see Young, *The General's General*, 246; McCallus, *The MacArthur Highway and Other Relics of American Empire in the Philippines*, 152–53; Dos Passos, *Tour of Duty*, 161; *New York Times*, January 26, 1945; *Atlanta Journal*, January 26, 1945; McManus, *To the End of the Earth*, 35–37; YOM, vol. 2, 627; Rogers, *The Bitter Years*, 248–49.   **291**   "Five bitter": O. W. Griswold, Diary, January 26–31, 1945, USAHEC, online.   **292**   "As soon as": Carl Mydans, *More Than Meets the Eye* (New York: Harper, 1959), 183. For Palawan and the raid, see Sides, *Ghost Soldiers*, 7–17, 20, and 270–318; DMREM, 246; McManus, *To the End of the Earth*, 39–45.   **292**   "First in Manila": Chase, *Front Line General*, 80–93. For other details, see YOM, vol. 2, 631–32; Dunn, *Pacific Microphone*, 289–94; Luvaas, ed., *Dear Miss Em*, 230; McManus, *To the End of the Earth*, 46–47; Carl Mydans, "My God! It's Carl Mydans," *Life*, February 19, 1945, 20–21; Scott, *Rampage*, 131 and 142; Knox, *Death March*, 108.   **293**   "They're frightened": Egeberg, *The General*, 131–39. For details of the visit, see *Los Angeles Examiner*, February 8, 1945; *New York Times*, February 8, 1945; Chase, *Front Line General*, 95–97.   **296**   "I would have": *Los Angeles Examiner*, February 8, 1945.   **296**   "restless": Egeberg, *The General*, 139. While Egeberg and Chase remembered visiting Santo Tomas second, newspaper accounts suggest MacArthur made it his first stop.   **296**   "I looked": DMREM, 248. For the visit, also see Chase, *Front Line General*, 96; Norman and Norman, *Tears in the Darkness*, 266–67; Scott, *Rampage*, 172–74; *Los Angeles Examiner*, February 8, 1945.   **297**   "I owe you": *Atlanta Journal*, February 7, 1945.   **297**   "My boys": Egeberg, *The General*, 136–40. For Malacañan, see Chase, *Front Line General*, 93 and 97–98.   **297**   "imminent": *New York Times*, February 6, 1945. For the parade and the bridges, see Scott, *Rampage*, 99, 130, 167, and 181; Bonner Fellers to Dorothy Fellers, February 3, 1945, Bonner Frank Fellers Papers, HILA.   **299**   "He does not": O. W. Griswold, Diary, February 7 and 19, 1945, USAHEC, online. For other details, see Scott, *Rampage*, 92, 221, 225, 251, and 288; McManus, *To the End of the Earth*, 59–60 and 64–66.   **300**   "The general": Dunn, *Pacific Microphone*, 306.   **300**   "put off": Luvaas, ed., *Dear Miss Em*, 216.   **300**   "The use": YOM, vol. 2, 643. For other details, see Scott, *Rampage*, 84 and 317.   **300**   "We know": O. W. Griswold, Diary, February 11–17, 1945, USAHEC, online. For other details, see Scott, *Rampage*, 298, 310, and 351–53; McManus, *To the End of the Earth*, 83.   **300**   "Block after": *New*

York Times, February 21, 1945. For other details, see Scott, *Rampage*, 316–17, 375, and 390–93; Smith, *Triumph in the Philippines*, 249–50 and 263–64; YOM, vol. 2, 634; Rogers, *The Bitter Years*, 263. **301** "Your situation": O. W. Griswold, Diary, February 18–22, 1945, USAHEC, online. For other details, see Smith, *Triumph in the Philippines*, 303; Scott, *Rampage*, 395–405; *New York Times*, February 25, 1945. **301** "I'm not going": Kenney, *The MacArthur I Know*, 98–99. For the fate of the people inside Intramuros, see Scott, *Rampage*, 201, 211, 237–40, and 400–405; Smith, *Triumph in the Philippines*, 299–300. **302** "Do not": Scott, *Rampage*, 405–6. **302** "temporarily pinned": DMREM, 247. For the books, see Manchester, *American Caesar*, 416. **303** "churches, monuments": DMREM, 197–98 and 251–54. For other details, see Special Investigating Mission, *Survey of War Damage in the Philippines* (Washington, DC: Government Printing Office, 1945), 14; Whitney, *MacArthur*, 192; *New Orleans Daily Picayune*, September 7, 1912; McManus, *To the End of the Earth*, 81 and 88; Scott, *Rampage*, 68–75 and 416–19; Toll, *Twilight of the Gods*, 89; YOM, vol. 2, 671 and 737–51. **304** "You can't": Egeberg, *The General*, 145–47. For other details, see *Washington Post*, February 19, 1945. **304** "No": *Atlanta Journal*, February 18, 1945. For the aides and the jump, see Egeberg, *The General*, 144–50; YOM, vol. 2, 650; *Washington Post*, February 19, 1945. **305** "They made it": *Denver Post*, March 2, 1945. For other details, see DMREM, 250; *New York Times*, March 3, 1945; Belote and Belote, *Corregidor*, 239–40 and 248; YOM, vol. 2, 650–52. **305** "I am home": *New York Times*, March 3, 1945. **306** "unfriendly": Luvaas, ed., *Dear Miss Em*, 225–26. For other details, see Kenney, *The MacArthur I Know*, 128–29; Interview with JM, New York City, August 17, 1984, RG 13, MMLA; Scott, *Rampage*, 434; Egeberg, *The General*, 160. **306** "to aid": *New York Times*, March 8, 1945. For the visit to Santo Tomas and the real reason, see Interview with JM, New York City, August 17 and 23, 1984, RG 13, MMLA; Egeberg, *The General*, 184–86. **306** "George": YOM, vol. 2, 657–58. **307** "I think": Interview with JM, New York City, August 23, 1984, RG 13, MMLA. For the silver and the houseboy, see Huff, *My Fifteen Years*, 38, 99, and 100–101. **307** "Build me": Whitney, *MacArthur*, 546–47. For Arthur's talents, see Huff, *My Fifteen Years*, 85 and 93–94. **308** "valuable": Luvaas, ed., *Dear Miss Em*, 238 and 295.

CHAPTER THIRTEEN **The Other Return**

309 "to indicate": JMW, Diary, May 6, 1945, JMWP, USAHEC. For other details, see JMW, Diary, August 5, 1945, JMWP, USAHEC. **309** "Christmas!": JMW, Diary, December 25, 1944, JMWP, USAHEC. For other details, see JMW, Diary, December 1, 1944, JMWP, USAHEC; GWS, 225 and 250. **309** "This is a": JMW, Diary, December 1, 1944, JMWP, USAHEC. For the steam and partitions, see JMW, Diary, February 23 and 25, 1945, JMWP, USAHEC. **310** "Groundhog": JMW, Diary, February 2, 1945, JMWP, USAHEC. For other details, see JMW, Diary, January 31, February 6, March 5, 15, 21, and 23, and April 1, 2, and 3, 1945, JMWP, USAHEC. **310** "Well, I":

JMW, Diary, April 2, 1945, JMWP, USAHEC. **310** "That is": JMW, Diary, March 8, 1945, JMWP, USAHEC. For monitoring the seconds, see JMW, "Regulation of Hamilton Watch," Diary, JMWP, USAHEC. **310** "my old bones": GWS, 253–56. For other details, see JMW, Diary, January 1 and 21 and February 18, 1945, JMWP, USAHEC. **311** "I do NOT": JMW, Diary, March 4, 1945, JMWP, USAHEC. For razors, see GWS, 255; Hal Leith, *POWs of Japanese Rescued* (Victoria, Canada: Trafford, 2003), 39. **311** "I have spoken": JMW, Diary, February 18, 1945, JMWP, USAHEC. For other details, see JMW, Diary, February 11 and May 6, 1945, JMWP, USAHEC; GWS, 256. **311** "I cannot": JMW, Diary, March 4, 1945, JMWP, USAHEC. For credit previously given, see POTRS, 157. **312** "the only palatable": JMW, Diary, February 25, 1945, JMWP, USAHEC. For the protest, see JMW, Diary, April 4, 1945, JMWP, USAHEC. **312** "As usual": JMW, Diary, April 22, 1945, JMWP, USAHEC. **312** "39th anniversary": JMW, Diary, June 12, 1945, JMWP, USAHEC. For the injury, also see JMW, Diary, May 14, 20, 22, and 27, 1945, JMWP, USAHEC. **312** "Carroll": JMW, Diary, June 19, 1945, JMWP, USAHEC. For his weight, see JMW, Diary, July 16, 1945, JMWP, USAHEC. **313** "There seems": JMW, Diary, June 24, 1945, JMWP, USAHEC. For his recovery, see JMW, Diary, July 8 and 15, 1945, JMWP, USAHEC. **313** "I realize": JMW, Diary, February 18, 1945, JMWP, USAHEC. For the anniversary of his farewell to Adele and plans for the future with her, also see JMW, Diary, May 14 and August 5, 1945, JMWP, USAHEC. **313** "There is": JMW, Diary, August 18, 1945, JMWP, USAHEC. For other details, see JMW, Diary, February 18 and August 5, 10, 12, 16, and 17, 1945, JMWP, USAHEC; GWS, 257–58; Edward King, Diary, August 9, 1945, National American Defenders of Bataan & Corregidor Museum, online. **314** "I congratulate": GWS, 258–59. **314** "the war was": GWS, 213 and 254–59. For other details, see JMW, Diary, July 19, 1944, May 6 and 10 and August 19, 1945, JMWP, USAHEC; Kennedy, *Freedom from Fear*, 745 and 809; Toll, *Twilight of the Gods*, 336–39, 343–50, 529, 663, 705–7; David D. Lowman, "The Treasure of the Awa Maru," *Proceedings* (August 1982), online; Spector, *Eagle Against the Sun*, 503–5, 532, and 542–43; YOM, vol. 2, 768–70 and 775–76. **315** "[to] bear": Toll, *Twilight of the Gods*, 723 and 734–38. **315** "By order": GWS, 251 and 259–60. **316** "Are you": William Craig, *The Fall of Japan* (New York: Dial, 1967), 276. For other details, see Leith, *POWs of Japanese Rescued*, 27–28; GWS, 260. **316** "looked like": Leith, *POWs of Japanese Rescued*, 28. **316** "He must": Craig, *The Fall of Japan*, 126–27, 221–35, and 271–78. For other details, see Ronald H. Spector, *In the Ruins of Empire: The Japanese Surrender and the Battle for Postwar Asia* (New York: Random House, 2007), 7–14; Leith, *POWs of Japanese Rescued*, 8–32; GWS, 260–61. **317** "The general": Leith, *POWs of Japanese Rescued*, 42. For the news about Roosevelt, see *Chicago Daily News*, September 1, 1945. **318** "The prospect": JMW, Diary, August 23, 1945, JMWP, USAHEC. **318** "notice": Leith, *POWs of Japanese Rescued*, 39–42. **318** "We were": GWS, 261–63. **318** "Officially released": JMW, Diary, August 24, 25, 26, and 27, 1945, JMWP, USAHEC. For the reunion with other officers, see LCB, "Personal Experience Sketches," 1945, Beebe Papers, USAHEC; TBAB, 172; GWS, 269–70. **319** "delighted":

GCM to Albert C. Wedemeyer, Washington, DC, August 22, 1945, in George C. Marshall, *The Papers of George Catlett Marshall*, ed. Larry I. Bland and Sharon Ritenour Stevens (Baltimore: The Johns Hopkins University Press, 2003), vol. 5, 283. For other details, see GCM to John J. McCloy, Washington, DC, August 20, 1945, in Marshall, *The Papers of George Catlett Marshall*, vol. 5, 285; GWS, 269. **319** "All this group:" *New York Times*, August 29, 1945. For the flight and tears, see JMW, Diary, August 26 (with flight manifest) and 27, 1945, JMWP, USAHEC; JRP, Diary, August 28, 1945, PC; LCB, "Personal Experience Sketches," 1945, Beebe Papers, USAHEC. **319** "You should have": Roger B. Jeans, ed., *The Letters and Diaries of Colonel John Hart Caughey, 1944–1945: With Wedemeyer in World War II China* (Lanham, MD: Lexington, 2018), 147. For other details, see GWS, 273; Oral Reminiscences of Albert C. Wedemeyer, July 6, 1971, D. Clayton James Papers, MMLA. **320** "Chocolate": JRP, Diary, August 28, 1945. **320** "The utterances": Jeans, ed., *The Letters and Diaries of Colonel John Hart Caughey*, 147. **320** "It was a": GWS, 273–74. For his photograph back, see *New York Post*, August 31, 1945. **320** "gaunt": *New York Times*, August 29, 1945. For the flight to Manila, see GWS, 275–76; JRP, Diary, August 30, 1945, PC. **321** "Give them": *Washington Evening Star*, August 30, 1945. For flying over Bataan, see JRP, Diary, August 30, 1945, PC. **321** "Manila was": GWS, 276–77. For the schedule, see JMW, Diary, August 31, 1945, JMWP, USAHEC. **321** "of all": Willoughby, *MacArthur*, 295; YOM, vol. 2, 785. For other details, see Egeberg, *The General*, 197; DMREM, 269–70. **321** "If the Japs": Kenney, *The MacArthur I Know*, 180–81. **322** "[would] be subject": DMREM, 264–65 and 271. For other details, see Dunn, *Pacific Microphone*, 351; YOM, vol. 2, 776 and 786. **322** "General Wainwright walked": *New York Times*, November 16, 1964. For arrival time, see JMW, Diary, August 31, 1945, JMWP, USAHEC; *New York Times*, November 18 and 25 and December 1, 1964; TBAB, 173. **322** "I was just": DMREM, 271. For the Wainwright family, see Betty Mears Wainwright, "Skinny," unpublished manuscript, WP, USMA, 215. **322** "I washed": GWS, 277. **323** "was haggard": DMREM, 271–72. **323** "Well, I'm": *New York Times*, September 1, 1945. For the delay and seating, see GWS, 278; *New York Post*, August 31, 1945; Dunn, *Pacific Microphone*, 355; DMREM, 271; *New York Times*, November 18, 1964; Egeberg, *The General*, 206; Oral Reminiscences of Colonel Sidney F. Mashbir, September 1, 1971, D. Clayton James Papers, MSSUL. **323** "Shocked": DMREM, 272. **323** "I want": Oral Reminiscences of Colonel Sidney F. Mashbir, September 1, 1971, D. Clayton James Papers, MSSUL. For James accepting this version, see YOM, vol. 2. 788. **324** "Why, Jim": Whitney, *MacArthur*, 217. For MacArthur's exact recollections and Wainwright's reaction, see DMREM, 272. **324** "The emotion": DMREM, 272. For the recovered documents and Wainwright's statement after, see DM to GCM, April 16, 1945, Surrender of American Forces in the Philippines, Records of the War Department's Operations Division, 1942–1945, NARA, ProQuest History Vault; *New York Times*, September 1, 1942; GWS, 278. **324** "I simply": GWS, 279–80. For the flags and feeling sick, see McManus, *To The End of the Earth*, 317; Rhoades, *Flying MacArthur to Victory*,

452.   **325**   "We are gathered": DMREM, 274–75; Dunn, *Pacific Microphone*, 361. For drafting the remarks and the proceedings, see Egeberg, *The General*, 206 and 210–12; Toll, *Twilight of the Gods*, 761.   **326**   "[about] the unpreparedness": Egeberg, *The General*, 212–13.   **326**   "When halfway": GWS, 280.   **326**   "These proceedings": DMREM, 275–77.   **327**   "I hear": Considine, *It's All News to Me*, 276. For Wainwright's son and the memoirs, also see GWS, 282; Elfrida Wainwright to Jack Wainwright, August 14, 1945, WP, USMA; Oral Reminiscences of Colonel Sidney F. Mashbir, September 1, 1971, D. Clayton James Papers, MSSUL.   **327**   "the shoe": *New York Times*, September 1, 1945.   **327**   "This might seem": GWS, 284–86. For other details, see *Atlanta Journal*, August 29, 1945; Scott, *Rampage*, 40–42, 442–47, and 503; *New York Times*, September 3, 1945.   **328**   "The war in the": *New York Times*, September 3, 1945.   **328**   "I will come": JMW, Diary, September 5, 1945, JMWP, USAHEC. For other details, see Interview with JM, New York City, June 24, 1984, RG 13, MMLA; GWS, 287–88; JRP, Diary, September 3, 1945, PC.   **329**   "Hello, darling": *Washington Evening Star*, September 10, 1945. For other details, see *San Francisco Chronicle*, September 9 and 10, 1945; *Washington Post*, September 7 and 11, 1945; JMW, Diary, September 6, 1945, JMWP, USAHEC; GWS, 256, 288, and 290; Pogue, *George C. Marshall: Organizer of Victory*, 38.   **329**   "You, my friends": *Washington Post*, September 11, 1945. For other details, see *Washington Post*, September 10, 1945.   **330**   "made a triumph": *Washington Evening Star*, September 10, 1945.   **330**   "During the half-hour": *Washington Post*, September 11, 1945.   **330**   "As I stood": *Washington Post*, September 11, 1945.   **331**   "I don't see": Harry S. Truman, Longhand Note, June 17, 1945, President's Secretary's Files, HSTLM, online. For other details, see GWS, 295; Michael Schaller, *The American Occupation of Japan: The Origins of the Cold War in Asia* (New York: Oxford University Press, 1987), 21.   **331**   "If he'd": Robert H. Ferrell, *Harry S. Truman: A Life* (Columbia: University of Missouri Press, 1994), 330–31.   **331**   "prima donna": Harry S. Truman, Longhand Note, June 17, 1945, President's Secretary's Files, HSTLM, online.   **332**   "super secret": 201 Wainwright, RG 165, NARA.   **332**   "The possibility": Henry Lewis Stimson, Diary, September 6, 1945, Stimson Papers, YU.   **332**   "firing line": Citation for the Medal of Honor, September 10, 1945, PPF 4261, HSTLM.   **333**   "more pleasure": *Washington Post*, September 11, 1945. For other details, see Mears, *The Medal of Honor*, 45.   **333**   "Come on": GWS, 295.   **333**   "General Jonathan": Citation for the Medal of Honor, September 10, 1945, PPF 4261, HSTLM.   **333**   "magic words": GWS, 295. For the smiles, see *Washington Post*, September 11, 1945.

EPILOGUE   **When Men Have to Die**

335   "[of] the extraordinarily": YOM, vol. 3, 5 and 22. For the road in, see DMREM, 280.   **335**   "an economist": DMREM, 281–82 and 291–93. For the commission, see Herman, *Douglas MacArthur*, 638–39.   **336**   "Never before": Manchester, *American Caesar*, 470.   **336**   "new shogun": YOM, vol. 3, 4, 58–61, 358, 362, and 371. For other details, see Herman, *Douglas MacArthur*, 676–77. **336** "I tried": DMREM, 282–83, 287–88, 294–95, 298–305, and 308–14. For the reforms, also see YOM, vol. 3, 129–39 and 165–92; Manchester, *American Caesar*, 478. **338** "Indefensible": W. Averell Harriman and Elie Abel, *Special Envoy to Churchill and Stalin, 1941–1946* (New York: Random House, 1975), 544. For other details, see *New York Times*, October 29, 1945; YOM, vol. 3, 94–95; Norman and Norman, *Tears in the Darkness*, 348–49 and 359–60; Scott, *Rampage*, 468–90; *United States of America v. Masaharu Homma*, vol. 16, 2281, and vol. 18, 2364. **338** "grant quarter": *United States of America vs. Masaharu Homma*, vol. 30, 3364–65. For the part of the dissent about the Geneva Conventions, see In re Yamashita, 327 U.S. 1 (1946), 72–78. **338** "That double bastard": JMW to JRP, February 22, 1950, WP, USMA. **338** "That is too": JMW to JRP, February 12, 1946, JMWP, USAHEC. **338** "There are few": DMREM, 296–98. For Homma's death, see Norman and Norman, *Tears in the Darkness*, 381–85. **338** "For forty-eight": *New York Times*, July 4, 1946. **339** "perpetuity": DMREM, 236–37 and 265–66. For other details, see YOM, vol. 2, 691–701; H. W. Brands, *Bound to Empire: The United States and the Philippines* (New York: Oxford University Press, 1992), 205–30; Karnow, *In Our Image*, 326–30. **339** "greatest person": YOM, vol. 3, 197–98, 206, and 208. For other details, see Smith, *Eisenhower in War and Peace*, 455–58 and 466–67; *Washington Evening Star*, June 20, 1948; Perret, *Old Soldiers Never Die*, 530. **340** "shortest of the": *Washington Post*, June 25, 1948. **340** "MacArthur is probably": *Official Report of the Proceedings of the Twenty-Fourth Republican National Convention* (Washington, DC: Judd & Detweiler, 1948), 252–54. For the second ovation, see *Washington Evening Star*, June 24, 1948. **340** "When I": JMW to DM, San Antonio, July 14, 1948, RG 10, MMLA. **340** "The professional": JMW to DM, Cincinnati, August 24, 1948, RG 10, MMLA. **340** "kill him": *Washington Post*, September 11, 1945. For the New York parade, see *New York Times*, September 14, 1945. **341** "I would bring": Considine, *It's All News to Me*, 273–77. For other details, see JMW, Diary, September 19–20, 1945, JMWP, USAHEC; *Albany Times-Union*, September 22, 1945; *New York Times*, May 15, 1946; James K. McGuinness to Robert Considine, Culver City, September 25, 1945, Bob Considine Papers, SU; McCarten, "General MacArthur: Fact and Legend," 12. **341** "my very bad": JMW to George Moore, May 11, 1946, JMWP, USAHEC. **341** "stood at attention": Considine, *It's All News to Me*, 274–76. **342** "hysterical": Elfrida Wainwright to Jack Wainwright, August 11, 1945, WP, USMA. For details, see Jack Wainwright to JMW, December 4, 1945, WP, USMA; Elfrida Wainwright to JMW, December 16, 1945, WP, USMA. **342** "had hoped": Elfrida Wainwright to JMW, December 16, 1945, WP, USMA. For other details, see C. C. Burlingame to JMW, February 26, 1946, WP, USMA; Jack Wainwright to JMW, December 4, 1945, WP, USMA. **342** "Try to": Betty Mears Wainwright, "Skinny," unpublished manuscript, WP, USMA, 224–25. For his weight, see JMW to Richard F. Watson, January 17, 1946, JMWP, USAHEC. **342** "social obligations": JMW to Cortland Parker, January 24, 1946, JMWP, USAHEC. For his "no comment" explanation, see *San Antonio Evening News*,

January 21, 1946. **343** "She worried": *Jacksonville Florida Times-Union*, January 4, 1946. For letters to Adele, see Jack Wainwright to JMW, December 4, 1945, WP, USMA. **343** "hero stuff": Jack Wainwright to JMW, December 4, 1945, WP, USMA. For company in Texas, see *San Antonio Evening News*, January 21, 1946; JMW to JRP, February 12, 1946, JMWP, USAHEC; JMW to Louise Pugh, July 2, 1948, WP, USMA; *New York Times*, November 4, 1945; James T. Patterson, *Grand Expectations: The United States, 1945–1974* (New York: Oxford University Press, 1996), 13–14. **343** "Lonesome": JMW to Jack and Elfrida Wainwright, May 24, 1946, WP, USMA. For other details, see JMW to Jennie Mears, March 28, 1946, JMWP, USAHEC; *Boston Herald*, March 25, 1946; C. C. Burlingame to JMW, February 26, 1946, WP, USMA; C. C. Burlingame to Jack Wainwright, May 20, 1946, WP, USMA; *The State of Texas v. Adele Wainwright*, 90 Day Commitment, May 7, 1946, WP, USMA; Guy F. Witt to JMW, Dallas, July 8, 1946, WP, USMA; E. James Brady, Report, October 7, 1953, WP, USMA; Franklin G. Ebaugh to JMW, December 23, 1946, WP, USMA. **343** "Get out": JMW to Betty Mears, August 6, 1946, JMWP, USAHEC. **343** "hell of a time": JMW to Jack Wainwright, Fort Sam Houston, July 18, 1947, WP, USMA. For other details, see Schultz, *Hero of Bataan*, 428; *Long Beach Independent*, January 15, 1946; JMW to AW, February 15, 1944, WP, USMA; *Dallas Morning News*, August 31, 1947. **344** "Halfway down": J. H. S., "Fiddlers' Green and Other Cavalry Songs," *The Cavalry Journal* 32, no. 131 (April 1923), 196–97. **344** "We will have": JMW to JRP and Louise Pugh, June 12, 1950, WP, USMA. For other details, see Warwick & Legler to JMW, January 13, 1949, WP, USMA; *Life*, September 20, 1948, 102; JMW to Herbert G. West, February 7, 1946, JMWP, USAHEC; JMW, "Notes on What I Do," JMWP, USAHEC; JMW, Diary, "Travellers Club," JMWP, USAHEC; JMW to Dorothy, March 19, 1951, WP, USMA. **345** "I don't think": JMW to Elfrida Wainwright, April 10, 1951, JMWP, USAHEC. For details, see *San Antonio Express*, February 6, 1948; Jack Wainwright to Lawrence M. Rich, June 4, 1952, WP, USMA; JMW to Viola Livingston, March 30, 1950, WP, USMA; E. James Brady, Report, October 7, 1953, WP, USMA; Betty Mears Wainwright, "Skinny," unpublished manuscript, WP, USMA, 225–27. **345** "Now I'm": *Dallas Morning News*, September 14, 1947. **345** "keep out": JMW to W. J. Campbell, July 25, 1950, JMWP, USAHEC. **345** "I know of no": *New York Times*, August 21, 1948. **346** "Everyone wants": JMW to Harold H. Lowy, January 4, 1950, WP, USMA. For details, see JMW, "Notes on What I Do," JMWP, USAHEC; Gloria Kowalski to JMW, March 30, 1951, WP, USMA. **346** "swear box": JMW to Helen, July 10, 1951, WP, USMA. For the pitch to MacArthur and other details, see JMW to DM, San Antonio, July 14, 1948, RG 10, MMLA; Betty Mears Wainwright, "Skinny," unpublished manuscript, WP, USMA, 226. **346** "near ragged": JMW to Louise Pugh, July 2, 1948, WP, USMA. **346** "really": Betty Mears Wainwright, "Skinny," unpublished manuscript, WP, USMA, 227. **346** "Among the great": JMW to Ruth B. Milliken, October 11, 1950, WP, USMA. For Lee and Grant, see JMW to Cyril Clemens, July 24, 1951, JMWP, USAHEC. **346** "No one's": Betty Mears Wainwright, "Skinny," unpublished manuscript, WP, USMA, 227. **346** "as a modest": JMW to Lyndon Johnson, July 30, 1951, JMWP, USAHEC. For Little Boy on the desk, see JMW to JRP, November 17, 1949, WP, USMA. **347** "laying a field": DMREM, 384–99; YOM, vol. 3, 560–604. For summaries of the war, see Herman, *Douglas MacArthur*, 704–816; Patterson, *Grand Expectations*, 207–42; David Petraeus and Andrew Roberts, *Conflict: The Evolution of Warfare from 1945 to Ukraine* (New York: Harper, 2023), 11–36. **348** "because they feel": Huff, *My Fifteen Years*, 140. **348** "Old soldiers": DMREM, 400–405. For the election, see YOM, vol. 3, 642–55; Perret, *Old Soldiers Never Die*, 575–76. **349** "Hello, Skinny": *Greensboro Record*, April 19, 1951. **349** "never want": Jack Wainwright to AW, September 17, 1953, WP, USMA. For other details, see Jack Wainwright to AW, August 14, 1953, WP, USMA; Betty Mears Wainwright, "Skinny," unpublished manuscript, WP, USMA, 232; *Washington Post*, September 2, 1953; Jack Wainwright to E. James Brady, August 14, 1953, WP, USMA; E. James Brady to Jack Wainwright, Colorado Springs, August 14, 1953, WP, USMA. **349** "I believe": Elfrida Wainwright, "Notes on Death," JMWP, USAHEC. For other details, see *Washington Post*, September 9, 1945; JMW to Wilhelm D. Styer, Fort Sam Houston, October 21, 1946, John Toland Papers, LC; JMW to Gordon L. Harris, Fort Sam Houston, January 28, 1947, USAHEC, online; JMW to Jack Wainwright, January 12, 1949, JMWP, USAHEC; Betty Mears Wainwright, "Skinny," unpublished manuscript, WP, USMA, 233; *New Orleans Times-Picayune*, September 9, 1953. **350** "I am glad": YOM, vol. 3, 655–62. **350** "What do": *Life*, July 14, 1961. For other details, see YOM, vol. 3, 676–77; *New York Times*, July 2, 1961. **350** "biggest ever": *Manila Times*, July 5, 1961. For the state of the city and MacArthur's death, see *Chicago Daily News*, June 18, 1960; *New York Times*, April 7, May 4, and November 16 and 22, 1964; YOM, vol. 3, 686–88; Perret, *Old Soldiers Never Die*, 585.

Illustration Credits

10 Courtesy of the National Archives and Records Administration
11 Courtesy of the Library of Congress
12 Courtesy of the Naval History and Heritage Command
13 Courtesy of the Naval History and Heritage Command
14 Courtesy of the National Archives and Records Administration
15 Courtesy of the Naval History and Heritage Command
16 Courtesy of the MacArthur Memorial Archives, Norfolk, Virginia
17 Courtesy of the Library of Congress
18 Courtesy of the National Archives and Records Administration (111-SC-334281*)
19 Courtesy of the National Archives and Records Administration
20 Courtesy of the Naval History and Heritage Command

PHOTO INSERT 2

1 Courtesy of the Naval History and Heritage Command
2 Courtesy of the Naval History and Heritage Command
3 Courtesy of the National Archives and Records Administration (319-PW-31a*)
4 Courtesy of the Naval History and Heritage Command
5 Courtesy of the Naval History and Heritage Command
6 Courtesy of the National Archives and Records Administration
7 Courtesy of the National Archives and Records Administration
8 Courtesy of the National Archives and Records Administration
9 Courtesy of the Naval History and Heritage Command
10 Courtesy of the National Archives and Records Administration
11 Courtesy of the Harry S. Truman Library and Museum
12 Courtesy of the National Archives and Records Administration
13 Courtesy of the National Archives and Records Administration
14 Courtesy of the National Archives and Records Administration
15 Courtesy of the National Archives and Records Administration
16 Courtesy of the National Archives and Records Administration
17 Courtesy of the Harry S. Truman Library and Museum
18 Courtesy of the Library of Congress
19 Courtesy of the National Archives and Records Administration
20 Courtesy of the National Archives and Records Administration

* Number included by request of the National Archives and Records Administration

Index

About the Author

Jonathan Horn is an author and former White House presidential speechwriter whose books include *Washington's End* and the Robert E. Lee biography *The Man Who Would Not Be Washington*, which was a *Washington Post* bestseller. He has written for outlets including *The Wall Street Journal, The Washington Post, The New York Times* Disunion series, *New York Post, The Daily Beast, National Review,* and *Politico Magazine,* and has appeared on *CBS Sunday Morning,* CNN, Fox News, MSNBC, and *PBS NewsHour.* A graduate of Yale, he lives in Bethesda, Maryland, with his wife, two children, and dog.